THE FATE OF THI

The Book of Martyrs by John Foxe written in the 16th century has long been the go-to source for studying the lives and martyrdom of the apostles. Whilst other scholars have written individual treatments on the more prominent apostles such as Peter, Paul, John, and James, there is little published information on the other apostles.

In *The Fate of the Apostles*, Sean McDowell offers a comprehensive, reasoned, historical analysis of the fate of the twelve disciples of Jesus along with the apostles Paul, and James. McDowell assesses the evidence for each apostle's martyrdom as well as determining its significance to the reliability of their testimony. The question of the fate of the apostles also gets to the heart of the reliability of the kerygma: did the apostles really believe Jesus appeared to them after his death, or did they fabricate the entire story? How reliable are the resurrection accounts? The willingness of the apostles to die for their faith is a popular argument in resurrection studies and McDowell offers insightful scholarly analysis of this argument to break new ground within the spheres of New Testament studies, Church History, and apologetics.

To my three kids: Scottie, Shauna, and Shane. My hope is that you will live your lives with as much boldness and sacrifice as the apostles.

The Fate of the Apostles

Examining the Martyrdom Accounts of the Closest Followers of Jesus

SEAN MCDOWELL
Biola University, USA

Routledge
Taylor & Francis Group

LONDON AND NEW YORK

First published 2008 by Ashgate Publishing

2 Park Square, Milton Park, Abingdon, Oxfordshire OX14 4RN
711 Third Avenue, New York, NY 10017

Routledge is an imprint of the Taylor & Francis Group, an informa business

First issued in paperback 2018

British Library Cataloguing in Publication Data
A catalogue record for this book is available from the British Library

The Library of Congress has cataloged the printed edition as follows:
McDowell, Sean.
 The fate of the apostles : examining the martyrdom accounts of the closest followers of Jesus / by Sean McDowell.
  pages cm
 Includes index.
 ISBN 978-1-4724-6520-7 (hardcover) – ISBN 978-1-4724-6521-4 (ebook) –
 ISBN 978-1-4724-6522-1 (epub) 1. Apostles–Death. 2. Christian martyrs–Death. I. Title.

BS2440.M443 2015
272'.10922–dc23

2015009323

ISBN 978-1-4724-6520-7 (hbk)
ISBN 978-1-138-54913-5 (pbk)

Contents

Acknowledgments

From beginning to end, my time researching and writing this project was possible only because of a team of generous supporters who surrounded and encouraged me. More than anyone else, my wife, Stephanie, gave me the strength to persevere when I was too tired and too frustrated to move forward, believing in me, encouraging me, reminding me I could do it. We did it, Love!

Tim and Kay Winn provided financial support through the Lampstand Foundation. I could not have done it without you. At different times, both Kim Van Vlear and John Nettleton have each provided unbelievable help so I could focus on this project.

Dr. Jim Parker was my doctoral advisor at Southern Baptist Theological Seminary, where I began the research that resulted in this book. Thanks for guiding me through and for making it enjoyable along the way! J. Warner Wallace helped me remain focused throughout the writing process and provided exceptional feedback. Thanks for all the phone calls where we discussed the nuances of the *Stromata* by Clement of Alexandria, the best way to calculate the martyrdom accounts for various disciples, and how to evaluate evidence. You are a colleague and a friend.

There are many other professors and friends who have been helpful along the way. Thanks to Andre Murillo, Dr. Victor Velazquez, and Dr. Alan Gomes for help with translation from German, French, and Latin sources. Dr. Thomas Schmidt responded to many of my email questions in relation to his research on the various apostles. And thanks to Dr. Ken Berding for guiding me through issues related to Polycarp and John, and for suggesting I connect with Dr. Charles E. Hill, who was incredibly helpful. I am indebted to Dr. Ted Cabal and Dr. Michael Haykin for providing positive feedback and direction. And thanks to Carlos Delgado and Chris Bosson for insightful criticism and amazing edits.

Dr. Michael Licona provided significant feedback throughout the entire process. Thanks for the various phone calls and constructive feedback. You're a true friend.

Scott Lindsey and the team at Logos Bible Software made much of my research possible. I could not have done this without the incredible resources they made so easily available or the personal direction they provided.

I thank my colleague and friend, Dr. Craig Hazen, head of the MA Christian Apologetics program at Biola University. Craig hired me to begin teaching in the fall of 2014, before I finished my doctorate, even freeing me up significantly to commit to research and study. Thank you, Craig. I am honored to be part of the program, and forever grateful for the support.

Chapter 1

Introduction

How can we trust in the historical resurrection of Jesus? A commonly used argument points to the apostles' willingness to become martyrs. Popular apologists frequently cite their deaths as good reason to trust the sincerity of their testimony, since it is difficult to believe they would go willingly to such gruesome deaths for the sake of empty deceit.

Credentialed scholars also make a similar argument. E.P. Sanders, for instance, in his *The Historical Figure of Jesus*, argues that "many of the people in these lists [of eyewitnesses] were to spend the rest of their lives proclaiming that they had seen the risen Lord, and several of them would die for their cause."[1]

And Michael R. Licona notes:

> After Jesus' death, the disciples endured persecution, and a number of them experienced martyrdom. The strength of their conviction indicates that they were not just claiming Jesus had appeared to them after rising from the dead. They really believed it. They willingly endangered themselves by publicly proclaiming the risen Christ.[2]

Further, in *The Historical Jesus of the Gospels*, Craig S. Keener argues:

> The disciples' testimony was not fabricated. Ancients also recognized that the willingness of people to die for their convictions verified at least the sincerity of their motives, arguing against fabrication. People of course die regularly for values that are false; they do not, however, ordinarily die voluntarily for what they believe is false. Intentional deception by the disciples is thus implausible.[3]

Still, despite the popularity and importance of this argument to historical Jesus studies, little scholarly work focuses primarily on *evaluating the evidence for their martyrdoms*.[4] Questions naturally remain, then, which strike to the heart of the

---

[1]   E.P. Sanders, *The Historical Figure of Jesus* (New York: Penguin, 1993), 279–80.

[2]   Michael R. Licona, *The Resurrection of Jesus: A New Historiographical Approach* (Downers Grove, IL: InterVarsity Press, 2010), 366.

[3]   Craig S. Keener, *The Historical Jesus of the Gospels* (Grand Rapids, MI: Eerdmans, 2009), 342.

[4]   For various books that explore the lives of the apostles, see William Barclay, *The Master's Men* (London: SCM Press, 1960); Pope Benedict XVI, *The Apostles* (Huntington,

apostolic message: Were the apostles hopelessly biased? Did they really believe Jesus had appeared to them after his death, or did they fabricate the entire story? Do the deaths of the apostles provide positive evidence for the resurrection accounts? And perhaps most importantly, most fundamentally: How strong is the actual historical evidence that the apostles of Jesus died as martyrs? In offering this study, I hope to answer these questions.

In fact, we do have reliable historical evidence to trust the ancient and uniform testimony that (1) all the apostles were willing to die for their faith, and (2) a number of them actually did experience martyrdom.

The argument itself is quite simple: The apostles spent between one and a half and three years with Jesus during his public ministry, expecting him to proclaim his kingdom on earth. Although disillusioned at his untimely death, they became the first witnesses of the risen Jesus and they endured persecution; many subsequently experienced martyrdom, signing their testimony, so to speak, in their own blood. The strength of their conviction, marked by their willingness to die, indicates that they did not fabricate these claims; rather, without exception, they actually believed Jesus to have risen from the dead. While in and of themselves these facts prove neither the truth of the resurrection in particular nor Christianity as a whole, they do demonstrate the apostles' sincerity of belief, lending credibility to their claims about the veracity of resurrection, which is fundamental to the case for Christianity.

In other words, *their willingness to face persecution and martyrdom indicates more than any other conceivable course their sincere conviction that, after rising from the dead, Jesus indeed appeared to them.*

IN: Our Sunday Visitor, 2007); Ronald Brownrigg, *The Twelve Apostles* (New York: Macmillan, 1974); John R. Claypool, *The First to Follow: The Apostles of Jesus* (Harrisburg, NY: Morehouse, 2008); E. Dale Click, *The Inner Circle* (Lima, OH: CSS, 2000); Edgar Goodspeed, *The Twelve: The Story of Christ's Apostles* (Philadelphia, PA: John C. Winston, 1957); J.G. Greenhough, *The Apostles of Our Lord* (New York: A.C. Armstrong & Son, 1904); Morris Inch, *12 Who Changed the World: The Lives and Legends of the Disciples* (Nashville, TN: Thomas Nelson, 2003); George F. Jowett, *The Drama of the Lost Disciples* (Bishop Auckland, England: Covenant, 2004); Emil G. Kraeling, *The Disciples* (Skokie, IL: Rand McNally, 1966); Herbert Lockyer, *All the Apostles of the Bible* (Grand Rapids, MI: Zondervan, 1972); F. Townley Lord, *The Master and His Men: Studies in Christian Enterprise* (London: Carey, 1927); Marianna Mayer, *The Twelve Apostles* (New York: Phyllis Fogelman, 2000); William Steuart McBirnie, *The Search for the Twelve Apostles*, rev. ed. (Carol Stream, IL: Tyndale, 1973); C. Bernard Ruffin, *The Twelve: The Lives of the Apostles After Calvary* (Huntington, IN: Our Sunday Visitor, 1997); Thomas E. Schmidt, *The Apostles After Acts: A Sequel* (Eugene, OR: Cascade, 2013); Asbury Smith, *The Twelve Christ Chose* (New York: Harper & Row, 1958); H.S. Vigeveno, *Thirteen Men Who Changed the World* (Glendale, CA: G/L Publications, 1967).

Of course, however, many often misstate or misunderstand the argument from the deaths of the apostles to the truth of Christianity. Candida Moss, for example, claims that Christians "like to think of their martyrs as unique. The fact that early Christians were willing to die for their beliefs has been seen as a sign of the inherent truth of the Christian message .... Christianity is true, it is said, because only Christians have martyrs."[5] Two points are important to make in response. First, as I demonstrate, there *are* many martyrs outside Christianity; I don't claim that *only* Christians have martyrs, but that *the apostles died uniquely for the belief that they had actually seen the risen Christ*, which demonstrates the sincerity of their convictions. The deaths of others for their religious causes in no way undermine the evidential significance of the fate of the apostles. Second, the apostles' willingness to die for their beliefs does not demonstrate "the inherent truth of the Christian message," but that the apostles *really believed* that Jesus had risen from the grave. The apostles could have been mistaken, but their willingness to die as martyrs establishes their unmistakable sincerity. The apostles were not liars; rather, they believed they had seen the risen Jesus, they were willing to die for this claim, and many actually did die for it.

Methodology

I am primarily concerned with the historical evidence for the martyrdom of the apostles, which involves studying the earliest available sources, including New Testament documents, with particular focus on the book of Acts, the writings of the early church fathers, pseudepigraphical writings such as the *Acts of the Apostles*, Gnostic sources, and other extra-biblical accounts.

While there are some valuable later sources for the fate of some of the apostles, this investigation focuses primarily on what Markus Bockmuehl has dubbed "living" memory. First- and second-century writers emphasized that they were passing on a shared "living" memory of the apostles, which is to make a stronger claim than saying they were simply passing on a shared tradition or cultural memory. Instead, they believed they were transmitting personal memory of events that trace back to the apostles themselves.[6] This living memory extended until the end of the second century, after which it could no longer

---

[5]   Candida Moss, *The Myth of Persecution: How Early Christians Invented a Story of Martyrdom* (New York: HarperCollins, 2013), 17, 81.

[6]   Markus Bockmuehl, "Peter's Death in Rome? Back to Front and Upside Down," *Scottish Journal of Theology* 60 (2007): 7–13. The belief in living memory can be seen in church fathers including Ignatius, Papias, Polycarp, Justin, Irenaeus, and possibly even Tertullian.

be accurately appealed to as a means of understanding the apostolic Gospel.[7] This prevents neither the development of legendary material about the apostles nor theological disagreements. According to Bockmuehl, living memory simply means that "until the end of the second century there were living individuals who personally, and sometimes vividly, remembered the disciples of the apostles—and that such memory was still thought to carry weight in debates about how to interpret the bearers of apostolic faith."[8]

According to Bockmuehl, living memory involves three generations: (1) Peter and his contemporary associates, assumedly dead by roughly AD 70, (2) the direct followers of the apostles, the last of which died by about AD 135, and (3) the second-generation followers of the apostles, who would have died by about AD 200.[9] Of course, by focusing on living memory I do not mean to imply that later history necessarily becomes suspect and unreliable. On the contrary, one can know many things independently of living memory. Indeed, for some apostles no chain of living memory exists, and for these cases one will need to rely upon the merits of later tradition.

Historians have recognized a spectrum of epistemological confidence for the examination of historical events. For the purposes of this inquiry, I adopt the following scale for evaluating the historical evidence for the martyrdom of individual apostles:

- *not possibly true*—certainly not historical;
- *very probably not true*—doubtfully historical;
- *improbable*—unlikely;
- *less plausible than not*—slightly less possible than not;
- *as plausible as not*—plausible;
- *more plausible than not*—slightly more possible than not;
- *more probable than not*—likely;
- *very probably true*—somewhat certain;
- *the highest possible probability*—nearly historically certain.

---

[7]   Bockmuehl provides an example from Irenaeus, who as a boy had personal contact with Polycarp, an eyewitness and companion of the apostles. Irenaeus insists that Polycarp would have soundly rejected Florinus's Valentinian understanding of Christian origins: "I can attest before God that if that blessed and apostolic presbyter had heard anything of this kind he would have cried out and covered his ears, sand said according to his custom, 'O good God, for what a time have you preserved me that I must endure this?' He would have fled the very place where he was sitting or standing, when he heard such words" (Eusebius, *Ecclesiastical History* 5.20.7). Irenaeus believed there was a short chain of personal contacts tracing back to the apostles that revealed a personal recollection in his own day. See Eusebius, *Ecclesiastical History* 5.20.9.

[8]   Ibid.

[9]   Ibid. 5.20.7, 12–13.

The reliability of the historical evidence for each apostle will be analyzed individually and assessed based upon the quantity and quality of the available historical data.

If the terms were put into a numeric scale, the probabilities look like this:

1. *not possibly true*—0–1;
2. *very probably not true*—2;
3. *improbable*—3;
4. *less plausible than not*—4;
5. *as plausible as not*—5;
6. *more plausible than not*—6;
7. *more probable than not*—7;
8. *very probably true*—8;
9. *the highest possible probability*—9–10.

To help determine where each apostle falls on the numeric scale, a few specific questions will be asked. First, how many sources are there? Multiple sources, when they are independent, provide greater confidence the claim is true. Second, how early are the sources? Generally speaking, earlier sources are considered more reliable than later sources. Third, are there sources from varying perspectives? For instance, a martyrdom account has greater credibility if it is supported by Christian, Gnostic, and secular sources. And a written account may also find support from oral tradition. Fourth, is there a historical nucleus even if secondary details disagree? Various accounts often fail to match up on some particulars, yet historians confidently believe they can ascertain a historical core. This claim is true even if an account has legendary and miraculous details.[10]

Defining Martyrdom

What, precisely, is a martyr? In its original Greek setting, "martyr" simply means one who testifies in a legal manner, a "witness."[11] Later, it came to refer to one whose testimony for Jesus results in death, which is now the standard Christian understanding of "martyr."[12]

---

[10]   A popular example is the crossing of the Rubicon by Julius Caesar, which led to his taking control of the Roman Empire. There is considerable debate about when and where he crossed the river. Some of the various accounts seem to contradict, and one even has a miraculous story. Yet classicists are confident the account is historical. See Craig Blomberg, *Can We Still Believe the Bible?* (Grand Rapids, MI: Baker, 2014), 138.

[11]   Mark Allan Powell, "Martyr," in *HarperCollins Bible Dictionary*, rev. ed., ed. Mark Allan Powell (New York: HarperCollins, 2011), 608.

[12]   David Noel Freedman, ed., *Eerdmans Dictionary of the Bible* (Grand Rapids, MI: Eerdmans, 2000), s.v. "Martyr," by Edward P. Myers.

But does martyrdom require death, or can one's suffering qualify one as a martyr? Are martyrs only those who confess certain beliefs, or might they be persons singled out, say, for moral acts? While these are worthwhile questions, I limit this discussion to the traditional understanding of Christian martyrdom, perhaps the strictest possible definition, as *involving death for confession of the Christian faith*.[13]

I should note that this understanding of martyrdom includes the idea that death is voluntary. Even though martyrdom can be avoided through one's renunciation of belief, the martyr *chooses* death. This applies even if the confessor is not given an official opportunity to recant, for he or she continues in the faith with knowledge of the outcome that may result from such belief. Thomas Wespetal concludes: "Thus individuals like John the Baptist, Zechariah (2 Chr 24:20–22) and Uriah (Jer 26:20–23), although they were given no formal opportunity to recant, could have forestalled their deaths had they taken the initiative to retract their accusations against their king."[14]

There are no early and reliable historical accounts to indicate the apostles were given the opportunity of recanting their faith at the moment of their deaths. The earliest record of executions for merely bearing the name "Christian" comes from a letter the governor Pliny wrote to Emperor Trajan (AD 112), long after the death of the last apostle:

> I interrogated these as to whether they were Christians; those who confessed
> I interrogated a second and a third time, threatening them with punishment;
> those who persisted I ordered executed. For I had no doubt that, whatever the

---

[13]   Thomas Wespetal defends this traditional conception of martyrdom with a few clarifications. First, at times the church has recognized non-fatal martyrdoms, such as monasticism or being sent to work at mines. However, the church continued to distinguish between those who died and those who did not. Fatal and non-fatal cases were not designated with a single term, which would have abolished the difference. There is substantial historical evidence for reserving "martyr" for those who have died (1 Clement 5:3–7, *The Martyrdom of Polycarp* 1.1, 2.1–2, 13.2, 14.2, 15.2, 17.3, 18.3, 19.1, 21.1, and Origen, *Commentary on John* 2.28). Second, some have applied "martyr" to those who have died defending the poor and oppressed of the world. But as Wespetal observes, this runs contrary to what seems to be the majority Christian view since the early church through the time of the Reformation. Third, while one must die for the faith to be considered a martyr, this death need not occur immediately, but can occur soon afterward because of the harm caused by the persecution. Fourth, martyrdom must end in death. Daniel, Meshach, Shadrach, and Abednego demonstrated a willingness and readiness to face death for their convictions until God saved them. Nevertheless, they cannot technically be considered martyrs, as some have tried to do. Thomas J. Wespetal, "Martyrdom and the Furtherance of God's Plan: The Value of Dying for the Christian Faith" (Ph.D. diss., Trinity Evangelical Divinity School, 2005), 19–33.

[14]   Ibid., 34.

nature of their creed, stubbornness and inflexible obstinacy surely deserve to be punished .... Those who denied that they were or had been Christians, when they invoked the gods in words dictated by me, offered prayer with incense and wine to your image ... and moreover cursed Christ ... these I thought should be discharged.[15]

Although Pliny's represents the first *explicit* reference to the mere bearing of the name "Christian" as being sufficient to warrant death, there is good reason to believe the practice existed much earlier, even into the mid-to-late first century, when the apostles engaged in missionary activity.[16] Peter urges Christians to expect and accept persecution for the *name* of Christ: "Yet if anyone suffers as a Christian, let him not be ashamed, but let him glorify God in that name" (1 Pet 4:16).[17] In his classic study on persecution in the early church, Geoffrey de Ste. Croix argues that persecution "for the Name" likely began during the time of Emperor Nero (AD 54–68):

The onus is on those who deny the early importance of this long-lasting element to produce reasons why it should have arisen only after Pliny's day, when all that we know of Roman religion would lead us to expect its appearance very soon after Christianity first attracted the attention of the government.[18]

---

[15] Pliny the Younger, *Letters* 10.96–97, as cited in *Roman Civilization: Selected Readings*, 3rd ed., ed. Naphtali Lewis and Meyer Reinhold, vol. 2 (New York: Columbia University Press, 1990), 551–53.

[16] Candida Moss disagrees: "The fact that Pliny has to make inquiries about this indicates that, before this point, there were no measures in place for the treatment of Christians" (*Myth of Persecution*, 140). As a result, she concludes that Christians were not the ancient Roman equivalent of "enemies of the state." But the fact that Pliny makes inquiries of Trajan could be for a host of other equally compelling reasons than the lack of measures for the treatment of Christians. Consider an alternative view: maybe the laws exist, but Pliny is unsure of how he is to apply them in his particular circumstances. Even in contemporary America there are state and federal laws that are regularly ignored and not enforced for political reasons. Immigration is a case in point. There are fierce debates about whether federal border laws should be enforced. The problem is not a lack of laws, but the political climate that makes it difficult to enforce them. Thus, even though there are federal and state laws on immigration, it would be completely feasible for a modern-day version of the Pliny–Trajan discussion to take place between a state governor and the President of the United States regarding how to treat illegal immigrants.

[17] Unless otherwise indicated, all Scripture quotations are from the English Standard Version of the Bible.

[18] G.E.M. de Ste. Croix, *Christian Persecution, Martyrdom, and Orthodoxy*, ed. Michael Whitby and Joseph Streeter (Oxford: Oxford University Press, 2006), 150.

Oscar Cullman believes Christians came into conflict with the state *before* Nero: "The whole Neronic persecution would be incomprehensible, unless the Roman State had come to know the Christians earlier. It was on the basis of previous experiences of them that they were declared state enemies."[19]

Candida Moss, on the other hand, believes the lack of official records of the apostles being given the opportunity to recant and live undermines the validity of their testimony. This is the missing element, she claims, required to make the argument they died *for* Christ.[20] She is right that there is not a record of the apostles being offered the opportunity to recant, but they ministered in potentially caustic environments with full awareness of the possible consequences for their actions.[21] The fact that their founding leader was a crucified criminal of the Roman Empire also certainly plays a part of their collective consciousness. Jesus even warned his disciples that the world would hate and even persecute them, as they did him (John 15:18–25).[22] Every time the apostles proclaimed the name of Christ, then, they knowingly risked suffering and death. Even so, they continued to teach and preach the risen Jesus. Given their active proclamation of Christ, and their full awareness of the cost of such proclamation, if some of the apostles died for their faith, they qualify under the traditional definition of "martyr."[23]

---

[19]   Oscar Cullman, *The Earliest Christian Confessions*, trans. J.K.S. Reid (London: Lutterworth Press, 1949), 30. Cullman points to passages in 2 Cor and Acts 17:7, which indicate that those brought to the faith by Paul were accused by the Jews before civic authorities.

[20]   Moss, *Myth of Persecution*, 137.

[21]   See Acts 4, 5, 6:8–8:3, and 12:1–5.

[22]   This is not to presume the truth of Jesus's martyrdom predictions as recorded by John. While I do not hold that the NT authors simply fabricated sayings for Jesus based on subsequent events, those who do believe this will find that they are unable to avoid the conclusion that the statements (which they will tend to think are late fabrications) nevertheless describe the real state of affairs—to wit, the persecution of the apostles. William Paley aptly observed:, "One side or other of the following disjunction is true; either that the evangelists have delivered what Christ really spoke, and that the event corresponded with the prediction; or that they put the prediction into Christ's mouth, because, at the time of writing the history, the event had turned out to be so." Either way, the apostles were likely persecuted for their faith. William Paley, *A View of the Evidences of Christianity* (London: John W. Parker & Son, 1859), 59.

[23]   There is considerable debate as to whether Christians were the first martyrs. G.W. Bowersock argues that martyrdom was entirely new to the second, third, and fourth centuries of the Christian faith. He says, "There is no reason to think that anyone displayed anything comparable to martyrdom before the Christians ... martyrdom was alien to both the Greeks and the Jews" (G.W. Bowersock, *Martyrdom and Rome* [Cambridge: Cambridge University Press, 1995], 7–8). Candida Moss agrees with Bowersock that *The Martyrdom of Polycarp*, traditionally dated AD 157, was the first time the term "martyrs" was indicative of the concept of martyrdom. The problem with this approach, says Moss, is that it makes

Challenges for the Historical Investigation

Critics frequently challenge the claim that the death of the apostles provides significant evidence for the veracity of their testimony, usually along two lines. First, the lack of early historical data undermines the trustworthiness of the accounts.[24] Second, the *Apocryphal Acts*, which record the lives and deaths of many of the apostles after the *Acts of the Apostles*, are filled with legendary accounts, and thus undermine the credibility of the tradition.[25] Candida Moss concludes: "The result is that the fact of the apostles' deaths cannot be used as evidence for the truth of Christianity, the resurrection, or any other detail of Jesus's ministry."[26]

Lack of Information

These two challenges raise important issues. As for the first challenge, it is true that there is little information on the lives and deaths of *some* of the apostles shortly after the inception of the church. But the lack of information does not undermine the significance of what does exist. As I will show, the evidence for individual apostles varies considerably. And it is certainly possible that future evidence will arise that sheds further light on the fate of the apostles.

---

the *idea* of martyrdom synonymous with the particular term. A group may value death for a specific reason without having a corresponding word for the person who dies. She says: "If terminology is divorced from theme, the search for the beginning of martyrdom takes us into the expanses of the Greco-Roman and ancient Jewish literature, to the tales of the Maccabees, the epic poems of Homer, and the paradigmatic death of Socrates" (Candida R. Moss, *Ancient Christian Martyrdom* [New Haven, CT: Yale University Press, 2012], 5). As Moss observes, early Christians did not necessarily see dying for their faith in Christ as new and unique (see Heb 11:32–38). The key issue for this book is not whether the term *martyrs* was in use during the time of the deaths of the apostles. This book will utilize a functional definition of martyr that incorporates examples of martyrdom even if the corresponding technical term was not yet in use.

[24] In a debate with William Lane Craig, Bart Ehrman questioned the quality of the historical evidence for the martyrdom of the apostles: "And an earlier point that Bill made was that the disciples were all willing to die for their faith. I didn't hear one piece of evidence for that. I hear that claim a lot, but having read every Christian source from the first five hundred years of Christianity, I'd like him to tell us what the piece of evidence is that the disciples died for their belief in the resurrection" ("Bart D. Ehrman—Opening Statement," in William Lane Craig and Bart D. Ehrman, "Is There Historical Evidence for the Resurrection of Jesus?", debate at Holy Cross, Worcester, MA, March 28, 2006, accessed November 5, 2013, http://www.reasonablefaith.org/is-there-historical-evidence-for-the-resurrection-of-jesus-the-craig-ehrman#section_2).

[25] Robert M. Price, "Would the Apostles Die for a Lie?" *Free Inquiry* 21 (Fall 2001): 20.

[26] Moss, *Myth of Persecution*, 137.

Two reasons may help explain why there is so little detailed early explication of the lives and deaths of the apostles. First, during the inception of the church, Christians did not write primarily to chronicle their own history, but to address specific issues and problems in the church. Paul does not aim to write a history of the church or develop a systematic theology. Rather, he addresses particular issues within individual churches. The same is true for a period in the post-apostolic age. On his way to martyrdom, for instance, Ignatius wrote his letters to individual churches to address issues they were currently facing, such as unity, suffering, and the danger of false teachers. The *Didache*, also known as *The Teaching of the Twelve Apostles*, is a handbook with instructions for Christian behavior. And the *Shepherd of Hermas* deals with real issues people confronted, including the problem of sin after baptism. There is no systematic history of the church until Eusebius in the fourth century. The one exception to this point is the book of Acts, which records important church history. But even the focus of Acts is more on chronicling the spread of the Gospel (cf. Acts 1:8) than on recording the history of the church for its own sake.

Second, we should remember the purpose for which Jesus called 12 apostles. James Dunn notes: "The only obvious way to interpret the significance of Jesus' choice of twelve disciples was that he saw them as representing (the twelve tribes of) Israel, at least in God's eschatological intent."[27] This same reasoning lies behind the emphasis in early Christianity upon "the Twelve," as seen in passages such as 1 Corinthians 15:5 and Revelation 21:14. The calling of the 12 disciples was a prophetic sign that God was sovereignly initiating a new era for Israel. Craig Keener writes:

> Although these witnesses were foundational (cf. similarly Eph 2:20), from the standpoint of Luke's theology, such choices did not exalt the individuals chosen *as* individuals (hence the emphasis on their backgrounds, e.g., Luke 5:8; 22:34; Acts 8:3); rather, these choices highlighted God's sovereign plan to fulfill the mission effectively ... apart from Jesus, all the protagonists would be like David, who passed from the scene after fulfilling God's purpose in his generation (Acts 13:36).[28]

This may help explain why the Gospels pay so little attention to some of the apostles. The importance of the Twelve is found less in the individuals who composed the group than in the theological transformation their existence signified. For these two reasons, one may expect little historical explication of their lives in the writings of the early church.

---

[27] James D.G. Dunn, *Beginning from Jerusalem: Christianity in the Making* (Grand Rapids, MI: Eerdmans, 2009), 2:206.

[28] Craig S. Keener, *Acts: An Exegetical Commentary* (Grand Rapids, MI: Baker, 2012), 1:662.

Legendary versus History

As for the second challenge, Candida Moss completely dismisses the evidence for the deaths of the apostles because "our sources for these events are the stuff of legend, not history."[29] There are two problems with this sweeping dismissal. First, evidence for some of the apostles is not contained in legendary documents, such as Clement of Rome's accounts of the deaths of Peter and Paul, and Josephus's account of the death of James. Second, while many legendary accounts of the lives and deaths of various apostles occur in the early writings of the church, including some seemingly unbelievable[30] legends contained in *Apocryphal Acts*,[31] the key question is not whether they contain some legends, but whether they contain a historical core. Hans-Josef Klauck observes: "From the fourth and fifth centuries onward, in the West and especially in the East, the relevant material becomes more and more copious and crosses the always fluid border into pure legend and hagiography."[32] Moss agrees: "It was ... during the fourth century that Christians became more interested in telling romantic fictions than preserving historical facts."[33] If Christians started telling romantic fictions around the fourth century, without any ties to historical truth, then it seems to imply that before that time they *were* concerned with preserving at least a remnant of historical truth. And sometimes it may be reasonable to conclude that a kernel of historical truth has been preserved even *after* this time as well. We must examine each account individually, not, as Moss does, merely sweep them aside collectively.

The *Apocryphal Acts of the Apostles*, then, written before the fourth century, may contain some remnants of a reliable historical tradition. Most scholars seem to assume the *Apocryphal Acts* are entirely fictional and incapable of providing veridical historical data on the lives and martyrdoms of the apostles. However, two points raise questions about the dogmatism with which this position is often

---

[29] Moss, *Myth of Persecution*, 136.

[30] Even in court cases, jurors are instructed that they may not believe a particular portion of an eyewitness account, but can still accept some other isolated piece. The juror simply has to try to determine why the witness might speak truthfully in one area of testimony, while lying or being incorrect in another.

[31] For example, in *The Acts of John* a group of bedbugs pester the apostle John. They annoy him so much that he commands them to stay far away from "the servants of God." They wake in the morning and find the bugs patiently waiting at the door of the room. The bugs continue to obey the voice of John. In the *Acts of Philip*, a huge leopard prostrates itself at the feet of three apostles and speaks to them with a human voice. And in *The Acts of Paul*, milk splashes on the tunics of the executioners at the beheading of Paul.

[32] Hans Josef Klauck, *The Apocryphal Acts of the Apostles*, trans. Brian McNeil (Waco, TX: Baylor University Press, 2008), 231.

[33] Moss, *Myth of Persecution*, 234.

held. First, archaeological finds have provided support for at least one significant *Act*.[34] Second, there may be a living memory of an earlier reliable tradition that some of the *Acts* contain.[35] Of course, then, while they would not be treated with the same credulity as other ancient writings, such as those of Tacitus or Josephus, still these accounts should not, without careful analysis, be dismissed as entirely fictitious. Instead of simply dismissing apocryphal accounts that contain legend, I intended carefully and cautiously to use them in historical analysis.

Additional Historical Challenges

Two final challenges hinder an ability to discern the lives and fates of individual apostles. First, beginning late in the second century, various major cities began claiming apostolic origins. Justo Gonzalez observes:

> In its rivalry with Rome and Antioch, the church in Alexandria felt the need to have a founder with apostolic connections, and thus the tradition appeared that Saint Mark had founded the church there. Likewise, when Constantinople became a capital city in the empire, its church too needed apostolic roots, and thus it was claimed that Philip had preached in Byzantium, the ancient site on which Constantinople was later built.[36]

There are multiple traditions surrounding the apostle Andrew, involving Scythia (southern Russia), Greece, as well as Ephesus and Asia Minor. These traditions may appear contradictory, and attempts have been made to reconcile them.[37] Perhaps an overly zealous church invented one or more of the traditions to give itself apostolic authority. It may be difficult to know for sure. The mere fact that multiple traditions exist does not, however, mean there is no knowable truth about Andrew's mission. And it does not follow that a reasonable conclusion cannot be drawn by analyzing the quality and quantity of evidence. At worst, the various traditions simply raise the difficulty of investigation and the care with which the evidence must be handled.

The second challenge for the investigation into the deaths of the apostles relates to the fact that in the Greco-Roman world, dying a courageous death was both a sign of virtue as well as a mark of manliness. A good death could transform one into a model of patriotism or heroism.[38] This was doubly true for

---

[34]   See Chapter 9 for a significant archaeological finding that supports *The Acts of Thomas*.

[35]   See the analysis of *The Acts of Peter* in Chapter 5.

[36]   Justo Gonzalez, *The Early Church to the Dawn of the Reformation*, The Story of Christianity, revised and updated ed. (New York: HarperCollins, 2010), 1:37.

[37]   McBirnie, *The Search for the Twelve Apostles*, 52.

[38]   Moss, *Ancient Christian Martyrdom*, 28–29.

Christians since Jesus, who died as a martyr, founded Christianity.[39] Clement of Alexandria said: "We call martyrdom perfection, not because the man comes to the end of his life as others, but because he has exhibited the perfect work of love."[40] According to Tertullian: "The death of martyrs also is praised in song."[41] Thus, martyrdom stories served both edifying and apologetic purposes in the early church, especially in the West.[42]

Does this mean the martyrdom stories were fabricated? Some may have been. Multiple stories for certain apostles include their dying in different places, at different times, and in different ways. Clearly they cannot all be true. But it hardly follows that *all* stories were invented simply because they elevate the status of the martyr and served an apologetic function in the early church. Just because a fact may have an apologetic function does not mean it was invented. The writer could be equally motivated by concern for truth. The onus, then, is on those who claim the stories were *all* invented; what evidence exists to warrant the claim? In fact, if the church felt free to invent martyrdom stories, then one wonders why more stories of the martyrdoms of the apostles were not invented in the first two centuries of the church. The silence of history is telling.

I uphold, then, that the disciples fully understood the cost of following Jesus. In his farewell address to his disciples, Jesus spoke both of the world's hatred for them and of the witness that the Holy Spirit and the disciples will provide for him. The result of this witness, Jesus warned his disciples, would be their suffering and death (John 15:18–16:4). Thus, they expected and anticipated their own deaths for the sake of the Gospel. In doing so, they were following the example of Jesus, and providing the greatest possible witness for their belief in the risen Jesus. William Weinrich concludes:

> Jesus' love, shown in his death, leads to the disciples' giving their life for the brethren. The suffering and death of the disciples, occasioned by the hate of the world, is "witness" to Jesus and therefore gives sustenance to the community of believers. This element was fundamental in the early Christian view of martyrdom

---

[39] G.W.H. Lampe, "Martyrdom and Inspiration," in *Suffering and Martyrdom in the New Testament*, ed. William Horbury and Brian McNeil (Cambridge: Cambridge University Press, 1981), 118.

[40] Clement of Alexandria, *Stromata, Miscellanies* 4.4, as cited in *Ante-Nicene Fathers: Fathers of the Second Century: Hermas, Tatian, Athenagoras, Theophilus, and Clement of Alexandria*, ed. Alexander Roberts and James Donaldson, rev and chronologically arranged by A. Cleveland Coxe (Buffalo, NY: Christian Literature Co., 1885), 2:412.

[41] Tertullian, *Scorpiace* 7, as cited in *The Ante-Nicene Fathers: Latin Christianity: Its Founder, Tertullian*, ed. Alexander Roberts and James Donaldson, rev. A. Cleveland Coxe (Buffalo, NY: Christian Literature Co., 1885), 3:639.

[42] Herbert Musurillo, *The Acts of the Christian Martyrs* (Oxford: Oxford University Press, 1972), liv.

and lies at the bottom of the Acts of the Martyrs whose principal function was to exhort and encourage those who read them.[43]

Jesus was the great exemplar for his disciples. He called his disciples not merely to follow his doctrines or teachings, but to follow *him*. He willingly laid down his life for those he loved (John 10:14–18). Christians are urged to follow his example (Mark 8:31–38; Heb 12:1–3; 1 Pet 2:18–25; 1 John 2:6). Paul called believers to him as he imitated Christ (1 Cor 11:1; Phil 3:17; 1 Thess 1:6; 2 Thess 3:7). Paul suffered greatly for his faith (2 Cor 23–33). He saw this suffering as honoring Christ, but also testifying to His name. Ignatius saw martyrdom as an imitation of the example of Jesus: "Permit me to be an imitator of the passion of my God."[44] While the ancient world revered as heroes those who died a good death, the church did not need to invent all the martyrdom stories, for the apostles willingly faced death as an act of imitating Christ, so their message would have the greatest impact.

Research Outline

Even though there are undeniable impediments to the investigation, careful historical analysis revealed that the apostles were willing to die for their faith, and that in fact many did. The strength of their convictions demonstrates that they were not fabricating their claims about Jesus, but that they actually believed their claims that Jesus had risen from the grave.

Before examining the historical evidence for individual apostles, a few steps need to be established. The subsequent chapters address the following issues:

1. What was the apostolic kerygma? Chapter 2 makes the case that the Christian faith was a "resurrection movement" since its inception. People joined the church because they believed in the resurrection, and the apostles, as well as other early Christians, willingly suffered for their conviction that Jesus rose from the grave. There is no record of an early Christianity in which belief in the resurrection was missing.
2. Who were the Twelve? Were they really eyewitnesses to the resurrection? Chapter 3 explains what is known about the apostles and provides evidence they were genuinely eyewitnesses. Focus is placed on the original 12 disciples—with Matthias replacing Judas—as well as Paul and James

---

[43]   William C. Weinrich, *Spirit and Martyrdom: A Study of the Work of the Holy Spirit in Contexts of Persecution and Martyrdom in the New Testament and Early Christian Literature* (Washington, DC: University Press of America, 1981), 30–31.

[44]   Ignatius, *Epistle to the Romans*, 6.13.

the brother of Jesus, since they were also witnesses of the resurrection (1 Cor 15:3–8). It is important to demonstrate that they were actually eyewitnesses because this separates them from others who suffered and died for their beliefs, including modern day martyrs.

3. Did Christians really suffer and die for their faith in the early decades of the church? How extensive was the persecution? In order to establish that the apostles died as martyrs it was demonstrated that Christians were in fact tortured and killed in significant numbers during the early church. Chapter 4 demonstrates the historical evidence for the persecution of Christians in the first century. Among the sources for this evidence are the New Testament, early Christian writers, and Roman and Jewish historians.

4. Is there evidence the apostles died as martyrs for their faith? Chapters 5–18 are the core of the book and the linchpin of the argument. The chapters begin with the most attested apostles, such as Peter and Paul, move to the moderately attested apostles, such as Andrew and Thomas, and conclude with the least attested apostles, such as Simon the Zealot and Matthias. After the historical evidence is presented, each apostle is analyzed with a historical rating from *not possibly true* (certainly not historical) to *the highest possible probability* (nearly historically certain).

5. The concluding chapter summarizes the evidence from the investigation and draws broad conclusions concerning the fate of the apostles regarding the evidence it provides for the resurrection. Three pressing objections are considered and rebutted. Once all the evidence is considered, it is clear the apostles were willing to die for reporting what they believed to be true, and that many in fact did.

Chapter 2
The Centrality of the Resurrection

We can count the deaths of the apostles as evidence for the sincerity of their convictions about the risen Jesus only if the apostles had a *resurrection* faith. That is, (1) the resurrection must lie at the heart of the earliest Christian *kerygma*, and (2) the faith of the disciples must be based upon their belief that Jesus truly rose from the grave.

While some critics doubt the centrality of the resurrection,[1] the majority of scholars accept that Christianity was a resurrection faith since its inception. In *The Resurrection of The Messiah*, New Testament scholar Christopher Bryan begins his inquiry with the assumption that three established facts can be considered "historical certainties," one of which is the centrality of the resurrection in the earliest Christian self-definition.[2] Bryan is not alone in his estimation. According to ancient historian Paul Barnett: "It was this twin conviction, that Jesus was the Christ and that God had raised him alive from the dead, that drove and energized the first disciples and that alone accounts for the rise of Christianity as we encounter it in the historical records."[3]

What gives these scholars such confidence? To see the centrality of the resurrection in the first Christian *kerygma*, the evidence is considered from early Christian creeds, preaching in Acts, Paul's letters, and the Apostolic Fathers.

Early Christian Creeds

Early Christological creeds, verbal proclamations of the faith that circulated *before* their inclusion in various New Testament books, are often considered the most promising glimpse into the earliest Christian beliefs before the composition of the New Testament writings (beginning *c.* AD 50).[4] These creeds

---

[1]   Robert M. Price, "Would the Apostles Die for a Lie?" *Free Inquiry* 21 (Fall 2001): 20

[2]   Christopher Bryan, *The Resurrection of the Messiah* (Oxford: Oxford University Press, 2011), 3–4. According to Bryan, the other two "historical certainties" are the existence of the Christian church in the years following the crucifixion and the belief, among both Jews and Gentiles, that dead people stayed dead.

[3]   Paul Barnett, *The Birth of Christianity: The First Twenty Years* (Grand Rapids, MI: Eerdmans, 2005), 186.

[4]   Gary R. Habermas, *The Historical Jesus: Ancient Evidence for the Life of Christ* (Joplin, MO: College Press, 1997), 143–70. I credit Gary Habermas for many of the insights that guide the formulation of this section.

provide a window into the earliest known Christian beliefs that motivated the proclamation of their faith, the most common elements of which were the death and resurrection of Jesus, which demonstrate the present Lordship of Christ.[5]

An example many scholars consider a Christological creed is Romans 1:3–4: "Concerning his Son, who was descended from David, according to the flesh and was declared to be the Son of God in power according to the Spirit of holiness and by his resurrection from the dead, Jesus Christ our Lord." Rudolph Bultmann says this passage relies upon a pre-Pauline traditional formula from the early church, which dated the Messiahship of Jesus from the resurrection.[6] Paul is proclaiming that the man, Jesus, was born of human descent through the lineage of David and was declared the Son of God, Christ the Lord, because of his resurrection.

Romans 4:24b–25 contains another possible early creed: "It will be counted to us who believe in him who raised from the dead Jesus our Lord, who was delivered up for our trespasses and raised for our justification." Bultmann considers this "a statement that had evidently existed before Paul and had been handed down to him."[7] According to this creed, justification for sins is provided to those who have faith in the one who raised Jesus from the dead. Again, one finds the resurrection at the heart of earliest Christian belief. The important point about these creeds is that there is testimony to the centrality of the resurrection that likely pre-dates the writing of Romans—typically dated between AD 55 and 58.

Another strong candidate for an early creed can be found in 1 Thessalonians 4:14: "For since we believe that Jesus died and rose again." This is the basic Christian confession of the early church. Paul taught this same creed when the Thessalonian church was founded (Acts 17:3). The introductory statement "we believe," the atypical reference to "Jesus" without a title, and the rare translation "rose again" (anestē) in the writings of Paul indicate this is a pre-Pauline creed. Gene Green writes: "These characteristics suggest that the apostle appeals to a pre-Pauline creed that had been handed over to the church and that both the apostolic company and the Thessalonians confessed. The centrality of the death and resurrection of Jesus as the cornerstone of the apostolic proclamation can hardly be disputed."[8]

By the time Paul wrote the letter to the Thessalonians (c. AD 49/50), the heart of the creedal proclamation—the resurrection—was in a fixed form. Paul

---

[5]   Oscar Cullmann, The Earliest Christian Confessions, trans. J.K.S. Reid (London: Lutterworth Press, 1949), 58–64.

[6]   Rudolf K. Bultmann, Theology of the New Testament, trans. Kendrick Grobel (New York: Charles Scribner's Sons, 1951), 1:27, 50, 82.

[7]   Ibid., 82.

[8]   Gene Green, The Letter to the Thessalonians, The Pillar New Testament Commentary (Grand Rapids, MI: Eerdmans, 2002), 219–20.

is not arguing for the truth of the resurrection to the church at Thessalonica. Rather, he mentions the resurrection in passing, which indicates there was already agreement upon its centrality and importance.

Early creeds can also be found outside the letters of Paul. Oscar Cullmann considers 1 Peter 3:18 such an example: "For Christ also suffered once for sins, the righteous for the unrighteous, that he might bring us to God, being put to death in the flesh but made alive in the spirit." In light of 1 Peter 3:18, and other such creeds, Cullmann concludes: "It is, then, the *present* Lordship of Christ, inaugurated by His resurrection and exaltation to the right hand of God, that is the centre of the faith of primitive Christianity."[9]

First Corinthians 15:3–7

Perhaps the most crucial creedal text for understanding early Christian *kerygma* is found in 1 Corinthians 15:3–5:

> For I delivered to you as of first importance what I also received: that Christ died for our sins in accordance with the Scriptures, that he was buried, that he was raised on the third day in accordance with the Scriptures, and that he appeared to Cephas, then to the twelve.

Paul goes on to describe an appearance of Jesus to the 500, to James, to all the apostles, and then to himself. The core of this tradition is the death, burial, resurrection, and appearances of Jesus.

The chief value of this creed is its early dating. First Corinthians is typically dated AD 54–5, roughly twenty-five years after the death of Jesus (*c.* AD 30). Thus, this formulation reveals a pre-Pauline tradition even closer to the time of Jesus than the writing of 1 Corinthians. In the preceding verses, Paul says: "Now I would remind you, brothers" (1 Cor 15:1). Paul intends to *remind* them of the core Gospel facts they already knew. Thus, Paul did not invent this creedal formula, but faithfully passes on the tradition he had previously received.

Gary Habermas offers five reasons why the creedal nature of this passage is accepted by the vast majority of critical scholars across a diverse theological spectrum.[10] First, Paul uses the words "delivered" (*paradidōmi*) and "received" (*paralambanō*), which are technical terms for the transmission of tradition. Second, many of the words in the creed are non-Pauline, indicating a distinct origin. Third, the creed is likely organized in a stylized, oral form. Fourth, there

---

9   Cullmann, *The Earliest Christian Confessions*, 58. See pp. 41, 45, 53, and 57–62 for the creedal nature of this passage.

10   Habermas, *The Historical Jesus*, 153–54.

are internal indications of a Semitic source, such as the reference to Peter with the Aramaic "Cephas." Finally, the triple usage of "and that" as well as the reference to the fulfillment of Scripture indicate ancient Hebraic narration.

There is good reason to believe the origin of this tradition is Jerusalem. In the list of appearances, Paul specifically mentions Cephas and James (1 Cor 15:5, 7). It cannot be mere coincidence that these are the only two apostles Paul mentions visiting in person on his first trip to Jerusalem. Nevertheless, the key question is *when* Paul received the tradition. Two main possibilities present themselves. First, Paul received the tradition during his stay with Ananias and other disciples in Damascus after his conversion (Acts 9:19). Paul immediately began proclaiming Christ, and gained in his ability to confound the opposition with evidence that Jesus was the Christ (Acts 9:20–22). Second, he received the tradition during his first visit to Jerusalem three years later (Acts 9:26–28; Gal 1:18). Paul stayed with the apostles for fifteen days, which is plenty of time to learn about the life, death, resurrection, and appearances of Jesus. Paul uses the term "visit" (*historeō*) to describe his stay in Jerusalem, which implies he went to interview Peter. It has the same root word as the modern term "history." It was important for Paul to get to know the apostles, specifically Peter. According to F.F. Bruce, it should go without saying that Paul sought firsthand accounts of the life, death, and resurrection of Jesus from the apostles. One piece of information Bruce says Paul "most probably" received is the appearance of Jesus to Peter (Luke 24:34).[11]

Paul Barnett prefers the first option, that Paul received the tradition during his stay in Damascus. After all, what else was Paul preaching in Damascus besides the death and resurrection of Jesus?[12] Nevertheless, other possibilities exist as to when Paul received the tradition.[13] There may not be certainty when Paul received the tradition, but long before the writing of 1 Corinthians he had ample opportunity through contact with leading Jerusalem figures. Michael R. Licona writes:

> Moreover, even if Paul received the tradition embedded in 1 Corinthians 15:3–7
> from someone outside of the Jerusalem leadership, his constant interaction with
> these leaders in and outside of Jerusalem coupled with his high regard for tradition
> virtually guarantees that the details of the tradition in 1 Corinthians 15:3–7 are

---

[11]   F.F. Bruce, *The Epistle to the Galatians*, The New International Greek Testament Commentary (Grand Rapids, MI: Eerdmans, 1982), 98.

[12]   Paul Barnett, *Jesus and the Rise of Early Christianity* (Downers Grove, IL: InterVarsity Press, 1999), 182. He notes that the phrase "I delivered to you as of *first importance*" can equally be rendered as "I delivered to you what I also received *at first*," which would have been at Damascus.

[13]   Paul visits Jerusalem on at least two more occasions before writing his first letter (Acts 11:27; 15:2; Gal 2:1–10). Paul could also have received the tradition from Barnabas, James, Silas, or another apostle on a separate occasion.

precisely in line with what the Jerusalem leadership was preaching (1 Cor 15:11). We have what amounts to a certifiably official teaching of the disciples on the resurrection of Jesus.[14]

We have, then, firm and unambiguous evidence that the resurrection was at the heart of the earliest Christian *kerygma*. The fact that Paul mentions the apostles in the 1 Corinthians 15:3–7 creed—"the Twelve," "all the apostles"—indicates that belief in the resurrection of Jesus was not simply a Pauline idea, but belonged to the entire circle of first believers.

The Resurrection in Acts and the Letters of Paul

We also find evidence for the centrality of the resurrection of Jesus in the apostolic preaching in Acts. Speeches in Acts make up approximately one-third of the book's content. In contrast to Luke's contemporary writers, such as Tacitus, Herodotus, and Josephus, Luke chronicles events propelled largely by the spoken word. Luke seems to want his audience to know that the Spirit-filled preaching of Jesus, as opposed to other macrohistorical events such as wars, paved the way for the church's explosive growth.[15]

In his Pentecost speech, Peter describes how God appointed Jesus to do wonders but he was killed by lawless men, and yet "God raised him up, loosing the pangs of death, because it was not possible for him to be held by it" (Acts 2:24).[16] The resurrection is mentioned in most evangelistic speeches, to both Jews and Gentiles, as well as in other passages throughout Acts.[17] James Dunn concludes:

> The claim that Jesus had been raised from the dead is the central and principal message of the preaching in Acts .... We can be quite confident, then, that Jesus'

---

[14]   Michael R. Licona, *The Resurrection of Jesus: A New Historiographical Approach* (Downers Grove, IL: InterVarsity Press, 2010), 232.

[15]   Ben Witherington III, *The Acts of the Apostles: A Socio-Rhetorical Commentary* (Grand Rapids, MI: Eerdmans, 1998), 116–18.

[16]   C.K. Barrett makes the observation that this speech, which is characteristic of Acts as a whole (except at 20:28), shows no developed theology, especially in comparison with the letters of Paul. There is no suggestion that Jesus is the incarnate Son of God and no positive effect is ascribed to his death. Thus, Barrett concludes: "There is no question that this speech and those that resemble it present an elementary, undeveloped, theology and Christology." He concludes that the speeches must be early. See C.K. Barrett, *A Critical and Exegetical Commentary on the Acts of the Apostles* (New York: T. &T. Clark, 1994), 1:131–32.

[17]   Acts 1:21; 2:24, 31–32; 3:15; 4:2, 10–11, 33; 5:30; 10:40; 13:30, 33–34; 17:3, 18, 31; 23:6; 24:15, 21; 25:19; 26:8, 23.

resurrection was from the first a prominent and distinctive feature of earliest Christian belief and functioned as a defining identity marker of the new sect which gathered round his name.[18]

Paul fills his letters, especially the book of Romans, with affirmations of the resurrection as well. N.T. Wright observes:

> Squeeze this letter [Romans] at any point, and resurrection spills out; hold it up to the light, and you can see Easter sparkling all the way through. If Romans had not been hailed as the great epistle of justification by faith, it might easily have come to be known as the chief letter of resurrection.[19]

Paul's letters confirm the central place the resurrection held in the early preaching of Peter in the book of Acts. Yet the theme of resurrection is not limited to Acts and the letters of Paul. With the exception of Hebrews, all the major books of the New Testament make resurrection a central focus.[20]

Resurrection in the Apostolic Fathers

The resurrection is at the heart of the biblical and pre-biblical proclamation of the earliest Christians. Yet it is also central to many of the generation of believers shortly after the apostles, known as the Apostolic Fathers. For instance, *1 Clement* 42:3 says: "When, therefore, the apostles received his commands and were fully convinced through the resurrection of our Lord Jesus Christ and persuaded by the word of God, they went forth proclaiming the good news that the Kingdom of God was about to come."

In his *Letter to the Magnesians* 11, Ignatius wrote: "You should be fully convinced of the birth and suffering and resurrection that occurred in the time of the governor Pontius Pilate."[21] Resurrection permeates many of the rest of his letters.[22] In the *Letter of Polycarp to the Philippians*, Polycarp says: "He [Jesus] persevered to the point of death on behalf of our sins; and God raised him up

---

[18]   James D.G. Dunn, *Beginning from Jerusalem: Christianity in the Making* (Grand Rapids, MI: Eerdmans, 2009), 2:212–13.

[19]   N.T. Wright, *The Resurrection of the Son of God* (Minneapolis, MN: Fortress Press, 2003), 241.

[20]   Ibid., 476.

[21]   Bart D. Ehrman, ed. and trans., *The Apostolic Fathers* (Cambridge, MA: Harvard University Press, 2004), 1:253.

[22]   *To The Ephesians* 20; *To The Trallians* intro., 9; *To The Philadelphians* intro., 9; *To The Smyrneans* 1, 12.

after loosing the labor paints of Hades."[23] His belief in the resurrection helped Polycarp face martyrdom boldly.

The *Letter of Barnabas* offers a critique of Jewish practices—such as circumcision, fasting, kosher food laws, Sabbath, and so on—in contrast to the new life in Christ. The whole point of the book is that Jewish practices are no longer necessary for salvation because of the death and resurrection of Jesus. Thus, *The Letter of Barnabas* 5:6 says: "He [Jesus] allowed himself to suffer in order to destroy death and to show that there is a resurrection of the dead."[24] The resurrection is the heart of the earliest Christian *kerygma*, from the pre-biblical creeds to the Apostolic Fathers.

Conclusion

The resurrection was central to Christian proclamation from the inception of the church to at least the generation after the death of the apostles. Craig Keener writes: "Paul and his predecessors were united on the basic Gospel message (1 Cor 15:1–12); we lack any evidence, except for secondary scholarship reflecting speculation, for "Jesus communities" that did not affirm Jesus as Messiah (and hence King and Lord) or that denied his resurrection."[25]

For all the first-century disagreements within the church, the lack of any evidence for disputation on the resurrection speaks loudly as to its centrality and universality among the first believers. James Dunn observes:

> It is an undoubted fact that the conviction that God had raised Jesus from the dead and had exalted Jesus to his right hand transformed Jesus' first disciples and their beliefs about Jesus. It is also natural that they should have focused their earliest preaching and teaching on filling out the consequences of that basic belief.[26]

It is important to grasp the significance of the earliest Christian *kerygma* for the lives of the disciples. Although they were Galileans and their lives were in danger since the arrest and death of Jesus, they stayed in Jerusalem to proclaim the resurrection. This shows their understanding and acceptance of the basic meaning of the crucified and risen savior. Otherwise, they would hardly have engaged in missionary work. If they wanted to persuade Jews in Jerusalem to

---

[23] *Letter of Polycarp to the Philippians* 1.2, in *The Apostolic Fathers*, 1:333–34.

[24] Bart D. Ehrman, ed. and trans., *The Apostolic Fathers* (Cambridge, MA: Harvard University Press, 2004), 2:27. Other passages in the *Letter* highlight the importance of the resurrection, including 1:6–7, 15:9, and 16:2–3.

[25] Craig S. Keener, *Acts: An Exegetical Commentary* (Grand Rapids, MI: Baker, 2012), 1:565.

[26] Dunn, *Beginning from Jerusalem*, 2:1,169.

believe in Jesus, it would be counterproductive to invent fictitious stories whose falsehood could easily be discovered. Thus, their preaching only makes sense if they truly believed Jesus had risen from the dead, and if the evidence was there to confirm it.

Chapter 3

The Twelve Apostles

Very early on in his public ministry, Jesus reached out to 12 individuals, inviting them to be his personal disciples. Mark offers two purposes for the selection of the Twelve. First, they were to "be with him" (Mark 3:14a). They ate with him, travelled with him, ministered with him, watched him do miracles, and listened to his teachings; some even observed his arrest, trial, and execution.[1] During their time with Jesus, they experienced a rigorous apprenticeship patterned after the approach Judaism took towards the Old Testament.[2] Second, Jesus selected the Twelve that he "might send them out to preach and have authority to cast out demons" (Mark 3:14b–15). Through the Twelve, Jesus was multiplying his effectiveness. Even more importantly, though, he was preparing them to carry on his work after he was gone.

Who Were the Twelve?

The term "the Twelve" appears in all four Gospels.[3] The Synoptic Gospels and Acts provide the names for the Twelve (see Table 1.1).

The Gospel of John offers no list, but does refer to some of them, including Andrew, Peter, Philip, Nathanael, Thomas, Judas (not Iscariot), Judas Iscariot, the "son of Zebedee," who are not mentioned by name, and the disciple "whom Jesus loved."

How, if at all, can we reconcile the different names mentioned as members of the Twelve? Some scholars have suggested that differences among the lists indicate that the original names were forgotten when the Gospels were written down, making the tradition unreliable.[4] However, differences in the lists are minimal, and their similarities offer a potentially decipherable pattern. In all

---

[1] Peter, James, and John were with Jesus in the Garden of Gethsemane at his arrest (Mark 14:32–50; Matt 26:36–56; Luke 22:39–53; John 18:1–11). Peter followed Jesus into the courtyard (Mark 14:54). John was present at the cross (John 19:26–27). This, of course, assumes the apostle John is "the beloved disciple."

[2] Ronald Brownrigg, *The Twelve Apostles* (New York: Macmillan, 1974), 33–34.

[3] Matt 10:1–25; 11:1; 20:17, 47; Mark 3:14, 16; 4:10; 6:7; 9:35; 10:32; 11:11; 14:10, 17, 20, 43; Luke 6:13; 8:1; 9:1, 12; 18:31; 22:3, 47; John 6:67, 70–71; 20:24.

[4] For instance, see Joseph A. Fitzmyer, *The Gospel according to Luke I–IX: Introduction, Translation, and Notes*, The Anchor Bible, vol. 28 (Garden City, NY: Doubleday, 1981), 620.

Table 1.1   Apostolic lists

Matthew 10:2–4	Mark 3:16–19	Luke 6:13–16	Acts 1:13
Simon (Peter)	Simon (Peter)	Simon (Peter)	Peter
Andrew	James, son of	Andrew	John
James, son of	Zebedee	James	James
Zebedee	John	John	Andrew
John	Andrew	Philip	Philip
Philip	Philip	Bartholomew	Thomas
Bartholomew	Bartholomew	Matthew	Bartholomew
Thomas	Matthew	Thomas	Matthew
Matthew	Thomas	James, son of	James, son of
James, son of	James, son of	Alphaeus	Alphaeus
Alphaeus	Alphaeus	Simon the Zealot	Simon the Zealot
Thaddaeus	Thaddeus	Judas, son of James	Judas, son of James
Simon the Zealot	Simon the Zealot	Judas Iscariot	
Judas Iscariot	Judas Iscariot		

four lists, for example, the names occur in three groups of four names—except Acts omits the then-deceased Judas Iscariot—and the first name in each group is the same: Peter always tops the first group, Philip the second, and James, son of Alphaeus, the third; the order of the subsequent names varies. Richard Bauckham provides a plausible explanation: "It is quite intelligible that a list of this kind should be remembered as consisting of three groups, with the first name in each group a fixed point in the memory, but with the order of other three names in each group variable."[5] In addition, the slight variation in the lists may also suggest that the Twelve was more widely known than a standardized list of names.[6]

One difference that requires explanation is the variation between Thaddaeus and Judas, son of James. There are two possible explanations. First, Thaddaeus might have been an original member of the Twelve who dropped out for an unknown reason, whom Judas, son of James, replaced some time later. Some have suggested that the exact composition of the Twelve may have varied from time to time.[7] It seems unlikely, however, that Matthew and Mark would include in the list a dropout instead of his replacement. This differs from the case of Judas, since Judas was essential to the furtherance of the story and his

---

[5]   Richard Bauckham, *Jesus and the Eyewitnesses: The Gospels as Eyewitness Testimony* (Grand Rapids. MI: Eerdmans, 2006), 98.

[6]   Craig S. Keener, *The Historical Jesus of the Gospels* (Grand Rapids, MI: Eerdmans, 2009), 246.

[7]   Leon Morris, *The Gospel According to Matthew*, The Pillar New Testament Commentary (Grand Rapids, MI: Eerdmans, 1992), 243–44.

betrayal is indicated in the list. Second, Judas, son of James, and Thaddaeus[8] might have been the same person. It was not uncommon for Palestinian Jews to have both Semitic and Greek names.[9] Furthermore, Judas, son of James, needed to be distinguished in some way from Judas Iscariot. He is referred somewhat awkwardly as "Judas, not Iscariot" in John 14:22, yet it seems unlikely this was his usual designation.

The difference also appears in the names between Bartholomew, as mentioned in the four lists, and Nathanael, mentioned in John 1:45–52. Bartholomew has traditionally been identified as Nathanael. Three reasons have been offered to justify this conclusion. First, Bartholomew is a family name, not a proper name. Bartholomew comes from the Hebrew for "son of Talmai." Second, Bartholomew immediately follows Philip in the three Gospel lists, and Philip is the one in the Gospel of John who brought Nathanael to Jesus (John 1:45). Third, Nathanael never appears by name in the Synoptic Gospels, and equally Bartholomew never appears by name in the Gospel of John. It seems reasonable to conclude that Bartholomew and Nathanael are the same person.[10]

Finally, there is the question of the identification of Matthew and Levi. Although Matthew occurs in all four lists, there is the distinct call of Levi (Mark 2:13; Luke 5:27), which parallels Matthew's call (Matt 9:9). The similarity in wording between the three accounts as well as the chronology of preceding event—healing the paralytic—and subsequent event—a shared meal with "sinners"—indicates these refer to the same occasion. Thus, the traditional view is that Matthew and Levi are the same person. Robert Stein finds this view reasonable since first-century Jews often had two or more names. He concludes the tax collector could have been called "Levi Matthew." Another possibility is that Levi was Matthew's name prior to conversion. Still, identifying Matthew with Levi has its detractors. However, this issue does not need to be resolved to proceed with the investigation, for the name Matthew appears in all four lists of the Twelve regardless of the identity of Levi.

---

[8] There is early textual evidence that "Lebbaeus" should replace the name Thaddaeus. Some Greek manuscripts even combine the two forms of the text: "Thaddaeus who was called Lebbaeus" or "Lebbaeus who was called "Thaddaeus" (Barclay M. Newman and Philip Stine, *Matthew: A Handbook on the Gospel of Matthew* [New York: United Bible Societies, 1988], 284–85).

[9] Bauckham, *Jesus and the Eyewitnesses*, 100.

[10] Perhaps counting slightly against this tradition is the apostolic list found in the *Epistle of the Apostles* (c. AD 150–175), which lists Bartholomew and Nathanael as separate apostles. The reason this evidence is only slight is that it also has Peter and Cephas as separate apostles, yet virtually all scholars recognize Cephas is another name for Peter.

The Historicity of the Twelve

An impressive case can be made for the historicity of the Twelve as a group Jesus personally formed. Three primary arguments have been offered for the existence of the Twelve during the ministry of Jesus. First, references to the Twelve appear in various sources and forms.[11] The different lists of names for the Twelve indicate they may represent independent tradition. Second, by the criterion of embarrassment, the early church would have been very unlikely to invent a story of Jesus personally choosing Judas to be a member of the Twelve. This is one reason why E.P. Sanders considers the existence of the Twelve among the "(almost) indisputable facts about Jesus."[12] Third, if the tradition of the Twelve were invented, one would expect early church records to be filled with examples of the Twelve's powerful influence and leadership in the church. Yet the opposite is the case. Neither Luke nor Paul has much to say of the Twelve. While the lack of early information on the Twelve makes it difficult to determine the historicity of their martyrdom accounts, this same absence is an indication that the group was not a mere invention of the early church.

Richard Bauckham recently completed an onomastic study of Jewish names of this time that lends additional support to the authenticity of the Twelve.[13] Among Jews in first-century Palestine there were a small number of very popular names and a large number of rare ones. As would be expected, if the tradition of the Twelve were reliable, a combination of common and rare names would be on the lists. This is exactly what we find. Taken together, these facts make it highly likely the Twelve existed as a special group of disciples who formed an inner circle around Jesus.

The Apostolic Witness

The basic sense of "apostle" (*apostolos*) refers to one "sent out" as an authorized emissary on behalf of a superior. In Luke and Acts, the term *apostle* predominantly designates the Twelve.[14] The ministry of these apostles principally involved proclaiming the resurrection of Jesus (Acts 1:22; 2:32; 3:15; 4:33; 5:32; 10:39–41; 13:31), teaching (Acts 2:42), and prayer (Acts 6:2–4). Many signs and

---

[11] Mark mentions the Twelve at least ten times: 3:14; 4:10; 6:7; 9:35; 10:32; 11:11; 14:10, 17, 20, 43. John, who has no special interest in the Twelve, directly mentions the group in 6:67–71. John also refers to Thomas as "one of the Twelve" (20:24). In addition, there may be an indirect reference to the Twelve in the Q tradition of Matt 19:28/Luke 22:30. Paul also has a brief mention of the Twelve in 1 Cor 15:5.

[12] E.P. Sanders, *Jesus and Judaism* (London: SCM Press, 1985), 101.

[13] Bauckham, *Jesus and the Eyewitnesses*, 67–88

[14] Luke 6:13; 9:1, 10; 22:14, 30; 24:9–10; Acts 1:26; 2:37, 42–43; 4:33–37; 5:2, 12, 18, 29, 40; 6:6; 8:1, 14–18; 9:27; 11:1.

wonders were enacted through the apostles as testimony to the truth of their proclamation (Acts 2:43; 3:1–10; 5:12–16). Given that they were commissioned directly by Jesus, the earliest Christian writings portray the apostles as having the authority of Christ himself.[15]

Specific criteria for inclusion in the Twelve include, as Peter makes clear, that he must be "one of the men who have accompanied us during all the time that the Lord Jesus went in and out among us, beginning from the baptism of John until the day when he was taken up from us—one of these men must become with us a witness to his resurrection" (Acts 1:22) Thus, according to Peter, a member of the Twelve must have been with Jesus from the time of his baptism until his ascension, and he would become a witness (*martyrs*) of his life, and specifically to his resurrection. The book of Acts makes repeated claims that the mission and authority of the apostles come from the personal appearances of the risen Jesus.[16] This value for eyewitness testimony is consistent with ancient Greco-Roman culture. The best evidence was believed to come from eyewitnesses, and reports further removed from the events were considered weaker.[17]

The Gospel of John offers additional support to the Lukan idea that an apostle gained authority to proclaim the risen Jesus by having been with Jesus from beginning to end. In his final speech to his disciples after the last supper, Jesus said: "But when the Helper comes, whom I will send to you from the Father, the Spirit of truth, who proceeds from the Father, he will bear witness about me. And you also will bear witness, because you have been with me from the beginning" (15: 26–27). Luke and John agree that true witnesses to the work of Jesus have "been with [Jesus] from the beginning." Richard Bauckham believes this idea was widespread in the early church beyond these two authors: "Evidently in the early Christian movement a special importance attached to the testimony of disciples who had been eyewitnesses of the whole ministry of Jesus, from its beginning when John was baptizing to Jesus' resurrection appearances."[18] Support for Bauckham's thesis can be found in the Apostolic Fathers.[19] The apostles' confidence to suffer in their proclamation of the Gospel came from the belief that they had personally seen the risen Jesus.

The Twelve provide an important link between the time of Jesus and the early church. They provided the initial witness to the risen Jesus (Acts 2:14; 4:33;

---

[15]   Passages that indicate the apostles had the very authority of Christ himself include the earliest biblical texts (Mark 3:14–15; Matt 10:14, 20; John 14:26; 17:8, 18; Acts 10:41–42; 2 Pet 3:2) and the apostolic fathers (*1 Clement* 42:1–2; 47:1–3; Ignatius, *Letter to the Magnesians* 7:1; *Letter to the Romans* 4:4; Justin Martyr, *1 Apology* 39; Irenaeus, *Against Heresies* 3.1.1).

[16]   Acts 1:22; 2:32; 4:20; 5:32; 10:39; 13:31; 22:15.

[17]   Craig S. Keener, *Acts: An Exegetical Commentary* (Grand Rapids, MI: Baker, 2012), 1:768.

[18]   Bauckham, *Jesus and the Eyewitnesses*, 116.

[19]   For instance, see First Clement 42:1–3 and Ignatius, *Letter to the Smyrneans* 3.

5:29–32) and authenticated the mission work to the Samaritans and Gentiles (Acts 8:14; 11:1–18). After accomplishing these tasks, the Twelve disappear from Acts. Although Matthias is chosen to replace Judas early in Acts, there is no attempt to fill the vacancy created by the death of James about a decade later (Acts 12:1–2). After the Twelve accomplish their task, Acts shifts to focus on Peter, James the brother of Jesus, then Paul.

All of the Apostles

The New Testament refers to "all the apostles" in a broader sense, beyond the Twelve (1 Cor 15:7, 9), which had its basis in appearances of the risen Jesus, and thus they are considered "witnesses." Candidates for this group include Barnabas (Acts 14:14; 1 Cor 9:5–6), Stephen (Acts 22), Andronicus and Junias (Rom 16:7), Timothy and Silas (1 Thess 1:1; Col 1:1), Apollos (1 Cor 4:6, 9), and last of all Paul (1 Cor 9:1; 15:8). Authority of this group of apostles came not simply from Christ, but from *the risen Christ*.[20] This group of apostles, which includes the Twelve, was to publicly proclaim the risen Jesus, and they were expected to suffer in the course of being witnesses.

While Paul and James did not belong to the Twelve, they did have apostolic authority from having seen the risen Jesus (1 Cor 15:7–8).[21] Neither believed in Jesus during Jesus's own lifetime: the brothers of Jesus, including James, rejected him (John 7:5), and Paul had even persecuted the church (Acts 8:3; Gal 1:13). So while James and Paul were not part of Jesus's inner circle during his public ministry, they were eyewitnesses of the risen Jesus; their martyrdoms, then, in terms of providing support for their testimony as that of the Twelve, would be equally significant. This is why they are considered *apostles* along with the Twelve for the sake of this investigation.

Did the Apostles Engage in Missionary Work?

While the apostles undoubtedly engaged in their first missionary work to the people of Israel, some doubts exist regarding whether they engaged in missionary work to various nations of the world *after* ministering to the Jews. Mark's Gospel,

---

[20]   Paul makes this claim twice: 1 Cor 9:1, "Am I not an apostle? Have I not seen Jesus our Lord?", and in 15:8 Paul says, "Last of all, as one untimely born, he appeared also to me."

[21]   Rosenblatt argues that the details of Saul as a young man witnessing the death of Stephen (Acts 7:58) were not meant to indict Paul as an accessory to murder, but to make the theological point regarding the integrity of Paul's identity as a witness to Jesus. Marie-Eloise Rosenblatt, *Paul the Accused: His Portrait in the Acts of the Apostles* (Collegeville, MN: Liturgical Press, 1995), 26.

which was likely the first to be written and circulated, contains little reference to a universal commission.[22] The writings of Matthew and Luke, however, both likely written after AD 70, emphasize that the apostles are to "make disciples of all nations" and to be witnesses "in Jerusalem, and in all Judea and Samaria, and to the end of the earth" (Matt 28:19; Acts 1:8). There is a clear shift in emphasis from Israel to the nations of the world.

There is little doubt the apostles first witnessed their faith to Israel. But what evidence is there that they engaged in missionary work *beyond* Israel? There is both internal and external evidence the apostles engaged in missionary work after their departure from Jerusalem.

Internal Evidence for a Universal Commission

Jesus called the Twelve with the specific purpose that they would be missionaries (Mark 3:14). After a period of preparation, Jesus sent the Twelve to minister in pairs, which involved healing the sick, casting out demons, and proclaiming the kingdom of God (Mark 6:7–13; Matt 10:5–16; Luke 9:1–6). This commission has the ring of historicity.[23] The mission was limited in duration, and focused specifically on the house of Israel. Yet, in the subsequent verses Jesus says: "Beware of men, for they will deliver you over to courts and flog you in their synagogues, and you will be dragged before governors and kings for my sake, to bear witness before them and the Gentiles" (Matt 10:17–18; Mark 13:9; Luke 21:12–13). Jesus warns his followers that their preaching will be deeply opposed and they will be brought before the highest authorities in the land. The emphasis on "governors and kings" indicates that Jesus is no longer speaking of their present mission, but the future mission to the Gentiles outside Palestine. This short-term trip is preparation for future missionary activity to all the nations. It is worth noting that Jesus views persecution positively as an opportunity for the apostles to "witness" to the truth of the Gospel. They expected to suffer for proclaiming the kingdom of God to all the nations.

If the mission is to be universal, why begin just with Israel? The reason was theological, not pragmatic.[24] Jesus always intended the kingdom of God to be universal, but he did begin with the Jews.

---

[22]   There is a reference to a universal commission in Mark 16:15: "And he said to them, 'God into all the world and proclaim the gospel to the whole creation.'" The final 12 verses in Mark, 16:9–20, do not appear in the earliest manuscripts and so are rejected by most scholars. If these verses should be included, as a minority of scholars suggest, it would only strengthen the case for a universal commission.

[23]   For a case for the historicity of the missionary endeavors of the Twelve, see John P. Meier, *A Marginal Jew* (New York: Doubleday, 2001), 3:157–63.

[24]   Eckhard J. Schnabel, *Early Christian Mission: Paul and the Early Church* (Downers Grove, IL: InterVarsity Press, 2004), 2:295.

The book of Acts shows the beginnings of the Christian mission. One of Luke's primary purposes is to show the development of Christian evangelism from a religious sphere to a larger secular sphere that includes governors and kings. Acts 1:8 functions as a summary statement, then, for the entire book: the mission begins in Jerusalem (1–7), but then spreads to Judea and Samaria (8–12), and finally to the ends of the earth, which in the story is Rome (13–28). The phrase "ends of the earth," however, is not limited to Rome, as the prophets often use the same phrase to indicate distant lands (Isa 49:6). Some specific events in Acts indicate the universal focus and expansion of the Gospel.

1. Philip the Evangelist proclaimed Christ in Samaria (Acts 8:4–8) and shared with an Ethiopian eunuch (Acts 8:26–40). The apostles in Jerusalem sent Peter and John to confirm the news (Acts 8:14–25).

2. Paul was specifically chosen by Jesus to be his emissary to the Gentiles (Acts 9:15), even while he continued to preach to the house of Israel. Paul was also aware of other Christians involved in missionary work, such as the apostles (1 Cor 9:5; 12:28–29) and other "brothers" who proclaimed the Gospel (Phil 1:12–18).

3. After his vision at Joppa, Peter concluded: "Truly I understand that God shows no partiality, but in every nation anyone who fears him and does what is right is acceptable to him" (Acts 10:34b–35). Peter then shared how he and the other apostles were witnesses to the risen Jesus, sent out to proclaim that message so that *everyone* who believes will be saved (Acts 10:43). Peter also preached the Gospel and saw people "turn to the Lord" as he traveled through Judea, Galilee, Samaria, and Lydda (Acts 9:32–35).

4. The church of Antioch also sent out missionaries to both Jews and Gentiles who had not been reached with the Gospel (Acts 11:19–22; 13:1–2).

5. Acts concludes with Paul preaching "with all boldness and without hindrance" in his final speech in Rome, suggesting the story continues and the witnessing is as yet incomplete.[25] Acts 28 is an intentionally open-ended conclusion to indicate that the worldwide witnessing of the Gospel must continue.[26]

The biblical precedent for the great commission is clear: Jesus trained his apostles to reach the nations, and even commanded them to do so, and the book of Acts recounts the effects of this teaching. The apostles not only

---

[25] John B. Polhill, *Acts*, The New American Commentary, vol. 26 (Nashville, TN: Broadman & Holman, 1992), 86.

[26] Ben Witherington III, *The Acts of the Apostles: A Socio-Rhetorical Commentary* (Grand Rapids, MI: Eerdmans, 1998), 111.

proclaimed the risen Jesus, but as their response to the missionary report from Samaria indicates, they personally directed the missionary efforts from Jerusalem.

External Evidence for a Universal Commission

The New Testament records the commission to reach the ends of the earth. But was such a task even possible in the first century AD? Could the apostles have made it to faraway places like Spain, Ethiopia, and India? In his massive two-volume work *Early Christian Mission*, Eckhard Schnabel provides multiple reasons to believe such a task was entirely possible.[27] While these facts do not *prove* the apostles engaged in missionary activity to distant lands, they do rebut objections meant to undermine the plausibility of such an endeavor. The apostles had the resources, training, and incentive to engage in missionary work. In addition, the Roman Empire was fairly stable during the time of Claudius (AD 41–54), which is the initial period the apostles would have engaged in missionary activity.[28] Not only was missionary activity possible in the first century AD, there is also positive external evidence for such endeavors.

The Twelve led the Jerusalem church until Herod Agrippa (AD 41–44) initiated a persecution that resulted both in the death of James, the son of Zebedee, and the arrest of Peter (Acts 12:1–4). It seems at this point that the Twelve left Jerusalem and transferred leadership to a group of elders led by James the brother of Jesus (Acts 11:30; 12:17; 15:12–21; 21:15–19; Gal 2:9). Acts 12 marks a significant turning point in the ministry of the Twelve and the Jerusalem church. After sharing about his escape from prison, Peter "departed and went to another place" (Acts 12:17). The other apostles likely left at this point as well—if not earlier. It is noteworthy that "the brothers," as well as James, are to be informed about Peter's departure. The other apostles are not mentioned. It seems likely they had already left Jerusalem. Given their awareness of the death of James and subsequent arrest of Peter, it seems abundantly probable the apostles would have fled Jerusalem to avoid the wrath of Herod Agrippa.[29]

The consistent testimony of the early church is that the apostles left Jerusalem to engage in missionary work. As demonstrated below, both orthodox and Gnostic sources see missions as the prime task of an apostle. It is impossible to

---

[27] Schnabel, *Early Christian Mission*, 1:470–99.

[28] The stability during the reign of Claudius is in contrast to the preceding reign of Caligula (AD 37–41), who was insane during part of his time in power, and the subsequent reign of Nero (AD 54–68), who launched the first official state persecution of Christians. See Earle E. Cairns, *Christianity Through the Centuries: A History of the Christian Church*, 3rd ed. (Grand Rapids, MI: Zondervan, 1996), 66.

[29] Polhill, *Acts*, 283.

say whether the persecution was the initial motivation for their mission work, or if the persecution simply put existing plans into motion. Regardless, we have considerable external support for the departure of the Twelve to engage in mission work. This list focuses on testimony within the living memory of the apostles:[30]

Clement of Rome 42:3–4b (c. AD 95–96):
Having therefore received their orders, and being fully assured by the resurrection of our Lord Jesus Christ, and established in the word of God, with full assurance of the Holy Ghost, they went forth proclaiming that the kingdom of God was at hand. And thus preaching through countries and cities.[31]

The Preaching of Peter (c. AD 100–120):
Jesus says to the disciples after the resurrection, "'I have chosen you twelve disciples, judging you worthy of me,' whom the Lord wished to be apostles, having judged them faithful, sending them into the world to the men on the earth, that they may know that there is one God."[32]

Ascension of Isaiah 3.17–18 (c. AD 112–138):
And the Beloved sitting on their shoulders will come forth and send out His twelve disciples; And they will teach all the nations and every tongue of the resurrection of the Beloved, and those who believe in His cross will be saved, and in His ascension into the seventh heaven whence He came.

The Gospel of Thomas 12 (c. AD 140):
The disciples said to Jesus, "We know that you will depart from us. Who is it who will be great over us?" Jesus said to them, "Wherever you have come, you will go to James the Righteous, for whose sake heaven and earth came into being."

---

[30]   There are many later examples which claim the apostles left Jerusalem to engage in missionary work: *Letter of Philip to Peter*; (Pseudo-)*Hippolytus on the Twelve*; Origen, *Commentary on Genesis*, vol. 3, as cited in Eusebius, *Church History* 3.1; *Fragments of Polycarp*; *The Acts of Peter and the Twelve Apostles*; *Epistle of Peter to Philip* 140.23–27; *Acts of Thomas* 1.1; *Didascalia Apostolorum* 24; Eusebius, *Ecclesiastical History* 3.1b–2a.

[31]   Clement of Rome, *The First Epistle of Clement to the Corinthians*, as cited in *Ante-Nicene Fathers: The Apostolic Fathers—Justin Martyr—Irenaeus*, ed. Alexander Roberts and James Donaldson, rev and chronologically arranged by A. Cleveland (Buffalo, NY: Christian Literature Co., 1885), 1:16.

[32]   Clement of Alexandria, *Stromata* 6.6, as cited in *Ante-Nicene Fathers: Fathers of the Second Century: Hermas, Tatian, Athenagoras, Theophilus, and Clement of Alexandria*, ed. Alexander Roberts and James Donaldson, rev. A. Cleveland Coxe (Buffalo, NY: Christian Literature Co., 1885), 2:491.

1 Apology 39.2–3, Justin Martyr (c. AD 155–157):
For from Jerusalem there went out into the world, men, twelve in number, and these illiterate, of no ability in speaking: but by the power of God they proclaimed to every race of men that they were sent by Christ to teach all the word of God.[33]

The Epistle of the Apostles (c. AD 150–175):
He answered and said to us, "Go and preach to the twelve tribes of Israel and to the gentiles and Israel and to the land of Israel towards East and West, North and South."[34]

The Acts of Peter 5 (c. AD 180–190):
While they were grieving and fasting God was already preparing Peter at Jerusalem for the future. After the twelve years had passed, according to the direction of the Lord to Peter, Christ showed to him the following vision, saying, 'Peter, Simon, whom you expelled from Judea after having exposed him as a magician, has forestalled you at Rome ... . But do not delay. Go tomorrow to Caesarea, and there you will find a ship read to sail to Italy ... . Instructed by this vision, Peter did not delay to mention it to the brethren and said, "I must go to Rome to subdue the enemy and opponent of the Lord and brethren."[35]

Apollonius (c. AD 200):
Moreover, he says, on the basis of tradition, that the Savior ordered his apostles not to leave Jerusalem for twelve years.[36]

The historical value of these individual sources undoubtedly varies, and while individual sources do disagree over the *particulars* of some of the apostles' lives, they generally agree the apostles stayed in Jerusalem for some time before embarking on world missions. The apostolic commission to world missions thus meets the criterion of multiple attestation.[37] Why do these sources not tell a

---

[33] Justin Martyr, *The First Apology of Justin*, as cited in *Ante-Nicene Fathers: Fathers of the Second Century: Hermas, Tatian, Athenagoras, Theophilus, and Clement of Alexandria*, ed. Alexander Roberts and James Donaldson, rev. A. Cleveland Coxe (Buffalo, NY: Christian Literature Co., 1885), 1:175–76.

[34] *The Epistle of the Apostles* 30, as cited in J.K. Elliott, *The Apocryphal New Testament* (Oxford: Oxford University Press, 2009), 575.

[35] *The Acts of Peter* 5, as cited in Elliott, *The Apocryphal New Testament*, 401–02.

[36] Eusebius, *History of the Church* 5.18.

[37] Support for the apostolic commission comes from a variety of genres, including letters (*1 Clement*), church order teachings (*Didascalia Apostolorum*), historical accounts (Eusebius, *Church History*), and historical novels (*Acts of Thomas, Acts of Peter*). See Meier, *A Marginal Jew*, 1:174–75.

more consistent and coherent tradition of exactly where each apostle went? Eckhard Schnabel offers important insight:

> If the sources from the second and third centuries presented a coherent and consistent tradition, then this would be used as an argument against the authenticity of such a conference in Jerusalem twelve years after Easter. It is a fact that no early Christian text that reports or claims to report historical events attempts to provide a comprehensive historical account. It is precisely the missing 'coherence' that may indicate that Christian authors of the second and third centuries had information about the ministry of the apostles. Since they did not write a comprehensive history of the early church, they passed on information that they had in a selective and uncoordinated manner.[38]

In sum, we have firm historical support for the missionary endeavors of the Twelve after Jerusalem.

The Testimony of the Twelve

The Twelve were the first witnesses to Jesus, and they spearheaded the initial missionary movement from Jerusalem. Assuming Acts preserves a historical core, the apostles boldly proclaimed their faith after Pentecost, willingly suffering and facing possible death. And if Acts preserves historical kernels in this regard, we see that after Pentecost they boldly proclaimed their faith even in the face of suffering and possible death.

The boldness of the apostles starkly contrasts with their character before Pentecost. Before Pentecost, the apostles regularly misunderstood the teachings of Jesus (Matt 13:1–23; 16:23), they bickered with one another (Mark 10:35–45), they lacked faith (Mark 4:40; Matt 14:31; Mark 9:18; Mark 9:19), and they abandoned Jesus at his arrest (Mark 14:50). What accounts for the radical change in the apostles? How could they go from an ordinary band of men with little courage to a bold group willing to suffer and die for their faith? How did they come to fear God more than men? Luke provides insight:

> But Peter and the apostles answered, "We must obey God rather than men. The God of our fathers raised Jesus, who you killed by hanging him on a tree. God exalted him at the right hand as Leader and Savior, to give repentance to Israel and forgiveness of sins. And we are witnesses to these things, and so is the Holy Spirit, whom God has given to those who obey him" (Acts 5:29–32).

---

[38]   Schnabel, *Early Christian Mission*, 1:531.

Chapter 4
Persecution in the Early Church

Even before the church's beginning, followers of Jesus—eventually called Christians—faced great difficulty and persecution. The forerunner of Christ, John the Baptist, was imprisoned and beheaded. Jesus of Nazareth himself was crucified. Stephen was stoned to death after his witness before the Sanhedrin (Acts 6–8). Herod Agrippa killed James the brother of John (Acts 12:12), which led to the departure of the rest of the Twelve from Jerusalem. This persecution was not simply brought on by the missionary work of Paul, but the preaching of the first apostles regarding the Messiahship and Lordship of the risen Jesus.

This persecution should have come as no surprise to the disciples of Jesus since he had instructed them to expect discrimination, betrayal, imprisonment, torture, and even death. When they accepted the invitation to follow Jesus, the Twelve knew the potential cost—and he reminded them of this cost throughout his ministry.

The Cost of Discipleship

Jesus told his disciples to expect persecution (Matt 10:16–23; Mark 13:9; John 15:18–27, 16:2–3, 33) and suffering for the sake of righteousness (Matt 5:10–11, 43–44; Luke 6:22–23). He even warned them they would be killed, as Israel had killed the prophets (Matt 21:33–40, 22:6, 23:30–31, 34, 37; Mark 12:1–11; Luke 6:22–23, 11:47–50, 13:34, 20:9–18). They expected persecution in the same manner Jesus experienced it himself (John 15:18–27) specifically because of their proclamation of the *name of Jesus* before men (Matt 24:9; Luke 21:12–13, 17). In turn, their deaths would testify to the truth of their proclamation, as the death of Jesus proclaimed the truth of his. Many Romans, when they saw Christians martyred for their faith, did in fact abandon their view of reality and choose to follow Jesus. Justin Martyr, for instance, considered the martyrdom of Christians a significant part of his journey to the Christian faith: "For I myself, too, when I was delighting in the doctrines of Plato, and heard the Christians slandered, and saw them fearless of death, and of all other things which are counted fearful, perceived that it was impossible that they could be living in wickedness and pleasure."[1]

---

[1] Justin Martyr, *Second Apology* 12, as cited in *The Ante-Nicene Fathers: The Apostolic Fathers with Justin Martyr and Irenaeus*, ed. Alexander Roberts and James Donaldson, rev. A. Cleveland Coxe (Buffalo, NY: The Christian Literature Company, 1885), 1:1,193.

Showing the relationship between martyrdom and mission, Jesus says: "Truly, truly, I say to you, unless a grain of wheat falls into the earth and dies, it remains alone; but if it dies, it bears much fruit" (John 12:24), so that the disciples expected to lose their lives for the sake of the advancement of the Gospel.

Mark cryptically clarifies the cost of discipleship by placing the martyrdom of John the Baptist (6:14–29) right between the commission of the Twelve (6:7–13) and their return (6:30). Mark's reader is forced to consider that those who follow Jesus may face the same fate as John.[2] Although the persecution of the disciples is not referred to during the ministry of Jesus, we see a hint of this persecution in John 9, where the blind man whom Jesus healed is cross-examined by the religious authorities and ejected from the synagogue for *confessing* Christ (9:22, 34). After Pentecost, however, when they were truly witnesses to the risen Christ (Acts 4:20), the apostles experience a wave of persecution from the religious authorities for confessing the name of Christ, which culminates in the arrest of Peter and the death of James (Acts 12:1–5).

Can these teachings of Jesus about suffering and persecution be trusted? John Meier provides three types of teachings that reliably trace back to the historical Jesus.

First, Jesus taught that losing one's life for the sake of the Gospel is necessary to save it. If parallel passages are considered, this teaching occurs six times in the four Gospels (Mark 8:35; Matt 10:39, 16:25; Luke 17:33, 9:24; John 12:25). Meier concludes: "Such a pithy, paradoxical proverb that is attested in variant forms in Mark, Q, and John has a very good chance of going back to the historical Jesus."[3]

Second, Jesus taught that his followers must deny themselves and take up their crosses and follow him. Meier observes: "Both the shocking imagery and multiple attestation of sources argue for Jesus as the source of the saying."[4] In the first century, a cross was an instrument of humiliation, degradation, punishment, cruelty, and shame. It was the ultimate symbol of Roman oppression. To pick up one's cross was to sacrifice one's entire life and allegiance to the cause of Christ. This saying has clear martyrological connotations.[5]

---

[2]   James R. Edwards, *The Gospel According to Mark*, The Pillar New Testament Commentary (Grand Rapids, MI: Eerdmans, 2002), 177.

[3]   John P. Meier, *A Marginal Jew* (New York: Doubleday, 2001), 3:63.

[4]   Ibid., 3:65. Multiple attestation for this teaching occurs in Mark 8:34; Matt 16:24; Luke 9:23, and also Q (Matt 10:38 and Luke 14:27). A similar saying also occurs in *The Gospel of Thomas* 55.

[5]   Thomas J. Wespetal, "Martyrdom and the Furtherance of God's Plan: The Value of Dying for the Christian Faith" (Ph.D. diss., Trinity Evangelical Divinity School, 2005), 83.

Third, Jesus warned his disciples to expect persecution from within their own families (Mark 10:29; Matt 10:37; Luke 14:26).[6] In essence, Jesus was simply calling his disciples to experience the same type of persecution he faced, for even his own family rejected him (Mark 3:20–35; John 7:5).

How should the disciples respond to the possibility of suffering and death? Rather than cower in fear, they should preach boldly, acknowledging God before men (10:32), knowing that God will reveal everything in the end (Matt 10:26). They should proclaim the Gospel loudly, publicly, from the rooftops (10:27), trusting that God is more powerful than the persecutors (10:28). After the death and resurrection of Jesus, this is exactly what they did.

Persecution in the Writings of Paul

At his conversion, Paul was told that, as part of his mission, he would suffer explicitly before Jews and Gentiles (Acts 9:15–16), and indeed he did suffer. Paul's second letter to the Corinthians lays out most explicitly the suffering he endured, which included being whipped, beaten, stoned, shipwrecked, near starvation, and in danger from various people and places (2 Cor 6:4–9).

Suffering is a central theme of the letters of Paul.[7] He not only suffered deeply for proclaiming the name of Jesus, but expected other believers to suffer as well (Rom 8:35–36; 1 Thess 3:3–4; Phil 1:29; cf. 2 Tim 4:5). Paul and Barnabas encouraged their newly won converts in Asia Minor to continue in the faith because "through many tribulations we must enter the kingdom of God" (Acts 14:22). It was through the suffering of disciples, not just the display of power, that Jesus would be manifest to the world (2 Cor 4:7; cf. John 17:1–5).

Paul faced the genuine possibility of death while ministering in Asia. He writes: "For we were so utterly burdened beyond our strength that we despaired of life itself. Indeed, we felt that we had received the sentence of death. But that was to make us rely not on ourselves but on God who raises the dead" (2 Cor 1:8b–9). At first, it appears this is another passage where Paul emphasizes God's strength in human weakness (2 Cor 12:10), but closer analysis reveals that Paul seems to be anticipating his pending death. Paul says they were "burdened beyond our strength, that we despaired of life itself," and "had received the sentence of death," which indicate Paul and his companions truly believed death was imminent and, humanly speaking, there was no possibility of escape.

---

[6] Meier, *A Marginal Jew*, 3:67–72.

[7] Paul discusses suffering and persecution in six of his seven undisputed letters: Rom 5:3–4, 8:18, 35, 12:12, 14, 14:8, 15:31; 1 Cor 4:9–13; 2 Cor 1:3–10, 4:8, 6:4–7, 7:5, 11:24–27, 12:10; Gal 4:29, 5:11; Phil 1:29; 1 Thess 2:1–2, 2:14–15, 3:3–4. Suffering is also a central idea of some of the disputed letters: Eph 3:1; Col 1:24; 2 Thess 1:4–9; 2 Tim 1:8, 12, 2:3, 8, 10–12, 3:12.

What gave Paul hope amidst his despair and pending death? Thomas Wespetal concludes: "Thus, the hope of the resurrection was a sustaining force for Paul in this 'non-fatal' trial of faith, which was a precursor to and foreshadowing of his ultimate test before Nero in Rome."[8]

Paul experienced persecution not only at the hands of the religious authorities, but also at the hands of Gentiles. He reports that the governor under King Aretas in Nabataea wanted to arrest him (2 Cor 11:32–33; Acts 9:23–25). This demonstrates two key points. First, even in this early stage, Paul did not limit his preaching to the Jews, but reached out to pagans as well. Second, non-Jewish governments were provoked by the public proclamation of Jesus in the earliest stages of the development of the church. The fact that the governor of King Aretas aimed to arrest Paul makes sense only if government officials considered Paul and his message provocative and threatening to public safety.[9] This is an important precedent. While persecution of Christians primarily began at the hands of the Jewish authorities, this incident indicates that non-Jewish governments could also be threatened by the public proclamation of the Christian faith.

Another incident shows how the actions of Christians could provoke governmental backlash. In Philippi, a slave girl with a spirit of divination followed Paul and Silas around for many days, crying out: "These men are servants of the Most High God, who proclaim the way of salvation" (Acts 16:17). After becoming annoyed, Paul cast the spirit out of her in the name of Jesus (v. 18). But when the slave owners saw she lost her powers, they dragged Paul and Silas before the magistrates and said: "These men are Jews, and they are disturbing our city. They advocate customs that are not lawful for us as Romans to accept or practice" (vv. 20b–21). The crowd joined in attacking them, and so they were beaten and thrown in prison. While Paul and Silas were persecuted for economic reasons, rather than for preaching the name of Jesus, this incident provides early evidence of the conflict between Christian practices and those of the Roman Empire. Local magistrates were not afraid to severely persecute those who disrupted the common good. Most persecutions before the time of Decius were the result of popular clamor, such as this, rather than planned governmental campaigns.[10]

---

8   Wespetal, "Martyrdom and the Furtherance of God's Plan," 87.

9   Eckhard J. Schnabel, *Early Christian Mission: Paul and the Early Church* (Downers Grove, IL: InterVarsity Press, 2004), 2:1,036.

10   The principal legal basis behind the persecution of Christians in the first few decades of its existence appears to have been the procedure of *coercitio*, which gave local authorities flexibility and discretion to enforce policies intended to maintain public order. Local magistrates were not forced to follow imperial judicial norms in breaches of civil peace. Provincial magistrates were given considerable latitude in judicial action. See Paul Achtemeier, *1 Peter*, Hermeneia Commentary Series (Minneapolis, MN: Fortress Press, 1996), 34.

Yet Paul himself connects this incident at Philippi to suffering for Christ, in Philippians 1:28–2:11. He tells the Philippians that they are not to be frightened in anything by their opponents, for it was granted for them to suffer for the sake of Christ, referring then in 1:29 to his own suffering which "you saw"—the flogging in Philippi—and moves immediately into Christ's own suffering on the cross for God's glory. Paul clearly believes that their, his, and Jesus's suffering is a part of the Christian call, and that his own suffering in Philippi was a part of suffering for Christ. While persecution was largely sporadic in the first three centuries, every Christian knew he might be called to testify to his faith at the cost of his life.

Persecution in the Rest of the New Testament

The expectation of suffering and persecution is not unique to the Gospel narratives or the letters of Paul. In fact, the expectation and importance of suffering is a central theme throughout the New Testament.

Hebrews

The epistle to the Hebrews was written to help Christians undergoing trials. As a result of great pressure amongst believers, many threatened to apostatize (3:12–13; 6:4–6; 10:26–29). Hebrews emphasizes the supremacy of Jesus, including his successful trials against temptation (2:9–10, 18), as well as the lives of those in the so-called "hall of faith" (11:4–38), as examples believers should imitate. What happened to many of those in the hall of faith? The author of Hebrews clarifies that the prophets:

> who through faith conquered kingdoms, enforced justice, obtained promises, stopped the mouths of lions, quenched the power of fire, escaped the edge of the sword, were made strong out of weakness, became mighty in war, put foreign armies to flight. Women received back their dead by resurrection. Some were tortured, refusing to accept release, so that they might rise again to a better life. Others suffered mocking and flogging, and even chains and imprisonment. They were stoned, they were sawn in two, they were killed with the sword. They went about in skins of sheep and goats, destitute, afflicted, mistreated—of whom the world was not worthy—wandering about in deserts and mountains, and in dens and caves of the earth. (Heb 11:33–38)

How should Christians respond to the reality of suffering? According to the author of Hebrews, they should follow the example of Jesus, who suffered profoundly for his faith—including hostility, violence, and death at the cross—

and who is now seated at the right hand of the throne of God (Heb 12:2). Hebrews 13:12–13 says: "So Jesus also suffered outside the gate in order to sanctify the people through his own blood. Therefore let us go to him outside the camp and bear the reproach he endured." Paul Middleton writes:

> The command is to go out and suffer, following the example of Jesus and the heroes of faith, especially the martyrs, who come at the climax of the list of faithful heroes. Now is the time for Church members who have not yet endured to the point of spilling their blood to do so, and in this context, the triple warning against apostasy becomes explicable.[11]

James

The book of James is often called "The Proverbs of the New Testament" because it provides practical wisdom for putting faith into action. And yet a background assumption of James is that the righteous will suffer for their faith (1:2, 12). James encourages his readers to be patient in suffering and to recall the example of the prophets who spoke *in the name of the Lord*:

> As an example of suffering and patience, brothers, take the prophets who spoke in the name of the Lord. Behold, we consider those blessed who remained steadfast. You have heard of the steadfastness of Job, and you have seen the purpose of the Lord, how the Lord is compassionate and merciful. (5:10–11)

Those who proclaim the name of the Lord should expect persecution just as the prophets did. God honored the prophets by making them his mouthpiece, but their lives were not always spared. Similarly, those who proclaim the name of the Lord should expect to suffer, but can find encouragement in the example of Job and other prophets.

First Peter

In the book of 1 Peter, Peter encourages Christians in the dispersion who faced persecution (1:6; 2:19–23; 3:14, 17; 4:1, 12–16, 19; 5:1, 9–10) to be willing to suffer for doing good, as Christ did (2:21; 4:1, 13), which accords with the will of God (3:17; 4:19). Peter calls these believers to stand strong in their faith and to be holy as Jesus is holy (1:15–16) even as they face the same kind of "fiery trial" Jesus faced, which included being beaten, insulted, reviled, and even killed (1:19–23; 4:12–16). There was early persecution *for the name of Christ* outside Jerusalem.

---

[11] Paul Middleton, *Radical Martyrdom and Cosmic Conflict in Early Christianity* (New York: T. & T. Clark, 2006), 158.

First John

The letter of 1 John is written to testify to the truth of the incarnation and to encourage Christians to turn from sin and love God and one another. First John may in fact have been written in part to help the church address those who had failed the trial of martyrdom and succumbed to the world.[12]

According to one interpretation, 1 John 5:6–8 refers to the martyrdom of Christians as testimony of the true faith, along with the Spirit and baptism.[13] While not required of the text, it must be conceded that this interpretation is indeed plausible. If correct, it would raise the expectation that the first witnesses—the Twelve—would in fact be martyred for their faith as testimony that they belonged to the true faith.

If this interpretation cannot be maintained, 1 John 3:13 *still* testifies to the expectation that believers will be hated for their faith: "Do not be surprised, brothers, that the world hates you." At the very least, 1 John teaches that true disciples of Jesus should expect vitriol, scorn, and hatred from the world for their belief that Jesus is the Son of God.

Revelation

The book of Revelation is undoubtedly one of the most controversial and difficult books to interpret. What is generally agreed upon, however, is that Revelation has the following as a central theme: that Christians must be prepared to face death for Christ's honor, a theme supported by the multiple references to the suffering and persecution of believers for their faith (1:9; 2:10, 13; 6:9; 11:7–8; 12:11, 17; 13:7, 10, 15; 14:12; 16:6; 17:6; 18:24; 19:2; 20:4, 9). While Satan is the true enemy, Christians are called to "witness" to their faith, even if it means death: "Do not fear what you are about to suffer. Behold, the devil is about to throw some of you into prison, that you may be tested, and for ten days you will have tribulation. Be faithful unto death, and I will give you the crown of life" (2:10). Without exception, those considered "witnesses" (*martyrs*) face a violent death (2:13; 11:7; 17:6). At this stage, "martyr" simply meant "witness," and did not yet signify one who dies in proclamation of the faith. Yet those who are "witnesses" in Revelation are killed for their faith, and thus are technically martyrs. In facing death, they stand firm in the faith and their lives testify against Satan and his followers (cf. 6:9–11; 12:11; 16:6; 17:6; 18:24; 19:2).

---

[12] M.J. Edwards, "Martyrdom and the First Epistle of John," *Novum Testamentum* 31 (1989): 164–71.

[13] William C. Weinrich, *Spirit and Martyrdom: A Study of the Work of the Holy Spirit in Contexts of Persecution and Martyrdom in the New Testament and Early Christian Literature* (Washington, DC: University Press of America, 1981), 71–73.

The writings of the New Testament make something very clear: suffering and persecution are to be accepted as part and parcel of the Christian faith.[14] Jesus was the founder and exemplar of the faith and he was crucified as a criminal. Since Christians are called to imitate him, they ought to expect the same hatred by the world, which may include their own persecution, and even death. While dying for the name of Jesus is unique to the New Testament era, dying for God has earlier roots in the Old Testament.

Martyrdom in the Old Testament

In the first century AD, a popular tradition was that even God's own people might kill the prophets. Jesus specifically cited this tradition,[15] and implied it in some of his parables (Matt 21:33–40; Mark 12:1–11; Luke 20:9–18; Matt 22:6). Paul, Luke, the author of Hebrews, and James also referred to this same tradition (1 Thess 2:14–15; Luke 7:51–52; Heb 11:32–38; Jas 5:10–11). Recent prophetic figures, such as Onias the high priest (2 Macc 4:34–36) and John the Baptist, shared this very fate.

The popularity of this tradition raises an important question: How many prophets were actually killed for their beliefs? The New Testament seems to indicate that all, or at least most, ended their lives as martyrs. However, the Old Testament only records two specific instances of a prophet being killed (Jer 26:20–23; 2 Chr 24:17–22). But additional stories indicate persecution, and even death, for prophets who spoke words of judgment (1 Kgs 18:4, 13; 1 Kgs 19:1–8; Jer 11:18–23; 20:1–6; 37:11–15; 38:1–9; Neh 9:26).

Non-canonical sources tell a similar story of the martyrdom of many of the prophets. *The Lives of the Prophets*, a first-century AD Palestinian Jewish work, records the brutal deaths of many Old Testament prophets.[16] According to this text, Manasseh ordered Isaiah be sawn in two.[17] The Jews stoned Jeremiah. Ezekiel was slain by Israelites in exile because he criticized their idol-worship. King Joram threw Micah off a cliff for rebuking him. Amos was beaten and

---

[14] Although it is impossible to prove the accuracy of the New Testament reports in light of the absence of multiple attestations, it is historically improbable that all of these reports would be invented whole cloth with no historical kernel behind them. Although it is important not to privilege the historical accuracy of the New Testament literature a priori when conducting historical research, to dismiss it a priori as biased propaganda would be to make as egregious an error in the opposite direction.

[15] Matt 22:37; Luke 13:34; cf. Matt 5:10–11; 23:30–31, 34; Luke 6:22–23; 11:47–50.

[16] Charles Cutler Torrey, ed. and trans., *The Lives of the Prophets: Greek Text and Translation* (Philadelphia, PA: Society of Biblical Literature and Exegesis, 1946).

[17] The tradition that Isaiah was sawn in two is also possibly hinted at in Heb 11:37 and reported in *The Martyrdom of Isaiah*. See *Pseudepigrapha of the Old Testament*, vol. 2, 162.

killed with a cudgel. Ignatius, too, wrote of the persecution of the prophets who were inspired by grace to convince unbelievers (cf. *The Epistle of Ignatius to the Magnesians* 8). The tradition of the martyrdom of the prophets underwent even further development in later Jewish tradition. According to John Pobee:

> At this stage martyrdom became a *sine qua non* of the prophetic vocation and, therefore, every prophet was regarded as having undergone a martyr's death .... Indeed, according to midrash standing in the name of R. Jose b. Nehonai, the following were the persecuted prophets: Abel, Noah, Abraham, Isaac, Jacob, Joseph, Moses, Saul, David, and Israel.[18]

Willingness to face persecution rather than forsake God has even earlier roots in the book of Daniel. The confidence of Daniel and his friends to face persecution boldly (Dan 3, 6) came from their belief in Yahweh, the one true sovereign God (5:23), who could resurrect them to eternal life (12:2–3). Yet even though Daniel and his friends are protected, the author of Daniel wants to portray that not everyone can expect a similar fate; however, they should not fear because their reward will come in the afterlife (Dan 12:1–3). From the earliest times, biblical stories such as Daniel provided models for how Christians could boldly face persecution.[19]

As Boudewijn Dehandschutter notes, 2 Maccabees also contains popular stories of martyrdom that may have influenced the first Christians. The people of Israel were facing great calamity at the hands of Antiochus Epiphanes (*c.* 215–164 BC). The temple was defiled, Jews were forced to eat sacrifices offered to false gods, and thousands were murdered (2 Macc 6:3–11; 8:3–4).[20] Yet some stood strong. The scribe Eleazar was forced to open his mouth and eat swine flesh, but he spit it out and chose to "die gloriously, than to live stained with such an abomination" (2 Macc 6:19). The incident concludes: "And thus this man died, leaving his death for an example of noble courage, and a memorial virtue, not only unto young men, but unto all his nation" (2 Macc 6:31).

Seven brothers and their mother were also constrained to break the Mosaic Law by eating swine flesh. But one of the brothers spoke up and said: "We are ready to die, rather than to transgress the laws of our fathers" (2 Macc 7:2). The

---

[18]   John S. Pobee, *Persecution and Martyrdom in the Theology of Paul*, Journal for the Study of the New Testament Supplement Series, ed. Bruce D. Chilton (Sheffield, England: JSOT Press, 1985), 28.

[19]   Boudewijn Dehandschutter, "Example and Discipleship: Some Comments on the Biblical Background of the Early Christian Theology of Martyrdom," in *Polycarpiana: Studies on Martyrdom and Persecution in Early Christianity*, ed. J. Leemans (Leuven, Belgium: Leuven University Press, 2007), 222.

[20]   Josephus, *The Wars of the Jews* 1:2.

seven brothers were slaughtered with the most brutal means of torture. The mother pleaded with her last living son to spare his life, but he replied:

> I will not obey the king's commandment: but I will obey the commandment of the law that was given unto our fathers by Moses. And thou, that hast been the author of all mischief against the Hebrews, shalt not escape the hands of God. For we suffer because of our sins. (2 Macc 7:30b–32)

The brothers not only suffered deeply for their commitment to the law, but they *expected* to suffer as a result of the sins of Israel. What gave these brothers the courage and willingness to die for the law? Belief in the resurrection (2 Macc 7:14) and belief that the tormentors would be punished (2 Macc 7:19, 36).

Josephus records another incident where the Jews refused to honor Caius with a statue, even to the point of death. They even threw themselves on the ground, stretched out their throats, and said they were willing to be slain.[21] The Jews suffered to testify that Yahweh is the one true God. Israel was called to bring this knowledge to the Gentiles (cf. 1 Sam 17:46). "You are my witnesses," declares the Lord (Isa 43:10), so that "my salvation may reach to the end of the earth" (Isa 49:6). The Israelites were chosen to declare the holiness and greatness of God to the Gentiles, and suffering was a necessary component of this prophetic witness (Isa 53).

There was precedent that such suffering could bring about conversion of the persecutor; in fact, that was the point. As a result of seeing the willingness of Shadrach, Meshach, and Abednego to face death in the fiery furnace, Nebuchadnezzar praised the God of Israel (Dan 3:28). And King Darius recognized the God of Daniel as well (Dan 6:25–28).

By the New Testament era, the Jews had fully embraced the value of dying for the truthfulness of the Law rather than recanting their beliefs. Although there are significant differences between Jewish martyrdom and Christian martyrdom, early Christians saw their lives and missions in light of this tradition.[22] Even in the face of persecution and probable death, the apostles would refuse to compromise their beliefs about God with the hope that their persecutors would

---

[21]   Josephus, *Antiquities of the Jews* 18.8.3.

[22]   Paul Middleton notes some significant differences between Jewish martyrdom and Christian martyrdom. First, the Maccabean heroes died for the Law, whereas Christians died because of their refusal to sacrifice to the gods. Second, while both types of martyrdom deal with a larger conflict, the Jewish form has a more temporal focus—the ransacking and defilement of the Temple. And third, Jews saw suffering as caused by God to correct the Jews for their wrongdoings. Christians, on the other hand, saw suffering as coming from Satan, therefore death involved defeating Satan. Middleton grants that Judaism is an important factor in the development of Christian martyrdom, but it is not sufficient. See Middleton, *Radical Martyrdom*, 112–15.

convert to the true faith. Jesus followed the example of the persecuted prophets, and after Pentecost, his apostles ministered in the same way, hoping their deaths would be a witness to the resurrection of Jesus Christ.

Persecution Began with the Jews

The Old Testament and Gospel narratives provide the necessary background to anticipate persecution of the apostles. The book of Acts, however, provides the initial accounts. The tradition of God's own people killing the prophets was correct, for the first systematic persecution of Christians began at the hands of the Jewish religious authorities. It was the Jewish leadership *of the time*[23] who had turned Jesus over to the Roman authorities to face crucifixion (Matt 27:1–2; Mark 15:1; Luke 23:1; John 18:28). As soon as the apostles begin preaching that this same Jesus was the resurrected Messiah, the Jewish leaders began to silence and persecute them, too. They imprisoned and threatened them (Acts 4:13–22), beat them (Acts 5:40), and killed Stephen, a witness for the faith (Act 7:54–60).

After the death of Stephen (*c.* AD 37), "there arose on that day a great persecution against the church in Jerusalem, and they were all scattered throughout the regions of Judea and Samaria, except the apostles" (Acts 8:1b).[24] The view was sometimes held within Judaism that scattering was a good thing. Second Baruch 1:4 says: "For this reason, behold I bring evil upon this city, and upon its inhabitants, and it shall be removed from before Me for a time, and I will scatter this people among the Gentiles that they may do good to the Gentiles."[25] Paul was responsible for this scattering because of his fierce persecution, which he further attests to after becoming a Christian (Gal 1:13; 1 Cor 15:9). Can this tradition be trusted historically? According to James Dunn,

---

[23] To claim that persecution began with the Jewish religious authorities of the first century is not to indict *all* ethnic Jews, and is limited to the Jews of the time who rejected Jesus as Messiah and who persecuted the first Christians. The Twelve were all Jewish, as were many of the first disciples. Even Jesus was Jewish! Jesus loved the Jews and focused his primary ministry on reaching out to them.

[24] The claim that a great persecution arose but somehow the 12 apostles were spared may seem implausible. It would seem more likely that the persecutors would specifically target the leaders. However, the key point is not that the apostles escaped persecution, since other passages in Acts make it clear they were targeted (4:1–3; 5:17–18; 12:1–19). Luke's primary point is that while some Christians had to emigrate permanently because of the persecution, the apostles stayed as leaders in Jerusalem for some time. See Richard Bauckham, "James and the Jerusalem Church," in *The Book of Acts in its Palestinian Setting*, ed. Richard Bauckham (Grand Rapids, MI: Eerdmans, 1995), 428–29.

[25] *Pseudepigrapha of the Old Testament*, vol. 2, ed. and trans. R.H. Charles (Oxford: Clarendon Press, 1913), 481.

an initial persecution directed by Paul from Jerusalem "can be readily envisaged on good historical grounds and with very plausible historical speculation."[26]

This was only the beginning of the persecution. Philip the Evangelist fled to Samaria because of persecution (Acts 8:4–5). Paul faced persecution from the Jews, and often had to flee for his life (9:23–25, 29–30; 13:45–50; 14:5, 19; 17:1–10, 13–15; 18:6–7; 20:3; 21:27–36; 23:12–15). James the brother of John was killed (12:2) and Peter was arrested because it "pleased the Jews" (12:3). Persecution by the Jews was also taking place in areas outside Jerusalem, such as Thessalonica (1 Thess 2:14–16). Persecution by the Jews continued until at least the middle of the second century.[27] In fact, according to Herbert Workman, the Jews could be detected in the background for virtually all persecutions against Christians, even after persecution became official policy of the state. This was possible because of how widespread the Jewish dispersion was throughout the Roman Empire.[28]

The first Christians were often protected from Rome (Acts 18:12–17; 19:23–41; 22:22–29; 23:23–28:31) as long as Christianity was considered a sect within Judaism—a *religio licita*—but once Christianity was considered a variant from Judaism, protection from persecution was no longer guaranteed. This is precisely what happened during the reign of Nero.

Persecution under Gentile Rulers

The Neronian Persecution

Nero was the first Emperor (AD 54–58) to persecute Christians; in AD 64, when rumors spread that Nero had started a fire that burned three entire quarters of the city of Rome and thousands lost their homes, Nero blamed Christians. Tacitus gives the details (AD 115):

> Therefore to eliminate this rumor he falsely produced defendants and inflicted the most extraordinary punishments upon those whom, hated for their crimes, the people called Christians. The origin of this name was Christ, whom the procurator Pontius Pilate put to death in the reign of Tiberius; crushed for a while, the deadly superstition burst forth again not only throughout Judea, the source of this evil, but even throughout Rome, to which all horrible and shameful

---

[26] James D.G. Dunn, *Beginning from Jerusalem: Christianity in the Making* (Grand Rapids, MI: Eerdmans, 2009), 2:275–76.

[27] Frend, *Martyrdom and Persecution*, 154, 184.

[28] Herbert B. Workman, *Persecution in the Early Church* (Cincinnati, OH: Jennings & Graham, 1906; reprint, Oxford: Oxford University Press, 1980), 45–47.

things flow from everywhere and are celebrated. Therefore the first persons arrested were those who confessed; then on their information, a great multitude was convicted not so much on the charge of setting fire as on hatred of the human race. Mockeries were added to their deaths, so that wrapped in the skins of wild animals they might die torn to pieces by dogs, or nailed to crosses they were burned to death to furnish light at night when day had ended. Nero made his own gardens available for this spectacle and put on circus games, mingling with the people while dressed in a charioteer's uniform or standing in his chariot. As a result there arose compassion toward those who were guilty and who deserved the most extraordinary punishments, on the grounds that they were being destroyed not for the public good but for the savagery of one man (*The Annals* 15.44.2–5).[29]

Several observations are necessary. First, these words are some of the most ancient indications of how pagans viewed Christians. Clearly Tacitus does not believe Christians set fire to Rome, but were being sacrificed "to the ferocity of a single man." Still, Tacitus believed the rumors that Christians were "a class of men, loathed for their vices" who believed a "superstition" and had a "hatred of the human race."

Second, the fire in Rome was not the source of the misgivings and hatred of Christians. Rather, this brought to a head the growing suspicion many Romans already had of this new religion. Conflict inevitably traces back even earlier. Suetonius (*c.* 70–*c.* 140) mentions the expulsion of the Jews from Rome in AD 49 "at the instigation of Chrestus." While conclusions must be drawn with a degree of tentativeness, it is historically probable that "Chrestus" refers to Jesus of Nazareth.[30]

The conflict in Rome was not caused by Chrestus, but by the teaching that Jesus was the Christ (Messiah), which generated opposition by the Jews, resulting in the expulsion of many from Rome.[31] Suetonius had also referenced the persecution by Nero that is consistent with the Tacitus account: "Punishments were also inflicted on the Christians, a sect professing a new and mischievous religious belief."[32] These references by Tacitus and Suetonius reveal the disgust and hostility Greco-Romans held towards Christians as early as the mid-first century.

---

[29]   Herbert W. Benario, "The Annals," in *A Companion to Tacitus*, Blackwell Companions to the Ancient World, ed. Victoria Emma Pagán (Chichester, England: Wiley-Blackwell, 2012), 114–15.

[30]   Robert E. Van Voorst, *Jesus Outside the New Testament* (Grand Rapids, MI: Eerdmans, 2000), 29–39.

[31]   Gary R. Habermas, *The Historical Jesus: Ancient Evidence for the Life of Christ* (Joplin, MO: College Press, 1997), 191. The account in Suetonius is not given a specific date. If the year is AD 49, it would cohere more or less with the account of Paul's visit to Aquila and Priscilla in Corinth, when "Claudius had commanded all the Jews to leave Rome" (Acts 18:2).

[32]   Suetonius, *Nero* 16.2.

Third, Tacitus assumes a considerable number of Christians live in Rome by the early 60s. For Tacitus to have noticed Christians' presence and been so apparently bothered by them—and for Christians to have provided a sufficient scapegoat for the fires—while certainly Nero killed a minority of all Christians at the time, he undoubtedly killed them in significant numbers.

Fourth, it appears the official persecution was confined to Rome, since there is no mention of persecution elsewhere. However, nothing was done to revoke the laws Nero had put in place against Christians. These laws thus provided sanction and precedent for the formal persecution of Christians by the state. From this point forward, the church was officially in opposition to the Roman state. Frend concludes: "In the 250 years that separate the Neronian persecution in 64 CE from the conversion of Constantine to Christianity, *c.* 312, Christianity was an illegal and suspect religion whose members were subject to arrest, condemnation and, in many cases, death."[33] Most of these persecutions were not at the hand of the emperor. Rather, most were police actions on the provincial level that went unrecorded in the archives of the nation.[34] While few governors would have the desire to instigate a persecution against Christians, if public opinion turned against Christians, governors would indeed put Christians on trial to acquiesce to public demand.[35]

Fifth, Tacitus reports that Christians were killed for confessing the *name* of Christ. Once Nero officially condemned Christians for confessing the name of Christ, nothing prevented other provincial governors from persecuting those involved, by definition, with the same deviant and potentially treasonous religion. Workman notes what this meant for Christians after the reign of Nero:

> To become a Christian meant the great renunciation, the joining a despised and persecuted sect, the swimming against the tide of popular prejudice, the coming under the ban of the Empire, the possibility at any moment of imprisonment and death under its most fearful forms. For two hundred years [after Nero] he that would follow Christ must count the cost, and be prepared to pay the same with his liberty and life. For two hundred years the mere profession of Christianity was itself a crime.[36]

Christians who minded their own affairs, who focused on living proper lives before outsiders, were often spared persecution from the state (cf. 1 Thess 4:11).

---

[33] W.H.C. Frend, "Persecution: Genesis and Legacy," in *The Cambridge History of Christianity: Origins to Constantine*, ed. Margaret M. Mitchell and Frances M. Young (New York: Cambridge University Press, 2006), 503.

[34] Workman, *Persecution in the Early Church*, 26.

[35] G.E.M. de Ste. Croix, *Christian Persecution, Martyrdom, and Orthodoxy*, ed. Michael Whitby and Joseph Streeter (Oxford: Oxford University Press, 2006), 121.

[36] Workman, *Persecution in the Early Church*, 42.

However, outspoken leaders of the faith, such as the apostles (cf. Acts 4:13, 5:21), were much more likely to stir resentment and thus face the wrath of the state (cf. Acts 12:2–3). The apostles consistently proclaimed the name of Jesus, putting themselves in the greatest possible danger of facing persecution and martyrdom.

Candida Moss questions the extent of the first Roman persecution against Christians, and even claims early Christians invented the idea of martyrdom.[37] She suggests caution in using the aforementioned passage by Tacitus, since he wrote "at least fifty years after the events he describes."[38] In response to Moss's claim, though, Paul Maier notes: "This is the same as suggesting that no one today can write accurately about what happened in the Kennedy administration!"[39] So while caution should be observed with the passage from Tacitus, as with any historical passage, many historical accounts are written over fifty years after the events, including the writings of Moss herself. In addition, Tacitus's hostility towards Christianity actually weighs in favor. Remarkably, not a word appears in Moss's book about the supporting passage in Suetonius (*Nero*, 16.2), which also mentions the punishment inflicted on Christians. Moss simply ignores the fact that persecution against Christians is mentioned not only by Christians, but also by two early Roman sources. This is why Maier concludes: "Rarely do both friendly and hostile sources agree on anything, but the persecution of Christians is one of them."[40]

Reasons for Persecution

Christians faced the hatred, disgust, and persecution of the Roman Empire for a number of reasons.[41] Perhaps the most prominent reason was that Christians refused to pay homage to the Roman gods. Because they worshipped an invisible deity that lacked physical representation, Christians were accused of atheism, which was akin to worshipping no god. In rejecting the gods of Rome, they rejected the legitimacy of the empire—which was sanctioned by the gods—and to deny proper honor to the gods was to be unpatriotic, compromising the health

---

[37]   Candida Moss, *The Myth of Persecution: How Early Christians Invented a Story of Martyrdom* (New York: HarperCollins, 2013), 13–22.

[38]   Moss, *The Myth of Persecution*, 139.

[39]   Paul Maier, "The Myth of Persecution: A Provocative Title, an Overdone Thesis," *Christian Research Journal* 36 (2013): 55.

[40]   Maier, "Myth of Persecution," 55.

[41]   Christianity was suspect since followers worshipped a crucified criminal. In addition, the fact that many of the first believers were uneducated peasants contributed to the narrative that Christianity was a religion of the ignorant, or as Tacitus put it, of people who believe a "pernicious superstition." And Christian rituals such as baptism, the Lord's Supper, and the giving of a holy kiss raised suspicion that Christians were a subculture in opposition to the empire.

of the entire empire. Earthquakes, floods, and pestilence were often blamed on people refusing to honor the gods. Tertullian wrote:

> If the Tiber rises as high as the city walls, if the Nile does not send its waters up over the fields, if the heavens give no rain, if there is an earthquake, if there is a famine or pestilence, straightway the cry is, "Away with the Christians to the lion!"[42]

Because the gods were considered the guardians of Rome, protection for the Roman people required they be given their proper honor and respect. The religious practices of the Roman people, then, could not be separated from the flourishing of the state.

The problem was not so much that Christians worshipped Jesus as God, but that they refused to show homage to other gods by offering sacrifices. According to Christians, Jesus had died on the cross as the ultimate sacrifice, so no further sacrifice was believed to be necessary. But the stability of the state, according to the Romans, depended upon all citizens offering obeisance to the gods. Exclusive worship of Jesus was believed to alienate the goodwill of the gods and disturb the *pax deorum*—the proper relationship between the gods and humanity. Christians thus bore the blame for various disasters affecting the community. Michael Haykin observes:

> Why would Christians, who preached a message of divine love and who were commanded to love even their enemies, be accused of such a vice? Well, if one looks at it through the eyes of Roman paganism, the logic seems irrefutable. It was, after all, the Roman gods who kept the empire secure. But the Christians refused to worship these gods—thus the charge of 'atheism' that was sometimes leveled at them. Therefore, many of their pagan neighbors reasoned, they could not love the emperor or the empire's inhabitants. Christians thus were viewed as fundamentally anti-Roman and so a positive danger to the empire.[43]

While the first Christians to address the charge of atheism were the Christian apologists of the second century, there is no reason to think the situation was previously different.[44]

---

[42]   Tertullian, *The Apology* 3:47.

[43]   Michael A.G. Haykin, *Rediscovering the Church Fathers* (Wheaton, IL: Crossway, 2011), 37.

[44]   De Ste. Croix, *Christian Persecution, Martyrdom, and Orthodoxy*, 133–40.

Conclusion

An ancient tradition that the prophets would suffer for their faith, especially in the books of Daniel and 2 Maccabees, anticipated the New Testament era when it was believed that prophets would suffer at the hands of their own people as well as secular authorities. And many did suffer persecution. Jesus both taught and modeled this tradition to his apostles, warning them also to expect persecution. Jesus took up his cross to his own crucifixion, and he called on his apostles to go and do likewise. Christians were first persecuted at the hands of their own people, then by Gentiles during the reign of Nero, officially persecuted by the Roman government. From at least that point forward, Christians could legally be persecuted *for the name of Jesus*. These factors make it not merely plausible, but likely that at least some of the apostles would face martyrdom for proclaiming the name of Jesus.

Chapter 5
The Martyrdom of Peter

The New Testament mentions Peter more than any other apostle, including Paul.[1] All four Gospels list him among the first called to follow Jesus (Mark 1:16–17; Matt 4:18–20; Luke 6:12–16; John 1:40–42). Along with James and John (sons of Zebedee), Peter was in the inner circle of Jesus, but even within this select group he is clearly the leader. Thus, he was uniquely present at the healing of Jairus's daughter (Mark 5:37; Luke 8:51), the transfiguration (Mark 9:2–13; Matt 17:1–8; Luke 9:28–36), and Jesus's agony in the Garden of Gethsemane (Mark 14:32–42; Matt 26:36–46). He is regularly depicted as the spokesman for the Twelve (e.g. Mark 10:28; Matt 19:27; Luke 12:41). And in all three Synoptics, only Peter confesses that Jesus is the Christ (Mark 8:29; Matt 16:16; Luke 9:20). Peter is also the primary character throughout the first 15 chapters of Acts.[2] Paul corroborates the leading role of Peter in his letters as well (1 Cor 15:13; Gal 1:18; 2:9). The significance of Peter is further portrayed in the sheer number of pseudepigraphical works attributed to him.[3] In light of these facts, Martin Hengel understandably considers Peter "the apostolic foundational figure of the church."[4]

Although Peter denied Jesus three times, he became emboldened in his faith after the resurrection. Acts reports his willingness to suffer for proclaiming the Christian faith (Acts 4:1–2). After being threatened by the Jewish authorities,

---

[1]   If the different names for Peter—Simon, Cephas, Peter—are taken into consideration, he is mentioned 75 times in the Synoptics and 35 times in John. He is mentioned a total of 181 times in the New Testament, which is four more times than Saul/Paul. See Martin Hengel, *Saint Peter: The Underestimated Apostle*, trans. Thomas H. Trapp (Grand Rapids, MI: Eerdmans, 2010), 10–11.

[2]   Peter takes charge of finding a replacement for Judas (Acts 1:15). He regularly speaks publicly on behalf of the apostles (2:14–41; 3:11–26; 4:1–22; 5:29; 10:34–48; 11:1–18; 15:7–11). Peter performs powerful miracles after Pentecost (3:1–8; 5:15; 9:32–34; 9:36–43). And Peter becomes a spokesman for the universality of the Gospel (8:14; 10:31–48; 11:1–18; 15:7–11).

[3]   Many non-canonical texts carry Peter's name, showing that Peter was considered the foremost apostle from the second to sixth centuries. These include the *Gospel of Peter*, *Apocalypse of Peter*, *The Acts of Peter*, *Preaching of Peter*, *The Acts of Peter and the Twelve Apostles*, *Acts of Peter and Paul*, *Passion of Peter and Paul*, *Letter of Peter to Philip*, and the *Martyrdom of Peter*.

[4]   Hengel, *Saint Peter*, 28–36.

Peter and John say: "Whether it is right in the sight of God to listen to you rather than to God, you must judge, for we cannot but speak of what we have seen and heard" (Acts 4:19b–20). When the apostles were arrested a second time and taken before the Sanhedrin, Peter responded: "We must obey God rather than men" (Acts 5:29b). Morris Inch concludes: "Peter was willing to die at that moment for his faith—not a bad turnabout for a man who went from tilting at windmills to having the faith of a child. Fortunately, his time to die for his faith wasn't for years to come."[5] Peter's clear willingness to suffer for proclaiming his faith came from his belief that he had personally witnessed the risen Jesus. The fear that overtook Peter at the arrest of Jesus has been replaced with a newfound boldness.

The Historical Question

Scholars disagree significantly over the fate of Peter. Arguably the most influential work defending the traditional view of Peter's martyrdom during the reign of Nero is Oscar Cullman's *Peter: Disciple, Apostle, Martyr*. Cullman concludes that the martyrdom of Peter in Rome "is relatively though not absolutely assured."[6] More recently, Richard Bauckham claims that Peter's crucifixion in Rome during the reign of Nero can be securely established with "high historical probability."[7] In contrast, F. Lapham believes the martyrdom tradition dates from the second century and is based on "the most slender of textual and archaeological evidence."[8]

In order properly to evaluate the strength of the case for Peter's martyrdom, we must evaluate each piece of evidence individually and then consider the overall strength of the case. This study focuses primarily on the literary evidence, since the archaeological evidence is far less conclusive. It is unlikely the bones discovered in the twentieth-century excavation at the Vatican actually belong to Peter. In any case, this cannot be proved.[9] While the biblical book of Acts

---

[5]   Morris Inch, *12 Who Changed the World: The Lives and Legends of the Disciples* (Nashville, TN: Thomas Nelson, 2003), 19.

[6]   Ibid., 114.

[7]   Richard J. Bauckham, "The Martyrdom of Peter in Early Christian Literature," in *Rise and Decline of the Roman World*, Part II, ed. Wolfgang Haase and Hildegard Temporini (New York: Walter De Gruyter, 1992), 26:588.

[8]   F. Lapham, *Peter: The Myth, the Man, and the Writings* (New York: T. & T. Clark, 2003), 3.

[9]   The earliest statement that Peter and Paul were buried in Rome comes from Gaius (AD 200), as found in Eusebius: "I can point out the trophies [monuments] of the apostles. If you will go to the Vatican or the Ostian Way, you will find the trophies of those who founded this church." Carsten Thiede considers this positive evidence tracing back to Peter's

reports neither the death of Peter nor Paul, and while no other early ancient text states it directly, nevertheless, a host of indirect witnesses help us determine the likelihood of Peter's martyrdom in Rome.

The Missionary Activity of Peter

The book of Acts portrays Peter preaching and teaching in Jerusalem (2:14–41), Judea, Galilee, Samaria (cf. 9:31–32), and Caesarea (10:34–43). First Peter was written to exiles of the dispersion in Pontus, Galatia, Cappadocia, Asia, and Bithynia (1:1). It is by no means impossible that Peter was engaged in missions to these churches. James Dunn observes: "Since we know nothing of the beginnings of Christianity in Pontus, Cappadocia, and Bithynia, we can hardly exclude the possibility that 1 Pet. 1.1 provides evidence for beginnings during Peter's life and mission."[10] Church tradition has Peter ministering in Syria, Greece, Anatolia, and Rome.[11] Larry Helyer notes:

> These traditions are not manufactured out of thin air. Paul's letters give evidence that Peter was indeed in Antioch of Syria and almost certainly visited Corinth .... There is good reason to believe that Peter addresses the believers in Anatolia because he is in some sense their apostle. It may be that many of these people were members of Roman house churches before being forcibly relocated to the eastern fringes of the empire. This correlates with the tradition that the apostle Peter actively served the church in Rome for some years. In short, it is likely that Peter evangelized among Jews and Greeks in the western Diaspora, including Rome, over a period of at least sixteen or seventeen years and possibly more.[12]

If Peter was in Rome for this period, why did Paul not mention him in his letter to the Romans (AD 56/57)? Scholars have offered a variety of explanations.[13]

---

martyrdom under Nero in Rome. See Carsten Thiede, *Simon Peter: From Galilee to Rome* (Grand Rapids, MI: Zondervan, 1988), 193. In contrast, Cullman considers the reasons against early Christians actually burying the bones of Peter in the vicinity of Nero's garden "almost overwhelming." See Oscar Cullman, *Peter: Disciple, Apostle, Martyr* (Waco, TX: Baylor University Press, 2011), 152–56. It is noteworthy, though, that Rome is the only place mentioned as the scene of Peter's death and the repository of his body. While the exact burial spot may be debatable, Rome is likely the correct city.

[10] James D.G. Dunn, *Beginning from Jerusalem: Christianity in the Making* (Grand Rapids, MI: Eerdmans, 2009), 2: 1152

[11] Eusebius and Jerome place Peter in Rome during the reign of Claudius (*c.* AD 42.). See *Church History* 2.14.16 and *On Illustrious Men* 1.

[12] Larry R. Helyer, *The Life and Witness of Peter* (Downers Grove, IL: InterVarsity Press, 2012), 101–02.

[13] For instance, see Hengel, *Saint Peter*, 63; Cullman, *Peter*, 79.

Yet regardless of the reason, Helyer offers an important perspective: "However we account for this omission, to pit an argument from silence against the widespread tradition linking Peter and Rome seems ill-advised."[14] At best, it seems one can only conclude that Peter was not in Rome when Paul wrote the letter. To make a further inference from this silence would go beyond the available evidence.

Much has been made of the "another place" that Peter went to after his escape from prison in Acts 12:17. John Wenham has argued that "another place" refers to Rome,[15] which most scholars have rejected, as Rome would have been too distant since Peter soon returned to Jerusalem (Gal 2:7–9). Others have suggested that "another place" is a metaphorical reference to Peter's death in prison in Jerusalem (*c.* AD 44).[16] The majority of scholars have rejected this thesis for a variety of reasons.[17] The point of the "another place" seems to be that while Agrippa martyred James, Peter escaped to a safe place. The specific location was unimportant to the larger narrative of Acts.

However, even if these critics were correct and "another place" refers to his death, this would not overturn Peter's *willingness* to face martyrdom and suffer for his beliefs. F. Lapham suggests Herod Agrippa executed Peter shortly after the death of James, the son of Zebedee (Acts 12:2).[18] If this were true, it would certainly undermine significant church tradition about Peter's mission and martyrdom in Rome, but it would not overturn the premise that Peter died as a martyr for his faith. In fact, early execution in Jerusalem would still demonstrate the martyrdom of Peter.

---

    14   Helyer, *The Life and Witness of Peter*, 103.
    15   John Wenham, "Did Peter Go to Rome in AD 42?" *Tyndale Bulletin* 23 (1972): 94–102.
    16   Guy M. Davis, Jr. "Was Peter Buried in Rome?" *Journal of Bible and Religion* 20:3 (July 1952): 168; Warren M. Smaltz, "Did Peter Die in Jerusalem?" *Journal of Biblical Literature* 71:4 (December 1952): 214; Donald Fay Robinson, "Where and When Did Peter Die?" *Journal of Biblical Literature* 64:2 (June 1945): 255–67.
    17   One problem for this thesis is that it requires that the Jerusalem Council (Acts 15) occur before Peter's escape from prison (Acts 12:5–11). Second, the narrative in Acts 12 reads like a straightforward account of Peter's departure away from Agrippa, not a metaphorical reference to death. Luke unequivocally cited the death of James (Acts 12:2), so why would he cryptically mention the death of Peter fifteen verses later? Third, there is early and consistent testimony that Peter visited Rome and was martyred there. Fourth, if Agrippa killed Peter, it is curious why Peter is mentioned three times in two chapters of Galatians without any indication he is dead (1:18; 2:6–10; 2:11–21). Even more troublesome is why Paul would have such harsh words about Peter if he were not alive (Gal 2:11–14).
    18   Lapham, *Peter*, 248.

Peter in Rome

First Peter 5:13 provides the earliest indirect evidence for Peter's stay in Rome: "She who is at Babylon, who is likewise chosen, sends you greetings, and so does Mark, my son." According to Richard Bauckham, all recent scholars recognize that "Babylon" refers to the church from which 1 Peter was written.[19] The Old Testament city of Babylon was in ruins, so he could not have been referring to that city.[20] Rather, it was a relatively common cryptic name for Rome, the enemy of God.[21] Like the Hebrews exiled in the Babylon of the Old Testament, Christians in Rome felt themselves exiles in a foreign land, a sinful city that oppressed the people of God. This fits Peter's earlier reference to their experience as "sojourners and exiles" (2:11). If conservative scholars are correct, this is a first-century reference to Peter's presence in Rome, dating possibly as early as the 50s. If Peter is pseudonymous, then it dates to the 80s or 90s at the earliest, most likely in the early second century. Even at this later date, 1 Peter 5:13 would still qualify as good evidence that Peter was in Rome at some time.

A second line of indirect evidence lies in the likelihood that Mark wrote his Gospel based on the testimony of Peter while in Rome. Papias reports that Mark was Peter's interpreter and wrote down accurately all that Peter remembered from his experience with Jesus.[22] Although Eusebius recorded the writings of Papias at the beginning of the fourth century, these writings date from two centuries earlier and are likely reliable tradition (c. AD 110). Irenaeus, who likely wrote from the Roman archives, also reports that Mark recorded Peter's experience with Jesus.[23] The only exception among the church fathers was Chrysostom (d. AD 407), who believed Mark recorded Peter's account while Peter was in Egypt.[24] Internal evidence also indicates that Mark was written in Rome. For instance, numerous Latinisms in Mark suggest a Roman origin.[25] Furthermore, the Roman "flavor" of the opening lines as well as the prominence of the centurion's confession (15:39) are consistent with the Gospel originating

---

[19] Bauckham, "The Martyrdom of Peter," 542.

[20] Paul Achtemeier, *1 Peter*, Hermeneia (Minneapolis, MN: Fortress Press, 1996), 353 n. 73.

[21] Craig S. Keener, *The IVP Bible Background Commentary: New Testament* (Downers Grove, IL: InterVarsity Press, 1993), 722. At a later time, Jewish and Christian and Jewish apocalyptic texts identify Rome as the oppressor during the end times (*Sibylline Oracles* 5:143, 149; *4 Ezra* 3:1–2, 28–31, *2 Baruch* 11:1–2; Rev 14:8; 16:9; 17:5, 6; 18:2ff.). But the reference in 1 Pet 5:13 focuses on the exilic nature of their experience in a foreign land, similar to the Hebrews in ancient Babylon.

[22] Eusebius, *Church History* 3.39.15.

[23] Irenaeus says: "After their departure, Mark, the disciple and interpreter of Peter, did also hand down to us in writing what had been preached by Peter" (Irenaeus, *Against Heresies* 3.1.1).

[24] Chrysostom *Homily on Matthew* 1.7.

[25] Hengel, *Saint Peter*, 40.

in Rome.[26] Paul's passing reference in 2 Timothy 4:11, "get Mark and bring him with you," as well as 1 Peter 5:13, where Mark sends his greeting, place Mark in Rome, most likely with Peter. Although not indisputable, this provides significant corroborative evidence that Peter did, in fact, go to Rome.

Since the middle of the second century, Christian writers unanimously concur that Peter visited Rome. In his *Letter to the Romans* (c. AD 106), Ignatius assumes that Peter had already ministered in Rome.[27] In the *Apocalypse of Peter* (c. AD 135), Jesus commands Peter to go to "the city of the west," which is undoubtedly Rome.[28] Dionysius of Corinth wrote a letter to Roman Christians (c. AD 170) in which he claims that "Peter and Paul sowed among Romans and Corinthians."[29] And Gaius, Roman presbyter in the early third century (c. 199–217), claims that Peter and Paul founded the Roman church. Towards the end of the second century (AD 170s), Irenaeus says that Peter and Paul preached at Rome and laid the foundation of the church (*Against Heresies* 3.1.1). Finally, the *Acts of Peter* (AD 180–190) explicitly mentions that Peter went to Rome to challenge Simon Magus. In sum, early Christian tradition unanimously puts Peter, towards the end of his life, in Rome.

F. Lapham remains skeptical of the credibility of these accounts. He suggests that in order to have "superior authority and greater theological credibility," the Roman church invented Peter and Paul as their apostolic founders.[30] However, this seems very doubtful since Ignatius, Irenaeus, and Dionysius of Corinth were not even from Rome.[31] While the specific date is conjectural, it is *historically very probable* that Peter was in Rome for at least some period of time.

Evidence for the Martyrdom of Peter

The traditional view is that Peter was crucified in Rome during the reign of Nero in AD 64–67. A minority of scholars doubt this account.[32] Since there is

---

[26] Paul Barnett, *The Birth of Christianity: The First Twenty Years* (Grand Rapids, MI: Eerdmans, 2005), 162.

[27] That Peter previously ministered in Rome is the assumption of Ignatius's claim in 4:3: "I do not command you as Peter and Paul did. They were apostles; I am free." See Bauckham, "The Martyrdom of Peter," 587–89.

[28] Dennis D. Buchholz, *Your Eyes Will Be Opened: A Study of the Greek (Ethiopic) Apocalypse of Peter* (Atlanta, GA: Scholars Press, 1988), 360.

[29] Eusebius, *Church History* 2.25.8.

[30] Lapham, *Peter*, 93.

[31] I owe this observation to F.J. Foakes Jackson, "Evidence for the Martyrdom of Peter and Paul in Rome," *Journal of Biblical Literature* 46 (1927): 77–78.

[32] Arthur Drews and Frank R. Zindler, *The Legend of Saint Peter: A Contribution to the Mythology of Christianity* (Austin, TX: American Atheist Press, 1997); Lapham, *Peter*; Michael D. Goulder, "Did Peter Ever Go to Rome?" *Scottish Journal of Theology* 57 (2004): 377–96.

such a plethora of sources for the fate of Peter from the first two centuries, this investigation focuses entirely on the period of living memory. The place to begin is within the pages of the New Testament itself.

John 21:18–19

The earliest reference to the death of Peter is found on the lips of Jesus in John 21:18–19:

> "Truly, truly I say to you, when you were young, you used to dress yourself and walk wherever you wanted, but when you are old, you will stretch out your hands, and another will dress you and carry you where you do not want to go." (This he said to show by what kind of death he was to glorify God). And after saying this he said to him, "Follow me."

The cryptic nature of this passage makes it likely an authentic saying of Jesus.[33] Some have considered John 21 to be a later addition to an already existing Gospel, but no manuscripts have been found lacking Chapter 21. Van Belle has made a solid case that Chapter 21 was part of the original Gospel.[34]

The context of this verse is important for proper interpretation. In verses 15–17, Jesus had just restored Peter from his threefold denial (18:15–18, 25–27). Three times Jesus asks Peter if he loves him, and after each response Jesus replies by commanding Peter to either "Feed my lambs," "Tend my sheep," or "Feed my sheep." The implication is clear—Peter, an undershepherd of Jesus, is called to care for the flock and sacrifice his life for them, just as Jesus did. Andrew Lincoln observes:

> The force is that Peter will demonstrate the genuineness of his love by caring for those who belong to Jesus, the good shepherd. Jesus has already described what it means to shepherd the flock in 10.1–18, 26–8 and has proved his identity as the good shepherd in laying down his life for the sheep before taking it up again (cf. 10.15b, 17–18). Now Peter is charged with the privilege and responsibility of being the undershepherd who will protect, nourish, and tend the flock of the good shepherd himself.[35]

---

[33] Craig L. Blomberg, *The Historical Reliability of John's Gospel* (Downers Grove, IL: InterVarsity Press, 2001), 278.

[34] Gilbert Van Belle, "Peter as Martyr in the Fourth Gospel," in *Martyrdom and Persecution in Late Antique Christianity: Festschrift Boudewijn Dehandschutter, ed. J. Leemans* (Leuven, Belgium: Peeters, 2010), 288–89.

[35] Andrew T. Lincoln, *The Gospel According to Saint John*, Black's New Testament Commentary (New York: Hendrickson, 2005), 518.

Peter had previously said that he would lay down his life for Jesus (13:36). But Jesus knew he was not ready, which his threefold denial evidences (13:38). Yet after the risen Jesus restores Peter for his failings, Peter, now truly ready to accept his role as shepherd of the flock, demonstrates his love for the flock by following Jesus even to the point of death (cf. 15:13). Gilbert Van Belle notes:

> From Jesus' prophecy and the evangelist's aside in 21:19 it is clear that Peter as shepherd will follow Jesus, the good shepherd, to his death. Just as Jesus gives his life for those who follow him (10:11, 15, 17–18; 15:13) and glorifies God, Peter will follow Jesus and die for it, and thereby glorify God.[36]

Commentators unilaterally agree that this passage predicts the martyrdom of Peter. Bart Ehrman concludes: "It is clear that Peter is being told that he will be executed (he won't die of natural causes) and that this will be the death of a martyr."[37] Most commentators agree that it incorporates a veiled reference to martyrdom by crucifixion.[38] Yet there is significant minority who are skeptical.[39] Bultmann has suggested that the prophecy of Jesus is an old proverb that merely contrasts the robustness of youth with the feebleness of old age: "In youth a man is free to go where he will; in old age a man must let himself be taken where he does not will."[40] In other words, at one time Peter was free to go where he

---

[36]   Van Belle, "Peter as Martyr," 295–96.

[37]   Bart Ehrman, *Peter, Paul, and Mary Magdalene: The Followers of Jesus in History and Legend* (Oxford: Oxford University Press, 2006), 84.

[38]   For instance, see George R. Beasley-Murray, *John*, Word Biblical Commentary, vol. 36 (Dallas, TX: Word, 1999), 408–09; Gerald L. Borchert, *John 12–21*, The New American Commentary, vol. 25B (Nashville, TN: Broadman & Holman, 2002), 338–39; D.A. Carson, *The Gospel According to John*, The Pillar New Testament Commentary (Grand Rapids, MI: Eerdmans, 1991) 679–80; William Hendriksen, *Exposition of the Gospel According to John*, New Testament Commentary (Grand Rapids, MI: Baker, 1953), 489–90; Craig S. Keener, *The Gospel of John: A Commentary* (Peabody, MA: Hendrickson, 2003), 2:1,237–38; Andreas J. Köstenberger, *John*, Baker Exegetical Commentary on the New Testament (Grand Rapids, MI: Baker, 2004), 599; Colin G. Kruse, *John: An Introduction and Commentary*, Tyndale New Testament Commentaries (Downers Grove, IL: InterVarsity Press, 2003), 387; Michael R. Licona, *The Resurrection of Jesus: A New Historiographical Approach* (Downers Grove, IL: InterVarsity Press, 2010), 366.

[39]   For instance, see Blomberg, *The Historical Reliability of John's Gospel*; Ehrman, *Peter, Paul, and Mary Magdalene*; J. Ramsey Michaels, *The Gospel of John* (Grand Rapids, MI: Eerdmans, 2010); Herman N. Ridderbos, *The Gospel According to John: A Theological Commentary*, trans. John Vriend (Grand Rapids, MI: Eerdmans, 1997), 667; Urban C. von Wahlde, *The Gospels and Letters of John*, Eerdmans Critical Commentary, vol. 2 (Grand Rapids, MI: Eerdmans, 2010), 905.

[40]   R. Bultmann, *The Gospel of John: A Commentary*, trans. G.R. Beasley-Murray, R.W.N. Hoare, and J.K. Riches (Hoboken, NJ: Blackwell, 1971), 713.

desired, but in his old age he will unwillingly be led by another. Thus, according to Bultmann, this passage is not supposed to be taken as a prediction of the crucifixion of Peter.

Even though many have accepted this interpretation, his reasoning is unconvincing. In the ancient world, the phrase "stretch out your hands" frequently referred to crucifixion.[41] Specifically, in the second century, certain Old Testament passages that involved the spreading out of arms or hands were often understood as prophetic types of Christ on the cross. For instance, in Exodus 17:12 Moses lifts up his hands in the battle against Amalek. The *Epistle of Barnabas* 12 and Justin Martyr's *Dialogue with Trypho* 90–91 interpret this as a type of the crucifixion of Christ. Another example comes from Isaiah 65:2b: "I spread out my hands all the day to a rebellious people." This was understood as a type of Christ in *The Epistle of Barnabas* 12, *First Apology of Justin* 35, and Irenaeus, *The Demonstration of the Apostolic Preaching* 79. The *Odes of Solomon* makes it clear that the stretching out of hands is a reference to crucifixion (27:1–3; 35:7; 41:1–2). There is also evidence that pagan authors considered spreading out the hands as a phase in crucifixion.[42]

Ramsey Michaels doubts the phrase "stretch out your hands" refers to crucifixion, and believes it is rather simply a gesture of helplessness before arrest and execution, first because neither Moses nor Isaiah literally died by crucifixion.[43] The Johannine editorial aside in John 21:19a, however, clarifies for the reader that the context is specifically about the death of Peter. Michaels' second reason is that, if it referred to crucifixion, the stretching out of the hands should come after Peter is taken where he does not want to go.[44] However, Bauer has argued persuasively that the Roman crucifixion victim would have first been forced to carry the *patibulum* (cross beam) on his back while his arms were stretched out and tied to it, and then forced to walk to the place of crucifixion,[45] precisely what happened to Jesus (cf. John 19:17).[46] Thus, the order in John 21:18 matches the known means of crucifixion. Nevertheless, it is important to remember that the form of crucifixion varied widely in the ancient world. No formula existed for how it was always done. Still, it seems the word order does not significantly undermine the likelihood that "stretch out your hands" is best

---

[41]   Carson, *The Gospel According to John*, 680.

[42]   Artemidorus, *Onirocriticus* 1.76; Epictetus, *Diatribai* 3.26.22; Josephus, *Antiquities of the Jews* 19.94; Seneca, *Ad Marciam de consolitione* 20.3; Dionysius Halicarnassensis, *Antiquitates Romanae* 7.69; Plautus, *Miles gloriosus* 2.4.7; Tertullian, *De bono pudicitiae* 22. See Van Belle, "Peter as Martyr," 303.

[43]   Michaels, *The Gospel of John*, 1,048.

[44]   Ibid.

[45]   W. Bauer, *Das Johannes-Evangelium* (Tübingen, Germany: Mohr-Siebeck, 1933), 232.

[46]   William D. Edwards, Wesley J. Gabel, and Floyd E. Hosmer, "On the Physical Death of Jesus Christ," *Journal of the American Medical Association* 255 (March 1986): 1,455–63.

understood as a reference to crucifixion. Even if this understanding is mistaken regarding Peter's death by crucifixion, the narrator's comments make it evident that it is a reference to Peter's martyrdom nonetheless: "This he said to show by what kind of death he was to glorify God (21:19a)."[47]

Jesus immediately followed his prediction of the martyrdom by simply saying to Peter, "Follow me" (21:19b), an allusion to a conversation between Jesus and Peter shortly before Jesus's arrest: Peter had asked Jesus where he was going, and Jesus replied: "Where I am going you cannot follow me, but you will follow me afterward" (13:36). Peter had volunteered to follow Jesus, but failed, not understanding that following Jesus meant facing death, because he did not grasp that Jesus was going to his own death. Now, after the death and resurrection, Jesus and Peter are revisiting this conversation, but from the perspective that Peter is finally ready to truly follow Jesus. To follow Jesus now means to shepherd the flock as Jesus did, even to the point of crucifixion—or at least death. Peter is now able to do what he could not do before—to lay down his life in love. William Hendriksen sums up what Jesus meant: "Be my disciple and apostle, and as such follow me in service, in suffering, and in death (by being willing to endure affliction and even martyrdom for my sake)."[48]

Peter must now live his life with the full reality that he will face martyrdom, just as Jesus did. Whether by crucifixion, which is very probable, or by another means, and even though the passage itself provides no details of when or where, Peter's coming death in this passage is undoubtedly the earliest reference to the martyrdom of Peter.

Second Peter 1:12–15

In 2 Peter 1:12–15, Peter provides his farewell address in the form of a testament. Death, the author knows, is pending, because of some sort of crisis. He desires, then, to leave a legacy of his core teachings. Scripture incorporates many such farewell speeches, including Jacob (Gen 49), Moses (Deut 31–32; Josephus, *Antiquities* 4.177–193), David (1 Kgs 2:1–9), Paul (Acts 20:17–35), and Jesus (Luke 22:24–38; John 13–17). Including a farewell address was also a common practice in Jewish literature.[49] Although formal elements of a testament have been difficult to establish because of the variety within the available examples, Jerome Neyrey has identified five common elements, which can all be found in 2 Peter 1:12–15.[50]

---

[47]   Lincoln, *The Gospel According to Saint John*, 519.
[48]   Hendriksen, *Exposition of the Gospel According to John*, 490.
[49]   *Testament of the Twelve Patriarchs*; *2 Baruch* 78–87; *Testament of Moses*.
[50]   Jerome H. Neyrey, *2 Peter, Jude: A New Translation with Introduction and Commentary*, The Anchor Yale Bible (New Haven, CT: Yale University Press, 1993), 164. First, the author predicts his pending death in 1:14, which is why he wrote 2 Pet. Second,

Peter's goal is straightforward—he is about to die, and wants to give a reminder to readers of what he has taught them:[51]

> Therefore I intend always to remind you of these qualities, though you know them and are established in the truth that you have. I think it right, as long as I am in this body [tent], to stir you up by way of reminder, since I know that the putting off of my body [tent] will be soon, as our Lord Jesus Christ made clear to me. And I will make every effort so that after my departure you may be able at any time to recall these things. (2 Pet 1:12–15)

The "tent" is a metaphor for the human body, which is common in Scripture (Isa 38:12; 2 Cor 5:1, 4; John 1:14). It indicates that Peter's remaining time on earth is short. Daniel Keating observes: "The image of a tent always spoke of what was passing and transitory, looking forward to what was stable and permanent."[52] And the reference to "departure" (*exodus*) is a euphemism for death.[53]

Peter, aware his death is imminent,[54] wants to stress early in the letter that his time for ministry is short and that Jesus directly revealed this to him (1:14). The key question is *how* Christ revealed this to Peter. And why did the author add this idea? It is impossible to rule out some unknown prophecy Peter received from Jesus, but this seems unlikely. Rather, Bauckham concludes: "The only plausible reason is that there was a well-known dominical prophecy of Peter's death which the readers of 2 Peter would know, and so it is natural for the writer to add a reference to this prophecy."[55] So, what is the prophecy to which Peter refers? Four common explanations have been offered:[56]

---

he predicts a future crisis for believers, which will involve attacks through false teachers and false prophets (2:1–3; 3:1–7). Third, given the nature of the impending crisis, he exhorts the believers not to fall into sin but to live godly lives (1:3–11; 3:11). Fourth, a commission is implied, in that Peter desires his words to be a continual reminder to the people, even when he is gone (1:12–15). Fifth, he leaves a legacy of staying faithful to Jesus the end (3:17–18).

51   Ruth Anne Reese, *2 Peter and Jude* (Grand Rapids, MI: Eerdmans, 2007), 138.

52   Daniel Keating, *First and Second Peter, Jude* (Grand Rapids, MI: Baker, 2011), 149.

53   Norman Hillyer, *1 and 2 Peter, Jude*, New International Biblical Commentary (Peabody, MA: Hendrickson, 1992), 173.

54   Some commentators have suggested that the Greek word *tachinē* means "suddenly." But *tachinē* is better translated as "soon." There is no sense that an imminent, violent death was already occurring. Rather, Peter senses the prophecy is set to take place soon. See Michael Green, *The Second Epistle General of Peter and the General Epistle of Jude*, Tyndale New Testament Commentaries, rev. ed. (Grand Rapids, MI: Eerdmans, 1987), 79; and Douglas J. Moo, *2 Peter and Jude*, The NIV Application Commentary (Grand Rapids, MI: Zondervan, 1996), 62.

55   Richard J. Bauckham, *Jude, 2 Peter*, Word Biblical Commentary, vol. 50 (Nashville, TN: Thomas Nelson, 1983), 199.

56   Some have also suggested the *Letter of Clement to James* as a possible source, but this writing is likely dependent upon either John or 2 Peter itself. See Bauckham, *Jude, 2 Peter*, 201.

1. John 13:36—In this passage, Peter asks where Jesus is going and Jesus replies: "Where I am going you cannot follow me now, but you will follow afterward." Although Peter had expressed his willingness to die for Jesus (v. 35), Jesus knew he was not yet ready. This passage is a prediction of Peter's future martyrdom, but since it is before the death and resurrection of Jesus, and few details are given, most scholars reject it as providing the primary background for 2 Peter 1:14.[57]

2. *Apocalypse of Peter*—In this mid-second-century document (*c.* AD 135) Jesus says to Peter: "I have spoken this to you, Peter, and declared it to you. Go forth therefore and go to the city of the west and enter into the vineyard which I shall tell you of, in order that by the sufferings of the Son who is without sin the deeds of corruption may be sanctified."[58] This passage unmistakably offers a *post eventum* prophecy after the martyrdom of Peter. Bauckham writes: "Since it follows a passage which seems dependent on 2 Pet 1:3–11, and precedes a passages which is dependent on the accounts of the Transfiguration, including 2 Pet 1:16–18, it is probable that the prophecy is inspired by 2 Pet 1:14."[59]

3. "Quo Vadis?" from the *Acts of Peter* 35—According to this story, Peter encounters Jesus while escaping arrest in Rome. Peter asks Jesus where he is going, and Jesus replies: "I go to Rome to be crucified." Jesus then ascends to heaven and Peter returns to Rome rejoicing that he can be crucified. The story clearly has the marks of legend and is likely a historical fabrication.[60] Furthermore, since the story is first attested in AD 180–

---

[57]   It seems that commentators who take 2 Pet as authentically Petrine as well as those who believe it is pseudepigraphal both agree that John 13:36–38 is not primarily in view here. Vinson, Mills, and Wilson, for instance, find this explanation unsatisfactory. They conclude: "Given our assessment that 2 Peter is pseudepigraphon, it is unlikely that the writer would rely upon part of the Petrine tradition that cast Peter in an unfavorable light, as is the case with John 13:36–38" (Richard B. Vinson, Richard F. Wilson, and Watson E. Mills, *1 & 2 Peter*, Smyth & Helwys Bible Commentary [Macon, GA: Smyth & Helwys], 312).

[58]   *The Apocalypse of Peter*, as cited in J.K. Elliott, ed., *The Apocryphal New Testament* (Oxford: Oxford University Press, 2009), 609.

[59]   Bauckham, *Jude, 2 Peter*, 200. Bauckham observes that this need not imply there that *The Apocalypse of Peter* presupposed an earlier prophecy. It is possible this passage relays an earlier traditional saying of Jesus prophesying the martyrdom of Peter, but the form of the saying cannot be determined.

[60]   Peter consistently waffled in his faith throughout the Gospels. For instance, even though Peter promised to lay down his life for Jesus (John 13:37), he shortly denied Christ three times. Yet after Pentecost, Peter boldly proclaimed his faith and willingly faced persecution. The "Quo Vadis" seems contrary to the character of Peter at this stage in his life. It is difficult to believe Jesus would need to chastise Peter once again and remind him of his need to face martyrdom before ascending once again to the Father.

190, even if it were historical, it is highly unlikely that it would be the source of revelation from Jesus in 2 Peter 1:14.

4. John 21:18—This is the most likely interpretation. As we have seen, this passage undoubtedly alludes to Peter's martyrdom, and is very probably a reference to crucifixion. Some have questioned this interpretation since it vaguely refers to a future death for Peter but gives no indication of time. John 21:18 indicates, though, that the prophecy will take place when Peter is "old," but no specifics are offered. "But," Douglas Moo observes, "we can surmise that Peter found himself in a situation where persecution had arisen and that he had drawn the conclusion that the Lord's prophecy about his death was shortly to be realized."[61] Peter has been living in the shadow of the prophecy for decades, yet now that he is substantially older, and persecution is likely increasing, he naturally infers the imminence of the prophecy.

If 2 Peter 1:14 is an allusion to the prophecy of John 21:18, then it is an indirect reference to the martyrdom of Peter. The author of 2 Peter portrays Peter as writing shortly before his death with full knowledge that his martyrdom is imminent. Even if 2 Peter were pseudepigraphical, it would be clear that the author portrayed Peter as likely going to die soon. And if it were written after AD 64, the Neronian persecution would have been well known. Thus, neither Peter nor another writer would need additional revelation, outside of the known tradition from John 21:18, to infer that Peter's death was imminent. Bauckham captures the significance of this passage: "This makes 2 Peter an early evidence of the Roman church's own tradition about Peter's martyrdom. That Peter is represented in 2 Peter as writing, from Rome, in the knowledge that his death was coming soon, strongly suggests, even if it cannot quite demonstrate, that Peter was known to have died in Rome."[62]

First Clement 5:1–4

First Clement is the first non-canonical document that refers to the martyrdoms of Peter and Paul. While some scholars have denied this claim entirely,[63] a significant number of scholars believe *1 Clement* 5.1–4 provides early attestation for their martyrdoms, including Bart Ehrman.[64]

---

[61]   Moo, *2 Peter and Jude*, 63.

[62]   Bauckham, "The Martyrdom of Peter," 553.

[63]   For instance, see Morton Smith, "The Report About Peter in I Clement V. 4," *New Testament Studies* 7 (1960–61): 86–88. See also Goulder, "Did Peter Ever Go to Rome?", 377–96.

[64]   Bart D. Ehrman, ed. and trans., *The Apostolic Fathers* (Cambridge, MA: Harvard University Press, 2004), 1:24.

Standard dating puts the letter toward the end of the first century (AD 95–96), although some scholars believe it was written much earlier.[65] This document has special significance because it is the only non-canonical document attesting the deaths of Peter and Paul within the first century, and it is written within one generation of the deaths of the apostles.[66] As Bockmuehl has noted, the references, "in quite recent time" and "of our own generation," refer to living memory.[67]

Early church tradition is unanimous that Clement of Rome is the author.[68] *First Clement* was commissioned to the church at Corinth by a small group of presbyters in Rome for which Clement was the likely secretary, which explains why his name was associated with the letter. And yet, scholarly research has revealed little knowledge of the ethnicity of the author.

The problems Clement addresses in the church of Corinth in the 90s appear to be similar as in the 50s, when Paul wrote 1 Corinthians.[69] After following Paul's example of highlighting the positive aspects of a church before offering criticism, Clement shifts directly to the shortcomings of the church at Corinth:

> From this came jealousy and envy, strife and faction, persecution and disorderliness, war and captivity. And so the dishonorable rose up against the honorable, the disreputable against the reputable, the senseless against the sensible, the young against the old. For this reason, righteousness and peace are far removed, since each has abandoned the reverential awe of God and become dim-sighted in faith, failing to proceed in the ordinances of his commandments and not living according to what is appropriate in Christ. Instead, each one walks

---

[65]   See Thomas J. Herron, *Clement and the Early Church of Rome: On the Dating of Clement's First Epistle to the Corinthians* (Steubenville, OH: Emmaus Road, 2008). If Herron is correct and *1 Clement* can be dated as early as AD 70, then the testimony of Clement regarding the martyrdoms of Peter and Paul would be enhanced.

[66]   Internal evidence reveals that one generation had passed from the lives of the apostles. *1 Clement* 44:2–6.

[67]   Markus Bockmuehl, "Peter's Death in Rome? Back to Front and Upside Down," *Scottish Journal of Theology* 60 (2007): 15.

[68]   *The Shepherd of Hermas* Vision 2.4.3, Eusebius, *Ecclesiastical History*, in *Nicene and Post-Nicene Fathers*, ed. Philip Schaff and Henry Wace, vol. 2.1 (New York: Christian Literature Co., 1890), 3.15–16; 4.22–23; Clement of Alexandria, *Stromata* 4.17; Irenaeus, *Against Heresies* 3.2–3.

[69]   Paul reports a number of problems in the Corinthian church, including quarrelling among Christian brothers (1:10–12), jealousy and strife among them (3:3), sexual immorality, greed, drunkenness, idolatry (5:1–11; 6:18), lawsuits among believers (6:1–8), liturgical abuse (11), abuse of spiritual gifts (12–14), and heretical teachings (15:1–49). In Phil 1:15–17, Paul also writes of how some people preach from envy and rivalry, which causes him affliction in prison.

according to the desires of his evil heart, which have aroused unrighteousness
and impious jealousy—through which also death entered the world (3.2–4).

The core problem Clement addresses is jealousy (*zēlos*) among the people of
God.[70] In his first example, involving Cain and Abel, Clement concludes: "You
see, brothers, jealousy and envy brought about the murder of a brother" (4.7).
The main purpose of the opening chapters of *1 Clement* is that jealousy among
believers brings about division, persecution, and even death.

Clement offers additional examples of the results of jealousy from the Old
Testament, including Jacob fleeing from Esau (4.8), Joseph being "persecuted to
the point of death" and then entering into slavery (4.9), Moses fleeing Egypt as
protection for his life (4.10), Aaron and Miriam being forced to sleep outside
the camp in the desert wilderness (4.11), Dathan and Abiram swallowed by the
earth as a part of Korah's rebellion (4.12), and David fleeing for his life while
being persecuted by King Saul (4.13). While not all of these conflicts resulted in
death, Clement is particularly interested in cases that end that way, which is why
he provides disproportionate detail in the first example of Cain and Abel. Clearly,
Clement believes that jealousy amongst the community of God leads to the danger
and threat of death. Whether death comes at the hands of a member of the Jewish
or Christian community (for example, King Saul) or at the hand of a secular ruler
(for example, Pharaoh),[71] the point is clear: jealousy amongst members in the

---

[70]   It is unclear precisely what the jealousy was that led to the death of Peter. Grant
proposes that it may have been ultraconservative Jewish Christian missionaries who demanded
circumcision and rejected the more moderate approach Peter had taken at Antioch, and
denounced him to the Roman authorities. Michael Grant, *Saint Peter: A Biography* (New
York: Scribner, 1994). Helyer concurs: "Since Peter championed Paul's law-free gospel, he
may also have encountered bitter Jewish Christian opposition. Is it going too far to suggest
that some of these opponents informed on Peter's whereabouts and were indirectly involved
in his arrest and martyrdom?" (Helyer, *The Life and Witness of Peter*, 274). This is in fact
similar to what happened to Jesus by his fellow Jews. Mark 15:10 reports: "For he perceived
it was out of envy that the chief priests had delivered him up."

[71]   The threat of death is clearly present in each of these cases: Jacob fled for his life
from Esau, who hated him and wanted to kill him (Gen 27:41). Joseph's brothers originally
wanted to kill him because of their jealousy, until Reuben has the idea to sell him into slavery
(Gen 37:18–24). Moses had to flee Egypt as Pharaoh sought to kill him for murdering the
Egyptian (Exod 2:11–15). For challenging Moses's prophetic authority, Miriam's skin was
turned leprous. Aaron pleaded with Moses: "Let her not be as one dead, whose flesh is half
eaten" (Num 12:12a). Dathan and Abiram, as well as their entire family, "went down alive
into Sheol, and the earth closed over them, and they perished from the midst of the assembly"
(Num 16:33). While David survived the attack on Saul, it is clear Saul was led by jealousy to
kill David (1 Sam 18:11, 25; 19:1; 20:33; 23:15).

community of God leads to death.[72] Clement cites these above examples without providing evidence they really happened. The reason is simple—*he did not have to*. He can safely assume they are common knowledge to the audience. He does the same for the fates of Peter and Paul—he assumes his audience is fully aware of their martyrdom accounts and accepts them as being true.

The context of the early chapters of *1 Clement* helps us understand the particular passage that focuses on the apostles Peter and Paul:

> But to stop giving ancient examples, let us come to those who became athletic contenders in quite recent times. We should consider the noble examples of our own generation. Because of jealousy and envy the greatest and most upright pillars were persecuted, and they struggled in the contest even to death. We should set before our eyes the good apostles. There is Peter, who because of unjust jealousy bore up under hardships not just once or twice, but many times; and having thus borne his witness he went to the place of glory that he deserved (5.1–4).

Clement tells that both Peter and Paul were persecuted and struggled in the contest "unto death." This likely refers to their martyrdom, although grammatical considerations are inconclusive.[73] Clement also says that Peter, after experiencing much hardship and persecution, had borne his "witness" and then went to the place of glory. It is possible, although unlikely, that "witness" is a reference to the death of Peter, since the term was not commonly used to mean a martyr's death until the martyrdom of Polycarp in the middle of the second century.[74]

---

[72] The theme of the destructive results of jealousy is carried up to chap. 14. In terms of how Christians should respond, Clement says: "For this reason we should obey his magnificent and glorious will and, as petitioners of his mercy and kindness, fall down before him and turn to his compassionate ways, leaving behind our pointless toil and strife and the jealousy that leads to death" (9.1). Clement then lists specific Old Testament figures that were spared death because they trusted God.

[73] See Licona, *The Resurrection of Jesus*, 366–68. Licona observes that "unto death" appears 16 times in the LXX and can mean dying or being on the verge of death. Jesus said, "My soul is very sorrowful, even to death." (Mark 14:34; Matt 26:38), yet he did not die from this intense grief. A generation later, Polycarp used the same phrase in a manner that undeniably referred to the death of Jesus: "He persevered to the point of death on behalf of our sins" (Polycarp, *Letter to the Philippians* 1.2).

[74] Boudewijn Dehandschutter, "Some Notes on 1 Clement 5, 4–7," in *Fructus Centesimus: Mélanges offerts à Gerard J.M. Bartelink à l'occasion de son soixantecinquième anniversaire*, ed. A.A.R. Bastiaensen, A. Hilhorst, and C.H. Kneepkens (Dordrecht, The Netherlands: Kluwer, 1989), 189–94. There are two possible earlier exceptions: first, Rev 2:13, "I know where you dwell, where Satan's throne is. Yet you hold fast my name, and you did not deny my faith even in the days of Antipas my faithful witness [*martyrs*], who was killed among you, where Satan dwells"; second, 1 Tim 6:13, "I charge you in the presence of God, who gives life to all things, and of Jesus Christ, who in his testimony before Pontius Pilate made the good confession."

Bockmuehl is much more confident of what a grammatical analysis can reveal.[75] Nevertheless, it can minimally be conceded that "witness" is more than "on the way to becoming the technical term for martyrdom."[76]

While a grammatical analysis of *1 Clement* 5:1–4 is favorable but inconclusive, the context strongly implies that Clement was referring to the martyrdom of Peter. *First Clement* 5 is part of the immediate context of the catalogue of examples in Chapters 4–6. Clement provides seven examples of jealousy from the Old Testament in Chapter 4, and then seven contemporary examples in Chapters 5–6. Of the final list, Peter and Paul are introduced as individuals, jointly in that order. Bockmuehl comments on the significance of this passage:

> At least for Christians in Rome and Corinth, it seems, that these two apostles are, at this stage, the most obvious, uncontroversial recent examples of faithful endurance in the face of jealousy and persecution .... Rhetorically, the writer seems able to assume that this is known and undisputed, not just in Rome but among his Corinthian readers too.[77]

Thus, I agree with Bauckham that "Clement probably knew that Peter was martyred, not from any written source but simply as a matter of common knowledge in the church at Rome when he wrote."[78]

Each example in Chapters 5–6 emphasizes the evil conclusions that come from jealousy between brothers and sisters. And yet the latter "contemporary" examples are distinguished from the first by their martyrological theme. Regarding the women Danaids and Dircae (6.2), Michael Holmes observes:

> In ancient mythology, the daughters of Danaus were given as prizes to the winners of a race; thus it is likely that *Danaids* is a reference to Christian women being raped prior to being martyred. Dirce died by being tied to the horns of a bull and then dragged to death.[79]

---

[75] He says: "The aorist participle, in both cases used of their 'witness' (*martyrēsas*), is clearly understood to mean their martyrdom; it falls under the heading of persecution and struggle 'unto death' (*1 Clem.* 5.2) and is the mode and means by which the apostles passed from this world to their place of glory" (Markus Bockmuehl, *Simon Peter in Scripture and Memory* [Grand Rapids: Baker, 2012], 110).

[76] Theodor Zahn, *Introduction to the New Testament*, vols. 2, 3, trans. Melancthon Jacobus (Edinburgh: T. & T. Clark, 1909), 71.

[77] Ibid., 109.

[78] Ibid., 560.

[79] Michael W. Holmes, ed. and trans., *The Apostolic Fathers: Greek Texts and English Translation*, 3rd ed. (Grand Rapids, MI: Baker, 2007), 53.

Clement indicates that a significant number of other persecuted Christians also became examples because of their faithful witness through suffering.[80] It seems highly doubtful Clement would have included Peter and Paul in this list if they were not martyred.[81]

Michael Goulder rejects that *1 Clement* provides any evidence for the martyrdom of Peter in Rome. He finds it improbable Peter ever made it to Rome, and believes Peter likely died in his bed about AD 55.[82] Goulder argues: "Peter was the prince of apostles, and if he was martyred at Rome, every Roman Christian would have known about it. If Clement shows knowledge of Peter's martyrdom at Rome, then he was martyred there. If Clement does not know about it, he was not so martyred."[83] Goulder finds it surprising how little Clement seems to know about Peter.

Goulder is right that if Peter had died in Rome, every Roman believer would have known about it. But the core problem with Goulder's position is that it is an argument from silence. There is simply no way of knowing for sure the extent of what Clement knew about Peter. There is record of what Clement *wrote*, but this is not necessarily the same as what Clement *knew*. To make his argument, Goulder must assume both that he was privy to what Clement knew about Peter *and* that Clement revealed everything he knew. However, Clement likely knew much more about Peter than he reveals and had reasons for not writing it explicitly here. In fact, if it was common knowledge, as Goulder suggests it may have been, then Clement would not need to mention it—he could simply take it for granted. Cullman notes:

> It is of course probable that not much was said of the particularly painful circumstances that contributed to those martyrdoms. The Christians who had caused the death of other Christians did not offer an edifying example for others .... Did the author, who wishes to show the working of the Holy Spirit in the Church of Christ, perhaps have scruples about speaking of this grievous and momentous jealousy?[84]

---

[80]   Tacitus also speaks of a "great multitude" in *Annals* 15:44. This is why many believe Peter and Paul were martyred during the reign of Nero, AD 64–67.

[81]   Cullman makes an additional point worth noting: The context of *1 Clement* 5 reveals that the examples of Peter and Paul are constructed in a quite similar way (even though the account of Paul is much longer). The account reveals that they both witnessed to their faith, and then provides a euphemistic portrayal of their deaths ("went to the place of glory" for Peter and "up to the holy place" for Paul). Parallelism in the account makes it clear that if one was martyred, the other must have been as well. Since it is universally recognized that Clement speaks of Paul's death, he must also speak of the death of Peter. See Cullman, *Peter*, 95–96.

[82]   Goulder, "Did Peter Ever Go to Rome?", 377–92.

[83]   Ibid., 384.

[84]   Cullman, *Peter*, 104.

Further, O'Connor suggests that *1 Clement* aims to promote better relations between the church and government, hoping to avoid future persecution: "Prudence may also have been a factor in the brevity of the notice; Clement may have refrained from mentioning details that would have endangered relations between Church and State."[85] It is not fair to assume, as Goulder suggests, that Clement knew merely what he revealed explicitly; clearly, Clement may have had strategic reasons for remaining reserved.

First Clement, then, provides strong evidence that the martyrdoms of Peter and Paul were part of the living memory of Christians in Rome, and likely in Corinth, towards the end of the first century. According to Bart Ehrman: "By the end of the first century and into the second it was widely known among Christians that Peter had suffered a martyr's death. The tradition is alluded to in the book of 1 Clement."[86] Cullman further suggests that since Clement wrote from Rome, we have good reason to believe Peter was martyred in Rome during the time of the Neronian persecution.[87] While this is possible, and certainly consistent with the other extant evidence, it seems to reach beyond what the text can deliver. Cullman also concludes that Clement reveals the place of martyrdom since he speaks of "among us" to the notice concerning Peter.[88] However, the "us" may just as likely refer to *both* the Roman and Corinthian churches, which would indicate it is a larger reference to the body of Christ—or at least Christians alive at that time—rather than simply Roman Christians. I agree with Bauckham that the only fact we can confidently ascertain from *1 Clement* is that of the martyrdom of Peter. Clement likely knew the specific time, location, and manner of his death, but he chose not to reveal it.[89]

Nevertheless, even if this interpretation is mistaken, *1 Clement* makes it clear that Peter and Paul were willing to suffer deeply and even face death for their belief in the risen Jesus. Clement says these "pillars" were persecuted because of "jealous and envy ... and they struggled in the contest even to death" (5.2). This does not mean they were persecuted as long as they were alive, but that the persecution ended in death. At the very least, this passage provides evidence that Peter and Paul were considered examples of faithful endurance for the Gospel, even in the midst of suffering, until their deaths.

---

[85] Daniel W. O'Connor, *Peter in Rome: The Literary, Liturgical, and Archaeological Evidence* (New York: Columbia University Press, 1969), 81.

[86] Ehrman, *Peter, Paul and Mary*, 84. Ehrman also says *1 Clement* "refers to the martyrdoms of Peter and Paul" (Ehrman, *The Apostolic Fathers*, 24).

[87] Cullman, *Peter*, 97.

[88] Ibid., 108.

[89] Bauckham, "The Martyrdom of Peter," 562.

Ignatius

Outside his letters and a few brief comments by Polycarp (*Letter to the Philippians* 9.1; 13.2), we know little about the life of Ignatius, an early second-century church father who, on his way to martyrdom in Rome, wrote letters to various churches.[90] His letters focus on rooting out doctrinal heresy within the churches and emphasize unity and harmony among believers. Ignatius claims to be the bishop of Antioch of Syria (*Letter to the Romans* 2.2). Most scholars accept the "middle recension," which includes seven letters to *Ephesians, Magnesians, Philadelphians, Romans, Smyrneans, Trallians,* and one to Polycarp (*c.* AD 100–118).[91] There are two texts in the letters of Ignatius that are relevant for our investigation regarding the martyrdom of Peter—*Letter to the Smyrneans* 3.1–3 and *Letter to the Romans* 4.3.

Letter to the Romans 4:3

This is another commonly cited passage regarding the possibility that Ignatius had knowledge of the martyrdom of Peter. It is the only letter from Ignatius not written to a church or bishop of Asia Minor. He shares his desire to be martyred so he can truly be a disciple of Jesus Christ, and then implores Roman Christians not to intervene (4.1; 6:1–2).

The key passage of interest is found in *Letter to the Romans* 4.3:

> I am not enjoining you as Peter and Paul did. They were apostles, I am condemned; they were free, until now I have been a slave. But if I suffer, I will become a freed person who belongs to Jesus Christ, and I will rise up, free, in him. In the meantime I am learning to desire nothing while in chains.

Ignatius, who willingly embraces his impending execution, distinguishes between his authority and the apostles—"I am not enjoining you as Peter and Paul did"—after pleading with the Roman Christians not to interfere in his martyrdom (4:1–2). Peter and Paul had authority to command Roman Christians simply because they were apostles; Ignatius, by contrast, is in chains and only becomes a full disciple through martyrdom.[92] He is well aware that his writings have less authority than the apostles. He has no idealistic expectations

---

[90] Ignatius was likely arrested with a group of Christians who were persecuted in Antioch and sent to Rome under guarded supervision. He was able to meet Polycarp while traveling through Smyrna. He also met representatives of many other churches, who came out to support him, and he wrote letters to them in return.

[91] Craig A. Evans, *Ancient Texts for New Testament Studies* (Grand Rapids, MI: Baker, 2005), 270.

[92] *Letter to the Ephesians* 1:2, 3:1; *Letter to the Romans* 4:1–2; *Letter to Polycarp* 7:1.

that he can become an apostle like Peter and Paul, because they have a greater authority to command believers regardless of their martyrdoms.

The letter does not say Peter and Paul were in Rome, but this is clearly the assumption since he is writing to Roman Christians. Bockmuehl writes: "Neither Ignatius nor any other ancient writer suggests that Peter, like Paul, 'instructed' the Roman church in *writing*. The only other possibility therefore, is that Ignatius evidently appeals to a local memory of the *personal* presence, ministry and, by implication, the martyrdom of both apostles in the capital."[93] This claim gains strength from the mention of Peter and Paul that occurs in a context in which Ignatius is addressing martyrdom (4:1–2). The fact that Ignatius singles out Peter and Paul among the various apostles indicates that he may have been aware of traditions related to their deaths in Rome, the city to which the letter is addressed.[94]

Ignatius's desire to be a "freed person" through his sufferings (4.3) and to realize "the things that constrain me" (6.3) have been taken by some to allude to his desire to share martyrdom with the apostles as well as ascend to heaven to be with them.[95] Ignatius says the apostles are free, but considers himself a slave (4.3). Thus, according to this view, he would suffer and experience martyrdom as the apostles did and then share in their freedom. While this is a possible interpretation, not all agree. Schoedel provides a much more convincing explanation:

> Surely Peter and Paul were thought of by Ignatius as "free" and capable of commanding obedience even apart from their martyrdom, and surely that is why the bishop recognizes his inability to speak to the Romans with the same authority as they (cf. *Eph*. 3.1; *Tr* 3.3). Ignatius differs from the apostles in that only through martyrdom can he become as they were.[96]

Ignatius certainly may have been aware of the martyrdoms of Peter and Paul, but *Letter to the Romans* 4:3 does not explicitly state so. At best, Ignatius assumes it.

Letter to the Smyrneans 3.1–2

The church at Smyrna and its bishop Polycarp were especially significant to Ignatius. Of all the cities and communities in Asia Minor, he chose Smyrna as his

---

[93] Markus Bockmuehl, "Syrian Memories of Peter: Ignatius, Justin, and Serapion," in *The Image of the Judaeo-Christians in Ancient Jewish and Christian Literature: Papers Delivered at the Colloquium of the Institutum Judaicum, Brussels 18–19 November, 2001*, ed. P.J. Tomson and D. Lambers-Petry (Tübingen, Germany: Mohr Siebeck, 2001),140, emphasis in original.

[94] Carl B. Smith, "Ministry, Martyrdom and Other Mysteries: Pauline Influence on Ignatius of Antioch," in *Paul and the Second Century*, ed. Michael F. Bird and Joseph R. Dodson (New York: T. & T. Clark, 2011), 39.

[95] Helyer, *The Life and Witness of Peter*, 276.

[96] William R. Schoedel, *Ignatius of Antioch: A Commentary on the Letters of Ignatius of Antioch* (Philadelphia, PA: Fortress Press, 1985), 177.

most prolonged visit en route to Rome. It is clear from this letter that Ignatius's chief concern for the church at Smyrna was Docetism,[97] although the primary interest is in 3:1–2:

> For I know and believe that he was in the flesh even after the resurrection. And when he came to those who were with Peter, he said to them, "Reach out, touch me and see that I am not a bodiless daimon." And immediately they touched him and believed, having been intermixed with his flesh and spirit. For this reason they also despised death, for they were found to be beyond death.

Ignatius adopts the canonical tradition of considering Peter the foremost apostle of the early church, both before and after the resurrection. Ignatius refers to "those who were with Peter," a reference to the other apostles. While the story of Jesus requesting the apostles reach out and touch him is reminiscent of Luke 24:39, it seems more likely they both rely upon a common tradition, since Ignatius provides no additional evidence of reliance upon Luke.[98] Thus, as Bauckham has observed: "He must have been able to assume, as common knowledge, that at least some of the twelve had died as martyrs."[99] It would be strange if Peter, the only apostle mentioned by name, were not one of these martyrs.

The fact that the apostles "despised death" indicates that Ignatius believed they were willing to suffer and even die for the belief that they had *physically* seen the risen Jesus. Ignatius mentions the apostles' willingness to suffer and face death as evidence for the reality of the resurrection. While we cannot be certain where Ignatius got his information, his letter does presuppose the martyrdom of many of the apostles, including Peter.

The Apocalypse of Peter

The *Apocalypse of Peter*, a pseudepigraphal work that begins with Jesus sitting upon the Mount of Olives as he teaches Peter and the disciples about the end of the world, clearly presents Peter as the lead disciple, just as in the Gospels and Acts. It is generally agreed that the *Apocalypse of Peter* dates from the first half of the second century (*c.* AD 135).[100]

We should distinguish, though, between the various documents often referred to as apocalypses of Peter.[101] Despite its shortcomings, the Ethiopic *Apocalypse*

---

[97]   *Letter to the Smyrneans* 1.1, 2; 2.1; 3:1–3; 5.2; 6.1; 7.1; 12.2.

[98]   Schoedel, *Ignatius of Antioch*, 226–27.

[99]   Bauckham, "The Martyrdom of Peter," 563.

[100]   Wilhelm Schneemelcher, ed., *New Testament Apocrypha*, ed. and trans. R.M. Wilson (Louisville, KY: Westminster John Knox Press, 2003), 2:622.

[101]   There is the Ethiopic *Apocalypse of Peter*, the Arabic *Apocalypse of Peter*, the Coptic *Apocalypse of Peter* (discovered in the Nag Hammadi library in 1945), and the Akhmim

of Peter, which provides the only complete text, is generally considered the best representation of the original.[102] Still, we remain uncertain of some of the exact wording and content at different points of the *Apocalypse of Peter*.[103] The passage that relates to the martyrdom of Peter is 14:4–6. A popular translation of the Ethiopic text:

> I have spoken this to you, Peter, and declared it to you. Go forth therefore and go to the city of the west and enter into the vineyard which I shall tell you of, in order that by the sufferings of the Son who is without sin the deeds of corruption may be sanctified. As for you, you are chosen according to the promise which I have given you. Spread my gospel throughout all the world in peace. Verily men shall rejoice; my words shall be the source of hope and of life, and suddenly shall the world be ravished.[104]

Since this chapter is the most corrupt of the Ethiopic text, Buchholz has provided a translation with corrections from the Greek text (Rainer fragment):

> Behold, I have shown you, Peter, and I have explained everything. And go into a city ruling over the west, and drink the cup which I have promised you at the hands of the son of the One who is in Hades in order that his destruction might acquire a beginning. And you ... of the promise ....[105]

The "city ruling over the west" is likely a reference to Rome. The phrase "drink the cup which I have promised" is clearly a reference to martyrdom. Jesus used the phrase with martyrological connotations when the Zebedee brothers requested they reign with Jesus (Mark 10:35–39; Matt 20:20–23). Jesus also uses the same saying in preparation for his own death (Matt 26:39; Mark 14:36; Luke 22:42; John 18:11). The author of the *Apocalypse of Peter* knew and used the Gospel of Matthew,[106] so it is likely he took this phrase directly from Matthew 20:22–23 and fully understood its martyrological association.

---

text (Greek). There are some theological differences between some of these versions. For instance, the Coptic version, which is more Gnostic, sees martyrdom negatively when compared with the Ethiopic and Greek texts. See Buchholz, *Your Eyes Will Be Opened*, 7–9.

[102] Elliott, *The Apocryphal New Testament*, 594.

[103] Terence V. Smith, *Petrine Controversies in the Early Church* (Tübingen, Germany: J.C.B. Mohr, 1985), 44.

[104] Elliott, *The Apocryphal New Testament*, 609.

[105] Buchholz, *Your Eyes Will Be Opened*, 345.

[106] Smith, *Petrine Controversies*, 46–48.

Though somewhat odd, the expression "the son of the One who is in Hades" likely refers to Nero.[107] In this statement, "in order that his destruction might acquire a beginning," Peter's preaching and martyrdom in Rome act as the channel through which God overcomes the power of Satan.[108] Buchholz summarizes the significance of this passage:

> This is possibly the oldest known unambiguous allusion to Peter's death in Rome. It witnesses to the idea that Peter's death must occur before Satan's destruction can begin, or to the idea that Peter's death must occur before Satan can really begin his (final) work of destruction (cf. 2 Th. 2:6–8). Either way, Peter's death is seen as a sign of the End, and surely this must be a very early idea, one which would not have arisen too long after Peter's (assumed?) death in Rome and one which would not be incorporated into new works at a date too far removed from that period of time.[109]

The *Apocalypse of Peter* provides additional early attestation for the martyrdom of Peter in Rome during the reign of Nero. It must be conceded that this is dependent upon the proper translation of the Rainer fragment, which is far from certain. Taken alone, the *Apocalypse of Peter* would provide modest evidence for the martyrdom of Peter in Rome. However, considered with the rest of the evidence, it is a significant piece of evidence for the traditional story concerning the fate of Peter.

The Ascension of Isaiah

We find another possible indirect witness for the martyrdom of Peter in the *Ascension of Isaiah*, an early second-century Old Testament pseudepigraphal apocalyptic text (*c.* AD 112–138).[110] Jonathan Knight has argued that the *Ascension of Isaiah* aims to address the Christians who feared that Rome would implement similar policies against Christians, just as Trajan had adopted in

---

[107] Bauckham, "The Martyrdom of Peter," 573. Bauckham observes that this is likely a relic of an early Christian reference to Nero as the antichrist, which is specifically related to the persecution of the church and Peter's martyrdom.

[108] Pheme Perkins, *Peter: Apostle for the Whole Church* (Minneapolis, MN: Fortress Press, 2000), 135. There is uncertainty about the exact meaning of this phrase.

[109] Buchholz, *Your Eyes Will Be Opened*, 360.

[110] The *Ascension of Isaiah* is known through only a dozen Ge'ez manuscripts, with the Ethiopic version being the primary witness because of its completeness. There is a possible further copy that belongs to the monastery of Dabra Bizen in Eritrea, but the political situation makes it unlikely this will surface any time soon. See Ted Erho, "New Ethiopic Witnesses to some Old Testament Pseudepigrapha," *Bulletin of the School of Oriental and African Studies* 76 (February 2013): 95–97.

Bithynia in the early part of the second century.[111] According to Knight, the death of Isaiah for witnessing to Jesus (chap. 5) brings to mind Trajan's policy of putting Christians to death who continued to proclaim the "name" of Christ. On the other hand, Greg Carey argues it is a polemic against the Jews for their ignorance and apostasy as well as a primary witness to Christ.[112]

The *Ascension of Isaiah* can be divided into two visions. The First Vision (chaps. 1–5) contains the narrative of the martyrdom of Isaiah. It includes the hope that the Beloved will return and destroy the oppressing forces (4.14–18). Beliar becomes angry with Isaiah and Manasseh has him sawn in two (5.1). The Second Vision (6–11) contains an apocalyptic account of Isaiah through the seven heavens, with a focus on the death and resurrection of Jesus and ultimate defeat of Beliar by the Beloved One (10).

The particular section often cited as a reference to the martyrdom of Peter is *Ascension of Isaiah* 4:2–3:

> Then will arise Beliar, the great prince, the king of this world, who has ruled it since its origin; and he will descend from his firmament in human form, king of wickedness, murderer of his mother, who himself is king of the world; and he will persecute the plant which the Twelve Apostles of the Beloved shall have planted; one of the Twelve will be delivered into his hands.[113]

The context of this passage is the prophecy that the Beloved One will return from heaven and send Beliar (Satan) to Gehenna while providing rest for the godly (4.14–21). All those who had supported Beliar will be destroyed (4.18), and hope is provided for those currently facing persecution.

In this passage, "Beliar" clearly refers to Nero, the one who descends in human form. This passage picks up the idea regarding the myth of Nero's return, which appears in other literature of the time.[114] It would seem possible to interpret this

---

[111] Jonathan Knight, *Disciples of the Beloved: The Christology, Social Setting and Theological Context of the Ascension of Isaiah* (Sheffield, England: Sheffield Academic Press, 1996), 33–39.

[112] Greg Carey, "The *Ascension of Isaiah*: An Example of Early Christian Narrative Polemic" *Journal for the Study of Pseudepigrapha* 9 (1998): 65–78.

[113] Robert Henry Charles, *The Ascension of Isaiah* (London: A. & C. Black, 1900), 95.

[114] The *Sibylline Oracles* identifies Nero with Beliar, as does the *Ascension of Isaiah*: "Then Beliar will come from the *Sebastenoi*, and he will raise up the height of mountains, he will raise up the sea, the great fiery sun and shining moon, for men. But they will not be effective in him. But he will, indeed, also lead men astray, and he will lead astray many faithful, chosen Hebrews, and also other lawless men who have not yet listened to the word of God. But whenever the threats of the great God draws nigh and a burning power comes through the sea to land it will also burn Beliar and all overbearing men, as many as put their faith in him" (3.63–74).

passage as referring to the execution of James (Acts 12:2), except that Beliar is considered the "murderer of his mother," which is a clear indication of Nero's murder of his mother Agrippina.[115] The image of Nero terrorized Christians and Jews, so he was considered a symbol for Jewish aversion to Rome. This is the symbolic sense in which the image of Nero is used in the *Ascension of Isaiah*.[116]

The claim that Beliar (Nero) will "persecute the plant which the Twelve Apostles of the Beloved shall have planted" refers to the persecution of the church. The key question involves the identity of "one of the Twelve" who will be delivered into the hands of Nero. Paul cannot be in mind here, because the author uses the same phrase to refer to the "twelve disciples" in 3:17 and 11:22. In addition, the *Ascension of Isaiah* never mentions Paul individually; it is unlikely, then, that he would be referred to cryptically as "one of the Twelve." Instead, the author has the same technical sense of "the Twelve" as in 1 Corinthians 15:5 and Mark 3:14–19, both of which clearly refer to the 12 apostles Jesus chose to join him in ministry.

Daniel O'Connor captures the most straightforward way of understanding this text: "If the passage is read without prejudice, the most convincing interpretation is that 'Beliar' is a cryptic name for Nero; 'the plant' stands for the Church; and Peter is the one of 'the Twelve" who is 'delivered into his hands.'"[117] The passage refers to an apostle who fell into Nero's hands, which most obviously refers to Peter, the only other apostle for whom there is any tradition about his martyrdom under Nero. Just as the "Beloved One" throughout the *Ascension of Isaiah* is a reference to Jesus, the "one" of the Twelve likely refers to Peter.

Why would the author(s) not specifically mention Peter? First, even Jesus often spoke in generic terms about his betrayer: "Truly, I say to you, one of you will betray me" (Matt 26:21). Prophecy is often generalized and vague, and this passage, which is part of the First Vision, is likely no exception. Second, as Bauckham concludes, because *The Ascension of Isaiah* was written during the living memory of Peter, the tradition of Peter's death in Rome under Nero would have been commonly known and easily identified by the first readers.[118]

Perkins argues, however, that the phrase "will be delivered into his hands" may not be a reference to martyrdom at all,[119] citing Paul's use of the same phrase in reference to a man who has sex with his father's wife. The church was to "deliver this man to Satan," which means they were to dismiss him from the fellowship (1 Cor 5.5). However, the phrase is a Semitism which often, although

---

[115] Philip Schaff, *History of the Christian Church* (Grand Rapids, MI: Eerdmans, 1955), 1:378. The incident of Nero killing his mother is recorded by Tacitus, *The Annals* 14.3–8; Suetonius, *Lives of the Caesars: Nero* 34; Dio Cassius, *Roman History, Epitome of Book* 61.12–13; Plutarch, *Antony* 87.4.

[116] Knight, *Disciples of the Beloved One*, 190.

[117] O'Connor, *Peter in Rome*, 69.

[118] Bauckham, "The Martyrdom of Peter," 568.

[119] Perkins, *Peter*, 139.

not always, implies destruction of the one who is handed over.[120] The context of the *Ascension of Isaiah* is clearly the persecution of those who oppose Beliar. In a similar context, when Jesus foretells his own death, he uses the same phrase. Matthew 17:22 says: "As they were gathering in Galilee, Jesus said to them, 'The Son of Man is about to be delivered into the hands of men, and they will kill him, and he will be raised on the third day.'" The author of the *Ascension of Isaiah*, then, likely used this phrase as a reference to martyrdom.

And even while this passage in *Ascension of Isaiah* does not explicitly state that Peter was martyred by Nero in Rome, when Beliar is identified as Nero, with the understanding that Nero's persecution was confined to Rome, and the likelihood that the "one" refers to Peter, this most likely refers to Peter's death in Rome under Nero. Cullman, therefore, may be right—the *Ascension of Isaiah* is likely the first and earliest document that attests to the martyrdom of Peter in Rome.

The Acts of Peter

Most, but not all, scholars[121] date the *Acts of Peter* to c. AD 180–190,[122] which falls within the living memory of the life of Peter and thus may have some historical value for this investigation. The *Acts of Peter* clearly contains substantial legendary material from earlier oral tradition,[123] and yet, despite the legendary accretions, as François Bovon and Eric Junod have observed, "their value as historical witnesses is not abolished."[124] Christine Thomas writes: "The mere fact that externally attested first-century individuals appear as protagonists in the pages of the *Acts of Peter* is sufficient to show that these narratives were not fictions completely divorced from historical memory."[125] She provides an important balance to the role of redactors in the *Acts of Peter*:

> Like the storytellers in the first phase, the author of the continuous narrative had limits to creative license: the basic characters, Peter, Agrippa, Nero, Eubula, and

---

[120] Bauckham, "The Martyrdom of Peter," 568.

[121] Matthew C. Baldwin, *Whose Acts of Peter? Text and Historical Context of the Actus Vercellensus* (Tübingen, Germany: Mohr Siebeck, 2005).

[122] Jan N. Bremmer, "Women, Magic, Place, and Date," in *The Apocryphal Acts of Peter*, ed. Jan N. Bremmer (Leuven, Belgium: Peeters, 1998), 17–18.

[123] Richard A Norris, Jr. "Apocryphal Writings and Acts of the Martyrs," in *The Cambridge History of Early Christian Literature*, ed. Frances Young, Lewis Ayres, and Andrew Louth (Cambridge: Cambridge University Press, 2004), 31.

[124] François Bovon and Eric Junod, "Reading the Apocryphal Acts of the Apostles," *Semeia* 38 (1986): 163.

[125] Christine M. Thomas, *The Acts of Peter: Gospel Literature, and the Ancient Novel* (Oxford: Oxford University Press, 2003), 47.

Marcellus, were already part and parcel of the narrative. The basic outline of the story was also given. As suggested above, however, this author was not consciously attempting innovation, but was striving to collect and preserve as much of the story of Peter as possible.[126]

The writer(s) of the *Acts of Peter* did not simply invent material, but were bound by received tradition. We have reason to believe earlier pre-existing traditions, and in particular *martyrdom* traditions, have been incorporated into the text.[127] The traditions behind the *Acts of Peter* trace back to the first century.[128] And yet the Apocryphal Acts also reflect the situation of the churches in the second and third centuries from which they were written.[129]

The most commonly repeated genre for the *Acts of Peter* and other Apocryphal Acts is the ancient novel.[130] While not disputing that the genre is novelistic in some capacity, Thomas says it should properly be called a "historical novel":

> The *Acts of Peter* embellish their characters using the same means as the novels, but the relationship to historiography differs considerably. The novels, both erotic and historical, avoid direct reference to commonly known historical events. Although the *minor* characters may be drawn directly from historical figures, neither the *main* characters nor the story refers to the events or public figures who populate historical discourse. In texts such as the *Acts of Peter*, however, the narrative focuses directly on figures of great public significance to the tradents. And it is precisely the most noteworthy events in the lives of the characters that become the province of the Christian writers and storytellers. This is certainly true of Simon and Peter, and even of secondary figures such as Marcellus. However

---

[126] Christine M. Thomas, "The 'Prehistory' of the Acts of Peter," in *The Apocryphal Acts of the Apostles*, ed. François Bovon, Ann Graham Bock, and Christopher R. Matthews (Cambridge, MA: Harvard University Press, 1999), 55.

[127] The mention of four soldiers in *Acts of Peter* 36 and four times four in Acts 12 suggests, according to István Czachesz, that both accounts of the arrest of Peter derive from a common pre-existing tradition. See István Czachesz, "The Gospel of Peter and the Apocryphal Acts of the Apostles," in *Das Petrusevangelium als Teil antiker Literatur*, ed. T. Nicklas and T.J. Kraus (Berlin, Germany: W. De Gruyter: 2007), 248, 261. Furthermore, Ralph Novak observes that "it is rather curious that the traditions concerning the deaths of Peter and Paul would have been preserved by orthodox Christians while the Acts containing the traditions were rejected, if the traditions first appeared in these two Acts" (Ralph Martin Novak, Jr., *Christianity and the Roman Empire* [Harrisburg, PA: Trinity Press, 2001], 27).

[128] Thomas, *The Acts of Peter*, 49.

[129] François Bovon, "Canonical and Apocryphal Acts of Apostles," *Journal of Early Christian Studies* 11 (Summer 2003): 184.

[130] See Hans-Josef Klauck, *The Apocryphal Acts of the Apostles*, trans. Brian McNeil (Waco, TX: Baylor University Press, 2008), 7–10.

historically worthless or distorted the information in the *Actus Vercellenses* may be, the objective is not to tell something that *may* have happened in the past, using history for décor, but to retell the most significant and well-known events from the public life of an individual; a narrative about noteworthy events of the past is the main objective. The Alexander romance provides the best generic parallel among the novelistic products of the Roman Empire. Alongside of the imaginative and improbable occurrences that form the fabric of the narrative, the romance also narrates all the best-known events of Alexander's life.[131]

Since the Apocryphal Acts contain both historical memory and legend, the difficulty is deciphering between the two. Is there a historical kernel we can trust? Some of the events in the *Acts of Peter* are clearly embellishment. For instance, Peter performs multiple miracles[132] that are narrative devices to prove that Peter represents the real Lord and that Simon is an impostor.[133] The feats of Simon Magus are clearly exaggerations as well. Nevertheless, all of the various versions of the *Acts of Peter*[134] tell a similar tale of Peter's activity and martyrdom in Rome, incorporating precisely the same characters: Peter, Simon, Marcellus, Agrippa, and Nero. The consistent reference to the martyrdom of Peter, which finds support from earlier sources both canonical and extracanonical, indicates a fixed tradition by the time the *Acts of Peter* appeared at the end of the second century. Before this time, the martyrdom accounts are very reserved and provide only indirect hints that he died in Rome under Nero. "However," says Perkins, "the later tradition quite strongly favors the fact of Peter's martyrdom under Nero, so we may assume that the earlier hints do point to that event as a fact as well."[135] Since there are no other accounts of Peter dying anywhere except Rome, it is likely the tradition of his martyrdom in Rome was so well known at this

---

[131]   Thomas, *The Acts of Peter*, 88–89.

[132]   Peter performed a number of miracles, including paralyzing half the body of Rufina, the adulterer (1.2), bidding a dog to condemn Simon (4.9), restoring a shattered statue of Caesar (4.11), ordering a dead tuna fish to come alive and swim again (5.13), giving a seven-month-old baby a voice to condemn Simon (5.15), and raising the son of the prefect (8.26), the widow's son (8.27), and Nicostratus from the dead (8.28). I am not adopting a naturalistic bias that assumes supernatural events must be legendary. Rather, the quantity and quality of the miracles sets them apart from the canonical Gospels and Acts and indicates they (as a whole) serve a literary and theological purpose and are not meant to be taken as historically veridical.

[133]   Magda Misset-Van De Weg, "'For the Lord Always Takes Care of His Own': The Purpose of the Wondrous Works and Deeds in the *Acts of Peter*," in *The Apocryphal Acts of Peter*, ed. Jan N. Bremmer (Leuven, Belgium: Peeters, 1998), 97–101.

[134]   Various versions of the Acts of Peter include the *Actus Vercellensus*, the Linus Text, Pseudo-Hegesippus, and the Marcellus text.

[135]   Perkins, *Peter*, 146.

point that the *Acts of Peter* was bound by this tradition. Thus, while the *Acts of Peter* does contain some stories that strain credibility, we should not ignore its testimony to the martyrdom of Peter.

The tradition surrounding his death by Nero, however, is less secure. Outside the *Acts of Peter*, only the *Ascension of Isaiah* and the *Apocalypse of Peter* allude, prior to the third century, to Peter's death by Nero. And it is interesting that Peter's arrest and death in the *Acts of Peter* have nothing to do with the Neronian persecution. No mention is made of the Roman fire or the blame Nero placed on the Christians. Nero only appears at the beginning of the narrative and briefly at the end, which indicates it could be a later addition to the text. In the *Acts of Peter*, Peter is arrested because of the jealousy of Agrippa and Albinus, whose wives and concubines will no longer have sex with them since their Christian conversions. Cullman believes this may be part of the historical core of the *Acts of Peter*, since *1 Clement* reports that the deaths of both Peter and Paul were occasioned by jealousy.[136] We remain uncertain how widely known the tradition of Peter's martyrdom under Nero had spread by the late second century, but it is significant that the author(s) fail to link them together. Thiede seems to come to a fair conclusion: "As far as the existing evidence is concerned, the death of Peter during Nero's fourteenth year cannot be ruled out, but neither, in the nature of the case, can it be proved beyond doubt."[137]

Was Peter crucified upside-down?

Given both the early reference in John 21:18 and the fact that crucifixion was a common form of punishment for slaves and non-Roman citizens, the crucifixion of Peter is historically likely. However, the claim that Peter was crucified upside-down is open to doubt. In the *Martyrdom of Peter*, when Peter approaches the place of execution, he gives a speech to the people and the cross (36.7–8). He concludes by saying: "But it is time for you, Peter, to surrender your body to those who are taking it. Take it, then, you whose duty it is. I request you therefore, executioners, to crucify me head-downwards in this way and no other." Peter gives a final speech while upside-down on the cross and then dies (40.11).

Many often assume that Peter's request shows humility, in that he did not consider himself worthy to die in the same manner as Jesus. But the text does not say this outright. Rather, Peter's upside-down state symbolizes that fallen humanity has now been restored through the cross.[138] The narrative indicates a

---

[136] Cullman, *Peter*, 109.

[137] Thiede, *Simon Peter*, 191.

[138] Monika Pesthy, "Cross and Death in the Apocryphal Acts of the Apostles," in *The Apocryphal Acts of Peter*, ed. Jan N. Bremmer (Leuven, Belgium: Peeters, 1998), 130. Pesthy notes that there is only one contemporary parallel with this account: the 23rd *Ode of Solomon*, where the Logos descends down to a wheel, understood as the cross, and the head and feet are reversed.

turning point in cosmic history, in the cross of Christ as well as the cross of Peter.[139] The world has been turned upside-down by sin, and so Peter can see the upside-down nature of the world clearly while hanging with his head downward on the cross. His speech makes clear that Adam, the "first man," fell head-downwards and turned the cosmos upside-down, but only through Christ can the world be seen "upright." Thus, the crucifixions of Jesus and Peter restore the creation, through the New Adam, to its intended functioning.[140]

Is the upside-down crucifixion of Peter a reliable tradition? The earliest church father to mention it, Origen, in Volume 3 of his *Commentary on Genesis* in the mid-third century (*c.* 230),[141] makes no mention of Peter's prolonged speech. It is uncertain whether Origen derived this from an independent tradition or from the *Acts of Peter*. We do have evidence Roman executioners varied their crucifixion practices for their own sadistic pleasure, however, so it is not intrinsically implausible Peter was crucified upside-down.[142] Still, while it is possible the tradition preserves an early memory of Peter's upside-down crucifixion, the evidence is simply inconclusive.

The Apocryphon of James

The *Apocryphon of James* is a pseudonymous text that describes the revelatory teachings of Jesus to James the brother of the Jesus, and Peter in the form of a letter to Cerinthus,[143] 550 days after his resurrection. The letter contains an *apocryphon* (secret writing) of teachings for James and Peter, but not the rest of the disciples. Unlike the four Gospels, the *Apocryphon of James* consists primarily of sayings delivered in parables and speeches. It was first discovered with other Gnostic texts in the Nag Hammadi Library in 1945. It contains a direct "prophecy" that James and Peter would be crucified for their faith:

---

[139] Jonathan Smith observes: "Rather than dealing with an exercise in humility, we have here an *act of cosmic audacity* consistent with an expressive of a Christian-gnostic understanding and evaluation of the structures of the cosmos and of the human condition .... For Peter to *request* to be crucified upside down was to deliberately dehumanize himself, to reverse the natural order, and to make of his death an act of rebellion against his manhood and the cosmos" (Jonathan Z. Smith, "Birth Upside Down or Right Side Up?", *History of Religions* 9 [1970]: 286, 293).

[140] Richard Valantasis, "Narrative Strategies and Synoptic Quandaries: A Response to Dennis MacDonald's Reading of *Acts of Paul* and *Acts of Peter*," *Society of Biblical Literature Seminar Papers* (1992): 238.

[141] Recorded by Eusebius, *Ecclesiastical History* 3.1.

[142] Martin Hengel, *Crucifixion* (Philadelphia, PA: Fortress Press, 1977), 22–26.

[143] The text is illegible, but it is typically taken to be Cerinthus, an early Christian heterodox teacher. See Eusebius, *Ecclesiastical History* 3.27–28.

Or do you not know that you have yet to be abused and to be accused unjustly; and have yet to be shut up in prison, and condemned unlawfully, and crucified without reason, and buried shamefully as I (was) myself, by the evil one? Do you dare to spare the flesh, you for whom the Spirit is an encircling wall? If you consider how long the world existed before you, and how long it will exist after you, you will find that your life is one single day, and your sufferings one single hour. For the good will not enter into the world. Scorn death, therefore, and take thought for life! Remember my cross and my death, and you will live![144]

James and Peter are specifically told by Jesus that they will "be shut up in prison, and condemned unlawfully, and crucified without reason." This passage was written specifically from Jesus to James and Peter, so it is likely the author was aware of their actual martyrdoms. Yet the text seems not to come from the tradition of their martyrdoms, especially since there is no known tradition that James was crucified, but on a creedal summary of the passion and death of Jesus.[145]

Our most pressing question involves the dating of this "prophecy." Ron Cameron has argued that the *Apocryphon of James* should be dated between the end of the first century and the middle of the second.[146] He essentially argues that the sayings in the *Apocryphon of James* are early and independent from the four Gospels, and in particular John. If so, this could be valuable early evidence for the martyrdom of Peter, even though there is no indication of when or where it took place. But not all scholars agree. Philip Jenkins writes: "Supposed parallels between the *Apocryphon* and the New Testament passages are tenuous, and it really takes the eye of faith to see these resemblances: often, passages cited as parallels are describing broadly similar ideas which were commonplaces of early Christian thought and rhetoric."[147] Rather than being an independent testimony to early Christian thought, Jenkins notes, the *Apocryphon* (and other secret texts) "could equally be seen as historical fictions which use the canonical gospels as a springboard for their speculative tales and theological discourses."[148]

The *Apocryphon of James* is written as a "remembrance" of the teachings of Jesus to James and Peter, which was a common technical term used in the early

---

[144] Translation by Francis E. Williams in *The Nag Hammadi Library in English*, ed. James M. Robinson, rev. ed. (San Francisco, CA: HarperCollins, 1990), 35.

[145] Bauckham, "The Martyrdom of Peter," 581.

[146] Cameron concludes: "The *Ap. Jas.'s* freedom in the use of sayings, the role given to James and Peter as authority figures in the transmission of the tradition, and the use of the technical term for 'remembering' strongly suggest that the composition of this non-canonical gospel dates from the first half of the second century" (Ron Cameron, *Sayings Traditions in the Apocryphon of James*, Harvard Theological Studies [Cambridge, MA: Harvard University Press, 2004], 34:123–24).

[147] Philip Jenkins, *Hidden Gospels* (Oxford: Oxford University Press, 2001), 97–98.

[148] Ibid., 98.

church to indicate the passing on of living memory from Jesus to the disciples.[149] Does this mean the *Apocryphon of James* contains early, independent sayings of Jesus? Not necessarily. Bockmuehl observes: "Here too we find an allusion to Peter's crucifixion (5.9–20), but the document's general tenor aims to subvert the traditional appeal to any apostolic memory of Jesus by appealing instead to Gnostic teachings."[150] Clearly, the author distinguishes himself from the wider Christian community by embracing certain Gnostic beliefs.[151] While the document appeals to the living memory of Jesus, this is likely a later literary device to convince readers of its credibility rather than a genuine tradition tracing back to the historical Jesus. The claim that the letter was written to James and Peter is another literary device meant to garner credibility for the document. It is certainly curious that no early church father quotes from the *Apocryphon of James*. Although some would like to date the *Apocryphon of James* early, the only secure date is that it was written some time before AD 314, when the threat of martyrdom and persecution of the church officially ended.

While the author of the *Apocryphon of James* likely knew of Peter's fate as a martyr, without convincing evidence for an earlier date, this text provides minimal corroboration for the martyrdom of Peter. At best, it shows that by the end of the second century *at the earliest*, the crucifixion of Peter was assumed by both Orthodox and Gnostic circles alike.

Dionysius of Corinth

Dionysius of Corinth wrote to the Roman bishop Soter around the year AD 170. While his goal was primarily pastoral, Dionysius writes to bolster the position of Corinth against the power of Rome.[152] In the letter, he mentions the martyrdoms of both Peter and Paul in Rome. Eusebius considers this letter confirmation that both Peter and Paul died as martyrs under the reign of Nero: "You have thus by such an admonition bound together the planting of Peter and

---

[149] Other early Christian writings, such as Acts 20:35, John 15:20, and *1 Clement* 13:1–2; 46:7–8, use the same technical term for "remembering," which was used to collect, compose, and transmit traditions of and from Jesus. Papias also used it to claim that Mark "remembered" the teachings of Peter and recorded them in his Gospel. See Eusebius, *Ecclesiastical History* 3.39.

[150] Bockmuehl, *Simon Peter*, 51.

[151] The audience of the letter likely rejected the doctrine of the atonement, ignored the second coming of Christ and the general resurrection, and desired to ascend without "flesh" to heaven, which they held to be within themselves. See Francis E. Williams, "The Apocryphon of James (I, 2)," in *The Nag Hammadi Library in English*, ed. James M. Robinson (Leiden, The Netherlands: Brill, 1977), 29–30.

[152] Richard I. Pervo, *The Making of Paul: Constructions of the Apostle in Early Christianity* (Minneapolis, MN: Fortress Press, 2010), 145–47.

Paul at Rome and Corinth. For both of them planted and likewise taught us in our Corinth. And they taught together in like manner in Italy, and suffered martyrdom at the same time."[153] The claim that Peter ministered in Corinth, while possible, is not explicitly stated in the New Testament. However, while it cannot be verified, it is certainly possible Peter visited Corinth as Dionysius suggests (1 Cor 1:12; 3:22; 9:5).[154]

The statement by Dionysius does not say they ministered *at the same time*, but simply that they both "taught us in our Corinth." Therefore, this claim is not intrinsically implausible that Peter visited and ministered in Corinth. However, the claim that both Peter and Paul founded the church at Corinth and Rome seems more like "ecclesial polemic,"[155] since only Paul is ever mentioned as the founder (1 Cor 3:10–15). Dionysius is also mistaken about Paul founding the church at Rome. This is verified by his letter to the Romans (AD 55–58), where he explicitly states that he had not yet visited Rome, much less been its founder (Rom 1:11–15; 15:20–29). In fairness, though, as Paul Maier writes: "Still, since both apostles were martyred very early in its history, it is understandable that they were quickly deemed honorable founders, so to speak."[156]

Nevertheless, we should doubt that they "suffered martyrdom at the same time." Since Dionysius may have been mistaken in his claim about the founding of both Corinth and Rome, we naturally ought to question his claim about the dual martyrdom of Peter and Paul in Rome. This is unlikely since Peter and Paul would have been executed with different methods. Most likely Dionysius meant that they suffered martyrdom in the same *era* rather than the exact same moment. This is consistent with tradition, and certainly more plausible.

It is interesting that Dionysius is writing *to* Rome and states that both apostles were martyred there. Since this is well within the living memory of the apostles, the church at Rome could easily have corrected this if it were not true. Were Peter and Paul not known to have died as martyrs in Rome, Dionysius's whole argument breaks down, yet he offers their place of martyrdom as known fact. The earlier hints of *1 Clement*, Ignatius, and Polycarp that Paul was martyred in Rome under Nero are made more explicit in Dionysius of Corinth (Eusebius).

---

[153]   Dionysius of Corinth, in Eusebius, *Church History* 2.25.4.

[154]   Simon Kistemaker, *Exposition of the First Epistle to the Corinthians*, New Testament Commentary (Grand Rapids, MI: Baker, 1993), 47. He observes that the Cephas faction (1 Cor 1:11–13) likely arose from personal contact with Peter, since this was likely the case with Paul and Apollos. Further, the church at Corinth was probably familiar with Peter since Paul mentions that Peter's wife accompanied him on his missionary journeys (9:5).

[155]   Perkins, *Peter*, 42.

[156]   Paul Maier, in Eusebius, *The Church History*, trans. Paul L. Maier (Grand Rapids, MI: Kregel, 2007), 79 n. 29.

Irenaeus

Irenaeus wrote his most famous work, *Against Heresies*, at the end of the second century (*c.* AD 180), placing it within the range of living memory of the apostle Peter. His task was to refute Gnosticism, which had become a significant competitor for the church by the late second century. Irenaeus claims to have personally listened to Polycarp, who was one of the last followers of the apostle John, as a young man in Asia. Eusebius records a letter Irenaeus wrote to Florinus:

> When I was still a boy I saw you [Florinus] in Lower Asia with Polycarp, when you had high status at the imperial court and wanted to gain his favor. I remember events from those days more clearly than those that happened recently—what we learn in childhood adheres to the mind and grows with it—so that I can even picture the place where the blessed Polycarp sat and conversed, his comings and goings, his character, his personal appearance, his discourses to the crowds, and how he reported his discussions with John and others who had seen the Lord. He recalled their very words, what they reported about the Lord and his miracles and his teachings—things that Polycarp had heard directly from eyewitnesses of the Word of life and reported in fully harmony with Scripture. I listened eagerly to these things at that time and, through God's mercy, noted them not on paper but in my heart.[157]

Irenaeus indirectly supports this claim elsewhere.[158]

Irenaeus provides a reference to the deaths of Peter and Paul in a section committed to defending the scriptural authority of the four Gospels:

> Matthew also issued a written Gospel among the Hebrews in their own dialect, while Peter and Paul were preaching at Rome, and laying the foundations of the Church. After their departure [death], Mark the disciple and interpreter of Peter, did also hand down to us in writing what had been preached by Peter.[159]

---

[157] Eusebius, *Ecclesiastical History*, 5.20

[158] In *Against Heresies* 3.1.1, Irenaeus says: "We have learned from none others the plan of our salvation, than from those through whom the Gospel has come down to us, which they did at one time proclaim in public, and, at a later period, but the will of God, handed down to us in the Scriptures, to be the ground and pillar of our faith" (*Against Heresies* 3.1.1). He goes on to explain that Mark was the interpreter of Peter, Luke was an associate of Paul who recorded Paul's experience in his Gospel, and how John, also a disciple of the Lord, published a Gospel while in Ephesus in Asia.

[159] Iranaeus, *Against Heresies* 3.1.1.

Some have contested that "departure" simply means Peter and Paul left Rome, but this is unlikely.[160] Like the reference in Dionysius of Corinth, we do not know precisely what Irenaeus meant by Peter and Paul "laying the foundations of the Church." If he meant that they founded the church, then he is mistaken. More likely, though, Irenaeus, like Dionysius, meant their deaths made them honorable founders.

Irenaeus mentions the deaths ("departures") of Peter and Paul, but provides no further details regarding their fate. He does not mention where, when, or how they died. In fact, natural deaths for both of them would be consistent with the statement in Irenaeus. However, given the strength of the tradition at this time concerning the preaching and martyrdom of Peter in Rome, it seems most likely that Irenaeus was well aware of the accounts and felt it unnecessary to repeat.

Tertullian

Tertullian, who comes just after the close of the living memory and who is the last writer we will consider here, wrote *The Prescriptions against Heretics* and *Scorpiace* near the turn of the third century (*c.* AD 208). In *The Prescriptions Against Heretics* 36, Tertullian explicitly mentions that Peter was crucified like Jesus:

> How happy is its church, on which apostles poured forth all their doctrine along with their blood! Where Peter endures a passion like his Lord's! Where Paul wins his crown in a death like John's [the Baptist] where the apostle John was first plunged, unhurt, into boiling oil, and then remitted to his island-exile![161]

It is true that this statement must be received with caution, especially since it occurs in the incredible story that John was plunged into boiling oil and emerged unhurt. Nevertheless, Tertullian is even more specific in *Scorpiace* 15, where he states, like the *Ascension of Isaiah*, that the martyrdoms of Peter and Paul took place under Nero:

---

[160] As Bauckham observed, there was sufficient precedent for the term "departure" to mean death in early Christian documents. In response to the claim that "departure" could simply mean leaving, Bauckham concludes: "Since not even later traditions provide the possibility of a time, which Irenaeus could have had in mind, when both Peter and Paul had been in Rome but had left, we must conclude that he meant to refer to their deaths" (Bauckham, "The Martyrdom of Peter," 585–86).

[161] Tertullian, *Against Heresies* 36, as cited in *Ante-Nicene Fathers: Latin Christianity: Its Founder, Tertullian*, ed. Alexander Roberts and James Donaldson, rev. A. Cleveland Coxe (Buffalo, NY: Christian Literature Co., 1885), 3:260.

And if a heretic wishes his confidence to rest upon a public record, the archives of the empire will speak, as would the stones of Jerusalem. We read the lives of the Caesars: At Rome Nero was the first who stained with blood the rising faith. Then is Peter girt by another, when he is made fast to the cross.[162]

Tertullian is so confident of his claims that he tells his doubters to examine "the archives of the empire." If there were no such public records, Tertullian would have automatically undermined his credibility. His appeal to them indicates his confidence that they existed and, if examined, would corroborate his testimony. Therefore, Tertullian was likely relying upon even earlier public records about the Neronian persecution and the fates of Peter and Paul.

Conclusion

The traditional view that Peter was crucified during the reign of Nero in AD 64–67 has been carefully analyzed. Additional later material that further confirms this tradition will not be analyzed in depth, for this analysis has focused on the period of living memory.[163]

This close examination of the evidence indicates that the following points can be regarded to have varying degrees of confidence from works written within the living memory of Peter until *c.* AD 200:

1. The martyrdom of Peter—*the highest possible probability* (John 21:18–19; *1 Clement* 5:4–5; Ignatius, *Letter to the Smyrneans* 3.1–2, Letter to the Romans 4.3; *Apocalypse of Peter* 14.4; *Ascension of Isaiah* 4:2–3; the *Acts of Peter*; Dionysius of Corinth, Eusebius, *Ecclesiastical History* 2.25; Tertullian, *Scorpiace* 15; lack of any competing narrative weighs favorably for the traditional view; the early and persistent tradition is that Peter was martyred for his faith.

2. The crucifixion of Peter—*very probably true* (John 21:18–19; Tertullian, *Scorpiace* 15).

3. Peter was in Rome—*very probably true* (1 Pet 5:13; 2 Pet 1:12–15; *Apocalypse of Peter* 14.4; *Ascension of Isaiah* 4:2–3; Ignatius, *Letter to the Romans* 4.3; Dionysius of Corinth, Eusebius, *Ecclesiastical History* 2.25; Irenaeus, *Against Heresies*, 3.1.1; *Acts of Peter*; Tertullian, *Scorpiace* 15).

---

[162] Tertullian clearly understands John 21:18 to be referring to the crucifixion of Peter.

[163] For instance, see the *Muratorian Canon* (*c.* AD 200); *Teachings of the Apostles* (*c.* third century); (Pseudo-)Hippolytus 1; *Letter of Clement to James* (fourth century); Lactantius, *De Mortibus Persecutorum* (*c.* AD 313); Eusebius, *Ecclesiastical History* 3.1 (*c.* AD 324); Aphrahat, *Demonstration XXI: Of Persecution* (§ 23); Macarius Magus III.22 (early fourth century); Jerome, *Lives of Illustrious Men* 1 (*c.* 392).

4. Martyrdom during the reign of Nero, AD 64–67—*more probable than not* (*Ascension of Isaiah* 4:2–3; *Apocalypse of Peter* 14.4; Tertullian, *Scorpiace* 15).

As seen, the individual components of the traditional view regarding the fate of Peter have varying degrees of historical probability. Yet when all the evidence is considered, the traditional view that Peter was crucified during the reign of Nero stands on solid historical ground.

Chapter 6
The Martyrdom of Paul

Next to Jesus, the apostle Paul is the premier figure at the beginning of Christianity. His influence has been so vast that some have suggested he is the true founder of Christianity.[1] Paul, born in the city of Tarsus, trained at the feet of Gamaliel (Acts 22:3), a highly honored teacher of the Torah who was a member of the Sanhedrin (Acts 5:34–39).[2] Luke tells that Paul was born a Roman citizen (Acts 22:28),[3] which would have given him boldness in his mission and ensured him proper juridical process.

Little doubt exists about Paul's Pharisaic Jewish roots, the lens through which Paul understood his newfound Christian faith (Phil 3:4b–5). While Paul spent his earliest years in a thoroughly Hellenistic city of the diaspora, he was clearly shaped by his family and synagogue with the utmost devotion to the Jewish faith. Udo Schnelle sums up the seminal details of Paul's background:

> Paul was a citizen of the Roman Empire who had grown up in significant metropolis of the realm, had disciplined himself in an intensive Pharisaic education (possibly in Jerusalem), and had worked for about three decades in a province of the empire where Hellenistic culture prevailed. He was thus no wandered between different cultural worlds; he united in himself—like Philo and Josephus—the cultures of Hellenistic Judaism and Greco-Roman Hellenism.[4]

Paul often stressed two priorities of his ministry: to evangelize Gentiles (Rom 11:13; Gal 1:16; 2:7) and to plant new churches rather than build on the foundations laid by another (Rom 15:20; 1 Cor 3:6; 4:15; Gal 4:19).[5] And yet

---

[1] William Wrede, *Paul* (London: Philip Green, 1907).

[2] Many scholars question whether Paul truly studied personally with Gamaliel. Even if Luke overstates Paul's connection to Gamaliel, Paul still would have been deeply influenced by Gamaliel since he influenced the practice of *every* Pharisee. See Bruce Chilton, *Rabbi Paul: An Intellectual Biography* (New York: Doubleday, 2004), 35.

[3] For an in-depth analysis of the citizenship of Paul, see Brian Rapske, *The Book of Acts and Paul in Roman Custody*, ed. Bruce W. Winter (Grand Rapids, MI: Eerdmans, 1994), 71–112.

[4] Udo Schnelle, *Apostle Paul: His Life and Theology*, trans. M. Eugene Boring (Grand Rapids, MI: Baker, 2003), 81.

[5] Klaus Haacker, "Paul's Life," in *The Cambridge Companion to St. Paul*, ed. James D.G. Dunn (Cambridge: Cambridge University Press, 2003), 27.

before his missionary endeavors, Paul fiercely persecuted the Christian church. Both Luke (7:58–8:3; 9:1) and Paul (1 Cor 15:9; Gal 1:13, 23; Phil 3:6) report these persecutions similarly, which provides little reason to doubt their veracity. And yet because of a personal appearance of the risen Jesus (Acts 9:1–19; 22:4–21; 26:12–18), the former persecutor became the church's foremost preacher and defender of the faith (1 Cor 15:8–11; Gal 1:11–16).

Beginning in Arabia, Paul took at least three missionary journeys throughout his life (2 Cor 11:32–33; cf. Acts 9:19–25). His trips included Cyprus and southern Asia Minor (Acts 13–14), Macedonia, Philippi, Thessalonica, Athens, Corinth (Phil 4:15ff.; 1 Thess 2:2; Acts 16–18), Antioch, Greece and Ephesus (Gal 2:11; Acts 18:18–20:38), and Rome via Jerusalem (Acts 21–28:31). Paul certainly intended to visit Spain[6] (Rom 15:24, 28), and some believe he evangelized Britain.[7]

When he was first called as an apostle, Paul was told he would suffer deeply for Christ (Acts 9:16), which he came to see as proof of his apostleship and devotion to God (Gal 6:17; 2 Cor 6:4–10; 11:16–33), as well as his imitation of Christ (1 Thess 1:6). Paul recounts his suffering firsthand:

> Five times I received at the hands of the Jews the forty lashes less one. Three times I was beaten with rods. Once I was stoned. Three times I was shipwrecked; a night and a day I was adrift at sea; on frequent journeys, in danger from rivers, danger from robbers, danger from my own people, danger from Gentiles, danger in the city, danger in the wilderness, danger at sea, danger from false brothers; in toil and hardship, through many a sleepless night, in hunger and thirst, often without food, in cold and exposure. And, apart from other things, there is the daily pressure on me of my anxiety for all the churches. (2 Cor 11:24–28)

This list of sufferings would not have been persuasive to Paul's audience unless it at least closely resembled his actual experience.[8] Luke also records that Paul was also stoned, beaten, and left for dead (Acts 14:19). He was attacked by crowds and dragged before magistrates (Acts 16:19–24). He was constantly in prison (2 Cor 6:4–5; Col 4:3; Eph 3:1; Philemon 1; Acts 21:33). In spite of these sufferings, he persisted in proclaiming the Gospel, expecting the same mistreatment wherever

---

[6]   Regardless of whether Paul made it to Spain or not, there is general agreement that Paul met his fate in Rome, which is key for establishing the traditional account of his martyrdom. For an analysis of the evidence for a Spanish mission, see Otto F.A. Meinardus, "Paul's Missionary Journey to Spain: Tradition and Folklore," *The Biblical Archaeologist* 41 (1978): 61–63.

[7]   George F. Jowett, *The Drama of the Lost Disciples* (Bishop Auckland, England: Covenant, 2004), 182–97.

[8]   Stephen C. Barton, "Paul as Missionary and Pastor," in *The Cambridge Companion to St. Paul*, ed. James D.G. Dunn (Cambridge: Cambridge University Press, 2003), 40.

he went (Acts 20:23). Sacrificing the pleasures of this life to advance the Gospel, he was unswayed by the difficulty of the task before him (Rom 1:14–16). After listing the suffering and persecution Paul endured, Jürgen Becker concludes: "Yet whatever details we may quote, and however we may take into account the meagerness of our tradition from this period, there can be no doubt that the apostle was subjected to conspicuously frequent and especially severe persecutions."[9]

How, amid such severe persecution and the possibility of death, could Paul so boldly proclaim the Gospel? The answer lies in his belief that the risen Jesus, whom he claimed to have personally seen, had already defeated death (1 Cor 15:55–56). Unlike later martyrs who suffered and died for resurrection reports that came *secondhand* from the testimony of others, Paul had seen the risen Jesus *firsthand*. He was an eyewitness of the resurrected Christ and suffered willingly for what he firmly believed to be true (1 Cor 15: 8; 9:1; Acts 9:1–6). Paul was convinced that Jesus had appeared to him after rising from the dead, and he willingly endangered himself for the sake of the Gospel.

The Historical Question

The traditional view holds that Paul was beheaded as a martyr in Rome some time between AD 62–68 during the latter part of the reign of Nero (AD 54–68). Scholars disagree significantly over the validity of this tradition. According to A.N. Wilson: "[T]here is certainly no hard evidence that Paul died the death of a martyr."[10] Rather, he suggests Paul died in the west while missionizing Spain. On the other hand, John McRay argues that "there is little doubt that he [Paul] died under Nero's reign in A.D. 67 or 68."[11] In order properly to evaluate the traditional view for the martyrdom of Paul, we must consider both the merits of each individual piece of evidence and the overall strength of the case. The Bible does not state the death of Paul directly, since all the writings cover earlier material.[12] But there are some strong biblical hints that Paul viewed his death as imminent, and there is a consistent extra-biblical tradition that can help determine the likelihood of Paul's martyrdom in Rome.

---

[9]   Jürgen Becker, *Paul: Apostle to the Gentiles*, trans. O.C. Dean, Jr. (Louisville, KY: John Knox Press, 1993), 170.

[10]   A.N. Wilson, *Paul: The Mind of the Apostle* (New York: W.W. Norton, 1997), 249.

[11]   John McRay, *Paul: His Life and Teaching* (Grand Rapids, MI: Baker, 2003), 257.

[12]   It is true that a majority of scholars accept the seven undisputed letters of Paul and believe that some of the letters, such as the Pastoral Epistles, were written after his death. But even if these letters are pseudepigraphical and written at the beginning of the second century, they still attempt to cover material from within the lifetime of Paul. It would make no sense for a pseudepigraphical author to include concrete evidence for Paul's death when it claims to be written by Paul himself!

This investigation focuses on the literary evidence, since archaeological remains concerning Paul are late and themselves dependent upon literary evidence and tradition.[13] And as with the case of Peter, this investigation focuses on what Markus Bockmuehl has dubbed "the living memory," which would end by about AD 200.

Paul in Rome

While the particular location is technically not critical for demonstrating Paul's death as a martyr, we should nonetheless consider the evidence for Paul's presence in Rome, since it is so central to the traditional account and since it provides the link to Nero. Unlike the case for Peter being in Rome, little scholarly debate exists regarding Paul. Nevertheless, Dwight Callahan doubts Paul's Roman journey and suggests he may have died in Philippi in fatal imprisonment.[14] However, even if Callahan is right, then Paul *still died as a martyr*, which is the critical piece for establishing the sincerity of his convictions. Even so, the traditional view that Paul made it to Rome is firmly established.

Philippians

Although a case can be made that all the prison epistles were written in Rome,[15] Philippians, of Paul's undisputed letters, provides the strongest case. Little doubt has been raised regarding Paul's authorship; that is, while Corinth, Caesarea, and Ephesus have more recently been suggested as the place from which Paul wrote Philippians, from the second-century Marcionite prologue to the eighteenth century, it was considered an established fact that Paul composed Philippians from Rome.[16] Evidence for Pauline authorship of Philippians in Rome can also be found through a careful internal analysis of the book.[17] Nevertheless, while a strong case can be made for Pauline authorship in Rome, given the significant

---

[13]   Ernst Dassmann, "Archaeological Traces of Early Christian Veneration of Paul," in *Paul and the Legacies of Paul*, ed. William S. Babcock (Dallas, TX: Southern Methodist University Press, 1990), 282.

[14]   Allan Dwight Callahan, "Dead Paul: The Apostle as Martyr in Philippi," in *Philippi at the Time of Paul and After His Death*, ed. Charalambos Bakirtzis (Eugene, OR: Wipf & Stock, 2009), 76.

[15]   Harry W. Tajra, *The Martyrdom of St. Paul* (Eugene, OR: Wipf & Stock, 1994), 51–72.

[16]   Gerald F. Hawthorne, *Philippians*, Word Biblical Commentary, vol. 43 (Nashville, TN: Thomas Nelson, 2004), xl.

[17]   Richard J. Cassidy, *Paul in Chains: Roman Imprisonment and the Letters of St. Paul* (New York: Crossroads, 2001), 126–35.

amount of scholarly disagreement as well as the additional arguments that can be fostered for a variety of locations,[18] Roman authorship of Philippians must be held tentatively. Thus, the likely authorship of Philippians provides only slight corroborative evidence for a Roman journey by Paul.

Second Timothy

The evidence from 2 Timothy is much more conclusive because Paul refers directly to his imprisonment in Rome (1:16–17; 2:9). Paul is either writing this account from Rome or based on a time when he was there. The difficulty arises as to how to place this imprisonment in the life of Paul. But the problem can be solved if Paul was released from his first imprisonment in Rome (Acts 28; Phil 1:18–19; 24–26: 2:24) and then later faced a more severe imprisonment in Rome, where he expected imminent death (cf. 2 Tim 1:16–17; 2:9; 4:6–8, 16–18).[19]

It may be objected that 2 Timothy is pseudepigraphical, and thus the reference to Rome is unreliable.[20] Nevertheless, even if Paul is not the author of the Pastorals, including 2 Timothy, it must have come from a group intimately connected to the apostle Paul. Therefore, whether pseudepigraphical or not, 2 Timothy provides a strong link to an early tradition that favors Paul's Roman occupation.

Acts

Perhaps Acts offers the strongest piece of evidence for Paul in Rome, where Paul says: "I was delivered as a prisoner from Jerusalem into the hands of the Romans" (Acts 28:17b). The book's climax tells of Paul arriving in Rome, to preach (Acts 28:31). Most scholars today date Acts between 70 and 85, with some into the 90s. Even at the latest reasonable date, Acts would still be within the living memory of eyewitnesses who could easily disconfirm a Pauline hiatus in Rome.

---

[18]   For a recent survey of the evidence for and against the various imprisonment options (Rome, Caesarea, Corinth, Ephesus), see Hawthorne, *Philippians*, xl–l.

[19]   Gordon D. Fee, *1 and 2 Timothy, Titus*, New International Biblical Commentary (Peabody, MA: Hendrickson, 1988), 3–5.

[20]   Some scholars have suggested that the author of the Pastoral Epistles made up the historical allusions to give the letters some degree of credibility. Thus, historical allusions are merely fiction. But, as Guthrie has observed, allusions in the Pastorals as well as the historical references have a sense of realism that is not accounted for by the fictional model, which is why many who take the fictional approach admit there is still a historical core. See Donald Guthrie, *The Pastoral Epistles: An Introduction and Commentary* (Grand Rapids, MI: Eerdmans, 1996), 28.

The lack of any early competing narrative for the demise of Paul elsewhere speaks strongly in favor of the traditional view that he was imprisoned in Rome.[21]

It cannot be objected that Rome is a mere add-on to the end of Acts. Acts 19:21 says: "After I have been there [Macedonia, Achaia, and Jerusalem], I must also go to Rome." Furthermore, the whole purpose of the book of Acts is to record the spread of the Gospel to "the ends of the earth" (Acts 1:8). In comparison with rural Galilee, Rome was considered "the ends of the earth."[22] Rome is not meant as an end in itself, but as representative of the entire world. In other words, if the Gospel could reach Rome, it could reach anywhere.

One way to escape the reality of Paul's trip to Rome is to consider Acts an ancient novel void of historical truth.[23] Although this approach does offer some fruitful literary insights, the genre of Acts presents considerable problems for this view. For one thing, most novels used fictitious characters, and when they used real historical figures, they had little knowledge about actual events in the figure's life; Acts, however, is filled with demonstrable historical events and characters.[24] Rather than fictional, then, Acts is best understood as an ancient historiographical work, similar in many ways to other ancient histories of the time.[25] Barring new arguments undermining the historical nature of Acts, the majority view that Acts is a historical text provides sufficient evidence that Paul was in Rome.

Extra-biblical Evidence

Along with the biblical testimony, unanimous evidence from the church fathers supports that Paul was in Rome. The first reference is in *1 Clement* 6:1 (*c.* AD 95–96), which shows Paul was remembered in Rome within one generation of his death. Similar testimony can be found in writings of both Ignatius (*The Letter to the Romans* 4:1–3) and Tertullian (*Scorpiace* 15:4–6). The *Acts of Paul* also indicates Paul journeyed to Rome. The details, however, vary significantly from the canonical Acts. They have different points of departure and land at

---

[21]   The Alexandrian and Western texts of Acts do vary in significant details regarding Paul's trip to Rome. But most significantly, they both agree that Paul ended up in Rome. For a comparison, see Jerome Murphy-O'Connor, *Paul: A Critical Life* (Oxford: Oxford University Press, 1996), 351–54.

[22]   Richard I. Pervo, *Acts: A Commentary on the Book of Acts*, Hermeneia (Minneapolis, MN: Fortress Press, 2009), 677.

[23]   Burton L. Mack, *Who Wrote the New Testament? The Making of the Christian Myth* (New York: HarperCollins, 1995), 11–15.

[24]   C.K. Barrett, "The Historicity of Acts," *Journal of Theological Studies* 52 (1999): 515–34; Colin Hemer, *The Book of Acts in the Setting of Hellenistic History*, ed. Conrad H. Gempf (Winona Lake, IN: Eisenbrauns, 1990).

[25]   Ben Witherington III, *The Acts of the Apostles: A Socio-Rhetorical Commentary* (Grand Rapids, MI: Eerdmans, 1998), 24–39.

different places, which likely indicates they provide independent testimonies to Paul's voyage to Rome.[26]

Paul's journey to Rome, then, is firmly established by the reference in 2 Timothy 1:16–17, the historical account in Acts 28:11–31, the likely authorship of Philippians—and other prison epistles—in Rome, and the early and unanimous tradition from the apostolic fathers. In addition, lack of a competing site for his final imprisonment means no good reason exists to doubt the traditional account of Paul's imprisonment in Rome.

Evidence for the Martyrdom of Paul

Scriptural Evidence

Even though Paul suffered deeply and considered his own death a reality (for example, 2 Cor 5:1–10), the New Testament does not directly state the martyrdom of Paul—which we, of course, should expect, since all the New Testament books cover only material from before his death.[27] Yet there are some strong hints that foreshadow his martyrdom in both the book of Acts and the Pastoral letters, where Paul strongly viewed his death as imminent.

Second Timothy 4:6–8
The majority of scholars consider 2 Timothy pseudepigraphical and written some time during AD 90–110. If this late dating were correct, it would not undermine the principal argument made here because the text shows how his close followers and disciples, just one generation removed, viewed his death. In fact, if it is pseudepigraphical, then the author(s) would have written 2 Timothy with awareness that Paul had died, since the letter is typically considered Paul's final will and testament.

Second Timothy portrays Paul in a Roman prison for preaching the risen Christ (1:11, 12; 2:8, 9). He has already undergone an initial hearing (4:16–18), and he firmly anticipates his own death (4:6–8). He writes to Timothy to offer instruction, admonition, and encouragement. Paul includes many details in the letter regarding changes he hopes to see in the life and ministry of Timothy, which reveals an underlying concern that he may never see him again.[28] In

---

[26]   Peter Wallace Dunn, "The *Acts of Paul* and the Pauline Legacy in the Second Century" (Ph.D. diss., Queens College, Cambridge, 1996), 32.

[27]   The one possible exception is the two witnesses who will give their testimony and then be conquered and killed by the beast (Rev 11:3, 7–8). However, scholars have almost universally rejected the idea that the two witnesses are Peter and Paul.

[28]   Murphy-O'Connor, *Paul: His Story* (Oxford: Oxford University Press, 2004), 232.

anticipation of his own death at the hands of authorities, Paul encourages Timothy to come to him quickly (4:9).

Whereas in his letter to the Philippians Paul considered that his imprisonment could end in death (Phil 1:20–24; 2:17, 23), in 2 Timothy he has an added sense of urgency:

> For I am already being poured out as a drink offering, and the time of my departure has come. I have fought the good fight, I have finished the race, I have kept the faith. Henceforth there is laid up for me the crown of righteousness, which the Lord, the righteous judge, will award to me on that Day, and not only to me but also to all who have loved his appearing. (2 Tim 4:6–8)

This passage is regarded as one of the most explicit references in the New Testament to Paul's looming martyrdom.[29] Paul expects his imprisonment will end in death (v. 6), he recognizes he has stayed faithful in his ministry, which is coming to an end (v. 7), and he anticipates his final heavenly reward (v. 8).

Paul uses two metaphors that indicate he views his death as imminent. First, he says he is "already being poured out as a drink offering" (v. 6). In ancient sacrificial systems, a liquid, such as oil or wine, was often poured out in sacrifice or consecration.[30] In the Old Testament, the sacrifice of animals involved the pouring out of blood in a similar manner (Lev 16:15–20). Paul undoubtedly believes his own blood will be poured out as a sacrifice for the sake of the Gospel. Ignatius used the same metaphor to indicate his own looming martyrdom.[31] Second, Paul says, "the time of my departure has come," which is a known euphemism for death.[32]

With his impending death in mind, then, Paul encourages Timothy to struggle for the Gospel and to suffer as Paul did (1 Tim 4:10; 2 Tim 2:3; 3:12; 4:5). Paul's "fight" has brought him to imprisonment in Rome, and as he now awaits execution, he calls Timothy, and other future believers, to follow his example amidst doctrinal error, godlessness, suffering, and even the prospect of martyrdom.

Finally, Paul anticipates the "crown" awaiting him for his life of faithful service (cf. Jas 1:12; Rev 2:10; 1 Pet 5:4). His crown is secured; it just awaits him to receive it. Even though Paul is unjustly sentenced to death, he will be declared righteous by the true judge—Christ. He is prepared to depart this world and

---

[29]   David L. Eastman, *Paul the Martyr: The Cult of the Apostle in the Latin West* (Atlanta, GA: Society of Biblical Literature, 2011), 141.

[30]   Homer, *Odyssey* 12.363; Plutarch, *Obsolescence of Oracles* 49; Num 15:5, 7, 10; 2 Sam 23:16–17; Ps 16:4.

[31]   Ignatius, *Letter to the Romans* 2:2.

[32]   William D. Mounce, *Pastoral Epistles*, Word Biblical Commentary, vol. 46 (Nashville, TN: Thomas Nelson, 2000), 578.

enter the next. Paul does not fear death, but views it as the climax of his ministry, the consummation of his apostolic calling.

So, while 2 Timothy does not explicitly state the martyrdom of Paul, we should remember that it would make no sense in a letter attributed to him. Still, it does clearly indicate that Paul believed his death was imminent, as he compared himself to a libation and said he was prepared to depart from this world. He was imprisoned and prepared to die as a martyr for the sake of the Gospel. Ironically for the conservative position, if 2 Timothy is pseudepigraphical, it *strengthens* the reference to his death, since the author would have known about his fate and would have been bound by the known tradition of the time and incapable of fabricating an account of his impending death. Regardless, 2 Timothy 4:6–8 sets the stage for the expectation that Paul would be executed in Rome.

Acts

Although the Acts narrative ends before Paul dies, it includes hints of the apostle's fate. A large number of English-speaking commentators—probably the majority—hold that the author of Acts was a traveling companion of Paul, so he would have known about Paul's experiences of persecution,[33] such as Paul's willingness to die in Jerusalem for the sake of Christ (Acts 19:13). Moreover, a comparison of Acts 19:21 with Luke 9:51 indicates that Luke believes Paul travels through Jerusalem on the way to martyrdom.[34] Stephen was charged in Jerusalem with defaming the temple and law (Acts 6:13). A similar charge is raised against Paul in Jerusalem (21:28). While these are probably trumped-up charges to condemn Paul,[35] he does incite animosity and opposition similar to what brought about the martyrdom of Stephen (v. 30), and is only saved by Roman troops. In Acts 20, Paul gathers the Ephesian elders at Miletus and warns them to be alert because "wolves" will bring heresy into the flock once he is gone (20:29). After explaining the uncertainty of what will happen to him in Jerusalem, except suffering and imprisonment (20:23), they weep because "they would not see his face again" (20:38). Luke also structures Paul's arrest and imprisonment in Acts after the account of Jesus in his Gospel,[36] which indicates they will both face a similar fate. David Eastman explains:

---

[33] Craig S. Keener, *Acts: An Exegetical Commentary* (Grand Rapids, MI: Baker, 2012), 1:407.

[34] Schnelle, *Apostle Paul*, 360.

[35] C.K. Barrett, *Acts of the Apostles*, Hermeneia, vol. 2, 2nd ed. (New York: T. & T. Clark, 2004), 1,020.

[36] Richard Longenecker, *Acts*, in vol. 9 of *The Expositor's Bible Commentary*, ed. J.D. Douglas and Frank E. Gaebelein [Grand Rapids, MI: Zondervan, 1981], 515); Dennis. R. MacDonald, "Apocryphal and Canonical Narratives about Paul," in *Paul and the Legacies of Paul*, ed. William S. Babcock (Dallas, TX: Southern Methodist University Press), 64–66.

Both Jesus and Paul go to Jerusalem despite a triple prediction that they will suffer there. Both receive a warm welcome and subsequently enter the temple, where they are seized. Both then endure a series of four trials, during which they are handed over to Gentiles, slapped, declared innocent three times, and subjected to a mob's cry of "Away with him." They submit themselves to God's will and are treated kindly or praised by a Roman centurion (Luke 9:51–23:47; Acts 20:1–27:43). By the end of the accounts, both have fulfilled the preaching ministry given to them. It is striking that Luke does not complete the parallel by recounting the death of Paul. Nonetheless, an audience familiar with Jesus' fate in Luke's Gospel might infer that Paul was headed down a similar road in Acts.[37]

If Luke anticipates the fate of Paul throughout Acts, and Acts was written after Paul's death—as most scholars agree—then why does Acts end with his imprisonment? Why does Luke not recount the fate of Paul? Scholars have ventured a number of possibilities,[38] the most promising of which considers the purpose for which Luke wrote Acts—to record the spread of the Gospel from Jerusalem and Judea through Samaria to the "ends of the earth" (Acts 1:8)— making sense of its ending quickly upon Paul's arrival in Rome: the purpose of Acts has been accomplished; Luke ends the narrative.[39] Acts is not a biography of Paul, a trial brief, or a martyrdom account, but a historical account of the spread of the church from Jerusalem to Rome. Since the Gospel had reached Rome, it could now be spread *everywhere*. George MacRae concludes:

> The journey of Paul in Acts first to Jerusalem and then to Rome analogously occupies a major part of the book (effectively 19:21–28:31) and represents the working out in the life of the model disciple the same journey toward suffering and death that was Jesus'. The difference is of course that Jesus has already made the journey. Paul can face the prospect of his fate with the confidence that was won for him by Jesus whose journey to death was crowned with resurrection and exaltation .... And perhaps it is the confidence of the divine assurance that enables

---

[37]   Eastman, *Paul the Martyr*, 18.

[38]   G.W. Trompf, "On Why Luke Declined to Recount the Death of Paul: Acts 27–28 and Beyond," in *Luke–Acts: New Perspectives from the Society of Biblical Literature Seminar*, ed. Charles H. Talbert (New York: Crossroad, 1984), 232–34.

[39]   Luke uses different characters in the story of Acts to further his end, and when that end is completed, Luke ceases to focus on them. If the life of the characters do not end in death (for example, John, Jesus, Stephen), they abruptly drop out of the narrative (Philip, Peter). Or in the case of Paul, since Luke has no further narrative interest in his fate, the story simply ends. See Daniel R. Schwartz, "The End of the Line: Paul in the Canonical Book of Acts," in *Paul and the Legacies of Paul*, ed. William S. Babcock (Dallas, TX: Southern Methodist University Press, 1990), 23.

the author of Acts to end his work not with the actual martyrdom of Paul but with
the serenity of the Christian mission being fulfilled in Paul's ministry in Rome.[40]

Another important reason for the abrupt ending of Acts may be that Luke wants
to indicate that Christianity and Rome are compatible. Acts ends during the
reign of Nero, but he had not yet begun his persecution of Christians. If Luke
wanted to portray peace between Christianity and Rome, it would be wise to
end the story before Paul's martyrdom.[41]

Acts does not report the death of Paul, but Luke leaves significant hints that he
is to be lead down a similar path as Jesus to martyrdom. Thus, while Acts cannot
offer direct evidence for Paul's fate, it provides the background expectation that
Paul would ultimately die as a result of proclaiming his faith. Since it was written
after Paul's death, and Luke would undoubtedly have been aware of his fate, Acts
provides supporting evidence for the traditional view that Paul died as a martyr
in Rome. But to fully substantiate the traditional rendition, a look outside the
New Testament for corroboration is needed.

First Clement 5:5–7

As stated previously, *1 Clement* (*c*. AD 95–96) is the first non-canonical
document that refers to the martyrdoms of Peter and Paul. Its greatest value
comes from its being an early account of Paul's violent death written in Rome,
where there could still be Christians alive who witnessed Paul's imprisonment
and death. Given that Clement only refers to Paul twice by name (5:5–7; 47:1),
it is noteworthy that one of them includes a reference to his martyrdom. This
is particularly significant since Clement is more concerned with drawing moral
lessons from known facts than providing the precision one may expect in a
historical work.[42]

While details regarding the manner of his fate are lacking, the immediate
context strongly implies that Clement was referring to the martyrdom of
Paul.[43] In the preceding verses, Clement refers to Peter as a pillar of the faith
who experienced profound suffering and was persecuted for his faith "even
unto death" (5:2). Richard Pervo notes that the reason Peter and Paul were

---

[40] George W. MacRae, "Whom Heaven Must Receive Until the Time: Reflections on
the Christology of Acts," *Interpretations* 27 (April 1973): 151–65.

[41] Luke does go out of his way to indicate how fairly Paul was treated as a prisoner in
Rome (28:16b, 30). He also indicates that the Romans had previously wanted to release him
in Caesarea (26:30–32; 28:18).

[42] F.F. Bruce, "Paul in Rome: 5 Concluding Observations," *Bulletin of the John Rylands
Library* 50:2 (1968): 270.

[43] See the discussion in Chapter 5 of this volume.

persecuted and ultimately martyred was because of "jealousy and envy."[44] And
the phrase in 5:7 that Paul was "set free from this world" implies he was put to
death. According to Bart Ehrman, this passage indicates the author was aware of
a tradition that Paul was put on trial and eventually executed for his faith.[45] *First
Clement* 5:5–7 focuses specifically on the fate of Paul:

> Because of jealousy and strife Paul pointed the way to the prize for endurance.
> Seven times he bore chains; he was sent into exile and stoned; he served as a herald
> in both the East and the West; and he received the noble reputation for his faith.
> He taught righteousness to the whole world, and came to the limits of the West,
> bearing his witness before the rulers. And so he was set free from this world and
> transported up to the holy place, having become the greatest example of endurance.

Clearly, the author of *1 Clement* wants to reveal Paul as a model of endurance
for others to imitate. Paul, then, is given considerably more space than Peter,
indicating he is the prominent person in this text.[46] Even though both Peter
and Paul are among the "pillars" of the faith, Paul is the greatest example of
endurance—he faced considerable persecution, yet continued to preach the
Gospel throughout the world, and was ultimately executed for his faith.

First Clement 6:1 also provides a clue as to *when* their deaths occur: "To these
men who have conducted themselves in such a holy way there has been added
a great multitude of the elect, who have set a superb example among us by the
numerous torments and tortures they suffered because of jealousy." Clement's
reference to "a great multitude" is almost identical in wording to Tacitus's reference
to vast numbers (*multitudo ingens*) who were convicted and ultimately killed by
Nero.[47] Bruce concludes: "That this is a reference to the persecution of Christians
in Rome under Nero is hardly to be doubted."[48] In sum, although one may wish
1 Clement 5:5–7 provided more details regarding circumstances surrounding the
fate of Paul, this in no way discounts the substantial evidence it does provide for
the traditional view that Paul was martyred under Nero in Rome.

---

[44]   Richard I. Pervo, *The Making of Paul: Constructions of the Apostle in Early Christianity*
(Minneapolis, MN: Fortress Press, 2010), 132. Pervo doubts the historical value of *1 Clement*,
as well as the rest of the Gospels and the book of Acts. But the salient point for this discussion
is that he interprets *1 Clement* 5:1–7 as referring to the martyrdoms of Peter and Paul.

[45]   Bart Ehrman, *Peter, Paul, and Mary Magdalene: The Followers of Jesus in History and
Legend* (Oxford: Oxford University Press, 2006), 173.

[46]   Andreas Lindemann, "Paul in the Writings of the Apostolic Fathers," in *Paul and the
Legacies of Paul*, ed. William S. Babcock (Dallas, TX: Southern Methodist University Press,
1990), 29.

[47]   *Annals* 15.44.2.

[48]   F.F. Bruce, *Paul: Apostle of the Heart Set Free* (Grand Rapids, MI: Eerdmans, 2000),
448.

Ignatius

Ignatius mentions Paul twice by name. Both instances have been taken as supporting the traditional view of Paul's martyrdom in Rome. For analysis and discussion of the first passage, *Letter to the Romans* 4:3, see Chapter 5 in this volume. The second passage, which applies uniquely to Paul, appears in *Letter to the Ephesians* 12:2:

> I know who I am and to whom I am writing. I am condemned, you have been shown mercy; I am in danger, you are secure. You are a passageway for those slain for God; you are fellow initiates with Paul, the holy one who received a testimony and proved worthy of all fortune. When I attain to God, may I be found in his footsteps, this one who mentions you in every epistle in Christ Jesus.

While Ignatius uses some hyperbole here, since Paul certainly did not mention the Ephesian church "in every epistle," his clear point is to make an intimate link between the church at Ephesus and the apostle Paul, *not* to give a precise word count on the number of times he specifically mentions the Ephesians in all his letters.[49]

In this passage, Ignatius may be referring to Paul's meeting with the Ephesian elders when they sent him off to imprisonment and eventual martyrdom (Acts 20:17–38), such that Ignatius sees his own impending martyrdom as following Paul's example. Ignatius clearly aims to imitate Jesus,[50] but practically he is following in the footsteps of Paul. Aageson concludes: "Ignatius holds Paul in the highest esteem, sees his own journey to martyrdom for God as following the pattern of Paul's journey, and visualizes the Ephesians as the passage way of those slain for the sake of God."[51]

But what does Ignatius mean by "proved worthy of all fortune"? Two reasons stand out to accept the phrase as a reference to Paul's martyrdom. First, the context reveals that Ignatius considers Ephesus a "passageway" for those who are "slain for God" (martyred). In the wider context, Ignatius points specifically to Paul as an example the Ephesians would recognize as one who was slain for God. And immediately afterward, Ignatius says: "When I attain to God, may I be found in his footsteps." In other words, Ignatius desires to face martyrdom with courage and commitment as Paul did. If Paul were not martyred, it would make no sense for Ignatius to raise him as his greatest example of imitation since he is en route to his own execution in Rome.

---

49   Lindemann, "Paul in the Writings," 36.
50   Ignatius, *Letter to the Ephesians* 10:3.
51   James W. Aageson, *Paul, the Pastoral Epistles, and the Early Church*, ed. Stanley E. Porter (Peabody, MA: Hendrickson, 2008), 124–25.

Second, to be "proved worthy of all fortune" was to deserve the reward of being with God, and Ignatius achieved this through imitation of the passion of Christ.[52] Ignatius says, "It is better for me to die in Jesus Christ than to rule the ends of the earth,"[53] echoing Paul (Phil 1:21). Ignatius sees his chains as a means of exhortation for other believers, which he bears on account of Christ so he may attain to God.[54] In *The Letter to the Magnesians*, Ignatius said: "If we do not choose to die voluntarily in his suffering, his life is not in us."[55] Therefore, to acquire the greatest reward of being with God, Ignatius must suffer and die at the hands of the ruler of this age. Thus, Ignatius lifts up Paul as an example to imitate because Paul was proved worthy of all fortune through his faithful witness, suffering, and martyrdom for his faith.

Ignatius clearly believes Paul was martyred, and he expects to follow his example. How did Ignatius gain such knowledge? Did he talk to someone who knew the apostles firsthand? Did he meet the apostles? Was he merely passing on legends about their deaths? Byzantium hagiography considers Ignatius the boy Jesus used as an example to teach his disciples about greatness in the kingdom of God (Matt 18:2–5). Jerome says that Ignatius knew Polycarp, who was a disciple of the apostle John.[56] While these claims are difficult to verify, chronologically and theologically speaking, Ignatius was undoubtedly close to the apostles.

Even at the latest possible date for his life and martyrdom (*c.* AD 135), Ignatius falls well within the window of living memory. Part of the significance of this letter is that Ignatius is writing to early Christians within the first generation after the death of Paul. If the tradition were not true, many believers would have corrected it. Yet Ignatius did not feel the need to exaggerate, ignore, or defend the martyrdom account of Paul. Instead, he simply assumes it in his *Letter to the Ephesians*—and possibly in his *Letter to the Romans*—as established fact. It seems reasonable to believe, then, that Ignatius was aware of an early tradition about the martyrdom of Paul in Rome.

Polycarp, Letter to the Philippians

Polycarp wrote this letter to the church at Philippi to encourage them to stay faithful to the core tenets of the faith (7:1), to live out the Christian faith (5:1), and to endure suffering as Christ, Paul, and the other apostles had (1:1; 2:3; 8:2; 9:2; 12:3). He apparently wrote his letter just after the death of Ignatius, since it

---

52   W.H.C. Frend, *Martyrdom and Persecution in the Early Church* (Oxford: Blackwell, 1965; corrected ed., Cambridge: James Clark, 2008), 198.

53   Ignatius, *Letter to the Romans* 6:1.

54   Ignatius, *Letter to the Trallians* 12:2.

55   Ignatius, *The Letter to the Magnesians* 5:2.

56   Saint Jerome, *On Illustrious Men*, trans. Thomas P. Halton (Washington, DC: Catholic University of America Press, 1999), 16:2.

appears Polycarp assumes Ignatius has died (1:1; 9:1), but has not received final confirmation (13:2). Polycarp encourages the church to follow the faith "that was delivered to us from the beginning" (7:2; cf. 3:1–3). Thus, Polycarp links the message he is delivering to the faith as taught by Jesus, Paul, and the first apostles.

Polycarp mentions Paul three times by name (3:2; 9:1; 11:3). Remarkably, one of those references makes it clear that Polycarp knew Paul and the other apostles had been martyred:

> Therefore I urge all of you to obey the word of righteousness and to practice all endurance, which you also observed with your own eyes not only in the most fortunate Ignatius, Zosimus, and Rufus, but also in others who lived among you, and in Paul himself and the other apostles. You should be convinced that none of them acted in vain, but in faith and righteousness, and that they are in the place they deserved, with the Lord, with whom they also suffered. For they did not love the present age; they loved the one who died for us and who was raised by God for our sakes. (*Letter to the Philippians* 9:1–2)

The specific context of this passage is Polycarp's guidance for Christians to imitate the model of Christ, even if they suffer for his name. The example of Paul is in the wider context of Jesus, who was crucified (8:1), and Ignatius, who died as a martyr (9:2). Then Polycarp refers to Paul and the other apostles, who "are in the place they deserved, with the Lord, with whom they also suffered" (9:2). The clear implication is that Paul suffered and faced a martyr's death as Jesus and Ignatius did. Polycarp links their examples together as models for the Philippian Christians to imitate. Bart Ehrman indicates that Polycarp was aware of a tradition in which Paul and the other disciples were in fact martyred.[57] Polycarp is confident that Christians at Philippi are as aware of the execution of Paul as of the crucifixion of Jesus—both by then matters of common knowledge and tradition, some time in the early to mid-second century, well within the range of living memory.

Dionysius of Corinth

For an analysis of the value of the writings of Dionysius of Corinth for the martyrdom of Paul, see Chapter 5 in this volume.

---

[57] Bart D. Ehrman, ed. and trans., *The Apostolic Fathers* (Cambridge, MA: Harvard University Press, 2004), 1:327.

Irenaeus

Irenaeus wrote his most famous work, *Against Heresies*, at the end of the second century (*c.* AD 180), placing it within the range of living memory of the apostle Paul. Irenaeus believes his authority comes directly from the teachings of Peter and Paul, which have been passed down faithfully through a line of unaltered succession.[58]

In a section committed to defending the scriptural authority of the four Gospels, Irenaeus references the deaths of Peter and Paul:

> Matthew also issued a written Gospel among the Hebrews in their own dialect, while Peter and Paul were preaching at Rome, and laying the foundations of the Church. After their departure [death], Mark the disciple and interpreter of Peter, did also hand down to us in writing what had been preached by Peter.[59]

Some have contested that "departure" simply means Peter and Paul left Rome, but the context makes this unlikely.

While Callahan, who discounts the significance of this reference, concedes that "departure" may refer to death, he argues that "early, unequivocal testimony of Paul's martyrdom, in Rome or anywhere else, is entirely lacking in early Christian literature."[60] Callahan is right that this passage does not provide "unequivocal" evidence that Peter and Paul were martyred under Nero. But why discount one important piece of evidence just because it does not make the *entire* case? Were historians to rely upon unequivocal evidence to make judgments, very little could be known about the past *at all*. Rather, historical reasoning and knowledge is based upon probability that comes from weighing the *totality* of the evidence and asking, "What best accounts for the available evidence?" And as we have seen, numerous other early writings help establish their fates as well. The passage in Irenaeus, then, must be read in light of the totality of knowledge regarding the fates of the apostles. In this case, Irenaeus does refer to the deaths of Peter and Paul, although he does not provide further details. It is true that natural deaths for both of them would be consistent with the statement by Irenaeus. However, Irenaeus was sufficiently close to the Roman church to know its local tradition. Given the strength of the tradition at this time concerning the preaching and martyrdom of Peter in Rome, it seems most likely that Irenaeus was well aware of the accounts and felt it unnecessary to repeat.

---

[58] See Chapter 5 in this volume.
[59] Iranaeus, *Against Heresies* 3.1.1.
[60] Callahan, "Dead Paul," 78.

The Acts of Paul

The *Acts of Paul* is typically dated AD 170–180. Yet some scholars have argued that the range of dates should be much larger, encompassing AD 140–200.[61] Peter Dunn has made a substantial case that it belongs in the first half of the second century.[62] If he is right, then there is a Pauline tradition incorporating his martyrdom only separated from him by two or three generations, well within the range of living memory, that thus may provide some historical value for this investigation.

However, these kinds of typical dates offered for the *Acts of Paul* assume that a coherent whole has been composed by one author, an assumption which has come under increasing criticism. Based on manuscript evidence from the fifth century, Glenn Snyder has argued that multiple, independent works circulated and developed into what we now call the *Acts of Paul*. The same is likely true for the *Martyrdom of Paul*, which contains the account of his execution by Nero.[63] Thus, Snyder concludes it was probably written during the reign of Trajan (AD 98–117).[64] If this is true, then there is a remembrance of Paul only one or two generations after his death. In addition, we have reason to believe earlier pre-existing traditions, and in particular *martyrdom* traditions, may have circulated prior to their incorporation into the text. With these considerations in mind, then, we cannot simply dismiss *Acts of Paul* as an entirely legendary account divorced from historical consideration.

The *Acts of Paul* clearly does contain some legendary material, though, such as Paul baptizing a lion and milk spurting from Paul's neck after decapitation (*Acts of Paul* 14). The characterization of Paul's appearance (*Acts of Paul* 1.3), for instance, is also likely motivated by the text itself rather than offering an independent testimony of his real appearance.[65] And yet Calvin Roetzel provides an important balance: "As fanciful and entertaining as these stories were, they enjoyed a tie, however loose it was, to history."[66]

---

[61] Tertullian refers to the *Acts of Paul* around AD 200, so it cannot be later than this date. A. Hilhorst, "Tertullian on the Acts of Paul," in *The Apocryphal Acts of Paul and Thecla*, ed. Jan N. Bremmer (Kampen, The Netherlands: Kok Pharos, 1996), 162.

[62] Dunn, "The *Acts of Paul*," 199.

[63] Glenn E. Snyder, *Acts of Paul: Formation of a Pauline Corpus*, ed. Jörg Frey (Tübingen, Germany: Mohr Siebeck, 2013), 15–17, 254.

[64] Ibid., 59–63.

[65] Jan N. Bremmer, "Magic, Martyrdom and Women's Liberation," in *The Apocryphal Acts of Paul and Thecla*, ed. Jan N. Bremmer (Kampen, Netherlands: Kok Pharos, 1996), 39. In the case of the martyrdom of Paul, there are earlier records of his death, as we have seen, that help establish its historical core. But the appearance of Paul is first recorded in this text, and seems to meet the needs of the author, and so it is likely a fabrication.

[66] Calvin Roetzel, *Paul: The Man and the Myth* (Minneapolis, MN: Fortress Press, 1999), 6.

Many of the characters, for instance, such as Paul, Onesiphorus, Judas, Titus, Luke, Peter, Barsabas Justus, Nero, and Tryphaena, are known historical figures. The author is bound, at least to a degree, to describe their lives and roles in ways that match the known historical tradition, and since these historically attested characters show the author is not completely divorced from historical memory. While there may be redaction, there is not free-flowing invention. Further, the enmity between Christians and Romans in the *Acts of Paul* matches the known historical situation from authors such as Tacitus, *1 Clement* 5–6, and *The Ascension of Isaiah* 4. Moreover, the mainstream, orthodox teaching of the *Acts of Paul* shows no significant signs of heresy or Gnosticism.[67] It accurately preserves some of the teachings of Jesus as well as important facts surrounding his life. The *Acts of Paul*, then, should not be taken as straightforward history—it is, similar to the *Acts of Peter*, probably best understood as historical novel, in which historical memory binds legendary embellishment.[68]

The same challenge arises for the *Acts of Paul* as the *Acts of Peter*: How is historical memory distinguished from legendary embellishment? It is true that the writer of the *Acts of Paul* was not aiming to write a straightforward historical narrative of the life, ministry, and death of Paul, but likely combined tradition, legend, and genuine history. Since the *Acts of Paul* matches the early and unwavering account of Paul's martyrdom in Rome, from both biblical and extra-biblical accounts, the tradition was undoubtedly fixed by the time of its composition.

Harry Tajra captures the likely historical core of the account of Paul's martyrdom in the *Acts of Paul*:[69]

1. Paul died in Rome.
2. Paul was martyred during the reign of Nero.
3. Paul was a Roman citizen.
4. Paul was put through some kind of trial and then faced a violent death.
5. Paul was arrested as a result of his preaching.

The *Acts of Paul*, then, provides an important testimony to the martyrdom of Paul in Rome, possibly within one or two generations of his death. With a probable date between the late first century and the early second century, and with a likely composition in Asia Minor, the *Acts of Paul* provides considerable support that the traditional view of Paul's fate had spread beyond the borders of Rome within a rather short time.

---

[67] Hans-Josef Klauck, *The Apocryphal Acts of the Apostles*, trans. Brian McNeil (Waco, TX: Baylor University Press, 2008), 74.

[68] Ibid., 7–10.

[69] Tajra, *The Martyrdom of Paul*, 131–33.

Was Paul Beheaded?

The uniform tradition has Paul executed by beheading. To establish that Paul was a martyr, it is not necessary to establish that he was in fact beheaded. Had he died by burning, for instance, he would still be a martyr. But since this is a core part of the tradition, it is important to consider its likelihood.

The first reference to Paul's death by beheading is found in the *Acts of Paul*, specifically in the *Martyrdom of Paul*. A few years later, at the turn of the second century, Tertullian became the first church father to state that Nero had Paul beheaded in Rome.[70] And then, in the early fourth century, Eusebius confirms this tradition.[71]

In the account in the *Acts of Paul*, Nero sends a decree that all Christians are to be put to death. Nero commands that prisoners be burned, but orders Paul beheaded according to Roman law. Schneemelcher finds this depiction not quite logical, since beheading was a less severe penalty.[72] However, this ignores that the text emphasizes the beheading as *according to Roman law*, which would require a different mode of execution for a Roman citizen such as Paul. The part of the narrative that is clearly embellishment is the milk that spurts out at his decapitation. The beheading narrative may have been driven by the theological conclusions the author intended readers to adopt from this episode. However, it seems more likely the tradition was already established by the time the author composed the *Acts of Paul* and the spurting milk was added to provide theological significance.

Romans had a variety of methods of execution.[73] In terms of beheading, Romans practiced *decollation*, which involved the use of a sword rather than decapitation with an axe.[74] It was a common form of execution. King Herod had John the Baptist beheaded (Mark 6:27). James the brother of John was "killed with the sword" under Herod Agrippa (Acts 12:2). The book of Revelation reports the beheading of those who gave testimony for Jesus and refused to worship the beast (Rev 20:4). Eusebius reports that Caesar "beheaded all who seemed to possess Roman citizenship and sent the rest to the beasts."[75] Eusebius later notes that after proclaiming his faith, Apollonius was beheaded according

---

[70] Tertullian, *Scorpiace* 15:4; *The Prescription Against Heretics* 36.

[71] Eusebius, *Ecclesiastical History* 2.25.

[72] Wilhelm Schneemelcher, ed., *New Testament Apocrypha*, trans. R.M. Wilson (Louisville, KY: Westminster John Knox Press, 2003), 2:231.

[73] Tacitus, *Annals* 15.44:2–5.

[74] Suetonius, *Nero* 49; Tacitus, *Annals* 2.32; John S. Pobee, *Persecution and Martyrdom in the Theology of Paul*, Journal for the Study of the New Testament Supplement Series, ed. Bruce D. Chilton (Sheffield, England: JSOT, 1985), 5.

[75] Eusebius, *Ecclesiastical History* 5.2.

to Roman law.[76] The sword, a symbol of power, brought fear into the hearts of people. Even Paul recognized that governing authorities do not bear the sword in vain (Rom 13:4).

Given that (1) there is no alternative claim of how Paul met his fate, (2) it was a common form of execution, and (3) it fits with what else is known about Paul (for example, his citizenship), it is more probable than not that Paul was beheaded. This cannot be held with the same degree of confidence as his martyrdom, but we have no good reason to doubt that the earliest accounts contain a tradition that dates back to his actual mode of death.

Tertullian

Tertullian wrote at the turn of the second century, and thus falls at the limit of the living memory of Paul. Like the author of *1 Clement* 5, Tertullian primarily depicts Paul as a model of resolute faithfulness and courage amidst suffering and of martyrdom.[77] Tertullian shows considerable interest in the martyrdom of Paul, since the church by his day had experienced both suffering and martyrdom. *Scorpiace* 15:5–6 provides a significant reference to the martyrdom of Paul:

> That Paul is beheaded has been written in their own blood. And if a heretic wishes his confidence to rest upon a public record, the archives of the empire will speak, as would the stones of Jerusalem. We read the lives of the Caesars: at Rome Nero was the first who stained with blood the rising faith. Then Peter is girt by another, when he is made fast to the cross. Then does Paul obtain a birth suited to Roman citizenship, when in Rome he springs to life again ennobled by martyrdom.

Tertullian reports that Paul was a Roman citizen, and links his death to the time of Nero. He is so confident of his claims that he tells his doubters to examine "the archives of the empire." If there were no such public records, Tertullian would have automatically undermined his credibility. His appeal to them indicates his confidence that they existed and, if examined, would corroborate his testimony. Therefore, Tertullian was likely relying upon even earlier public records about the Neronian persecution and the fate of Paul and Peter, James, and Stephen.

Tertullian makes two further allusions to the execution of Paul and Peter in Rome. In the first instance, Tertullian defends the equal apostolic status of Peter as compared to Paul: "It is a happy fact that Peter is on the same level

---

76   Ibid. 5.21.

77   Robert D. Sider, "Literary Artifice and the Figure of Paul in the Writings of Tertullian," in *Paul and the Legacies of Paul*, ed. William S. Babcock (Dallas, TX: Southern Methodist University Press, 1990), 106.

with Paul in the very glory of martyrdom."[78] Being on the "same level" does not require they face the same mode of execution, but that they were both apostles who died as martyrs in testimony for the faith. Tertullian is not trying to prove that either apostle was actually martyred, but to place Peter on equal footing with Paul. Tertullian assumes his audience are aware of the martyrdoms—he just makes sure they realize the implications of their equal fates. A few chapters later, Tertullian mentions again that Paul was beheaded like John the Baptist.[79] Eastman rightly concludes: "The shedding of apostolic blood was central to the foundation and spread of the Christian message in Rome. Because their deaths mirrored those of Jesus and John the Baptist, Peter and Paul became model martyrs who blessed the Roman church."[80] Tertullian's references to the apostle Paul show *minimally* that Paul was considered a model martyr by the end of the second century in North Africa.

Conclusion

The traditional view that Paul was beheaded during the reign of Nero, AD 64–67, has been carefully considered. There is additional later material that further confirms this tradition, but it will not be analyzed in depth, for this analysis has focused on the period of living memory.[81]

This close examination of the evidence indicates that the following points can be regarded to have varying degrees of confidence from works written within the living memory of Paul (until *c.* AD 200).

1. Paul was in Rome—*the highest possible probability* (possible authorship of Philippians from Rome; 2 Timothy 1:16–17; 2:9; Acts 28:17–31; 1 Clement 6:1; Ignatius, *The Letter to the Romans* 4:1–3; Tertullian, *Scorpiace* 15:4–6; *Acts of Paul*; the lack of any competing narrative).

2. The martyrdom of Paul—*the highest possible probability* (2 Tim 4:6–8; Acts 19:21–28:31; 1 Clement 5:5–7; Ignatius, *Letter to the Ephesians* 12:2; *Letter to the Romans* 4.3; *Letter to the Philippians* 7:1; Dionysius of Corinth [Eusebius, *Ecclesiastical History* 2.25]; Irenaeus, *Against Heresies* 3.1.1; *Acts of Paul*; Tertullian, *Scorpiace* 15:5–6; *The Prescription Against Heretics* 24, 36; the lack of any competing narrative weighs favorably for

---

78 Tertullian, *The Prescription Against Heretics* 24.

79 Ibid. 36.

80 Eastman, *Paul the Martyr*, 160.

81 Peter of Alexandria (AD 306), Aphrahat, *Demonstration XXI: Of Persecution* (§ 23); *Do Poenitentia: Epistola Canonica* 9; *The Acts of Peter and Paul* (AD 350); Jerome (AD 392), *Tractate on Psalm 96*, lines 176–83.

the traditional view; the early and persistent tradition is that Paul was martyred for his faith).

3. Martyrdom during the reign of Nero, AD 64–67—*very probably true* (*Acts of Paul*; Tertullian, *Scorpiace* 15:5–6; the chronology of Paul's life[82]).

4. The beheading of Paul—*more probable than not* (*Acts of Paul*; Tertullian, *Scorpiace* 15:4; *The Prescription Against Heretics* 36; *Hippolytus on the Twelve* 13; Eusebius, *Ecclesiastical History* 2.25; lack of any competing version of his death).

---

[82]   Robert Jewett, *A Chronology of Paul's Life* (Philadelphia, PA: Fortress Press, 1979).

Chapter 7
The Martyrdom of James, the Brother of Jesus

Until recent times, James, the brother of Jesus, was a largely forgotten figure in early Christianity. A cursory reading of the New Testament may give the impression that other figures such as Peter, Paul, Mary, and John are more important to understanding the early church. Yet in the past few years, significant studies have attempted to bring proper focus to the critical role James played in the origin and development of the Christian movement.[1]

Then who was James? Part of the difficulty in answering this question is the commonality of the name "James" in the New Testament.[2] The James focused on here is the eldest brother of Jesus, which is clear because James is listed first among the brothers and sisters of Jesus (Mark 6:3), a fact further confirmed in the early second-century document known as the *Gospel of Hebrews*, preserved by Jerome, where James is addressed as "my brother." Since Paul refers to the wives of the brothers of Jesus, James was likely married (1 Cor 9:5).

James was also an apostle. During his visit to Jerusalem, Paul says: "But I saw none of the other apostles except James the Lord's brother" (Gal 1:19). Attempts to translate Paul's passage to indicate that he did not consider James an apostle have been unsuccessful.[3] Unlike Luke, Paul does not limit the title "apostle" to the Twelve. Paul considered himself an apostle, equal in authority to those who were apostles before (cf. Gal 1:17). Those who were considered apostles had

---

[1]   For instance, see Jeffrey Butz, *The Brother of Jesus and the Lost Teachings of Christianity* (Rochester, VT: Inner Traditions, 2005); Bruce Chilton and Jacob Neusner, eds., *The Brother of Jesus: James the Just and His Mission* (Louisville, KY: Westminster John Knox Press, 2001); Patrick J. Hartin, *James of Jerusalem: Heir to Jesus of Nazareth* (Collegeville, MN: Liturgical Press, 2004); John Painter, *Just James: The Brother of Jesus in History and Tradition* (Columbia, SC: University of South Carolina Press, 1997); Pierre-Antoine Bernheim, *James, Brother of Jesus* (London: SCM Press, 1997).

[2]   The six most important people named James include: (1) James, the Lord's brother; (2) James, the son of Alphaeus, one of the 12 apostles; (3) James, the son of Zebedee, one of the 12 apostles; (4) James the Less, son of Mary, the wife of Clopas; (5) James, the father (or brother?) of Judas, one of the Twelve, and (6) Jude, the brother of James (identified author of the epistle of Jude).

[3]   Roy Bowen Ward, "James of Jerusalem in the First Two Centuries," in *Aufstieg und Niedergang der Römischen Welt* (Berlin, Germany: Walter de Gruyter, 1992), 780–81.

seen the risen Jesus (1 Cor 9:1), even if, like James and Paul, they were not part of the Twelve. Thus, according to Paul, "apostles" was a broader category that included Peter, the Twelve, James, the rest of the apostles, and finally himself (1 Cor 15:5–8).

Although James is never labeled "the Just" in Scripture, he is consistently painted in church tradition as being extraordinarily righteous. The first reference to James "the Just" is found in the *Gospel of Thomas* 12. The *Gospel of Hebrews*, in the fragment preserved by Jerome, also contains an early second-century reference to James as being righteous. The martyrdom of James also may have contributed to his being considered a righteous sufferer alongside Jesus and Stephen. The tradition of the righteousness of James comes to fruition in Hegesippus:

> He was called "the Just" by everyone from the Lord's time to ours, since there were many Jameses, but this one was consecrated from his mother's womb. He drank no wine or liquor and ate no meat. No razor came near his head, he did not anoint himself with oil, and took no baths. He alone was permitted to enter the sanctum, for he wore not wool but linen. He used to enter the temple alone and was often found kneeling and imploring forgiveness for the people, so that his knees became hard like a camel's from his continual kneeling in worship of God and in prayer for the people. Because of his superior righteousness he was called the Just and *Oblias*—meaning, in Greek, "Bulwark of the People" and "Righteousness"—as the prophets declare regarding him.[4]

This passage is clearly filled with exaggeration, as well as historical inaccuracies, but it captures the consistent and widespread tradition that James was considered righteous "from the Lord's time to ours."

James was one of the leaders of the early church. During his second trip to Jerusalem, Paul met with the three "pillars" of the faith—James, Cephas, and John (Gal 2:9). James is mentioned first to indicate his leadership in Jerusalem, as opposed to Peter (Cephas), the leading missionary to the Jews, which both coheres with the account in Acts where Luke singles James out as the leader of the elders, the key person Paul visits in Jerusalem (Acts 21:17–26), and matches the message sent by Peter to James before he departed for another place (Acts 12:17), indicating James was already the prominent figure among the brothers and likely already the principal leader (or at least the *burgeoning* leader) of the Jerusalem church. James demonstrates his leadership at the Jerusalem Council when he singlehandedly presides over the question of Gentiles and the law (Acts 15:14–21). The leadership of James is further corroborated in various early church fathers

---

[4]   Eusebius, *Ecclesiastical History*, in *Nicene and Post-Nicene Fathers*, ed. Philip Schaff and Henry Wace (New York: Christian Literature Co., 1890), 2.23.

and Gnostic writings.[5] While there is little debate about *whether* James led the early church,[6] scholars disagree about *when* James became the leader in Jerusalem.

The majority of theologians and scholars believe that the siblings of Jesus, including James, did not believe in Jesus during his pre-resurrection ministry. Certain passages in the Bible have traditionally been mustered to indicate that they were not disciples before the resurrection (for example, Mark 3:20–35; 6:2–4; John 7:3–5; 19:25–27). But a significant number of scholars have recently challenged the traditional view, suggesting these passages are open to divergent interpretations.[7] Even Richard Bauckham has held that it is more likely that before the crucifixion James had already belonged to the inner circle of disciples.[8] Butz concludes: "Jesus appeared to James after his resurrection not because James did *not* believe, but precisely because he *did*."[9]

However, Butz admits that the only evidence anywhere in the Gospels that Jesus's family may have been among his followers during his ministry is found in two passages in the Gospel of John. First, the brothers of Jesus are present when he turns water to wine (2:12). Butz says this gives "the impression that *the brothers were an essential part of the following of Jesus*."[10] Bauckham considers this the best evidence the family of Jesus were among his followers during his ministry.[11] However, as Licona has observed: "The occasion of Jesus' miracle apparently had no relation to his itinerant ministry. Jesus was simply present as a wedding guest and is even hesitant to perform a miracle."[12] The context would lead one

---

[5]   For instance, see the *Gospel of Thomas* 12; Hegesippus, *Ecclesiastical History* 2.23.4; Clement of Alexandria, *Ecclesiastical History* 2.1.3–4; Eusebius, *Ecclesiastical History* 2.23.1, *Apocryphon of James* 1:1–3; *Pseudo-Clementine Contestatio* 1:1.

[6]   For one exception, see S.G.F. Brandon, "The Death of James the Just: A New Interpretation," in *Studies in Mysticism and Religion presented to Gershom G. Scholem on His Seventieth Birthday by Pupils, Colleagues, and Friends* (Jerusalem, Israel: Central Press, 1967), 60.

[7]   Dale C. Allison, *Resurrecting Jesus: The Earliest Christian Tradition and its Interpreters* (New York: T. & T. Clark, 2005), 261–63; Bernheim, *James, Brother of Jesus*, 76–100; Butz, *The Brother of Jesus*, 20–47; Hartin, *James of Jerusalem*, 9–24; Painter, *Just James*, 11–41; Matti Myllykoski, "James the Just in History and Tradition: Perspectives of Past and Present Scholarship, Part I," *Currents in Biblical Research* 5:1 (2006); Ward, "James of Jerusalem," 786–91.

[8]   Richard Bauckham, *Jude and the Relatives of Jesus in the Early Church*, rev. ed. (New York: T. & T. Clark, 2004), 57.

[9]   Butz, *The Brother of Jesus*, 44.

[10]   Ibid., 37, emphasis in original.

[11]   Richard Bauckham, "James and Jesus," in Bruce Chilton and Jacob Neusner, eds., *The Brother of Jesus: James the Just and His Mission* (Louisville, KY: Westminster John Knox Press, 2001), 106–07.

[12]   Michael R. Licona, *The Resurrection of Jesus: A New Historiographical Approach* (Downers Grove, IL: InterVarsity Press, 2010), 452.

to believe Jesus was together with his siblings on a family outing rather than a ministry venture. This is clear because of Jesus's reluctance to perform his first miracle (2:4). Second, the most explicit statement to support the unbelief of the brothers is John 7:5: "For not even his brothers believed in him." Butz says this passage gives the impression that "Jesus' brothers were regularly in his company, and certainly not estranged from him."[13] Butz concludes that the brothers and *everyone else did not believe in him.* But John does make a distinction between the belief of his disciples and that of his family. While it may be true that full understanding and belief comes after the resurrection, John makes it clear that while the family of Jesus did not believe in him (7:5), his disciples did in fact believe as a result of seeing his first sign (2:11). Licona points out that this is why the world would hate the disciples, because they *did* believe in Jesus (15:18), and yet the world does not hate his brothers because they did *not* believe (7:7).[14] However, given that neither passage cited by Butz offers positive evidence for their belief during his ministry, it must therefore be conceded that the balance of the evidence favors unbelief.[15] Evidence for their nonbelief is multiply attested (John and Mark), and also fulfills the criterion of embarrassment. *Contra* Butz, when all the Gospel evidence is considered, more evidence exists to support that the brothers were not believers during Jesus's ministry, and became so on an appearance of the risen Jesus.

There is little doubt the risen Jesus appeared to James.[16] According to Paul, James had an appearance of the risen Christ (1 Cor 15:7). Most scholars consider it essentially certain that this refers to the brother of Jesus.[17] Paul had met James on multiple appearances and would have acquired firsthand information about his experience with the risen Jesus (Gal 1:19; 2:9; Acts 15:1–21; 21:18).

Unfortunately, the appearance to James is not recorded in the Gospels or Acts. But it is confirmed in the *Gospel of the Hebrews*[18] as well as the *Apocryphon of James*, which may contain an independent tradition of Jesus's sayings within a larger account of the risen Jesus appearing to James and Peter. Interestingly, the

13 Butz, *The Brother of Jesus*, 38.

14 Licona, *The Resurrection of Jesus*, 447.

15 Butz draws much of his arguments from Painter (*Just James*). This is true for many other scholars who reject the traditional position regarding the family of Jesus during his ministry as well, such as Hartin (*James of Jerusalem*). Thus, if Painter's position is unsustainable, then it will have a ripple effect on the arguments of later scholars who rely upon Painter. For a sharp critique of the position held by Painter, see Licona, *The Resurrection of Jesus*, 440–55.

16 William Lane Craig, *Assessing the New Testament Evidence for the Historicity of the Resurrection of Jesus* (Lewiston, NY: Edwin Mellen Press, 1989), 63–66.

17 Anthony C. Thiselton, *The First Epistle to the Corinthians: A Commentary on the Greek Text* (Grand Rapids, MI: Eerdmans, 2000), 1,207.

18 Jerome records this in *On Illustrious Men* 2.12.

Apocryphon concurs with Paul's list in 1 Corinthians 15:5–7, which identifies the same two individuals—Peter and James—as recipients of secret sayings from Jesus. Clement of Alexandria (*c.* AD 200) also preserves the tradition that Jesus appeared to James, John, and Peter and imparted higher knowledge to them.[19] The tradition that Jesus appeared to James is early, unanimous, and widespread, and there is no convincing reason to reject it.

The Martyrdom of James

Biblical Evidence

No biblical writer directly reports the death of James. Even Acts, which reports the martyrdoms of Stephen (7:54–8:1a) and James, son of Zebedee (12:2), ignores the death of James the Just. Why? Painter suggests Luke intentionally suppressed the role of James, whom Painter considers a hard-liner on the position of the law, and preferred to emphasize Paul's law-free Gospel.[20] Still, given that Luke does report the deaths of Stephen and James, son of Zebedee, why not also the death of James? Two points can be made in response. First, Painter's claim that Luke intentionally suppressed James is an argument from silence, since no good evidence exists demonstrating this was Luke's hidden intention; he must, then, provide more than a possible motivation. Second, there is a more convincing reason for Luke's silence: reporting the death of James did not advance the larger narrative Luke was telling about the expansion of the Gospel from Jerusalem, through Judea and Samaria, to the ends of the earth (Acts 1:8). Stephen's death was integral to get the disciples to minister beyond Jerusalem to Judea and Samaria (8:1b–2). And the death of James, son of Zebedee (12:2), provides the link to the arrest of Peter and the persecution by Herod, which led to Peter's departing to another place (12:17), and the shift to focusing on the missionary activity of Saul/Paul (Acts 12:25). As already seen, Luke drops key characters when they have served his purposes; given his larger goal in Acts, then, it seems good reason exists *not* to include the death of James.

James 5:6 has sometimes been understood as a reference to martyrdom: "You have condemned and murdered the righteous person. He does not resist you." According to Painter, the reference to the "righteous one" is an autobiographical account by the author. Since Painter assumes the epistle of James is pseudonymous and appears after his death, he believes this passage should be understood in relation to his martyrdom.[21] If the letter is pseudonymous, then this may be a

---

19   Eusebius, *Ecclesiastical History* 2.1.4.
20   Painter, *Just James*, 56.
21   Ibid., 259.

possibility. But this raises a host of other difficulties.[22] While the "righteous" person could be an individual such as Christ, Stephen, or James, it is likelier a general reference to a certain class of people. In 5:16b, James says: "The prayer of a righteous person has great power as it is working." This is meant as a generic truth about the power of prayer. James then uses Elijah as a specific example of a righteous one whom God answered his fervent prayers (5:17–18). While James and Jesus would fall under the general category of "righteous" ones, the reference in 5:6 is unlikely to be to either of them, since there is no tradition that their deaths came at the hands of the rich. Thus, it is necessary to look outside the canonical books for evidence for the martyrdom of James.

Josephus

Jewish historian Josephus provides the earliest account of the death of James in *Antiquities* 20.197–203 (*c.* 93/94). In the wider context, he offers a discussion about the difficulties Rome was having with its residents, which led to the invasion and destruction of Jerusalem in AD 70. The specific passage regarding James allows the dating of his execution to AD 62, since Josephus places his death between two Roman procurators, Festus and Albinus.[23] Upon the death of Festus, Nero appointed Albinus as the next procurator, but during the brief transition period, Ananus, who was appointed high priest by Herod Agrippa II, seized the opportunity provided by the vacancy in the procuratorial government to have James the brother of Jesus, and others with him, stoned to death.

While many scholars have disputed the statement by Josephus about Jesus in *Antiquities* 18, the reference to the death of James in *Antiquities* 20.197–203 is largely undisputed:[24]

> And now Caesar, upon hearing the death of Festus, sent Albinus into Judea, as procurator; but the king deprived Joseph of the high priesthood, and bestowed the succession to that dignity on the son of Ananus, who was also himself called Ananus. Now the report goes, that this elder Ananus proved a most fortunate man; for he had five sons, who had all performed the office of a high priest to God, and he had himself enjoyed that dignity a long time formerly, which had never happened to any other of our high priests: but this younger Ananus, who, as we have told you already, took the high priesthood, was a bold man in his temper, and very insolent; he was also of the sect of the Sadducees, who are very rigid

---

[22]   Douglas J. Moo, *The Letter of James*, The Pillar New Testament Commentary (Grand Rapids, MI: Eerdmans, 2000), 9–21.

[23]   E. Mary Smallwood, "High Priests and Politics," *Journal of Theological Studies* 13 (1962): 25–26.

[24]   Craig A. Evans, *Ancient Texts for New Testament Studies* (Grand Rapids, MI: Baker, 2005), 178.

in judging offenders, above all the rest of the Jews, as we have already observed; when, therefore, Ananus was of this disposition, he thought he had now a proper opportunity [to exercise his authority]. Festus was now dead, and Albinus was but upon the road; so he assembled the sanhedrin of judges, and brought before them the brother of Jesus, who was called Christ, whose name was James, and some others, [or, some of his companions]; and when he had formed an accusation against them as breakers of the law, he delivered them to be stoned; but as for those who seemed the most equitable of the citizens, and such as were the most uneasy at the breach of the laws, they disliked what was done; they also sent to the king [Agrippa], desiring him to send to Ananus that he should act so no more, for that what he had already done was not to be justified; nay, some of them went also to meet Albinus, as he was upon his journey from Alexandria, and informed him that it was not lawful for Ananus to assemble a sanhedrin without his consent;—whereupon Albinus complied with what they said, and wrote in anger to Ananus, and threatened that he would bring him to punishment for what he had done; on which king Agrippa took the high priesthood from him, when he had ruled but three months, and made Jesus, the son of Damneus, high priest.[25]

Eusebius also records this account similarly to Josephus's account,[26] both of which provide historical support for the existence of James, indicate that he was well known and influential among Christians and Jews in Jerusalem, and establish his death at the hands of religious leaders. And Josephus, who had become a Pharisee six years earlier and was likely serving as a priest at this time in Jerusalem, was in a good position to know the details surrounding these reported events.

Scholars in the early twentieth century disputed the passage by Josephus more than they do now. Today, most scholars accept the authenticity of this extended passage.[27] The reasons are twofold. First, we have no reason to suspect what would have motivated a possible forgery. Why would a Christian forging this passage invent the death of James without, so to speak, *finishing the job*? The passage lacks commitment, lacks *Christianity*—such as a clear and compelling confessional statement.[28] Second, James is introduced as "the brother of Jesus, who was called Christ." This is precisely the type of designation that would be expected for a Jew. If a Christian interpolated the passage, it would likely say "the brother of Jesus, who *was* the Christ."

[25] Jospehus, *The Works of Josephus: Complete and Unabridged*, trans. William Whiston (Peabody, MA: Hendrickson, 1987).

[26] Eusebius, *Ecclesiastical History* 2.23.21–24.

[27] Gerd Luedemann, *Opposition to Paul in Jewish Christianity*, trans. M. Eugene Boring (Minneapolis, MN: Fortress Press, 1983), 62.

[28] Paul Winter, "Josephus on Jesus," *Journal of Historical Studies* 1 (1968): 289–90.

Josephus does not indicate why James was put to death. He merely indicates that Ananus "formed an accusation against them as breakers of the law, he delivered them to be stoned." The *reasons* for his death are considered next. For now, it is sufficient to indicate that Josephus bears early and reliable testimony to the execution of James in AD 62.

Hegesippus

A more detailed account of the trial and execution of James appears in Hegesippus, who according to Eusebius, "came in the generation after the apostles" (*c.* AD 170). His writings about James are in Book 5 of his *Memoirs* (*Hypomnemata*), which have been preserved in Eusebius:

> Now some of the seven sects, which existed among the people and which have been mentioned by me in the Memoirs, asked him, "What is the gate of Jesus?" and he replied that he was the Saviour. On account of these words some believed that Jesus is the Christ. But the sects mentioned above did not believe either in a resurrection or in one's coming to give to every man according to his works. But as many as believed did so on account of James. Therefore when many even of the rulers believed, there was a commotion among the Jews and Scribes and Pharisees, who said that there was danger that the whole people would be looking for Jesus as the Christ. Coming therefore in a body to James they said, "We entreat thee, restrain the people; for they are gone astray in regard to Jesus, as if he were the Christ. We entreat thee to persuade all that have come to the feast of the Passover concerning Jesus; for we all have confidence in thee. For we bear thee witness, as do all the people, that thou art just, and dost not respect persons. Do thou therefore persuade the multitude not to be led astray concerning Jesus. For the whole people, and all of us also, have confidence in thee. Stand therefore upon the pinnacle of the temple, that from that high position thou mayest be clearly seen, and that thy words may be readily heard by all the people. For all the tribes, with the Gentiles also, are come together on account of the Passover."

> The aforesaid Scribes and Pharisees therefore placed James upon the pinnacle of the temple, and cried out to him and said: "Thou just one, in whom we ought all to have: confidence, forasmuch as the people are led, astray after Jesus, the crucified one, declare to us, what is the gate of Jesus." And he answered with a loud voice, "Why do ye ask me concerning Jesus, the Son of Man? He himself sitteth in heaven at the right hand of the great Power, and is about to come upon the clouds of heaven." And when many were fully convinced and gloried in the testimony of James, and said, "Hosanna to the Son of David," these same Scribes and Pharisees said again to one another, "We have done badly in supplying such

testimony to Jesus. But let us go up and throw him down, in order that they may be afraid to believe him."

And they cried out, saying, "Oh! oh! the just man is also in error." And they fulfilled the Scripture written in Isaiah, "Let us take away the just man, because he is troublesome to us: therefore they shall eat the fruit of their doings." So they went up and threw down the just man, and said to each other, 'Let us stone James the Just.' And they began to stone him, for he was not killed by the fall; but he turned and knelt down and said, "I entreat thee, Lord God our Father, forgive them, for they know not what they do." And while they were thus stoning him one of the priests of the sons of Rechab, the son of the Rechabites, who are mentioned by Jeremiah the prophet, cried out, saying, 'Cease, what do ye? The just one prayeth for you." And one of them, who was a fuller, took the club with which he beat out clothes and struck the just man on the head. And thus he suffered martyrdom. And they buried him on the spot, by the temple, and his monument still remains by the temple. He became a true witness, both to Jews and Greeks, that Jesus is the Christ. And immediately Vespasian besieged them.[29]

The account in Hegesippus is considerably different from the one in Josephus. In Josephus, James is a secondary figure to the Sadducean high priest Ananus, whereas in Hegesippus, the focus is clearly on the righteousness and martyrdom of James. Hegesippus replaces Josephus's account of James breaking the law with his innocence, even at the hands of his executioners. And Hegesippus adds that James was thrown from the temple and beaten to death to Josephus's claim that he was condemned to stoning.

Scholars disagree widely on the integrity of this passage by Hegesippus.

Close analysis of the text reveals tensions that call for caution in determining its historical value. First, after James testifies to Jesus, Hegesippus says: "Many were convinced and rejoiced at James's testimony." If so, why would they not try to save James? If, as the narrative makes clear, the events took place over a considerable period, then it seems they would have at least tried to stop the death of James, even if attempts were unsuccessful. Second, the account seems to be patterned after the deaths of Stephen and Jesus. James prays a prayer similar to the one delivered by Stephen at his death (Acts 7:59–60) and Jesus before his crucifixion (Luke 23:34). On the other hand, while this could be chalked up as Christian invention, it seems at least possible that James would have chosen to die by repeating the same lines as his brother, whom he had faithfully followed for the last three decades. Third, the claim "They buried him on the spot by the

---

29   Eusebius of Caesarea. *Ecclesiastical History* 2.23.8–18, as quoted in *Nicene and Post-Nicene Fathers*, ed. P. Schaff and H. Wace, trans. A.C. McGiffert (New York: Christian Literature Co., 1890): 1:125–27.

temple, and his gravestone is still there by the temple" seems questionable. Butz believes this claim has a "genuine element of veracity," since it could have been verifiable by examining the temple.[30] In contrast, since it seems to contradict Jewish law, many scholars have felt uneasy about affirming this.[31] The temple was destroyed in AD 70, a century before the time Hegesippus wrote his account, and so the gravesite could likely not in fact be confirmed as Butz suggests.

These points certainly lead to caution in evaluating the historical value of the account in Hegesippus, but they provide no reason to discount the entire tradition. The key points to be drawn from Hegesippus are the corroboration that James was stoned to death and that the cause of the action taken against him was his witness to Jesus. This final point could not have been gleaned from Josephus, although it is consistent with what he reports.[32] Even though there are exaggeration and historical inaccuracies in this account, a historical kernel can be ascertained. F.F. Bruce considers that:

> when the embellishments are stripped of, the story amounts to this: the high
> priest and his colleagues, alarmed at the growth of militant messianism, which
> threatened to embroil the nation with the Roman power, demanded that James
> should disown his Nazarene claim that Jesus was the Messiah. His refusal to do
> so lead to his death.[33]

Clement of Alexandria

A second Christian account of the death of James can be found in the writings of Clement of Alexandria (*c.* AD 150–215). The account of Clement is preserved by Eusebius[34] and is purportedly found in Clement's seventh book of the *Hypotyposes*. Eusebius places the quotation at the beginning of his chapter on the apostles, right after the ascension, but long before the extended quote by Hegesippus. Eusebius first cites Clement to establish that James was selected as the "bishop" of Jerusalem (*Hypotyposes*, Book 6), and then provides the quote indicating his death:

---

[30]   Butz, *The Brother of Jesus*, 112.

[31]   Yaron Z. Eliav, "The Tomb of James, Brother of Jesus, as *Locus Memoriae*," *Harvard Theological Review* 97 (2004): 42. Strict Halakhic rules forbid any sort of impurity in the area of the temple, which makes use of the temple area for a grave site very unlikely.

[32]   James D.G. Dunn, *Beginning from Jerusalem: Christianity in the Making* (Grand Rapids, MI: Eerdmans, 2009), 2:1,095.

[33]   F.F. Bruce, *Peter, Stephen, James and John: Studies in Non-Pauline Christianity* (Grand Rapids, MI: Eerdmans, 1979), 116.

[34]   Eusebius, *Ecclesiastical History* 2.1.4–5.

The Lord after his resurrection imparted knowledge to James the Just and to John and Peter, and they imparted it to the rest of the apostles, and the rest of the apostles to the seventy, of whom Barnabas was one. But there were two Jameses: one called the Just, who was thrown from the pinnacle of the temple and was beaten to death with a club by a fuller, and another who was beheaded.[35]

Little concludes that this passage has virtually no similarity to the account in Josephus, except the name James. He even suggests the different titles could indicate they are referring to two different men.[36] Given that Clement appears not to mention the stoning, it has been assumed that the original Christian account of the death of James used by Hegesippus, Clement, and the *Second Apocalypse of James* lacked the reference to stoning found in Josephus, and thus would indicate that Clement may have preserved an independent Christian tradition.[37] Luedemann suggests that Josephus's account and Clement's account, which he calls the purest form of the Christian tradition, are themselves mutually exclusive.[38]

But this conclusion may be too hasty. While Clement does not explicitly mention stoning, he does mention that James was "thrown down from the parapet." Being pushed down from a significant height is one of the initial and integral steps of execution by stoning.[39] It is certainly possible that Clement, in his shortened version, only included the first and last parts of the execution of James as recorded in Hegesippus. Bauckham concludes:

> There is no need to postulate either an earlier version of Hegesippus' own text or an original version of the source common to Hegesippus and the *Second Apocalypse of James* which lacked the stoning, and so nor is there any need to postulate dependence on Josephus at any stage. Josephus and the Christian tradition which we have in two forms (Hegesippus and the *Second Apocalypse of James*) are completely independent accounts of the death of James. The one element they have in common (that he was executed by stoning) shows that the Christian tradition, like Josephus, had some access to historical fact.[40]

---

[35]   Eusebius of Caesaria, *Ecclesiastical History* 2.1.4b–5, as quoted in *Nicene and Post-Nicene Fathers*, ed. P. Schaff and H. Wace, trans. A.C. McGiffert (New York: Christian Literature Co., 1890), 1:104.

[36]   Henry D. Little, "The Death of James, the Brother of Jesus" (Ph.D. diss., Rice University, 1971), 13.

[37]   Hartin, *James of Jerusalem*, 120–21.

[38]   Luedemann, *Opposition to Paul*, 173.

[39]   Little, "The Death of James," 87–89.

[40]   Richard Bauckham, "For What Offence Was James Put to Death?", in *James the Just and Christian Origins*, ed. Bruce Chilton and Craig A. Evans (Leiden, Netherlands: Brill, 1999), 205–26.

As a few recent scholars have suggested, while Clement undoubtedly had some access to historical fact, the evidence is not compelling that he provides an early independent account of the death of James. It is for good reason, then, that the majority of modern scholars agree that Clement is dependent upon Hegesippus.[41] The account in Clement provides early third-century evidence for the tradition of the execution of James within Christian circles, but it is likely not independent of Hegesippus.

The First Apocalypse of James

The *First Apocalypse of James* is an early third-century Gnostic text based upon a series of personal revelations James receives from Jesus.[42] Clearly, the text refers to James the Just, as Jesus says: "I have given you a sign of these things, James, my brother. For not without reason have I called you my brother, although you are not my brother materially" (24.14–15). It may initially appear that Jesus is denying that James is his brother, but this is not so. Rather, this passage reveals the Gnostic belief that Jesus did not take on a physical body, a fact made clear later in the dialogue when Jesus appears to James after his crucifixion: "Never have I suffered in any way, nor have I been distressed. And this people has done me no harm" (31.15–24). Along with reporting an appearance to James, the *First Apocalypse* also reports the tradition that James was called "the Just" as well as that he was the principal leader in the early church. Clearly, it preserves some accurate history.

Stanley Jones, who offers only one point of contact between the *First Apocalypse of James* and the Hegesippus account, argues that no reasons exists to deny that the former depends upon the latter.[43] But concrete evidence is lacking to show that the *First Apocalypse* was dependent on Hegesippus, as Jones suggests.

While there were formerly debates about the damaged ending of the martyrdom account, the *First Apocalypse of James* is now considered an example of martyrdom literature.[44] In fact, the entirety of the text aims to prepare James, as well as the reader, for martyrdom.

---

[41]   F. Stanley Jones, "The Martyrdom of James in Hegesippus, Clement of Alexandria, and Christian Apocrypha, Including Nag Hammadi: A Study of Textual Relations," *Society of Biblical Literature Seminar Papers* 29 (1990): 328.

[42]   Only two extant versions of the *First Apocalypse of James* have been published. One of them is the Tchacos Codex, and the other from the fifth of the Nag Hammadi codices. Both versions are in Coptic, yet there was likely an original in Greek dating from the end of the second century to the beginning of the third. Mikael Caley Grams Haxby, "The *First Apocalypse of James*: Martyrdom and Sexual Difference" (Ph.D. diss., Harvard University, 2013), 21–26.

[43]   Jones, "The Martyrdom of James in Hegesippus," 334.

[44]   Candida R. Moss, *Ancient Christian Martyrdom* (New Haven, CT: Yale University Press, 2012), 159.

There is substantial debate about whether the *First Apocalypse of James* originated in Jewish Christian circles or whether it is primarily Gnostic. Either way, the martyrdom account in the *First Apocalypse* likely pre-dates the Gnostic influence.[45] The historical value of this text lies not in that it contains an independent early tradition of the martyrdom of James, although this may be a live option. Rather, the value lies in that it shows how the tradition of the martyrdom of James was embraced by Jewish, Christian, *and* Gnostic sources within a century and a half from the event, which suggests an early, widespread, and consistent tradition regarding the fate of James. The tradition of the martyrdom of James must have been quite strong at the time of the writing of the *First Apocalypse* for a Gnostic text to incorporate the execution of James rather than transforming the entire tradition.

The Second Apocalypse of James

The *Second Apocalypse of James* is part of tractate four of the Codex V of the Nag Hammadi Library. Scholars disagree about the dating of the *Second Apocalypse*; still, many scholars date it as early as the first half of the second century.[46] Little dates it some time between AD 400, when the manuscripts at Nag Hammadi were buried, and AD 62, when James was killed. Regardless of the precise date, the *Second Apocalypse* preserves an additional early Gnostic tradition of the martyrdom of James.

As in the *First Apocalypse of James*, the key figure is clearly James the Just, the brother of Jesus. The text contains two primary sections: (1) a discussion of the revelatory discourse James experienced with Jesus in Jerusalem after his resurrection, written by Mareim, one of the priests, and (2) a depiction of the martyrdom of James. James ends his revelatory discourse with a prediction of the destruction of the temple and its cult, which is the final offense that causes the priests and all the people and the crowd to have him stoned to death (60.15–63.32).

Two significant facts stand out for this investigation. First, James is stoned as part of his execution as in the tradition from Josephus and Hegesippus.[47] Thus, the stoning is preserved in Jewish, Christian, and Gnostic traditions. Second, as in the Christian tradition (Hegesippus), his death results from his

---

[45]   Painter makes the observation that while the text does have Gnostic elements, the persecution and martyrdom of James is decidedly non-Valentinian, and thus likely antedates Valentinian influence (for example, Tertullian, *Scorpiace* 10; Irenaeus, *Against Heresies* 4.33.9). See Painter, *Just James*, 169.

[46]   Matti Myllykoski, "James the Just in History and Tradition: Perspectives of Past and Present Scholarship, Part II," *Currents in Biblical Research* 6:1 (2007): 63.

[47]   James M. Robinson, ed., *The Second Apocalypse of James*, trans. Charles W. Hedrick, The Nag Hammadi Library in English (Leiden, The Netherlands: E.J. Brill, 1977), 254.

explicit proclamation of the teachings of Jesus.[48] Both accounts claim that those
who prosecute James have gone astray (*Second Apocalypse of James* 62.7 and
Ecclesiastical History 2.23.15). In the *Second Apocalypse*, the crowd seized James
and struck him, dragged him upon the ground, put a stone on his abdomen and
then said: "You have erred!" Specifically, it is his preaching against the temple
that riles the crowd, similar to the charge raised against Jesus (Mark 14:58),
which suggests it may rely upon an earlier tradition.

Because of these similarities, and a few more, Jones suggests that the author of
the *Second Apocalypse of James* is dependent upon Hegesippus, which he considers
the simplest explanation.[49] But while the accounts certainly have similarities, the
differences count heavily against dependency. For instance, although James is
stoned in both accounts, he is beaten to death with a fuller's club in Hegesippus,
which is missing in the *Second Apocalypse*. And the method of stoning in the
Second Apocalypse is much closer to Jewish law than in Hegesippus.[50] The
accounts also differ over who puts James to death. In the account in Hegesippus,
it is the "scribes and Pharisees," but in the *Second Apocalypse*, the priests execute
him. While there is not likely direct dependence, as Jones suggests, there is a
common tradition about the martyrdom of James.

According to Bauckham, this common tradition is likely an early second-
century Jewish Christian source.[51] Thus, he concludes there are *at least* two early
streams of tradition recounting the death of James. On the other hand, given
the complexity of the tradition, Painter believes the *Second Apocalypse* draws on
a tradition independent from Josephus and Hegesippus that flowed through
an early form of Jewish Christian Gnosticism.[52] If this were the case, there
would be at least three independent traditions of the death of James. Although
it is difficult to know for sure what the original sources were for the various
accounts, the *Second Apocalypse*, as well as the *First*, remind us that the tradition
of the martyrdom of James had to be early, widespread, and consistent for three
competing sects—Jewish, Christian, Gnostic—to proclaim it.

Pseudo-Clementines

The Pseudo-Clementines consist of two novels—*Recognitions* and
Homilies—addressed to James the Just in the voice of Clement, despite being
pseudepigraphical—containing a fictional account of the journeys of Clement

---

[48]   Of course, the *Second Apocalypse of James* has a Gnostic interpretation of these
teachings. The key point is that both accounts agree that James taught the message of Jesus,
which angered the crowds and religious leaders, and was put to death for it.

[49]   Jones, "The Martyrdom of James in Hegesippus," 331–33.

[50]   See Little, "The Death of James," 71–93.

[51]   Bauckham, "For What Offence?", 204.

[52]   Painter, *Just James*, 177.

of Rome. According to the *Recognitions*, Clement went on a spiritual journey that eventually led him to Christ. He met Barnabas and Peter, then joined Peter on a missionary trip.

The Pseudo-Clementines, in final form, were written between the end of the third and the beginning of the fourth centuries. Yet most scholars agree that both *Recognitions* and *Homilies* relied upon an earlier Jewish Christian source (*Grundschrift*) written in Syria in the third century.[53]

Section 1:66–1.71 of the *Recognitions* is a subsection of a larger text embedded within the Pseudo-Clementines, often referred to as *The Ascents of James*. The name comes from an incident where James ascends the Temple steps to join a public debate about whether Jesus is the Messiah. He uses Scripture to argue that the Messiah would come twice, once in humbleness and then again in glory. Through seven days of debate, James persuades the people and the chief priest to be baptized. But then an "enemy" comes and persuades the people in opposition to James, creating an uproar that leads to bloodshed and other violent acts. Eventually the enemy "threw James from the top of the stairs, and when he fell was as dead, so he did not strike him a second time" (*Ascents of James* 1.70.8).[54] It soon becomes evident the "enemy" is the pre-converted Saul, who is engaging in one of his violent persecutions of the Christian church. Some scholars consider this episode a redaction of the account of the martyrdom of James using the ravaging of Saul against the church in Acts 8:1–3 as a guide.[55]

Given the similarities and differences between the account of the martyrdom of James in Hegesippus and *The Ascents of James*, scholars have come to diverging conclusions regarding the original source(s). The most significant difference between the accounts is that James survives the fall in *The Ascents of James*, whereas in Hegesippus and the *Second Apocalypse of James*, he is subsequently killed—beaten with a club in the former, and stoned in the latter. His opponents leave, thinking he is dead, so they don't strike him again (*Ascents of James* 1.70.8). It could be suggested that this contradicts the account in Josephus, Hegesippus, and the *Second Apocalypse*. However, this section is clearly the result of redaction, since James needs to be kept alive for further events in the story.[56] It is interesting that both Hegesippus and the *Second Apocalypse of James* agree with *The Ascents of James* that James did not die as a result of this fall—the fatal blow came later.

As mentioned earlier, there is no consensus regarding the substantially similar martyrdom accounts in Hegesippus, the *Second Apocalypse of James*,

---

[53] Robert E. Van Voorst, *The Ascents of James: History and Theology of a Jewish-Christian Community*, Society of Biblical Literature Dissertation Series 112 (Atlanta, GA: Scholars Press, 1989), 2.

[54] This English translation of the Syriac comes from W. Frankenberg, as recorded in Voorst, *The Ascents of James*, 74.

[55] Myllykoski, "James the Just in History, Part II," 83.

[56] Luedemann, *Opposition to Paul*, 176.

and the Pseudo-Clementines. And yet, while some significant differences do occur, the similarities are most important for this investigation, since they likely indicate an early, common tradition. The three martyrdom narratives share the location of the events at the Temple, the significant number of spectators, a speech by James defending the teachings of Jesus which are ultimately rejected by the religious leaders who then decide to kill him, and his fall. The Pseudo-Clementines provide further support for the persistent tradition that James publicly proclaimed the message of Jesus and suffered persecution for his faith.

Why Was James Killed?

Given the reference to the death of James in Josephus, as well as later Christian and Gnostic sources, there is little doubt James was executed in AD 62. But a key question remains: Why was James killed? If he were killed for political reasons unrelated to his faith, he would hardly qualify under the traditional definition of a martyr. The accounts of the death of James in Hegesippus, the *Second Apocalypse of James*, and the Pseudo-Clementines indicate that James died as a result of his proclamation of the Christian faith, even though they differ on the particulars. Most scholars have embraced this traditional view.

Yet recently, some scholars have questioned the reliability of this tradition, and believe that focusing on the Josephus account renders a very different verdict.[57] Unlike Hegesippus and Clement, the *Second Apocalypse of James*, and the Pseudo-Clementines, Josephus does not explicitly tie the death of James to his Christian proclamation. Rather, Josephus reports that James and his companions were condemned to stoning as "lawbreakers." The accounts all agree, though, that James was executed at the hands of the Jewish authorities—similar to his brother Jesus. Condemnation as a lawbreaker would be consistent with a number of crimes according to Jewish law. Yet Michael R. Licona makes a keen observation: "However, in the New Testament, Christians were often regarded as lawbreakers by the Jewish authorities because they were perceived as promoting ideas that were contrary to the Jewish Law (Acts 6:13; 18:13; 21:28)."[58] The key factor for determining the nature of the "crime" is the penalty of stoning. Religious leaders attempted to stone Jesus on multiple occasions for blasphemy (John 8:58–59, 10:30–39, 11:8; cf. Luke 4:16–30). Darrell Bock rightly draws attention to this fact:

> What Law was it James broke, given his reputation within Christian circles as a
> Jewish Christian leader who was careful about keeping the Law? It would seem

---

[57]   James S. McLaren, "Ananus, James, and Earliest Christianity. Josephus' Account of the Death of James," *Journal of Theological Studies* 52 (2001): 1–25.

[58]   Licona, *The Resurrection of Jesus*, 457.

likely that the Law had to relate to his Christological allegiances and a charge of blasphemy. This would fit the fact that he was stoned, which was the penalty for such a crime, and parallels how Stephen was handled as well.[59]

Although Josephus does not provide the specific reason for the death of James, blasphemy is consistent with his condemnation as a lawbreaker. Even so, McLaren suggests that if Josephus wanted the readers to understand that the charge against James was religious, he would have stated this explicitly.[60] But this is an argument from silence. The reason Josephus may not give specific details as to the nature of the crime is that it was not integral to his larger focus on the reckless behavior of Ananus the high priest, which led to his quick dismissal by King Agrippa. One should not conclude that later Christian writers, because of an absence of details in Josephus, embellished stories of James dying as a martyr since Josephus was motivated by different interests in his report about James. Even though further details are lacking, Josephus considering James a lawbreaker for blasphemy remains consistent with later Christian accounts that he died as a Christian martyr.

McLaren also suggests that the crime may have been entirely "trumped up in order to score a victory over a rival faction."[61] This trumped-up charge could stem from either a personal grudge or competition with a contrary party within Jewish politics. Yet it seems unthinkable that Ananus would have acted contrarily to his understanding of Jewish Law. James must have been sentenced for a crime for which Jewish Law considered stoning an appropriate punishment.

Another possible reason for the stoning of James is that he was charged with seducing the people to idolatry (Deut 13:1–18), which is a clear violation of the second commandment. Deuteronomy 13 specifies three groups of people who are to be killed for "seducing" the people to worship other gods. The first group is false prophets (13:1–3a). A false prophet who leads people astray is to be put to death (v. 5). Technically, a prophet in the Old Testament was one who is a "proclaimer" and "forthteller."[62] While Jesus could have been understood as a prophet in this manner, it seems unlikely the same would hold true for James, since it is never reported he prophesied or worked miracles.[63]

---

[59] Darrell L. Bock, *Blasphemy and Exaltation in Judaism: The Charge against Jesus in Mark 14:53–65* (Grand Rapids, MI: Baker, 2000), 196 n. 30.

[60] McLaren, "Ananus, James, and Earliest Christianity," 16.

[61] Ibid., 17–18.

[62] Eugene H. Merrill, *Deuteronomy*, New American Commentary, vol. 4 (Nashville, TN: Broadman & Holman, 1994), 230.

[63] Bauckham, "For What Offence?", 226. I am heavily indebted to Richard Bauckham for my analysis of the reasons for the death of James. He provides the most promising and insightful explanation for his death.

The second category in Deuteronomy 13 is someone who secretly entices his or her own relatives to follow other gods. Deuteronomy 13:9–10 says such an offender is to be stoned to death "because he sought to draw you away from the LORD your God." As a public leader in the early church, James likely was not one who "secretly" led the people to worship other gods.

The third category regards towns led astray to worship other gods (Deut 13:14b–15). The focus in this passage is on the punishment to be merited by the town that is led astray by "worthless fellows." Punishment for those who lead the town astray is not described, though perhaps they are to be killed with the sword along with town members. This final category seems difficult to apply to James since the focus is on punishing the town gone astray, rather than the perpetrators of the idolatry.

The question is whether there is leeway in the application of these principles beyond the specific cases cited in Deuteronomy 13. In other words, while it is a stretch to include James in these particular examples, is there precedent for thinking he could have been stoned for enticing the people to "go after other gods"? Rabbinic literature considered one who led a town astray a *maddiah*—a term that had application beyond the specific examples in Deuteronomy 13.[64] Bauckham explains:

> In that case, the Mishna extends the punishment by stoning from the *mēsît* [one who secretly leads another astray] to include also the *maddiah*, but not the deceiving prophet, whose execution takes a less severe form. The Babylonian Talmud's comments on *m. Sanh.* 7:10 record two other rabbinic views: that all three categories in Deuteronomy 13 incur death by stoning, and that only the *mēsît* is to be stoned, while the deceiving prophet and the *maddiah* are both to die by strangulation (*b. Sanh.* 67a).[65]

Since the Talmud and Mishna were written much later and may not provide direct insight to the legal ruling regarding the death of James, Bauckham rightly questions applying them to the late Second Temple period. However, Bauckham observes that they do "illustrate the sort of halakhic differences that could easily have existed at that time."[66] The Talmud and Mishna provide a plausible explanation for why Josephus reports that James was condemned to death by stoning that broadly matches what is found later in Christian and Gnostic sources.

For instance, the account by Hegesippus describes four warnings that the people are "going astray" or have "gone astray" because of James's teachings about Jesus. The scribes and Pharisees specifically ask James to "persuade the crowd not

---

[64] Ibid., 228.

[65] Ibid., 228.

[66] Ibid.

to err regarding Jesus." The Greek term has the meaning not of erring morally, but of rejecting the God of Israel.[67] Clearly, in the account by Hegesippus, the primary concern of the religious leaders who condemn James is that he is leading the people to idolatry. A similar statement also appears in the *Second Apocalypse of James*. Right after throwing James down and placing their feet on him along with a large stone, the scribes cry out: "You have erred!" In Hegesippus, James leads the people astray, whereas in the *Second Apocalypse of James*, James himself is led astray. Both agree that James was killed specifically for his theological error that involved "going astray." Given that James's theological error appears in both Christian and Gnostic sources—that are likely independent—it must have been a part of an earlier tradition.

Both explanations entertained here can plausibly account for why Josephus described James as being condemned to death by stoning. And the idea that the execution of James was related to his proclamation of his Christian faith finds later support in both Hegesippus and the *Second Apocalypse of James*. This is why, in his recent monograph on James, Patrick Hartin concludes: "Taking the traditions of Josephus together with those of Hegesippus, Clement, and Eusebius himself, one concludes that there is a basic historical core that testifies to the fact that James did indeed die the death of a Christian martyr."[68]

Even if James did not die as a direct result of his faith, he certainly believed it sincerely and willingly put himself in danger to advance it. He ministered publicly in unstable times when his life could have been in danger at any moment. He was certainly aware of the cost many before him had paid for publicly embracing the new faith: Jesus (Mark 14:53–65), the Twelve (Acts 5:18), Stephen (Acts 6:14), and James the son of Zebedee (Acts 12:2). James may have had a more conservative view of the law, but he nevertheless publicly identified himself as the leader of this group, and in fact had now become one of the three pillars, along with Peter and John (Gal 2:9). The key point for our investigation is this: James willingly put himself in danger as the leader of the Christian church in Jerusalem, which was based on the identity of its executed leader—his brother—as an enemy of Rome, and where many of the original leaders suffered and were killed for their faith. The best explanation for James's willingness to suffer and die for his faith is that he believed he had seen the risen Jesus (1 Cor 15:7).

Conclusion

The traditional view that James was martyred in Jerusalem in AD 62 has been carefully analyzed. There is additional later material that further confirms this

---

[67] Ibid., 230.

[68] Hartin, *James of Jerusalem*, 147.

tradition,[69] but it will not be analyzed in depth, for this analysis has focused on material that falls within or close to the living memory of James.

This close examination of the evidence indicates that the following points can be regarded to have varying degrees of confidence from the early tradition regarding James:

1. James was executed by stoning—*the highest possible probability* (Josephus, *Antiquities* 20.197–203; Hegesippus, *Hypomnemata* Book 5, as recorded in Eusebius, *Ecclesiastical History* 2.23; Clement of Alexandria, *Hypotyposes* Book 7, as recorded in Eusebius, *Ecclesiastical History*, 2.1.4–5; *Second Apocalypse of James* 60.15–63.32).

2. James died as a Christian martyr—*very probably true* (likely interpretation of Josephus, *Antiquities* 20.197–203; Hegesippus, *Hypomnemata* Book 5, as recorded in Eusebius, *Ecclesiastical History* 2.23; Clement of Alexandria, *Hypotyposes* Book 7, as recorded in Eusebius, *Ecclesiastical History* 2.1.4–5; *First Apocalypse of James*; *Second Apocalypse of James* 60.15–63.32).

3. James was thrown down from a high structure at the Temple—*more probable than not* (Hegesippus, *Hypomnemata* Book 5, as recorded in Eusebius, *Ecclesiastical History* 2.23; *Second Apocalypse of James* 60.15–63.32; Clement of Alexandria, *Hypotyposes* Book 7, as recorded in Eusebius, *Ecclesiastical History* 2.1.4–5; Pseudo-Clementines 1.70.8; consistency with Josephus, *Antiquities* 20.197).

---

[69] For instance, see Eusebius, *Ecclesiastical History* 2.23; Origen, *Contra Celsum* I.47, II.13; *On Matthew* X.17; Epiphanius, *Panarion* 20.1; Jerome, *On Illustrious Men* II.7–9; the Manichaean Psalm Book.

Chapter 8
The Martyrdom of John, Son of Zebedee

John, the younger brother of James, son of Zebedee, was a fisherman in Galilee with his older brother and father until Jesus selected him to be among his closest followers (Mark 1:16; Matt 4:21–22, 10:21–22; Luke 5:1–11). Although there are four people named "John" in the New Testament,[1] the apostle John is often designated as the "son of Zebedee" or the "brother of James" to separate him from the others.

There is only one recorded scene in the Gospels in which John is singled out without reference to his brother (Mark 9:38–39). This story is often told as indicating that John was particularly intolerant among the disciples. However, it may be that John is simply speaking on behalf of *all* the disciples. That fact that John uses "we" indicates that he was speaking for the Twelve, although he certainly could have been the instigator. The larger point of this passage is that all the disciples, including the most privileged ones, such as John, fail to understand what the passion means for their life and mission.

John also appears in an important narrative alongside his brother, James, where the brothers ask Jesus if they should send fire down on a Samaritan village that rejected him (Luke 9:54b). But Jesus rebuked them and they went to another village (9:55). Is this seemingly harsh response why James and John were given the title "Sons of Thunder" (*Boanerges*)? Alan Culpepper suggests that it may not have been a disparaging nickname, but a promise of what they could become.[2] After all, Peter was certainly not rock-like in his faith when Jesus renamed him the "rock" (Matt 16:18).

John always appears among the top four names in the lists of the 12 disciples (Mark 3:14–19; Matt 10:2–4; Luke 6:14–16). He is even mentioned second in Acts, right after Peter (Acts 1:13). With Peter, John healed a man (Acts 3:1–7), and again with Peter, he spoke publicly with boldness about what they had "seen and heard" (Acts 4:20). John was an eyewitness of the risen Jesus (Acts 1:1–11; 4:20). He undoubtedly was willing to suffer and face persecution for this conviction. Seeing Jesus alive from the grave gave John, along with the rest of the

---

[1] There is John the Baptist (Mark 1:1–8; Luke 1:5–17; 3:2–20; 7:18–35; John 1:19–28), Simon Peter's father, named John (John 1:42; 21:15–19), John Mark (Acts 12:12; 13:4–5; 15:37–41; 2 Tim 4:11), and John, who was of the high priestly family of Annas (Acts 4:6).

[2] R. Alan Culpepper, *John, the Son of Zebedee: The Life of a Legend* (Minneapolis, MN: Fortress Press, 2000), 40.

apostles, the boldness to keep preaching the faith even after facing imprisonment (Acts 4:1–3, 13).

The last biblical report about John shows him becoming a missionary with Peter (Acts 8:14–25). Given his prominence in Acts alongside Peter, John was undoubtedly one of the leading apostles of the early church. Paul considers John one of the "pillars" of the church along with Peter and James, the brother of Jesus (Gal 2:9).

John was among the inner circle of the 12 disciples. The Gospel of Mark reports that Peter, James, John, and Andrew were present at the discourse at the Mount of Olives (13:3). Along with Peter and James, John uniquely witnessed the raising of the daughter of Jairus (Mark 5:37–42), the transfiguration (Mark 9:2–13; Matt 17:1–13; Luke 9:28–36), and joined Jesus in the Garden of Gethsemane (Mark 14:32–42). It is interesting that these three instances each relate to death—*preparing* for death (Jesus in Gethsemane), *rising* from the dead (Jairus's daughter), and *appearing* after death (Jesus, Moses, and Elijah). Could it be that Jesus is uniquely preparing the three of them to face martyrdom by showing them God's power over death? Brian Incigneri suggests that Mark presents the "inner three" as key figures in his narrative because the readers would have already known that they were faithful to the point of martyrdom.[3] There is solid evidence Peter and James, the son of Zebedee, died as martyrs, but what about John?

The traditional view is that the apostle John was the author of the five Johannine writings (Gospel of John, three epistles, and Revelation), was the "beloved disciple" who sat by the Lord's side at the Last Supper, and died a natural death at an advanced age in Ephesus (c. AD 103). Even though this is a minority position among scholars, this view has experienced a sort of resurgence.[4] Since scholars typically date the writing of the Gospel to the mid-90s, identifying John the apostle as the author remains consistent with the traditional view that he died a natural death as an old man in Ephesus. While John might have written the Gospel after returning to Ephesus from Patmos and then faced martyrdom

---

[3]   Brian C. Incigneri, *The Gospel to the Romans: The Setting and Rhetoric of Mark's Gospel*, Biblical Interpretation Series, vol. 65 (Leiden, The Netherlands: Brill, 2003), 348.

[4]   Recent proponents of the traditional view include Craig Blomberg, *The Historical Reliability of John's Gospel* (Downers Grove, IL: InterVarsity Press, 2001), 22–41; Gerald L. Borchert, *John 1–11*, The New American Commentary, vol. 25A (Nashville, TN: Broadman & Holman, 1996), 82–90; D.A. Carson, *The Gospel According to John*, The Pillar New Testament Commentary (Grand Rapids, MI: Eerdmans, 1991), 24–29; Craig S. Keener, *The Gospel of John: A Commentary* (Peabody, MA: Hendrickson, 2003), 1:81–139.; Andreas Köstenberger, *John*, Baker Exegetical Commentary on the New Testament (Grand Rapids, MI: Baker, 2004), 6–8; Colin G. Kruse, *John: An Introduction and Commentary* (Downers Grove, IL: InterVarsity Press, 2003), 23–30; Leon Morris, *The Gospel According to John*, rev. ed. (Grand Rapids, MI: Eerdmans, 1995), 4–25; John A.T. Robinson, *The Priority of John* (London: SCM Press, 1985).

at an advanced age, we have only inferential evidence for this.[5] The authorship of
the Gospel, therefore, is inextricably linked with John's fate. We should realize in
addition that questions about the authorship of the traditional Johannine texts
remain distinct from issues of inspiration and canonicity.[6]

Authorship of the Gospel of John

Proponents of the traditional position provide both internal and external
evidence.

Internal Evidence

The classic defense of internal authorship for the Gospel of John comes from B.F.
Westcott at the beginning of the twentieth century. In five stages, he argued the
author must be (1) Jewish, (2) from Palestine, (3) an eyewitness, (4) one of the
12 apostles, and (5) the apostle John.[7] His first two points are largely accepted,
but there is much more debate about the last three. The last two in particular
are critical points for establishing the internal case of authorship. And this
relies upon demonstrating that the author of the fourth Gospel, John, the son
of Zebedee, is the Beloved Disciple. Regardless of the identity of this disciple,
clearly he or she provides the source behind the Gospel: "This is the disciple who
is bearing witness about these things, and who has written these things, and we
know that his testimony is true" (21:24). We must discover, then, whether John,
the son of Zebedee, is the Beloved Disciple.

The traditional answer is yes. Many contemporary scholars, as we have seen,
defend this view. But many *conservative* scholars disagree. Thus, this is an issue
on which even conservative scholars differ among themselves. Candidates for

---

5   Robert Eisler believes a late martyrdom for John is "undoubtedly historical." He
claims it is more probable that "the real truth has survived in the legend of the Evangelist
John being given the poison-cup. That he survived this treatment, unharmed like another
Mithridates, is obviously a pious invention, but it may be true that he was sentenced to drink
the hemlock-poison by a human provincial governor wanting to preserve the venerable old
man from a worse fate." Robert Eisler, *The Enigma of the Fourth Gospel* (London: Methuen,
1938), 174–75. This is an interesting hypothesis, although it is almost entirely conjecture.

6   The Gospel of John, for instance, is anonymous. Revelation claims to have been
written by a "servant John" who bore witness to all he saw about Jesus (Rev 1:1–2). But
it does not indicate *which* John this is. Just as there is disagreement about the author of
Hebrews without questioning inspiration, there can be disagreement about the writings
typically attributed to John.

7   B.F. Westcott, *The Gospel According to St. John: The Authorized Version with
Introduction and Notes* (London: Cambridge University Press, 1882), v–xxviii.

the Beloved Disciple among conservative scholars include Lazarus,[8] John "the Elder,"[9] an unknown historical figure not part of the Twelve,[10] and a non-real literary device meant to draw in the reader.[11] While the evidence for identifying the apostle John as the Beloved Disciple is stronger than many scholars concede, the conclusions must be tentative as to the value internal evidence provides for authorship of the Gospel of John and thus his traditional fate in Ephesus.

John 21:21–23a is typically cited as a passage to indicate that the apostle John would live a long life. Of course, applying this to the longevity of John's life relies upon identifying John as the Beloved Disciple. If the Beloved Disciple is not John, then this passage loses its force. According to Frederick Weidmann, given the numerous questions surrounding the identity of the Beloved Disciple, our conclusions regarding the length of his lifespan from this text must be tentative, at best.[12]

A number of other possibilities, such as John Mark, Thomas, Nathanael, Matthias, the rich young ruler, Paul, Benjamin, and Gentile Christianity have been advanced and critiqued.[13] And yet the point should be clear: while a strong case can be made to identify the apostle John as the Beloved Disciple, internal evidence does not require it. The diversity of opinions among conservative scholars forces us to be cautious regarding conclusions as to the identity of the Beloved Disciple and to the extent internal evidence from the Gospel of John supports the traditional view regarding the fate of the apostle John.

External Evidence

Analysis of the external evidence must begin with the observation that the early church seems unanimously to identify the apostle John as the author of his respective Gospel. Nevertheless, this position has been challenged by both conservative and liberal scholars alike. D.A. Carson observes, for example, that from the end of the second century forward "there is virtual agreement in the church as to the authority, canonicity and authorship of the Gospel of

---

8   Ben Witherington III, *What Have They Done with Jesus?* (New York: HarperCollins, 2006), 141–66; J.N. Sanders, *A Commentary on the Gospel According to St. John*, Black's New Testament Commentary (London: A. & C. Black, 1968), 29–32.

9   Richard Bauckham, *Jesus and the Eyewitnesses: The Gospels as Eyewitness Testimony* (Grand Rapids, MI: Eerdmans, 2006), 368, 393–416.

10   George, R Beasley-Murray, *John*, Word Biblical Commentary, vol. 36 (Nashville, TN: Thomas Nelson, 1999), lxxii–lxxiv.

11   A.T. Lincoln, *The Gospel According to Saint John*, Black's New Testament Commentary (New York: Hendrickson, 2005), 20–26.

12   Frederick W. Weidmann, *Polycarp and John: The Harris Fragments and Their Challenge to the Literary Traditions* (Notre Dame, IL: Notre Dame Press, 1999), 139.

13   Culpepper, *John*, 72–85.

John."[14] According to Carson, the earliest unambiguous citation that the Gospel of John was written by "John" is found in Theophilus of Antioch (*c.* 180): "And hence the holy writings teach us, and all the spirit-bearing [inspired] men, one of whom, John, says, 'In the beginning was the Word, and the Word was with God.'"[15] Nevertheless, while Theophilus identifies "John" as the author, he does not explicitly indicate "John *the apostle.*" So we find that "John the apostle" is not necessarily Theophilus's "John," even as "John the apostle" might be the natural way to interpret Theophilus's passage.

The *Muratorian Canon* (*c.* AD 170–220) also identifies John the apostle (that is, the son of Zebedee) as the author of the Gospel: "The Fourth of the Gospels is that of John, [one] of the disciples .... In the same night it was revealed to Andrew, [one] of the apostles, that John should write down all things in his own name while all of them should review it" (lines 5, 15).[16] Eckhard Schnabel claims the context argues strongly for John, the son of Zebedee, although nothing is known of the author or what sources were used.[17] Interestingly, John is described as a "disciple," whereas Andrew is called an "apostle." But we simply do not know why the author designated them differently or what he meant by it. He may have simply used the titles interchangeably without difference, as does the New Testament (Luke 22:11, 14).

Irenaeus

The most important second-century support for the traditional view of the authorship of John comes from Irenaeus. In *Against Heresies*, Irenaeus says: "John, the disciple of the Lord, who also had leaned upon His breast, did himself publish a Gospel during his residence at Ephesus in Asia."[18] That this refers to John the apostle is considered "unmistakable"[19] since, in another section, Irenaeus mentions:

---

[14]   Carson, *The Gospel According to John*, 28.

[15]   Theophilus of Antioch, *Theophilus to Autolycus* 1.22, in *The Ante-Nicene Fathers: Fathers of the Second Century: Hermas, Tatian, Athenagoras, Theophilus, and Clement of Alexandria*, ed. Alexander Roberts and James Donaldson, rev. A. Cleveland Coxe (Buffalo, NY: Christian Literature Co., 1885), 2:103.

[16]   Eckhard Schnabel, trans., "Canon Muratori" (paper presented at the annual meeting of the Evangelical Theological Society, Baltimore, MD, November 20, 2013), 1.

[17]   Ibid.

[18]   Irenaeus, *Against Heresies* 3.1.1, as cited in *The Ante-Nicene Fathers: The Apostolic Fathers—Justin Martyr—Irenaeus*, ed. Alexander Roberts and James Donaldson, rev. A. Cleveland Coxe (Buffalo, NY: Christian Literature Co., 1885), 1:414.

[19]   Andreas J. Köstenberger and Stephen O. Stout, "'The Disciple Jesus Loved': Witness, Author, Apostle—a Response to Richard Bauckham's *Jesus and the Eyewitnesses*," *Bulletin for Biblical Research* 18:2 (2008): 224–25.

those who were conversant in Asia with John, the disciple of the Lord,
[affirming] that John conveyed to them that information. And he remained
among them up to the times of Trajan. Some of them, moreover, saw not only
John, but the other apostles also, and heard the very same account from them.[20]

Thus, Irenaeus believed in one John of the apostolic age (John the Baptist
would have been earlier) who was the son of Zebedee and one of the pillars of
the ancient church (Gal 2:9). This apostle John, according to Irenaeus, was the
Beloved Disciple who lived in Ephesus until the reign of Trajan (AD 98–117).

However, Bauckham rejects this understanding and believes Irenaeus was
referring to a different "John" as the author of the fourth Gospel. He observes
that Irenaeus used the term "apostles" for more than the Twelve, including Paul,
Barnabas, the Seventy, and even John the Baptist.[21] However, another passage
in Irenaeus helps us discern which John he referred to. According to Irenaeus,
John "referred to the primary Ogdoad, in which there was as yet no Jesus, and no
Christ, the teacher of John. But that the apostle did not speak concerning their
conjunctions, but concerning our Lord Jesus Christ, whom he acknowledges as
the Word of God."[22] Irenaeus clearly believes this John was the author of the
fourth Gospel, for he proceeds to cite John 1:1. He also considers this John an
apostle who was taught by Jesus. The most natural way to read Irenaeus upholds
his referring to the apostle John, one of the Twelve, as author of the fourth
Gospel. But as Bauckham observes, the case is not as straightforward as some
have taken it to be, and it must be conceded that it is at least *possible* Irenaeus
refers to another John.

The significance of Irenaeus's testimony dwells in his record, in several of his
writings, of Polycarp's association with John.[23] If Polycarp accurately records
the testimony of the apostle John, and if Irenaeus received his testimony from
Polycarp, then strong living memory directly connects the apostle to Irenaeus.
In suggesting that the apostle John may have been martyred in the early AD
40s, Boismard recognizes he must demonstrate that the traditional reading of
Irenaeus is "very questionable."[24] Three common approaches aim to undermine
the testimony of Irenaeus.[25]

First, Irenaeus was confused. Irenaeus mistakenly reported that the apostle
John was the author of the Gospel when, in fact, it was another. Could Irenaeus
have been confused about which John wrote the Gospel? Answering this question

---

[20]   Irenaeus, *Against Heresies* 2.22.5.

[21]   Bauckham, *Jesus and the Eyewitnesses*, 462.

[22]   Irenaeus, *Against Heresies* I.9.2.

[23]   Ibid. 4.14.1–8; 5.33.4, "Letter to Florinus" and "Letter to Victor."

[24]   Marie-Émile Boismard, *Le Martyre de Jean L'apôtre* (Pende, France: J. Gabalda, 1996), 77.

[25]   Weidmann, *Polycarp and John*, 126–33.

involves looking at the relationship between the apostle John and Papias, as well as the relationship between the apostle John, Polycarp, and Irenaeus.

While Irenaeus claimed that Papias was a "hearer of John,"[26] Eusebius rejects this interpretation.[27] According to Eusebius, Papias did not directly speak to the apostles, but received their words at third hand from those who personally knew the apostles. If so, there is a greater likelihood of confusion on the part of Irenaeus regarding the teachings of Jesus. Interestingly, however, in his *Chronicle* Eusebius states that Papias and Polycarp were contemporaries, and that Papias was a hearer of the apostle John.[28] Thus, Eusebius either contradicted himself or changed his mind. In addition, both Jerome (*c.* AD 342–420) and Philip of Side (*c.* fifth century) disagree with Eusebius and hold that Papias was a disciple or "hearer" of the apostle John.[29] Given that Jerome often closely followed the teachings of Eusebius, he must have had good reason to demur on this issue. And finally, there are at least 14 different Papian fragments from known authors, as well as two from unknown authors, all of which associate Papias with the apostle John.[30] Eusebius is in the minority regarding Papias's relationship to the apostle John. It seems unlikely Irenaeus was confused about the relationship between Papias and John. But could he have been confused about the relationship between John, Polycarp, and himself?

There is little debate that Papias and Polycarp lived and ministered at the same time in Asia. Both Irenaeus and Eusebius agree that these two great bishops were contemporaries.[31] The key issue in determining whether or not Irenaeus was confused regarding the testimony of John is the relationship between Irenaeus and Polycarp. Prominent scholars such as C.K. Barrett and R.H. Charles have concluded that Irenaeus was simply mistaken about which John influenced Polycarp.[32]

In his *Letter to Florinus*, Irenaeus claimed that as a boy he "listened eagerly" to the teachings of Polycarp, who recounted the experiences the apostle John had with the Lord.[33] Eusebius preserves an additional passage from *Against Heresies* where Irenaeus recounts his relationship to Polycarp:

---

[26] Irenaeus, *Against Heresies* 5.33.4.

[27] Eusebius, *Ecclesiastical History* 3.39.1.

[28] Michael W. Holmes, ed. and trans., *The Apostolic Fathers: Greek Texts and English Translation*, 3rd ed. (Grand Rapids, MI: Baker, 2007), 733.

[29] Jerome, *Lives of Illustrious Men* 18; Philip of Side, *Church History*.

[30] Monte A. Shanks, *Papias and the New Testament* (Eugene, OR: Pickwick, 2013), 291.

[31] See Irenaeus, *Against Heresies* V.33.4. For an in-depth analysis of this evidence, see Shanks, *Papias and the New Testament*, 70–73.

[32] C.K. Barrett, *The Gospel According to St. John: An Introduction with Commentary and Notes on the Greek Text*, 2nd ed. (Philadelphia, PA: Westminster, 1978), 105; R.H. Charles, *A Critical and Exegetical Commentary on the Revelation of St. John*, International Critical Commentary (New York: Charles Scribner's Sons, 1920), xlix.

[33] Irenaeus, *Letter to Florinus*, in Eusebius, *Ecclesiastical History* V.20.4–7.

But Polycarp also was not only instructed by the apostles, and acquainted with many that had seen Christ, but was also appointed by apostles in Asia bishop of the church of Smyrna. We too saw him in our early youth; for he lived a long time, and died, when a very old man, a glorious and most illustrious martyr's death, having always taught the things which he had learned from the apostles, which the Church also hands down, and which alone are true.[34]

After analyzing these two passages closely,[35] Shanks concludes:

The implication is that in Irenaeus's letter to Florinus we learn that his relationship with Polycarp began in his childhood, while in *Against Heresies* we discover that their association extended into the period that Irenaeus referred to as "our first maturity." Such a period could range from childhood to early adolescence or to early adulthood, and thus would have involved a number of very influential years. Consequently, this extended period would make Irenaeus a more than credible witness of not only Polycarp's character and orthodoxy, but also of individuals that Polycarp considered to be his "companions."[36]

It is unreasonable to discount the credibility of the testimony of Irenaeus simply because of his youth.[37] And given the tight connection between the apostle John, Polycarp, and Irenaeus, it seems unlikely Irenaeus was confused about which John was the author of the fourth Gospel.

There is another way Irenaeus could have been confused about which John wrote the Gospel—*there were two Johns*. Papias wrote:

And whenever anyone came who had been a follower of the elders, I asked about their words: what Andrew or Peter had said, or Philip or Thomas or James or John or Matthew or any of the other of the Lord's disciples, and what Aristion and the presbyter John, disciples of the Lord, were still saying.[38]

The primary question is whether Papias refers to the same John twice, or to two different Johns. Eusebius clearly takes Papias as referring to two different

---

34   Eusebius, *Ecclesiastical History* IV.14.3–4.

35   Shanks, *Papias and the New Testament*, 74–76.

36   Ibid., 78.

37   Charles Hill has argued quite extensively that the link between Polycarp and Irenaeus is stronger than typically assumed. See Charles E. Hill, *From the Lost Teaching of Polycarp* (Tübingen, Germany: Mohr Siebeck, 2006). For a response to a critique of his view, see Charles E. Hill, "The Man Who Needed No Introduction: A Response to Sebastian Moll," in *Irenaeus: Life, Scripture, Legacy*, ed. S. Parvis and P. Foster (Minneapolis, MN: Fortress Press, 2012), 95–104.

38   Eusebius, *Ecclesiastical History* 3.39.4.

Johns, the first referring to the apostle John, and the second to John the elder, author of Revelation. Does this tradition trace back to Papias himself, or was it a misreading or an invention of Eusebius? Conservative scholars have widely diverging opinions, although the traditional view is that there is only one John.

The key question regards what reading is most *natural* to the text. And this is where the traditional view emerges. Although some use the existence of the anaphoric article as evidence Papias referred to two different Johns, such an interpretation is deeply strained. Daniel Wallace writes:

> The anaphoric article is the article denoting previous reference .... The first mention of the substantive is usually anarthrous because it is merely being introduced. But the subsequent mentions of it use the article, for the article is now pointing back to *the* substantive previously mentioned. It is the most common use of the article and the easiest usage to identify .... Practically speaking, labeling an article as anaphoric requires that it have been introduced at most in the same book, preferably in a context not too far removed.[39]

Taken at face value, the text in Papias provides minimal evidence for the existence of a second John, and it provides good grammatical reason to think Papias referred to the apostle John first as an apostle, and then second as a living elder.

The external evidence is also lacking for the existence of John the elder. If he played such a foundational role in the early church, why would *no* source before Eusebius indicate his existence? This is admittedly an argument from silence, but given that John the elder is believed to hold a significant position in the early church, it is a silence with some force.[40]

Keener believes the tradition of two Johns stems from Eusebius, not Papias:[41] Keener indicates that Eusebius may have had incentive for interpreting Papias as he did. Since Eusebius rejected millenarianism and believed the kingdom had begun with Constantine, he had reason to separate the apostle John from authorship of Revelation. Given, then, that the traditional reading of Papias indicates he referred to one apostle twice, the lack of early corroborating external evidence, and the apparent theological bias of Eusebius, it seems most likely that John the elder—understood as an early influential figure who may have been the Beloved Disciple and author of the fourth Gospel—is a fiction. Thus, there

---

[39] Daniel B. Wallace, *The Basics of New Testament Syntax* (Grand Rapids, MI: Zondervan, 2000), 98. In personal conversation with Wallace, he explained that he firmly believes this grammar principle applies to the fragment of Papias and that Papias was referring twice to the same John rather than to two different Johns (November 20, 2013).

[40] John Chapman, *John the Presbyter and the Fourth Gospel* (Oxford: Clarendon Press, 1911), 49.

[41] Keener, *The Gospel of John*, 1:98.

is little convincing reason to conclude that Irenaeus was mistaken about which John stood behind the fourth Gospel.

Second, Irenaeus was a liar. According to this view, Irenaeus consciously imparts inaccurate information about Polycarp and John to further his own agenda. This would not imply Irenaeus was mistaken about everything, or even most things, but that he intentionally exaggerated or imparted false information about the connection between John and Polycarp. Helmut Koester recently suggested that identification of the apostle John with Ephesus "is due to a fiction that Bishop Irenaeus of Lyon created."[42] As indirect support for this view, Lincoln notes that Irenaeus would have been concerned to refute heresy by tracing his teachings through Polycarp to the apostle John, and may have stretched the truth to legitimize his position.[43] While it is not inconceivable that he might have stretched the truth, we should realize that in writing his *Letter to Florinus*, Irenaeus would have subjected himself to sharp criticism by Florinus if his information were fabricated, exaggerated, or incorrect in any significant way. Shanks rightly concludes, then, that "Irenaeus's assertions were not for personal promotion, rather they were provided as a foundation upon which he could defend orthodoxy; thus they were not made without significant risk."[44] Thus, it seems unlikely Irenaeus lied about his connection to Polycarp, and by default, the apostle John.

Third, Irenaeus transmits a tradition he received. From the middle of the second century onward, the apostle John is traditionally portrayed as ministering in Asia Minor. The *Epistle of the Apostles* (c. AD 150–175) identifies John, the son of Zebedee, as the author of the fourth Gospel, but makes no mention of his sojourn to Ephesus. The *Acts of John*, on the other hand, describes the apostle John throughout Ephesus and Smyrna. It is typically dated some time between the middle and end of the second century (c. 150–200). While the main purpose of the Acts of John lies in the mission, rather than history,[45] and while the book is filled with legendary accounts of the apostle John, the author likely preserved a historical core of John's excursus to Asia Minor, just as the authors of the *Acts of Paul* and the *Acts of Peter* accurately preserve the visit of Peter and Paul to Rome. If this tradition is mistaken, critics should provide a plausible account for how and why it developed so quickly. Hans-Josef Klauck concludes: "Clearly the knowledge that John had died a natural death was so firmly anchored in the tradition that it was impossible to work the story up into a more dramatic

---

[42]   Helmut Koester, "Ephesos in Early Christian Literature," in *Ephesos: Metropolis of Asia: An Interdisciplinary Approach to its Archaeology, Religion, and Culture*, ed. Helmut Koester (Valley Forge, PA: Trinity Press International, 1995), 138.

[43]   Lincoln, *The Gospel According to Saint John*, 19.

[44]   Shanks, *Papias and the New Testament*, 76.

[45]   János Bolyki, "Miracle Stories in the Acts of John," in *The Apocryphal Acts of John*, ed. Jan N. Bremmer (Kampen, The Netherlands: Kok Pharos, 1995), 34.

death such as martyrdom. Nevertheless, it was at this point that legends began to develop."[46] Irenaeus may be passing on a tradition similar to that found in the *Acts of John*, so those who reject this tradition would need to provide a plausible account for its origin.

We find additional external support in Clement of Alexandria (*c*. AD 150–215) and Polycrates (*c*. AD 130–196). In *The Rich Man Who is Saved*, Clement reports that "John the apostle" returned to Ephesus from the island of Patmos after the death of the tyrant (that is, Trajan).[47] According to Eusebius, Clement also reports John authored a "spiritual Gospel."[48] Yet it must be recognized that in seeming contradiction to this position, Clement indicates the ministry of the apostles ended during the reign of Nero, AD 54–68 (*Stromata* 7.17).

Around AD 190, Polycrates, bishop of Ephesus, indicates that the apostle John, whom he identifies with the Beloved Disciple, died in Ephesus.[49] This testimony is significant, but some scholars question its reliability. First, in the same passage Polycrates seems to confuse Philip the apostle with Philip the evangelist (Acts 21:8–9). If so, it may be possible Polycrates also confused the apostle John with another John (for example, the Elder or Prophet). Second, legitimate questions have been raised as to whether John could have become a "priest wearing the miter," as Polycrates reports.[50] Interestingly, Polycrates refers to the apostle John as a "witness" (*martyrs*), which is often translated as "martyr." Although this could be utilized to defend the view that John died as a martyr after exile in Ephesus, it seems more likely Polycrates used the term to indicate that John personally knew Jesus and testified for his faith. It is easy to see how later writers could have confused the meaning of *martyrs* and concluded John died as a martyr.

Even so, the cumulative strength of external evidence seems to support that John the apostle—and author of the Gospel—died a natural death at an advanced age in Ephesus. If Irenaeus simply passed on a tradition he received, he passed on a well-preserved tradition. Yet it must be conceded that significant qualifications and objections can be raised against each individual piece of evidence for the traditional view, which in turn undermines the strength of the overall case. In addition, many scholars believe positive evidence can be provided to demonstrate the likelihood of the martyrdom of John. Before considering the evidence that John died as a martyr, it is first necessary to consider another approach to Johannine authorship that could be consistent with an early martyrdom of John, the son of Zebedee.

---

[46]   Hans-Josef Klauck, *The Apocryphal Acts of the Apostles*, trans. Brian McNeil (Waco, TX: Baylor University Press, 2008), 38.

[47]   Clement, *The Rich Man Who is Saved*, in Eusebius, *Ecclesiastical History* 3.23.3.

[48]   Eusebius, *Ecclesiastical History* 6.14.7.

[49]   Ibid. 3.31.

[50]   F.F. Bruce, *Peter, Stephen, James and John: Studies in Non-Pauline Christianity* (Grand Rapids, MI: Eerdmans, 1979), 127–28.

A Johannine School

The existence of a Johannine School can be traced to influential writers such as Strauss, Renan, and J.B. Lightfoot.[51] Many modern scholars embrace some version of the Johannine School as well,[52] the idea that there was a community from which the writings of John emerged. Scholarly opinion varies as to the relationship of John to the community, and also varies regarding *which* John headed the school. Some posit John the apostle as the head of the school, others assume the leader was a student of the apostle, and others believe John the elder headed it. Still others assume different members of the community wrote the various Johannine books. Differences here are vast. While the existence of some type of Johannine School is generally accepted, a consensus has not been reached. Technically, one could still accept that John, the son of Zebedee, "authored" for the fourth Gospel, yet believe his traditions were later redacted by others before it reached its final form. Keener considers this a "workable compromise" that is "tenable but probably not necessary."[53] If some version of the Johannine School is correct, then John could have faced an early martyrdom and yet in some sense still have "authored" of the fourth Gospel.

Analyzing the Johannine School

Culpepper is one of the leading protagonists for the Johannine School. In his influential monograph, Culpepper identified nine common features found in various ancient "schools," such as the Pythagorean School, the Academy of Plato, and the school at Qumran. He concludes that the Johannine School shared these commitments and thus qualifies as an ancient school.[54] Other conservative scholars have embraced some version of the Johannine School as well.[55] While it does seem to be a live possibility, three points stand out as significant from analyzing the evidence behind it. First, it is hard to avoid the conclusion that evidence for the existence of the Johannine School is speculative, at least to a

---

[51] For a history of the Johannine school hypothesis, see R. Alan Culpepper, *The Johannine School: An Evaluation of the Johannine-School Hypothesis Based on an Investigation of the Nature of Ancient Schools*, Society of Biblical Literature Dissertation Series 26 (Missoula, MT: Scholars Press, 1975), 1–34.

[52] Barrett, *The Gospel According to St. John*, 132–34; Beasley-Murray, *John*, lxxiv; Raymond Brown, *The Community of the Beloved Disciple: The Life, Loves, and Hates of an Individual Church in New Testament Times* (Mahwah, NJ: Paulist, 1979), 22–24.

[53] Keener, *The Gospel of John*, 1:100.

[54] Culpepper, *The Johannine School*, 287–89.

[55] Bruce, *Peter, Stephen, James and John*; Martin Hengel, *The Johannine Question*, trans. John Bowden (Philadelphia, PA: Trinity, 1989); Oscar Cullmann, *The Johannine Circle*, trans. John Bowden (Philadelphia, PA: Westminster, 1976).

degree. There is simply no direct evidence for the existence of a formal Johannine community responsible for compiling and composing the fourth Gospel or other Johannine books. Even Cullmann has noted that all the evidence is *inferential*. And the evidence from the church fathers is minimal.

Second, scholars defend the existence of the Johannine School primarily with John 21:24: "This is the disciple who is bearing witness about these things, and who has written these things, and we know that his testimony is true." Many scholars consider this proof that the Beloved Disciple is not the author of the whole work, but accompanied by a wider circle of disciples corporately testifying to the truth of the Gospel witness. This may be the case, but Bauckham has provided a more plausible interpretation: that this passage contains the "we" of authoritative testimony, which has nothing to do with a numerical plural.[56] If Bauckham is right, then the author of the Gospel is not indicating the existence of a Johannine community, but using the plural "we" to highlight the trustworthiness of the testimony of the Beloved Disciple.

Third, Michael Kruger notes that for a document to have apostolic authority, it should meet two criteria.[57] First, an apostle—or someone who directly received information from an apostle—wrote it. Thus, there must be some *historical* connection to an apostle. He cites the book of Hebrews as an example. While it was not written by an apostle, the author does say: "It was declared at first by the Lord, and it was attested to us by those who heard" (2:3). This criterion raises no problem for any variety of the Johannine School hypothesis. Second, and potentially problematic, it was written while the apostles were still alive so they could oversee the transmission of the tradition. Kruger makes it clear that the early church only accepted books if they were composed while an apostle was alive to affirm it. Yet if a Johannine School composed the Gospel of John *after* his death, it would then violate this early church perception of the role of apostles. Perhaps the link to John was so well known in the early church that an exception was made, or perhaps John wrote most of it and the community simply redacted it before the final form. Countless such possibilities can be imagined. But this final point does raise challenges for the existence of a Johannine School that claims the Gospel was written from John's reminiscences after he was gone.

The point of this brief survey has been to highlight the substantive debate *within* conservative scholarly circles in regard to the source for the Gospel of John and the rest of the Johannine texts. While the existence of a Johannine circle is largely speculative, it is a live option that cannot simply be dismissed out of hand. If proponents of the Johannine School hypothesis are correct, then an early martyrdom of John becomes plausible. Even if John the apostle is the source behind the Gospel that was later compiled, then the apostle could have

---

56 Bauckham, *Jesus and the Eyewitnesses*, 370–83.

57 Michael J. Kruger, *The Canon Revisited* (Wheaton, IL: Crossway, 2012), 182–83.

experienced early martyrdom. The goal here has not been to settle the issue of the existence of the Johannine School, nor the identity of the author behind the tradition. Barring new discoveries or fresh arguments, the debate will likely continue for some time. The important point is that there are a variety of options for the authorship of the Gospel of John and the other Johannine writings, with differing degrees of probability, some of which are quite compatible with his early martyrdom.

Evidence for the Martyrdom of John

Both internal and external evidence are often cited as support for the martyrdom of John.

Internal Evidence

The Cup of Christ
Perhaps the most important passage for the martyrdom of John is found in Mark 10:35–40:

> And James and John, the sons of Zebedee, came up to him and said to him, "Teacher, we want you to do for us whatever we ask of you." And he said to them, "What do you want me to do for you?" And they said to him, "Grant us to sit, one at your right hand and one at your left, in your glory." Jesus said to them, "You do not know what you are asking. Are you able to drink the cup that I drink, or to be baptized with the baptism with which I am baptized?" And they said to him, "We are able." And Jesus said to them, "The cup that I drink you will drink, and with the baptism with which I am baptized, you will be baptized, but to sit at my right hand or at my left is not mine to grant, but it is for those for whom it has been prepared."

This third passion prediction in Mark (8:34–9:1; 9:33–37) clearly shows that the disciples do not understand the price of following Jesus, even though James and John do express an element of faith. All three predictions were given on the road to Golgotha, at Jerusalem, which indicates that the Gospel is about the way of the cross.[58] Given the embarrassment this passage would bring to the closest followers of Jesus, it is likely authentic. Boismard has argued that this prophecy would not have been retained in Matthew and Mark if it had only been half-fulfilled—if only James, but not John, died as a martyr.[59]

---

[58]   Ben Witherington III, *The Gospel of Mark: A Socio-Rhetorical Commentary* (Grand Rapids, MI: Eerdmans, 2001), 286.

[59]   Boismard, *Le Martyre de Jean l'apôtre*, 9–10.

In the passage, James and John—or in Matthew, their mother—desire to be in a place of honor when Jesus comes in his "glory." In response, Jesus asks them a simple question: *Can they drink the cup he is about to drink?* The key question, then, becomes what Jesus meant when he said that they would "drink the cup" and experience his "baptism." Scholars typically abide in one of two main interpretations, with most favoring the first. First, the Zebedee brothers must experience the sufferings of Jesus and be willing to face martyrdom. Second, they, like Jesus, will actually experience martyrdom. Some scholars adopt this second position, seeing it as evidence both James and John died early deaths as martyrs.[60]

The "cup" is often considered a metaphor for one's lot in life; what one has been given to "drink."[61] According to William Lane: "To share someone's cup was a recognized expression for sharing his fate."[62] In the Old Testament, the cup metaphor can refer to receiving a blessing (Ps 16:5; 23:5; 116:13), or to the bitter taste of God's wrath (Ps 75:8; Isa 51:17, 22; Jer 25:15–29; Lam 4:21; Ezek 23:31–32; Hab 2:15; cf. Rev 14:10).

While these broad insights are helpful, the key to interpreting this particular passage is the narrower context within the Gospel of Mark. Mark 14:22–23 says: "And as they were eating, he [Jesus] took bread, and after blessing it broke it and gave it to them, and said, 'Take; this is my body.' And he took a cup, and when he had given thanks he gave it to them, and they all drank of it." The red wine clearly represents the blood that Jesus shed to establish the new covenant (cf. Exod 24:6–8; Jer 31:31–34). In this context, the cup was not a reference to his suffering, but specifically to his death. We find the second Markan reference to the cup in 14:36: "And he said, 'Abba, Father, all things are possible for you. Remove this cup from me. Yet not what I will, but what you will.'" Jesus prayed this prayer in the Garden of Gethsemane right before his arrest. In this context, the cup refers to his suffering, death, *and* the wrath he would experience from the Father while completing his mission. Of course, the death of Jesus was uniquely vicarious for sin (Mark 10:45; cf. Ps 49:7). Nevertheless, the cup Jesus

---

[60]   F.P. Badham, "The Martyrdom of St. John," *American Journal of Theology* 4 (1899): 731; Boismard, *Le Martyre de Jean L'apôtre*, 9–10; Incigneri, *The Gospel to the Romans,* 347–48; Gilles Quispel, "The Fourth Gospel and the Judaic Gospel Tradition," in *Gnostica, Judaica, Catholica. Collected Essays by Gilles Quispel*, ed. Johannes Van Oort (Leiden, The Netherlands: Brill, 2008), 475–80; Johannes Weiss, *A History of the Period A.D. 30–150*, trans. Frederick C. Grant (New York: Harper & Brothers, 1937), 2:709–10; Ben Witherington III, "The Martyrdom of the Zebedee Brothers," *Biblical Archaeology Review* 33 (May/June 2007): 26.

[61]   Joel Marcus, *Mark 8–16: A New Translation with Introduction and Commentary*, The Anchor Yale Bible (New Haven, CT: Yale University Press, 2009), 747.

[62]   William L. Lane, *The Gospel According to Mark* (Grand Rapids, MI: Eerdmans, 1974), 379–80.

spoke of cannot be separated from his death, for that is the manner in which the
debt was paid. To say that James and John would drink the cup meant that they
would share his fate. Their deaths would have a different effect, but they would
be martyred nonetheless.

Close readers of Mark realize that the request of James and John ironically
foreshadows the crucifixion scene: "And with him they crucified two robbers,
one on his right and one on his left" (15:27). When James and John requested to
reign with Jesus in his glory, they did not realize this would involve sharing the fate
of both Jesus and the two robbers who died by his side. Although many scholars
disagree with this interpretation, it appears to be the most natural reading of
the passage. It finds general support in the early church's understanding that the
apostolic calling was to suffer and die like Jesus.[63]

Specifically, drinking the "cup" of Mark 10:39 has sometimes been taken
throughout the early church to indicate martyrdom.[64] After mentioning that
John lived in Ephesus, wrote a Gospel, and was "honored with martyrdom,"
George the Sinner wrote:

> For when the Lord said to them, "Are you able to drink the cup that I drink?"
> and they eagerly assented and agreed, he said, "You will drink my cup and will be
> baptized with the baptism with which I am baptized." And this is to be expected,
> for it is impossible for God to lie.[65]

By the end of the second century, church fathers began trying to compensate
for the lack of a martyrdom tradition for John. How could John, one of the
closest disciples of Jesus who was told he would drink the cup of Christ, not
have faced martyrdom? Tertullian wrote that John was plunged into boiling
oil, but survived and was sent to island exile.[66] This passage may have been
invented to show that John was put through the act of martyrdom, and thus
qualifies as a functional martyr even though he survived. Thus, according to
Tertullian, John was *willing* to die for his faith and was put to death as a martyr,
but God supernaturally spared him. For Origen, the exile of John accounts for
his "martyrdom."[67] The legendary story that John survived poisoning,[68] along
with the account by Augustine of Hippo that the ground above his grave seems

[63]   Karl Heinrich Rengstorf, *Apostolate and Ministry: The New Testament Doctrine of
the Office of the Ministry*, Concordia Heritage Series, trans. Paul D. Pahl (St. Louis, MO:
Concordia, 1969), 41.
[64]   *The Martyrdom of Polycarp* 14.2; John Chrysostom, *Homilies on Matthew* LXV.
[65]   Michael W. Holmes, *The Apostolic Fathers: Greek Texts and English Translation*, 3rd
ed. (Grand Rapids, MI: Baker, 2007), 745.
[66]   Tertullian, *The Prescription Against Heretics* 36.3.
[67]   Origen, *Commentary on Matthew* 16.6.
[68]   This legend is contained in the *Acts of John* 19–21.

to live and breathe upon the interred corpse,[69] may have been developed as a result of this same concern. Even today, William Hendriksen takes the cup John drank as banishment to Patmos, not martyrdom.[70] This is certainly a plausible interpretation. But it would be interesting to know how much belief in the traditional view that John was exiled to Patmos shapes how modern scholars interpret this passage. If there were a stronger tradition for the martyrdom of John, or even if there were no tradition either way, would scholars understand "the cup" as referring uniquely to martyrdom? It seems likely many would.

Although the natural reading of this passage is that Jesus was predicting the martyrdom of the Zebedee brothers, perhaps Jesus meant they would suffer for following him and must be *willing* to face martyrdom—an interpretation we cannot completely rule out. Nevertheless, while scholars disagree about whether Jesus specifically predicted their deaths in Mark 10:39, no debate exists about his prediction that they would suffer for their faith. Even though the Zebedee brothers misunderstood the prediction at the time, they inevitably would have reflected back upon this experience after the resurrection of Jesus and understood that they must suffer and be willing to die for their allegiance to him. While the martyrdom of John the apostle is debatable, his willingness to suffer and die for his faith is not.

The disappearance of John

Another reason to conclude John may have been martyred early is his sudden disappearance from Acts. After playing a central role in the opening chapters of Acts (3:1–11; 4:13–19; 8:14–25) John completely drops out of Luke's narrative. Even though he was one of the inner three disciples of Jesus, he is not even mentioned at the Jerusalem council (c. AD 50), which even Peter returned for (15:6–11). In addition, he goes unlisted among the apostles of 1 Corinthians 9. Why would Luke not tell more about John, one of the pillars of the faith? Ben Witherington believes John was martyred before the Jerusalem council.[71]

Although the disappearance of John is consistent with his early martyrdom, it hardly provides *positive* evidence for it, since Luke could have a variety of reasons for not mentioning John again in Acts. The most reasonable explanation is that John served no further purpose in advancing the larger narrative Luke was telling about the expansion of the Gospel (Acts 1:8). As demonstrated earlier, Luke frequently drops important characters after they have served their purpose within the larger narrative (for example, Philip, Peter, John Mark). Thus, it should come as no surprise that John disappears as well. Furthermore, even if John did disappear from the narrative because of his early demise, it remains

---

[69] Saint Augustine, *Tractates on John: Tractate* 124.3.

[70] W. Hendriksen, *Exposition of the Gospel According to Mark*, New Testament Commentary (Grand Rapids, MI: Baker, 1975), 412.

[71] Witherington, "The Martyrdom of the Zebedee Brothers," 26.

uncertain that he was killed for his faith. The disappearance of John, then, provides minimal evidence for his early martyrdom.

External Evidence

Philip of Side (AD fifth century)

Philip of Side offers the most intriguing external evidence for the martyrdom of John. In a comment regarding a fragment from Papias, Philip said: "Papias says in his second book that John the Theologian and James his brother were killed by Jews."[72] Critics often summarily dismiss this statement. Yet four factors lend it authenticity. First, Philip transmits other sources accurately. Thus, according to Boismard, he likely reproduces the original meaning of Papias accurately in this instance as well.[73] Second, the fact that it is stated incidentally without any apparent theological agenda or development gives it the ring of authenticity. The statement is part of a larger section about Papias being in error regarding the millennium and the claim that Barsabbas (Justus) survived drinking poison when put to the test. Philip includes it as if his readers know it is true and will agree with him. Third, Philip did not depend upon the fragments in Eusebius, but had likely read sections of Papias's *Expositions of the Sayings of the Lord* for himself. This is supported by Philip's inclusion of material from Papias that is not known from any other ancient source. Nevertheless, only fragments remain from his extensive work titled *Church History* (AD 434–439), so it is not possible to meaningfully assess his accuracy as a historian. Fourth, even though it appears in only one manuscript, and may have been interpolated from Philip of Side,[74] George the Sinner (c. AD 840) gave a similar report of the death of John the hands of the Jews:

> At that time he [the apostle John] was the sole survivor of the twelve disciples, and after writing the gospel that bears his name was honored with martyrdom. For Papias, the Bishop of Hierapolis, who had seen him with his own eyes, claim in the second book of the *Sayings of the Lord* that John was killed by Jews, thus clearly fulfilling, together with his brother, Christ's prophecy concerning them and their own confession and agreement about this.[75]

Nevertheless, most scholars consider Philip of Side an unreliable historian.[76] It bears comment that Philip does not directly quote Papias, but provides a

---

[72]   Holmes, *The Apostolic Fathers*, 743.

[73]   Boismard, *Le Martyre de Jean l'apôtre*, 57.

[74]   Bruce, *Peter, Stephen, James and John*, 137.

[75]   Holmes, *The Apostolic Fathers*, 745.

[76]   Ibid., 172. Two notable exceptions are Hengel, *The Johannine Question*, 21, and James H. Charlesworth, *The Beloved Disciple* (Harrisburg, PA: Trinity Press International, 1995), 240–41.

summary of what he believes Papias wrote. And it is not uncommon to find ancient writers quoted for claims they never made.[77] Philip also does not indicate *when* or *where* John was killed. The statement itself is consistent with an early martyrdom—presumably Jerusalem—or a late martyrdom—presumably Ephesus.

The natural reading seems to indicate that the Jews killed him early in Jerusalem along with his brother James (Acts 12:2), but two reasons rule out an early martyrdom. First, Philip had previously declared that Papias was a disciple of John. But this would be virtually impossible if John had faced an early martyrdom in the AD 40s or 50s. Papias was not born until around AD 70. Second, Eusebius would have had motivation to utilize evidence for an early martyrdom of John. Philip was aware of the *Ecclesiastical History*, and thus likely Eusebius's views that John lived a long life. Given Eusebius's desire to separate the apostle John from authorship of Revelation because of his distaste for chiliasm, if there were evidence in Papias for an early martyrdom of John, Eusebius likely would have utilized it. The aforementioned quotation from Eusebius in his *Commentary on the Psalms* indicates his belief that each of the 12 apostles would suffer and die like Jesus. *Contra* Hengel, it seems Eusebius would have had more motivation to include it than dropping the report.[78] Culpepper seems correct: "The latter [that Eusebius intentionally suppressed the martyrdom account] is difficult to accept since Eusebius assumes the five books of Papias are still available."[79] This scenario raises considerable doubt whether the alleged quote by Papias was in the original.

Another possibility is that Eusebius missed some important information related to the death of John when he first wrote his history of the church. This seems very unlikely, though. Shanks observes:

> Remembering, however, that the time between the first and last release of *Ecclesiastical History* was well over a decade, it seems reasonable to conclude that during the intervening years someone would have pointed out this glaring omission to Eusebius if Papias had clearly described the Jewish responsibility or participation in the apostle John's martyrdom.[80]

A further intriguing possibility is that Philip of Side misread the statement in Papias. J.H. Bernard notes that the statement in Papias, according to Philip, is technically not true of James, the son of Zebedee. He was not "killed by the Jews," but by Herod (Acts 12:2), which "pleased the Jews." On the other hand, *the*

---

77 Chapman, *John the Presbyter*, 78.
78 Hengel, *The Johannine Question*, 21.
79 Culpepper, *John*, 155.
80 Shanks, *Papias and the New Testament*, 223.

Jews did kill James, the brother of the Lord. After closely examining the Greek, Bernard supposes that Eusebius confused James, the brother of Jesus, with James, the son of Zebedee. According to Bernard, the name "John" came into the text because Eusebius thought "the brother of the Lord, James" referred to John, the brother of James, rather than as a title to designate James as the brother of Jesus. Thus, according to Bernard, Eusebius misread Papias as claiming that the Jews killed both sons of Zebedee. J.H. Bernard concludes:

> I submit, therefore, that the idea that Papias is an authority for the 'red martyrdom' of John the son of Zebedee must be dismissed. In the light of the universal belief of the Church, it would be very difficult to suppose that Papias gave currency to any such idea. And the only quotation from him which has been supposed to support it may quite naturally be explained as a misreading of a passage in which he had spoken of the martyrdom of James the Just, but had made no mention of John at all.[81]

While Bernard's hypothesis here is little more than educated guesswork, the most reasonable supposition is that Philip misread Papias *in some manner*, which raises a critical question: Given the unanswered questions about the passage in Philip, is it more likely that Philip preserved a reliable tradition unknown or ignored by Eusebius or any other early church father, or that he, either intentionally or unintentionally, misstated Papias. The latter is clearly more probable.

Church calendars
Additional evidence for the early martyrdom of John can be found in a variety of church calendars, martyrologies, and homilies. Boismard believes the liturgical and patristic evidence makes it "impossible to doubt that the apostle John was indeed martyred."[82]

The Calendar of Carthage (*c.* AD 505) celebrates the feast of John the apostle and the apostle James, who was killed by Herod. Even though the calendar refers to John as "the Baptist," there was likely confusion by the author, since John the Baptist was also celebrated later, on June 24. The author may also have conflated John the Baptist and the apostle, since both were beheaded (Acts 12:2). In a Syriac martyrology in the East (AD 411), a celebration of James and John (December 27) is sandwiched right between the martyrdom of Stephen (December 26) and the apostle Paul (December 28). There is a Gallic tradition, possibly as early as the fifth century, that celebrates the martyr death of James and John on December 27.[83] A similar commemoration can be found in the writings

---

[81]   John Henry Bernard, *Studia Sacra* (London: Hodder & Stoughton, 1917), 274–75.

[82]   My own translation from: "[I]mpossible de douter que l'apôtre Jean ait été effectivement martyrize" (Boismard, *Le Martyre de Jean l'apôtre*, 13).

[83]   Boismard, *Le Martyre de Jean l'apôtre*, 15–16, 33–34.

of Aphrahat (AD 344).[84] Interestingly, Aphrahat had previously referred to the stoning of Stephen and the martyrdoms of Peter and Paul, and yet he identifies James and John *not* as martyrs, but as walking in "the footsteps of their Master Christ." Why the difference? Did he still mean martyrdom?

This passage in Aphrahat raises an important distinction in how James and John have been remembered in comparison with the other apostles. While they were commemorated together shortly after Christmas in both the East and West, it is not clear that it was because of their mutual martyrdoms.[85] In fact, Bernard argues that the tradition of their mutual commemoration began with Gregory of Nyssa (*c.* AD 335–*c.* 395), who was careful to distinguish between commemorations of martyrs from apostles. Gregory recorded the crucifixion of Peter and the beheading of James, and yet with John he tells the story of the boiling oil and his willingness to suffer as his witness for Christ.[86] According to Bernard, James and John were honored as apostles, not martyrs. James honored Christ by his martyrdom, and John honored Christ by his *willingness* to die as a martyr.[87]

Even if these passages do refer to the martyrdom of the apostle John, as Boismard surmises, questions still remain as to the historical value of these accounts. Little evidence attests that these calendars and festivals date before the end of the fourth century (*c.* AD 400).[88] At best, these liturgies demonstrate John's death was *celebrated* at this time. Given that the tradition arises in the late fourth century, a time when tradition was often untethered to history, it is questionable how much historical value it provides for the martyrdom of John.

Given the scattered, inconsistent, and late evidence, it is difficult to conclude with much confidence that the evidence points to an early martyrdom of the apostle John. As convenient as it may be to overstate the case for the martyrdom of John, the current evidence simply does not warrant such a conclusion.

This close examination of the evidence indicates that the following two points can be regarded to have varying degrees of confidence from the early tradition regarding the apostle John:

1. John ministered in Ephesus—*very probably true* (*Acts of John* 18, 62; Polycrates, in Eusebius, *Ecclesiastical History* 3.31; Justin Martyr, *Dialogue with Trypho* 81; Irenaeus, *Against Heresies*, 3.1.1; Clement of Alexandria, *The Rich Man Who is Saved*, in Eusebius, *Ecclesiastical*

---

[84] Aphrahat, *Demonstration XXI: Of Persecution* (§ 23).

[85] Bernard, *Studia Sacra*, 280.

[86] Ibid., 281–82.

[87] Ibid., 283.

[88] Arthur John Maclean, *The Ancient Church Orders* (Piscataway, NJ: Gorgias, 2004), 128–31.

History 3.23; Pseudo-Hippolytus, *Hippolytus on the Twelve Apostles* 3; Eusebius, *Ecclesiastical History* 3.1.

2. John experienced martyrdom—*improbable* (Mark 10:35–45; disappearance of John from Acts; Philip of Side citation; church calendars and martyrologies).

Chapter 9

The Martyrdom of Thomas

The Synoptic Gospels provide no details about Thomas except his name, which means "twin."[1] He appears only in the lists of disciples (Matt 10:2–4; Mark 3:16–19; Luke 6:14–16; Acts 1:13). Yet in the Gospel of John, Thomas emerges as an important figure in three passages.

Thomas first appears as a bold disciple, willing to go to his death for Jesus (John 11:16). Jesus had just received word of his beloved friend Lazarus's falling ill (11:3). When Jesus announced to his disciples that he was going to Judea, they tried to stop him (11:8). But Thomas is not dissuaded. He boldly proclaims: "Let us also go, that we may die with him" (11:16). These actions paint a different picture of Thomas than the typical "doubting" motif. Rather than wavering in his commitment, Thomas was willing to face death for his master. Thomas certainly initially doubted the resurrection of Jesus (20:25), but in this earlier passage he shows greater devotion to Jesus than do the rest of the disciples. Thomas also appears as the spokesman for the disciples in this passage—a role typically reserved for Peter in the Synoptic Gospels.

Thomas appears again in the Gospel of John, in the upper room. After Jesus has addressed his disciples (John 14:1–4), Thomas immediately asks Jesus how they can know where he is going (14:5). Rather than complying, Jesus responds that he is the only way to get eternal life (11:6). Even though Jesus had just said that the disciples knew the way to where he was going (14:4), Thomas still seemed lost. Clearly he did not understand the spiritual point Jesus was making. These first two passages indicate that Thomas had remarkable love and devotion to Jesus, but did not understand his message—until after his resurrection.

The third time Thomas is mentioned in the Gospel of John involves his absence at the appearance of Jesus to his disciples (20:24–25). When they tell Thomas, he still refuses to believe (20:25). After eight days, when all the disciples are together, this time including Thomas, Jesus appears among them, and after seeing the risen Jesus, Thomas proclaims: "My Lord and my God!" (20:27–28). Thomas had always been a devoted follower of Christ. But now his devotion would be grounded in an accurate understanding of who Jesus really was (and is).

---

[1] "Thomas" is Hebrew for "twin," and "Didymus" means the same in Greek. Some scholars believe Matthew was a twin to Thomas, since they appear next to each other in the Synoptic lists of the disciples. Others argue that he was a twin to Jesus, since that is how he appears in *The Apocryphal Acts of Thomas*. In reality, the identity of the twin is unknown.

The Gospel of John makes it clear that Thomas *personally* saw Jesus after his death and believed that he was the Lord. Jesus appeared a second time to the disciples as they gathered indoors for the sole purpose of persuading Thomas; no other instance occurs in the Gospels where Jesus appears for the sake of convincing one person. Thus, Thomas not only has a special place in the Gospel of John, but also seemingly in relationship to Jesus.

This passage reveals another critical point: Thomas's convictions were not developed secondhand, but by coming face-to-face with the risen Jesus. Like the rest of the apostles, he was willing to suffer and face death for this belief. He was thrown in jail for preaching publicly about Jesus (Acts 5:17–25). And when threatened by the religious authorities, Thomas refused to stop preaching because he was a *witness* of the risen Christ (Acts 5:29–32).

Along with playing a significant role in the Gospel of John, Thomas went on to become a prominent figure in the Gnostic and apocryphal texts of the early church. Thomas is the central figure in the *Infancy Gospel of Thomas* (c. AD 140–170), the *Gospel of Thomas* (c. AD 150), the *Book of Thomas the Contender* (c. AD 150–225), the *Acts of Thomas* (c. AD 200–220), and the *Apocalypse of Thomas* (c. sixth century). Thomas's prominent appearance in the apocryphal tradition is noteworthy. Most observes: "No other character figures as the protagonist or putative author mentioned in them by name as frequently as Thomas is, with the sole exceptions of Jesus himself and the disciples Peter and John."[2] Thomas was such a significant figure in the early church that some have suggested there was a Thomas School, with some degree of organization, that may have produced some of the early Gnostic texts that feature Thomas.[3]

The Historical Challenge

While Peter and Paul are believed by the Western church to have evangelized and died in Rome, the Eastern church has consistently held that Thomas founded the church in India before his martyrdom. Alphonse Mingana explains:

> It is the constant tradition of the Eastern Church that the Apostle Thomas evangelised India, and there is no historian, no poet, no breviary, no liturgy, and no writer of any kind who, having the opportunity of speaking of Thomas, does not associate his name with India. Some writers mention also Parthia and Persia

---

[2]   Glenn W. Most, *Doubting Thomas* (Cambridge, MA: Harvard University Press, 2005), 90.

[3]   For an analysis and critique of the idea of a Thomas School, see Philip Sellew, "Thomas Christianity: Scholars in Quest of a Community," in *The Apocryphal Acts of Thomas*, ed. Jan N. Bremmer (Leuven, Belgium: Peeters, 2001), 11–35.

among the lands evangelised by him, but all of them are unanimous in the matter of India. The name of Thomas can never be dissociated from that of India.[4]

While scholars hold widely divergent views on the historicity of the Thomas tradition, they seem to agree that the evidence is not demonstrative either way.

One difficulty in assessing the Thomas tradition is that the historical record of India is unconventional by Western standards. No written history of India exists until the arrival of the Portuguese in the sixteenth century.[5] Thus, it has often been claimed that since India lacked historical writing, it also lacked a sense of history. Only recently has this assumption been challenged. While early India may have lacked extensive historical writings, it does not follow that it also lacked a historical consciousness.[6] History was simply preserved in a manner different from in the West. Frykenberg explains:

> Each community, from out of its own store of cultural and material resources, sought to preserve its own oral tradition, its own epic historical narratives (*itihasa-puranas*), and its own narrative genealogies or lineages (*vamshāvalis*). Family members told and retold their own stories—about how their own family and their own community first came into being; how much adversity they suffered or how great the good fortune that came to them or brought them honour and status; how their own people first settled onto special lands or gained special distinction; and, among other things, how they first developed their own unique institutions. From generation to generation, children listened: during evenings after the sun went down and in times before lights were abundant, enthralled by stories that told about their own ancestral origins. Embedded in what was heard, in the form of bardic songs and oral traditions—and in what eyes beheld, in epigraphic copper and stone inscriptions, as well as on palm-leaf manuscripts—were hallowed sources of narratives that were ritually celebrated, danced, and sung.[7]

The Thomas Christians, for instance, still strongly hold to oral traditions that claim they were founded by the apostle Thomas. In place of written documentation are songs and poems, such as the *Thomma Parvam*, which was not written down until the early seventeenth century. This is not a good reason

---

4   Alphonse Mingana, *The Early Spread of Christianity in India* (Manchester: Manchester University Press, 1926), 15–16.

5   Nectarias McLees, "Witness for an Apostle: The Evidence for St. Thomas in India," *Road to Emmaus* 6 (2005): 60.

6   Romila Thapar, "Historical Traditions in Early India: *c.* 1000 B.C. to *c.* AD 600," *The Oxford History of Historical Writing*, ed. Andrew Feldherr and Grant Hardy (Oxford: Oxford University Press, 2011), 553–58.

7   Eric Frykenberg, *Christianity in India: From Beginnings to the Present* (Oxford: Oxford University Press, 2008), 92.

to glibly dismiss their historical value.[8] In fact, Gillman and Klimkeit note a double standard among Western scholars who dismiss apostolic roots in India because the tradition is deemed too late and legend-filled, and yet are ready to overlook the fact that the earliest record of Patrick of Ireland comes from the late eighth century, roughly three centuries after his death.[9]

Undoubtedly, the tradition of Thomas in India is filled with legend and myth. Nevertheless, Indian scholars tend to approach the intersection of tradition and truth quite differently. For instance, in India, tradition is a significant source for preserving historical truth. F.E. Pargiter writes:

> Tradition therefore becomes all-important. It is the only resource, since historical
> works are wanting, and is not an untrustworthy guide. In ancient times men knew
> perfectly well the difference between truth and falsehood, as abundant proverbs
> and sayings show. It was natural therefore that they should discriminate what was
> true and preserve it; and historical tradition must be considered in this light.[10]

While it is uncritical to simply accept tradition, it is overly critical to glibly dismiss it. The key is to separate fact from fiction, remembering that myths and legends do not arise in a vacuum. The place to begin is to consider the practicability of Thomas traveling to India and ministering during the first century AD. Was such a trip even possible?

Travel to India in the First Century AD

In the first century, an apostolic mission from Jerusalem to India was entirely physically possible. India may have been more open to direct communication with the West during the first two hundred years of the Common Era than during any other period before the coming of the Portuguese in the seventeenth century.[11] Trade relations were just as close with southern India as with the north. And while this period experienced a boom in trade and communication, there had already been extensive contact between the Mediterranean world and India for a long time.[12]

---

[8]   Ian Gillman and Hans-Joachim Klimkeit, *Christians in Asia Before 1500* (Ann Arbor, MI: University of Michigan Press, 1999), 163–64.

[9]   Ibid., 166.

[10]   F.E. Pargiter, *Ancient Indian Historical Tradition* (London: Oxford University Press, 1922), 3.

[11]   Samuel Hugh Moffett, *Beginnings to 1500*, A History of Christianity in Asia, vol. 1 (New York: HarperCollins, 1992), 31.

[12]   For a detailed description of the ancient evidence for relations between India and the West, see Eckhard J. Schnabel, *Early Christian Mission: Paul and the Early Church* (Downers Grove, IL: InterVarsity Press, 2004), 1:479–99

Trade between Rome and India flourished in the first and second centuries, at least from the time of Claudius (*c.* AD 45) to the time of Hadrian (d. AD 138). Significant routes and gaps through the mountains could be traversed quite efficiently.[13] Romans had an insatiable desire for Indian pearls, spices, pepper, silk, ivory, and cotton goods, and Indians imported tin, lead, gold, silver coins, wine, coral, beryl, and glass from the West. Many Roman coins dating from the time of Tiberius (AD 14–37) to Nero (AD 54–68) have been found in southern India, proving that Rome trade relations were as common in southern India as in the north.[14] In addition, archaeological evidence bolsters the case for trade relations in the first century. Most notably, many Roman artifacts were found at the "Indo-Roman trading station" at Arikamedu, near Pondichéry. Based on the nature of the artifacts, including pottery, beads, glass, and terracotta, it seems likely the Romans were using Arikamedu between the first century BC and the early second century AD.[15]

Perhaps the most intriguing evidence for trade between India and Rome comes from a surviving first-century document, a mariner's manual by an unknown merchant, called *The Periplus of the Erythraean Sea*, also commonly known as, "Travel and Trade in the Indian Ocean by a Merchant of the First Century." Written roughly around the time of Thomas's mission and the first great missionary expansion of the Christian church, the *Periplus* is the first record of organized trading between Rome, Parthia, India, China, and many other smaller nations of the time. The report contains details about various ports, cities, articles of trade, as well as navigational and commercial details on the Indian Ocean, many of which have been confirmed to be accurate.[16] Strabo's *Geography*, along with the writings of Pliny the Elder (*Natural History*) and Ptolemy (*Geography*), confirm that a journey from Rome to India would not have been unusual in the first century.[17] These works also contain fairly detailed references to India.[18] Thus, independent of the destination and fate of the apostle Thomas, it seems likely Middle Eastern Christians followed Roman trade routes to northern and southern India in the first century, and certainly by the second, with the desire to be obedient to the Great Commission (Matt 28:18–20).

---

[13] L.W. Brown, *The Indian Christians of St. Thomas* (Cambridge: Cambridge University Press, 1956), 59–60.

[14] Gillman and Klimkeit, *Christians in Asia before 1500*, 157.

[15] Romila Thapar, *A History of India* (New York: Penguin, 1966), 1:115.

[16] John Keay, *India: A History* (New York: Atlantic Monthly, 2000), 121.

[17] Klaus Karttunen, "On the Contacts of South India with the Western World in Ancient Times, and the Mission of the Apostle Thomas," in *South Asian Religion and Society*, ed. Asko Parpola and Bent Smidt Hansen (London: Riverdale, 1986), 189–91.

[18] *Natural History* 5.9.47; 6.21.56–26.106; Ptolemy, *Geography* 7.1

Given the textual, archaeological, and geographical evidence for trade and communication between India and the Roman Empire in the first century, we have no reason to doubt that a trip by the apostle Thomas to India was entirely possible.

Thomas in India

While it is surely possible that Thomas could have gone to India—*is it probable*? An important line of evidence in examining this question is to consider the witness of the early church fathers. Outside the New Testament, there are no known references to Thomas in the first century. The various "Thomas" books of the second century focus on the life and ministry of Jesus rather than Thomas's ministry endeavors. While the record of the sojourn for Thomas is not as early as the corresponding records for some of the other apostles (for example, Peter and Paul), there is a substantial testimony that he was the apostle to the East. Early church writings consistently link Thomas to ministry in India and Parthia.[19] Many later writings continue this tradition as well.[20]

There are two distinct lines of tradition for the apostle Thomas, linking him to both Parthia and to India. Despite what some writers suggest,[21] these traditions are not necessarily in conflict. Thomas may have embarked on his missionary journey by the mid-40s at the earliest, and the traditional dating places his death in AD 72. Clearly, then, he had plenty of time for multiple missions in the East. Another factor recognizes the flexibility of the name "India" in the first century AD. Moffett explains: "If Gundaphar was a Parthian Suren, as seems possible, a mission to India might loosely but not incorrectly be referred to as a mission to Parthians."[22] There is no good reason to discount this tradition as contradictory, especially since Parthia and India are both East of Jerusalem and proximate to one another. If Thomas really did go to the East, it may help explain why there is a silence in the first two centuries of the church regarding his ministry and fate.[23]

---

[19] *Acts of Thomas* 1 (c. AD 200–220); *Teachings of the Apostles* 3 (third century); *Hippolytus on the Twelve* (c. third century); Origen, *Commentary on Genesis*, vol. 3 (d. c. 254); *Clementine Recognitions* 9.29 (c. AD 350); St. Gregory of Nazianzen, *Oration* 33.11 (c. AD 325–390).

[20] Some of these later writers include St. Ephrem (c. AD 373), Gaudentius (387), Gregory of Nyssa (389), St. Ambrose of Milan (397), and Jerome (340–420).

[21] John N. Farquhar, "The Apostle Thomas in South India," in *Bulletin of the John Rylands Library* (Manchester: Manchester University Press, 1926), 11:41.

[22] Moffett, *A History of Christianity in Asia*, 33.

[23] For a response to the claim that Thomas simply disappeared altogether, see James F. McGrath, "History and Fiction in the Acts of Thomas: The State of the Question," *Journal for the Study of Pseudepigrapha* 17 (2008): 297–311.

Three points stand out from the early church fathers regarding their witness to Thomas. First, the testimony that he went to India is unanimous, consistent, and reasonably early. Second, we have no contradictory evidence stating Thomas did *not* go to India or Parthia or that he went elsewhere. Third, fathers both in the East and in the West confirm the tradition. Since the beginning of the third century it has become an almost undisputable tradition that Thomas ministered in India. While the case for Thomas in India is more provisional than for Peter and Paul in Rome, it does seem more probable than not.

The case may be slightly strengthened by evidence for the existence of early Christians in India. Eusebius claims that Pantaenus, the great Egyptian scholar in charge of the Alexandrian School, traveled to preach the Gospel of Christ to people in the East and went as far as India. When Pantaenus arrived in India (AD 189), he found that Bartholomew had already ministered there and left the Gospel of Matthew in Hebrew.[24] Jerome confirms this tradition, adding that Demetrius, the bishop of Alexandria, sent Pantaenus at the request of the people.[25]

There should be nothing surprising about Pantaenus finding Christians in India if Thomas, and *possibly* Bartholomew, had already preached there. Mingana rejects this story, claiming that the India Eusebius referred to "is without doubt Arabia Felix."[26] Yet according to Stephen Neill, a missionary in India who studied the expansion of Christianity in India for four decades: "When ships in hundreds were going from Egypt to South India, it is unlikely that anyone in Alexandria would be the victim of such a confusion .... It must be taken as probable that South India is the India of Pantaenus."[27]

Another early missionary to India is Theophilos the Indian (AD 354–425), sent by Constantius, the Arian emperor, as an ambassador to the Yemen, in hopes of getting permission to build churches for locals as well as Roman travelers. It is believed that he traveled to his native island Divus, as well as many other Indian districts. While it may be impossible to know whether he made it to India itself, he likely encountered an indigenous Indian church. He discovered resident congregants, regular church services where the Gospel was read in Syriac, a ministering clergy, and uniquely Indian customs, such as listening to the Gospel in a sitting posture.[28] This is an unmistakably Indian form of listening that is unlikely to have come from another place.[29] There is good reason to believe Theophilus encountered a uniquely Indian congregation in the mid-fourth century.

---

[24]   Eusebius, *Ecclesiastical History* 5.10.3.

[25]   Saint Jerome, *On Illustrious Men*, trans. Thomas P. Halton (Washington, DC: Catholic University of America Press, 1999), 36.

[26]   Mingana, *The Early Spread of Christianity*, 17.

[27]   Stephen Neill, *A History of Christianity in India: The Beginning to AD 1707* (Cambridge: Cambridge University Press, 1984), 40.

[28]   A.E. Medlycott, *India and the Apostle Thomas* (London: Ballantyne, 1905), 197–201.

[29]   Brown, *The Indian Christians of St. Thomas*, 67.

Another line of support comes from the *Book of Fate* (AD 196) by Bardaisan. In one section, he compares the customs of Christians with those of various pagan groups. While he mentions pagan customs in Parthia, he does not refer to any Christians living there. But he does mention Christians living in the midst of the Kushans, an empire that extended into Western India from the beginning of the second century to the end of the fourth.[30] If this evidence is considered in lieu of the claim by Eusebius that Pantaenus came to India in 189, there is considerable reason to accept the presence of Christians in India in the late second century.

We also know that bishops were in India at the end of the third and the early fourth centuries. The first identified bishop of India is David (Dūdi), who left Basrah by ship around AD 295. Though the location in India cannot be identified for sure, it was likely in southern India.[31] The second reference to a bishop is John, bishop of Persia and Great India (AD 325). Some have suggested that this solitary bishop from the East is an invention to emphasize the genuinely ecumenical nature of the council. But such skepticism is unwarranted. Eusebius, who was present at the council, noted that a Persian bishop was a participant.[32] This may suggest that the Indian church was well established before the Council of Nicea.[33]

If we combine the aforementioned evidence with the literary evidence of the *Didascalia Apostolorum* and the *Acts of Thomas*, traditions such as the *Thomma Parvom*, and with the Taxila Cross that may date to the second century,[34] then we have no good reason to doubt the existence of a Christian community in India by the late second century *at the latest*.[35] The next step is to consider the reliability of the earliest literary evidence that Thomas preached and died in India—the *Acts of Thomas*.

---

[30] Edward James Rapson, *The Cambridge History of India* (Cambridge: Cambridge University Press, 1922), 1:585.

[31] Neill, *A History of Christianity in India*, 41.

[32] Mingana, *The Early Spread of Christianity*, 63.

[33] James Kurikilamkatt, *First Voyage of the Apostle Thomas to India* (Bangalore, India: Asian Trading Corporation, 2005), 135.

[34] In 1935, a small cross on black stone was found outside the city of Sirkap, where the palace of king Gondophares once stood. The precise date is unknown, but it is commonly dated to the second century AD. Of course, if it is an early Christian cross it reveals nothing about a sojourn of Thomas to India. At best, it would reveal the existence of a Christian community in India in the second century. See John Rooney, *Shadows in the Dark: A History of Christianity in Pakistan Up to the 10th Century* (Rawalpindi, Pakistan: Christian Study Centre, 1984), 42–43.

[35] Aziz S. Atiya, *History of Eastern Christianity* (Notre Dame, IN: University of Notre Dame Press, 1968), 363.

The *Acts of Thomas*

The *Acts of Thomas*, the earliest literary account of the preaching ministry and martyrdom of Thomas in India, was likely composed in the early third century (*c.* AD 200–220), but may have originated as early as the second century.[36] The *Acts of Thomas* is the only ancient apocryphal Act that has survived in its entirety, although not in its original form.[37] It was likely written in Syriac and then translated into Greek.[38]

The *Acts of Thomas* begins with the apostles in Jerusalem dividing up the world for missions. According to lot, Thomas was assigned to go to India, but he reluctantly objected, even though Jesus appears to him at night. Shortly thereafter, a merchant named Abban came from India looking for a carpenter to work for King Gondophares. Jesus offers to sell him Thomas as a slave, and this time Thomas enthusiastically agrees. Once he arrives in the city, Gondophares assigns Thomas to build him a palace outside the city gates. Thomas agrees, but instead of using the money to build the palace, he gives it away to the poor and afflicted. Gondophares, furious when he hears how Thomas has used the money, casts him in prison, contemplating how he will kill him. That very night, the king's brother Gad dies and is taken by an angel to see the palace Thomas has built in heaven. Gad is allowed to return to life the next day and tell his brother all he had seen. As a result, both Gondophares and Gad seek the forgiveness of Thomas, and decide also to follow the Lord. Thomas travels to another land, and after preaching, casting out demons, and performing miracles, he is eventually thrown in prison by King Misdaeus (Mizdai). Thomas prays as he is escorted to his death by four guards, who kill him with spears.

There are two general positions regarding the historicity of the *Acts of Thomas*, largely determined by whether the apostolate of Thomas in India is accepted or rejected. The first position is to write it off as entirely fictional. The second position recognizes the legendary nature of the *Acts of Thomas*, but admits that it contains a historical core. According to McGrath, it is a tendency in Western scholarship to *assume* the legendary character of the *Acts of Thomas*, rather than to argue for it.

Some scholars have pointed to certain incidental details in the narrative that imply an Indian origin. For instance, Medlycott has argued that the practice of bathing or washing before meals was a uniquely Hindu custom that traced to southern India.[39] While this custom was Indian by nature, there is at least some

---

[36]   Frykenberg, *Christianity in India*, 93.

[37]   Hans-Josef Klauck, *The Apocryphal Acts of the Apostles*, trans. Brian McNeil (Waco, TX: Baylor University Press, 2008), 141.

[38]   Jan N. Bremmer, "The Acts of Thomas: Place, Date, and Women," in *The Apocryphal Acts of Thomas*, ed. Jan N. Bremmer (Leuven, Belgium: Peeters, 2001), 76.

[39]   Medlycott, *India and the Apostle Thomas*, 277–79.

evidence a similar custom was practiced in the Greco-Roman world, and thus it was not *uniquely* Indian.[40]

Part of the difficulty in ascertaining the truth about the Thomas tradition is that our earliest source (*Acts of Thomas*) is roughly 130–150 years removed from the events. Historically speaking, it must be admitted that this provides a significant challenge to the evidence. Even Benedict Vadakkekara, who strongly defends the apostolic roots of the St. Thomas Christians, recognizes that the lack of contemporary written accounts poses a challenge for the tradition.[41] He proceeds to suggest various reasons for the lack of written historical record, including the fact that for the first three thousand years of Indian history, there are many volumes on philosophy, religion, and poetry, but very few contemporary written historical accounts.[42] Whether or not his reasons are adequate, the reality still remains that the earliest written documents are at least two full generations removed from his death (AD 72). What value can it provide for this investigation?

It would be premature—simply because it was written in the early third century, at least two to three generations removed from the events—to dismiss the *Acts of Thomas* as lacking any historical value. While earlier sources are certainly preferred, later sources often provide valuable historical information. A helpful example comes from comparing the *Acts of Thomas* with the writings of Plutarch. In his *Lives*, Plutarch wrote over sixty biographies, fifty of which have survived. For several subjects in the *Lives*, Plutarch is treated as seriously as earlier sources. He is the main source for a number of ancient figures, many of whom lived hundreds of years before his writing (for example, Pelopidas, Timoleon, Dion, Eumenes, Agis, Cleomenes). Donald Russell writes: "The *Lives*, despite the pitfalls for the historian which have sometimes led to despair about their value as source-material, have been the main source of understanding of the ancient world for many readers from the Renaissance to the present day."[43] Later sources *can* provide valuable historical information, and must not simply be dismissed. The *Acts of Thomas* must be examined on its own merits to see if it contains any discernible historical information.

---

[40]   McGrath, "History and Fiction," x.

[41]   Benedict Vadakkekara, *Origin of India's St. Thomas Christians: A Historiographical Critique* (Delhi, India: Media House, 1995), 327.

[42]   Vadakkekara notes that Indians commonly wrote on palm leaves, which do not preserve well. Heavy rainfall and humid climate also dampen the preservation of written texts. He also speculates that the Europeans may have destroyed many ancient documents. See ibid., 327–36.

[43]   Simon Hornblower, Antony Spawforth, and Esther Eidinow, eds., *The Oxford Classical Dictionary*, 4th ed. (Oxford: Oxford University Press, 2012), s.v. "Plutarch," by Donald A. Russell.

One way to approach this question is to consider the genre of the *Acts of Thomas*. Christine Thomas has suggested that the various Acts of this period, and other similar novels, are best categorized as historical fiction.[44] The mere fact that the *Acts of Thomas* contains known historical figures such as Thomas, Gondophares, Gad, and *possibly* even Habban and Xanthippe,[45] Mazdai,[46] and the city of Andrapolis,[47] indicates that it is not entirely divorced from a historical memory. Rather than inventing a narrative for the apostle, the authors of the Acts would elaborate upon a known historical tradition. In the romance novels of this time, focus was placed on retelling the most significant and well-known events from the public life of the individual, even though legendary material was clearly added. Christine Thomas provides a helpful comparison: "The Alexander romance provides the best generic parallel among the novelistic products of the Roman Empire. Alongside of the imaginative and improbable occurrences that form the fabric of the narrative, the romance also narrates all the best-known events of Alexander's life."[48]

The content of the *Acts of Thomas* can be compared with the other four ancient Acts—Peter, Paul, John, and Andrew.[49] When it comes to the *Acts of Peter*, *Acts of Paul*, and the *Acts of John*, even though they contain clear embellishment, external evidence indicates that they reliably convey the travels, preaching, and fate of each apostle. If there were no external corroboration for the post-Jerusalem lives of these apostles, many scholars would likely reject them as entirely fictional. And yet external evidence indicates they retain a historical nucleus. The *Acts of Thomas* is of the same genre and time period as the other aforementioned Acts. Even though we have no similar early external corroboration for *Acts of Thomas*, its reliability—on the core facts of the narrative, including the travels, preaching, and death of the apostle Thomas—seems at least more probable than not.[50] Kurikilamkatt asks an important question:

---

[44] Christine Thomas, *The Acts of Peter: Gospel Literature, and the Ancient Novel* (Oxford: Oxford University Press, 2003), 88–89.

[45] John N. Farquhar, "The Apostle Thomas in North India," in *Bulletin of the John Rylands Library*, 11:9; Farquhar, "The Apostle Thomas in South India," 11:46.

[46] F.A. D'Cruz suggests that king Mazdai may be identified with *Mahadeva*, a common name among kings of south India. F.A. D'Cruz, *St. Thomas, the Apostle in India: An Investigation on the Latest Researches in Connection with the Time-Honored Tradition Regarding the Martyrdom of St. Thomas in Southern India* (Madras, India: Hoe & Co., 1922), 50–51.

[47] Kurikilamkatt argues that the city of Andrapolis (Syriac calls it Sandruk Mahosa) is likely the city of Barygaza. He argues that there is etymological, linguistic, geographical, and historical evidence in favor of this conclusion. He even argues there was likely a Jewish presence in the first century. See Kurikilamkatt, *First Voyage*, 44–53.

[48] Thomas, *The Acts of Peter*, 88–89.

[49] A.F.J. Klijn, *The Acts of Thomas: Introduction, Text, and Commentary*, rev. ed. (Leiden, The Netherlands: Brill, 2003), 4.

[50] C.B. Firth, *An Introduction to Indian Church History* (Delhi, India: ISPCK, 2012), 12.

If the story did not have a historical background and if the readers of the book knew Thomas had gone to some places other than those mentioned in the *Ath* [*Acts of Thomas*], how could the author of the *Ath* believe that any credibility would be given to his story?[51]

Later tradition, as well as the lack of any competing tradition for his journeys and fate, helps confirm this conclusion.

Gondophares

The most significant find convincing many scholars of the historical core of *Acts of Thomas* was the discovery in 1834 of a collection of ancient coins in the Kabul Valley of Afghanistan. Ancient coins often provide similar information to modern coins, including the names of various rulers and kings. Among the many forgotten kings whose images christened these coins was the name "Gondophares" in a variety of spellings, including "Gundaphar," "Gundaphara," "Gondophernes," and "Gondapharasa." Many other coins were soon found in different regions, confirming the existence of Gondophares, and his family as well.[52] In addition, ruins have been discovered that many consider his former palace.[53] Subsequent research dated the coins to the first century AD. More specific dating became possible with the discovery of a stone tablet among the ruins of a Buddhist city near Peshawar that contained six lines of text in an Indo-Bactrian language. Moffett concludes: "Deciphered, the inscription not only named King Gundaphar, it dated him squarely in the early first century A.D., making him a contemporary of the apostle Thomas just as the maligned *Acts of Thomas* had described him."[54]

King Gondophares was not the creative imagination of an early third-century Edessan Christian, but a real king who ruled the north Indian region from the early to mid-first century, right during the time it is believed Thomas traveled to India. As valuable as this finding is, it does not prove that Thomas went beyond Parthia to India, especially since trade relations made knowledge of Gondophares and his kingdom readily available.[55] Even so, this remarkable finding does demonstrate the possibility that Thomas visited the court of Gondophares. The story is not necessarily a fictional tale about distant lands.

---

[51] Kurikilamkatt, *First Voyage*, 86.

[52] Medlycott, *India and the Apostle Thomas*, 14.

[53] Rooney, *Shadows in the Dark*, 38.

[54] Moffett, *A History of Christianity in Asia*, 29.

[55] George Huxley, "Geography in the *Acts of Thomas*," *Greek, Roman, and Byzantine Studies* 24 (1983): 75.

An additional point strengthens the credibility of the account. The *Acts of Thomas* mentions Gad, the brother of Gondophares. As many scholars have observed, Gad may also match the name "Gudana" that was found on some coins alongside Gondophares. While Gondophares may have been "specially memorable" outside northwest India, the same would not have been true for his brother Gad, of which there is no corroborative evidence beyond the *Acts of Thomas* and the coins.

Lourens van den Bosch objects to the significance of this find, proposing that the expression "Gudana" is an adjective derived from Gad. He claims that the coins marked with "Gudana" merely refer to one king, namely Gondophares. Thus, he concludes that Gad is a historical invention.[56] While this possibility cannot be completely ruled out, McGrath provides two helpful objections to the assertion.[57] First, the majority of scholars of Indian history understand "Gudana" as a proper name, rather than an adjective. If Indian scholars accept Gad as a historical person, says McGrath, Western scholars should not express an inordinate amount of skepticism. Second, if this line of reasoning were pressed even further, Gondophares might also be considered an adjective, since it is an alternative pronunciation of the Persian name Vindapharna, which means "The Winner of Glory." In addition, what strengthens the credibility of the encounter about Thomas and Gondophares is that it is one of the few narratives in the *Acts of Thomas* that is not focused on sexual abstinence.[58]

Yet if Thomas made it to northwest India, as the *Acts of Thomas* suggests, why is there no remnant of his labors in that particular locale? Why does no contemporary Christian community in northwest India claim descent from Thomas? Scholars have proposed various reasons for the absence of such a tradition.[59] Yet when it comes to southern India, there is an unmistakable community that claims to have apostolic roots.

St. Thomas Christians

Perhaps the most accurate rendition of the tradition surrounding Thomas in southern India is that of *The St. Thomas Christian Encyclopaedia of India*:

> According to Indian tradition, St. Thomas came by sea, and first landed at Cranganore about the year 52 A.D.; converted high case Hindu families in Cranganore, Palayur, Quilon and some other places; visited the Coromandel coast,

---

[56] Lourens P. van den Bosch, "India and the Apostolate of St. Thomas," in *The Apocryphal Acts of Thomas*, ed. Jan N. Bremmer (Leuven, Belgium: Peeters, 2001), 134.

[57] McGrath, "History and Fiction," x.

[58] Schnabel, *Early Christian Mission*, 1:883.

[59] Vadakkekara, *Origin of India's St. Thomas Christians*, 309; Kurikilamkatt, *First Voyage*, 179–206.

making conversions; crossed over to China and preached the Gospel; returned to India and organized the Christians of Malabar under some guides (priests) from among the leading families he had converted, and erected a few public places of worship. Then he moved to the Coromandel, and suffered martyrdom on or near the Little Mount. His body was brought to the town of Mylapore and was buried in a holy shrine he had built. Christians, goes the tradition, from Malabar, the Near East and even from China used to go on pilgrimage to Mylapore and venerate the tomb.[60]

Rather than being preserved in written text, the tradition of the St. Thomas Christians has been transmitted through songs, stories, legends, customs, and celebrations of the people. These various forms of oral tradition were how Indians at this time recorded their history. The St. Thomas Christians are utterly convinced that their heritage traces back to the apostle Thomas himself, including introduction of the Syriac or Chaldaic (East Syriac) language. The community has preserved many ancient antiquities that testify to their traditions.[61] Some of the names of the converts of Thomas have been preserved as part of this tradition, and are still remembered today in Kerala.[62] When the Portuguese landed in Malabar around 1500, they found an indigenous community of Christians who had already held for centuries that Thomas was their founder. Like the tradition contained in the *Acts of Thomas*, the southern tradition contains numerous legends, exaggerations, and conflicting episodes. But the core of the tradition remains: that Thomas travelled to southern India, preached to the people, established a community, and was martyred and buried at Mylapore.

This southern tradition is not necessarily in conflict with the northern tradition. There was political turmoil in the northern kingdom of Gondophares around AD 50, which provides a convenient explanation for why Thomas, according to tradition, arrived in the south around AD 52. The traditions, then, may be complementary rather than contradictory.

Indian scholar Benedict Vadakkekara provides five supporting reasons for the credibility of the tradition.[63] First, the mere existence of a community claiming apostolic roots speaks to the genuineness of the tradition. There must have been some significant reason, says Vadakkekara, why the Indian Christians chose Thomas. Second, the St. Thomas Christians are unique in claiming Thomas as

[60] George Menachery, ed., *The St. Thomas Christian Encyclopaedia of India* (Madras, India: BNK Press, 1982), 1:5.

[61] For a detailed study of early Christian antiquities in India, see H. Hosten, *Antiquities from San Thomé and Mylapore* (Mylapore, India: The Diocese of Mylapore, 1936).

[62] Placid J. Podipara, *Thomas Christians* (Bombay, India: Darton, Longman & Todd, 1970), 18–20.

[63] Vadakkekara, *Origin of India's St. Thomas Christians*, 125–43.

their founding apostle. The lack of competing traditions is a sign of the reliability of the St. Thomas tradition. Third, the community has passed down the tradition with consistency. Marco Polo notes (1288–98) the pilgrimages that Christians were making to the tomb of the apostle Thomas at Mylapore.[64] Fourth, the tradition has been unanimous among both Christians and non-Christians sources. There have been some denominational splits among the St. Thomas Christians, but they unanimously share the conviction that their community has apostolic roots. Fifth, while there are undeniable embellishments, the tradition has retained its pristine simplicity.

While these points are noteworthy, they are certainly not conclusive. Perhaps the most significant detail for many Indian scholars in helping to establish the voyage and fate of Thomas in India is that the tradition of the St. Thomas Christians shows some signs of being independent of the *Acts of Thomas*. The *Acts of Thomas* tells nothing of a south India mission, although it does indicate that he preached "the word of God in all India." The southern tradition contains vague hints of a northern mission, mentioning the land of Kusaya, but in the St. Thomas tradition we find not even a slight echo of the Gnostic and encratic theology of the *Acts of Thomas*. And perhaps most interesting is that the *Acts of Thomas* refers to Thomas as "Judas" or "Judas Thomas," the name by which he was known in the Syriac tradition. On the other hand, the south Indian tradition knows the apostle only as Thomas. This is significant, since the entire tradition rests upon the name and person of the apostle Thomas. Although he notes that there may have been an awareness of the *Acts of Thomas* in the south Indian tradition, Kurikilamkatt highlights the differences between the two:

> There is not a single story in the South Indian tradition that is borrowed from the *Ath* [*Acts of Thomas*]. Nor is there one in the *Ath* which is taken from the South. But the ones in the *Ath* are embellished with great amount of romantic descriptions and catechetical homilies. The missionary methods of the apostle also is quite differently characterised in the two traditions. No king is converted in the South, while in the *Ath* the conversion begins with royal folk. In the *Ath* the apostle is often found in the company of the royal personages. He is involved in intrigues, rivalries and festivities, all centered around royal palaces and the royalty. But, in the South, it is the Brahmins who have the leading role in the narratives.[65]

---

[64] The possibility of the existence of the tomb at Mylapore would not prove his martyrdom, since there is no debate that Thomas eventually died and must have been buried *somewhere*. But it would help support the reliability of the southern Indian tradition. There is no evidence the St. Thomas Christians ever venerated another site for his remains. For an analysis of the evidence the tomb of Mylapore offers for the Thomas tradition, see A. Mathias Mundadan, *From the Beginning up to the Middle of the Sixteenth Century up to 1542*, History of Christianity in India, vol. 1 (Bangalore, India: Theological Publications in India, 1984), 49–60.

[65] Kurikilamkatt, *First Voyage*, 178.

While the historical data tracing either Indian tradition all the way back to Thomas is elusive, the existence of two traditions that show signs of being independent weighs in favor of the basic details they share in common—that *Thomas was a missionary, preacher, and martyr in India.*[66]

Thomas the Martyr

While the evidence is not conclusive, a few reasons seem to indicate that it is at least *probable* that Thomas was martyred in India. First, we have no doubt a mission from Jerusalem to Rome was physically possible in the first century. Second, Thomas had seen the risen Jesus (John 20:26–29), was zealous in his willingness to suffer and die for him (John 11:16), had received the missionary call from Jesus (Matt 28:19–20; Acts 1:8), and, given all we know of him, fits the profile of someone who would take part in such an endeavor. Third, while the earliest written record in the *Acts of Thomas* clearly contains embellishment, it likely preserves a historical core of the apostle's journey and fate. Fourth, both the written tradition (*Acts of Thomas*, early church fathers) and the oral tradition agree on the general mode of how Thomas was killed.[67] Fifth, no other more compelling narrative exists for the travels and fate of Thomas. These points are far from conclusive, but they do move the critical scholar to the following observations:

1. Thomas traveled to India—*more probable than not* (*Acts of Thomas* 1; *Didascalia Apostolorum* 24; *Hippolytus on the Twelve*; Origen, *Commentary on Genesis* vol. 3; Clementine, *Recognitions* 9.29; St.

---

[66] Indian scholars consistently note that the two traditions regarding Thomas are independent. Yet it must be recognized that local traditions, such as the *Thomma Parvam*, share common stories with the *Acts of Thomas*. Thus, questions of dependency may not be as simple as Kurikilamkatt and Vadakkekara suggest. See Brown, *The Indian Christians of St. Thomas*, 48–52.

[67] The St. Thomas tradition claims that Brahmans killed Thomas with a single spear. According to the *Acts of Thomas*, the king ordered four soldiers to pierce him with spears. They differ over *who* killed Thomas, and the number of spears that were used, but they both agree on the manner of his death. The death of Thomas by a single spear is preserved in the Edessene, Nestorian, and Monophysite traditions, as well as the records of Assemani, the eighteenth-century scholar from the East. There is one popular exception that seems to contradict this. When Marco Polo landed in India (AD 1293), he reported that a stray arrow meant for a peacock accidentally killed Thomas. Nevertheless, a close inspection of his description of India reveals that Marco Polo regularly confused fact and fiction, and relied heavily on hearsay. See Medlycott, *India and the Apostle Thomas*, 20–42; and van den Bosch, "India and the Apostolate of St. Thomas," 147.

Gregory of Nazianzen, *Oration* 33.11; physical possibility of travel; lack of competing tradition; evidence for early Christians in India; St. Thomas Christians tradition).

2. Thomas experienced martyrdom—*more probable than not* (*Acts of Thomas*; early church fathers beginning in the third century; lack of competing tradition; St. Thomas Christians tradition).

Chapter 10

The Martyrdom of Andrew

The apostle Andrew, probably best known as Peter's brother (Mark 1:16), was a fisherman like his brother. Both Andrew and Peter became disciples of Jesus after he said, "Follow me, and I will make you fishers of men" (4:19b). Andrew first brought Peter to Jesus, making a remarkable Christological confession (John 1:41). This essential material regarding Andrew, that he was a fisherman in Galilee who followed the call of Jesus, seems to reflect an authentic Jesus tradition.[1]

The name Andrew is Greek for "manly." He was originally from Bethsaida, a city about twenty-five miles east of Nazareth on the Sea of Galilee (John 1:44), but he moved to Capernaum with his family. Before becoming one of the Twelve, he was a disciple of John the Baptist (John 1:3–42). Jesus undoubtedly made a powerful impression upon him. Andrew must have been utterly convinced that Jesus was the Messiah. While not all of John's disciples followed Jesus (John 3:25–27), Andrew did. And he immediately brought Peter to him, saying: "We have found the Messiah" (John 1:41b). Andrew likely received a similar education to his brother, but because he lived with Peter and his family at the beginning of his ministry, he may not have been married.

The Synoptics provide little information about Andrew. Mark reports one instance where Andrew joins Peter, James, and John in hearing Jesus's teaching on the Mount of Olives (13:3–37), where Jesus proclaims the destruction of the temple and its precincts. While most scholars conclude that Andrew was not among the inner circle, he may have been on the fringes of the group. Interestingly, there is an early tradition that Andrew was a member of the inner circle, perhaps even more prominent than his brother Peter. This finds support from a quote by Papias in his *The Sayings of the Lord Interpreted*, in which he lists Andrew as the first apostle he sought to learn about the words of Jesus (*Ecclesiastical History* 3.39). The *Muratorian Canon* also links Andrew to the origin of the Gospel of John. James Patrick believes these traditions, along with internal evidence from the Gospel of John, reveal that Andrew was in fact the closest disciple to Jesus, and was the Beloved Disciple.[2] While Patrick

---

[1] Craig S. Keener, *A Commentary on the Gospel of Matthew* (Grand Rapids, MI: Eerdmans, 1999), 148–50.

[2] James Patrick, *Andrew of Bethsaida and the Johannine Circle* (New York: Peter Lang, 2013), 58–59.

believes the presbyter John wrote the fourth Gospel, he credits Andrew and the rest of the Johannine circle as being the source behind the stories.[3] While this hypothesis has not met with widespread approval in the scholarly community, it does raise interesting questions about the role and significance of Andrew in the early church.

Andrew is mentioned three times in the Gospel of John. On two of these occasions, he is mentioned along with Philip (6:8; 12:12). And the third time, he is mentioned right before Philip (cf. 1:40, 1:44). Clearly, there was some special connection between these two.

Every time Andrew appears in John, he is bringing someone to Jesus. The first time, he brings Peter to Jesus (1:41–42). In the second instance, Andrew brings to Jesus a small boy who has five small loaves of bread and two fish (6:8). The third time involves some Greeks who want to worship Jesus. They first approach Philip, who tells Andrew about their request, and Andrew decides the two of them should tell Jesus together (12:20–22). It may seem that Philip went to Andrew because he was closer to Jesus, but Colin Kruse suggests he approached Andrew with the request because he was the only other member of the Twelve who had a Greek name.[4] Philip may have been unsure whether Jesus would accept Gentiles, so together they approached Jesus.

Some have even speculated that Andrew first brought Philip to Jesus.[5] If so, then Andrew would be indirectly responsible for Nathanael hearing about Jesus as well (John 1:45). Whether or not this is true, Andrew is unmistakably characterized as having a missionary mindset from the moment he meets Jesus.

Ronald Brownrigg captures what can seemingly be known about the character of Andrew:

> Compared with his bombastic brother, Andrew emerges as a sensitive and approachable man who always had time and patience to listen to enquiries, even from children and foreigners. He was a selfless and considerate man, who did not resent the leadership of his brother. If his brother, Peter, was the skipper of the crew, Andrew was indeed the "ferry man" always willing to take people to Jesus. He was a kindly and faithful disciple, not fearful of ridicule even though he offered a picnic basket to feed five thousand. Although himself a Jew, he enabled Greeks to meet Jesus and he has been called the first "home missionary" as well as the first "foreign" missionary of the Christian church.[6]

---

3   Patrick, *Andrew of Bethsaida and the Johannine Circle*, 68.

4   Colin G. Kruse, *John: An Introduction and Commentary*, ed. Leon Morris, Tyndale New Testament Commentaries (Downers Grove, IL: InterVarsity Press, 2003), 264.

5   William LaSor, *Great Personalities of the New Testament* (Westwood, NJ: Revell, 1952), 58.

6   Ronald Brownrigg, *The Twelve Apostles* (New York: Macmillan, 1974), 46–47.

Beginning in the second century, Andrew became a popular figure in apocryphal writings such as the *Acts of Andrew*, the *Acts of Andrew and Matthias,* the *Acts of Peter and Andrew*, the *Acts of Andrew and Bartholomew*, and the *Pistis Sophia*.

As with the other disciples, Andrew was an eyewitness of the risen Jesus (1 Cor 15:5; Matt 28:9–10; Luke 24:36–53; John 20:19–23). He is one of the chief disciples mentioned in John, and witnessed the events the Gospel records, as well as many more that were not recorded (John 20:30, 21:25). He was willing to suffer for his conviction that Jesus is the Messiah (Acts 5:17–42). And many ancient traditions state that Andrew was in fact persecuted for his faith.[7] Despite a substantial record of his travels and persecutions, there is no record he ever wavered in his commitment to Jesus Christ.

Missionary Endeavors of Andrew

The earliest information about the missionary travels of Andrew comes from Origen, who states that he went to Scythia, in southern Russia.[8] Eucherius of Lyons (d. *c.* 450) and *Hippolytus on the Twelve* also mention Andrew preaching in Scythia. There were Jews in the surrounding area of Scythia from the time of the first century BC, and given the easy route of access to Scythia from Jerusalem, it was a logical place for Andrew to missionize. In their heyday, the nomadic Scythians were a vital political and economic force.[9] They were polytheistic and deeply superstitious.[10] Tertullian includes Scythia in his list of nations the Gospel has reached by the time he writes at the end of the second century.[11] Given the date of the tradition, as well as the plausibility of travel to Scythia in the first century AD, Francis Dvornik concludes that this tradition by Origen "seems to be well founded."[12]

While many scholars agree Andrew traveled to Scythia, substantial disagreement exists regarding the remaining traditions, including his martyrdom. Stewart Lamont believes evidence is lacking for the martyrdom tradition.[13] On the other hand, William Barclay concludes: "Even if we doubt the details, we

---

[7]   See George Alexandrou and Nun Nectaria McLees, "The Astonishing Missionary Journeys of the Apostle Andrew," *Road to Emmaus* 4 (2010): 48.

[8]   "Commentary on Genesis," in Eusebius, *Ecclesiastical History* 3:1.

[9]   Tamara Rice, *The Scythians* (New York: Frederick A. Praeger, 1957), 23.

[10]   Rice, *The Scythians*, 85–86.

[11]   Tertullian, *An Answer to the Jews* VII.

[12]   Francis Dvornik, *The Idea of Apostolicity in Byzantium and the Legend of the Apostle Andrew* (Cambridge, MA: Harvard University Press, 1958), 199.

[13]   Stewart Lamont, *The Life of Saint Andrew* (London: Hodder & Stoughton, 1997), 41.

cannot doubt that Andrew died a martyr for his Master."[14] Yet, as will be seen, the truth is likely somewhere between these two perspectives.

Greek scholar George Alexandrou wrote a 1,000-page book on the missionary travels of Andrew called *He Raised the Cross on the Ice*.[15] His goal was not to critique the traditions, but to begin with the assumption that all the evidence is at least possible.[16] He then lined up all the traditions of Andrew to see if he could trace his missionary travels with any level of probability. Alexandrou concluded: "It was like a train, one car after another, until I had only twenty years missing from St. Andrew's return to the Black Sea from Valaamo until he went to Sinope—and from there to Patras in Achaia, to his martyrdom."[17] Alexandrou eventually found a tradition of Andrew living in a cave in Romania for twenty years that fit the gap in his timeline exactly. Perhaps the most interesting finding from his studies is how smoothly the traditions fit together when they are lined up chronologically and geographically.[18]

According to Alexandrou, ancient traditions reveal four missionary journeys of Andrew that include locations such as Constantinople, Pontus, central Asia, Ethiopia, Georgia,[19] southern Russia, and more. Given the travel conditions of the first century, Alexandrou concludes that there is nothing intrinsically impossible about each of these missionary journeys. Given the current state of information, it is impossible to determine the validity of every single account, yet it seems overly skeptical to dismiss them entirely as legendary.

The first tradition that Andrew was in Patrae (Greece), the traditional site of his martyrdom, is found in the *Acts of Andrew*, which is typically dated between the middle of the second century and the beginning of the third. Four other

---

[14]   William Barclay, *The Master's Men* (London: SCM Press, 1960), 43.

[15]   At the time of this writing, Alexandrou had not yet published his book. He has worked with over fifty different languages to chronicle all the traditions surrounding the travels of the apostle Andrew and to see if they could plausibly fit together. He revealed some of his preliminary findings in his article. See Alexandrou and McLees, "The Astonishing Missionary Journeys," 3–55.

[16]   Ibid., 13.

[17]   Ibid.

[18]   The one exception Alexandrou notes is the tradition that Andrew went to Scotland, which likely originated in the seventh century. See Marinell Ash and Dauvit Brown, "The Adoption of Saint Andrew as Patron Saint of Scotland," in *Medieval Art and Architecture in the Diocese of St Andrews*, ed. John Higgit (London: British Archaeological Association, 1994), 16–24. Also, see Peter Ross, *Saint Andrew: The Disciple, the Missionary, the Patron Saint* (New York: The Scottish American, 1886).

[19]   According to tradition, Andrew visited Georgia three times. On his third journey, he was joined by Simon the Zealot and Matthias. See Giuli Alasania, "Twenty Centuries of Christianity in Georgia," *IBSU International Refereed Multi-Disciplinary Scientific Journal* 1 (2006): 117–18.

sources mention his sojourn in Greece before the dawn of the sixth century.[20] Thus, the tradition that Andrew ministered in Greece is consistent, widespread, and relatively early. Ursula Hall finds the tradition of Andrew visiting Greece doubtful, because it was the missionary field of other men, in particular Paul.[21] It is not clear, however, why it is implausible for a number of men to minister in the same region. Paul often visited cities such as Corinth that already had an established community of believers. Peter and Paul both went to Rome. Some claim that both Thomas and Bartholomew visited India. Whether this tradition is true or not is irrelevant. The point is that there is nothing implausible about two or more apostles ministering in the same place, as Hall suggests was the case for Andrew and Greece.

According to the Syriac *Teaching of the Apostles*,[22] Andrew ministered in Nicaea, Nicomedia, Bithynia, and inner Galatia. This is similar to where Peter ministered (1 Pet 1:1). Given that the disciples often went out in twos (Mark 6:7; Luke 10:1), some scholars have suggested that Andrew may have ministered for a period with his brother Peter.[23] Lamont questions this tradition, since earlier traditions place him in the region of the Black Sea.[24] There is nothing chronologically or geographically impossible about Andrew ministering in both regions. As for the apostles, the *Teaching of the Apostles* also cites that James wrote in Jerusalem, Simon [Peter] in Rome, John from Ephesus, and Judas Thomas from India. Given that the author got these ascriptions correct, at least according to my assessment, it is at least probable he also got the tradition correct about Andrew.

A few factors make at least *some* missionary travels of Andrew highly likely, even if we cannot currently ascertain the probability of every individual tradition. First, multiple traditions exist involving Andrew. Unlike the apostle Thomas, who was consistently considered an apostle of the East or greater India, Andrew has multiple traditions throughout Judea, Africa, central Asia, and Europe. The chances that all of them are fictional seem remote. Second, as Alexandrou observes, even though the traditions developed independently, they naturally line up chronologically and geographically. Third, the earliest accounts of Andrew, found in the Gospels, reveal Andrew as having a missionary mindset; it is within the known character of Andrew to engage in missions.

---

[20] Philastrius, *de Haeresibus liber* 88; Gregory of Nazianzen, *Oration* 33.11; Jerome, *Ad Marcellum*; Evodius, *de Fide contra Manichaeos*; Theodoretus, *Interpretatio in Psalmos* 116.

[21] Ursula Hall, *The Cross of St. Andrew* (Edinburgh, Scotland: Birlinn, 2006), 13.

[22] William Cureton, *Ancient Syriac Documents* (London: Williams & Norgate, 1864), 34.

[23] Thomas E. Schmidt, *The Apostles After Acts: A Sequel* (Eugene, OR: Cascade, 2013), 154.

[24] Lamont, *The Life of Saint Andrew*, 43.

Fourth, archaeological evidence has been found to support certain traditions.[25] When these four considerations are combined with the commission by Jesus to evangelize the world (Matt 28:19–20; Acts 1:8), and the early textual evidence that the apostles actually carried out this commission, we have convincing reason to believe Andrew was a missionary who advanced the Gospel of Christ.

Evidence of the Martyrdom of Andrew

The earliest known written source reporting the martyrdom of Andrew is the *Acts of Andrew* (*c.* AD 150–210), which begins with the summoning of Andrew by Maximilla, the wife of the proconsul Aegeates, to cast a demon out of a servant boy. After seeing Andrew deliver the boy, Stratocles, the brother of Aegeates, joins Maximilla in becoming a disciple of Andrew. With Andrew's encouragement, Maximilla began to resist the sexual advances of her husband in an attempt to love God alone. Knowing he would be upset, Maximilla devised a plan to have a servant girl named Euclia sleep with Aegeates in her place, which lasted about eight months until Aegeates discovered that Andrew was behind the change in his wife—for which Aegeates had Andrew thrown in prison, promising to release him only if Maximilla would sleep with him and bear his children. But Andrew refused to back down, proclaiming that he would rather be killed. Aegeates had Andrew crucified, but without nails, so he would experience the torment of being eaten by dogs if he were still alive at night. In perhaps the most memorable scene from the *Acts of Andrew*, Andrew speaks to the cross as he approaches the site of crucifixion, and commands the executioners to carry out their orders. He preaches for four days from the cross until a large crowd demands Aegeates release him. But Andrew refuses to accept the pardon, and dies by crucifixion.[26] After the death of Andrew, Maximilla leaves Aegeates, and he commits suicide by leaping from a tall height. Unlike Peter, Paul, and Thomas in their respective Acts, Andrew does not appear again after his death.

There is significant debate about when to date the *Acts of Andrew*, ranging from the middle of the second century to the beginning of the third. The *Acts of Andrew* may very well fall within the range of living memory, but we cannot be sure. Many later written accounts exist of the death of Andrew, but they can be

---

[25]   See Vakhtang Licheli, "St. Andrew in Samtskhe—Archaeological Proof?", in *Ancient Christianity in the Caucasus*, ed. Tamila Mgaloblishvili (New York: Curzon Press, 1998), 37.

[26]   The *Acts of Andrew* does not mention the "St. Andrew's cross," which is shaped like an X. That was first associated with him in the fourteenth century. See Frederick W. Norris, "Acts of Andrew," in *Encyclopedia of Early Christianity*, ed. Everett Ferguson (New York: Garland, 1997), 1:11.

traced back only through the *Acts of Andrew*.[27] This is also likely true for ancient calendars as well as liturgical prayers such as the *Irish Palimpsest Sacramentary* and the *Missale Gothicum* (*c.* AD 700).[28]

One possible independent early source, *Hippolytus on the Twelve*, attributed to Hippolytus, a third-century bishop,[29] says: "Andrew preached to the Scythians and Thracians, and was crucified, suspended on an olive tree, at Patrae, a town of Achaia; and there too he was buried."[30] This account confirms the mission to Scythia as reported by Origen, but also the crucifixion in Patras as stated by the *Acts of Andrew*. Interestingly, it mentions Andrew was crucified "upright on an olive tree," which may indicate it is an independent tradition.[31] Even if Hippolytus did not write this work, it may be early. Nevertheless, given the questions that remain about this text, the matter of the reliability of the martyrdom account of Andrew rests largely upon the trustworthiness of the tradition behind the *Acts of Andrew*.

Between the third and ninth centuries, the *Acts of Andrew* was widely read and diffused in such diverse places as Africa, Egypt, Palestine, Syria, Armenia, Asia Minor, Greece, Italy, Gaul, and Spain.[32] Its original form has not survived, but scholars have reconstructed a version that likely comes close to the earliest version.[33] Judging from the various versions of the *Acts of Andrew*, the original text consisted of the missionary travels of Andrew and his journey to Patras, where he was executed. Fernando Lanzilotta observes that "the textual witnesses

---

[27]   Peter M. Peterson, *Andrew, Brother of Simon Peter: His History and His Legends* (Leiden, The Netherlands: Brill, 1958), 14–23, 40–43.

[28]   Els Rose, "Apocryphal Tradition in Medieval Latin Liturgy: A New Research Project Illustrated with the Case of the Apostle Andrew," *Apocrypha* 15 (2004): 115–38.

[29]   Hippolytus is often considered one of the most important church figures of the third century, but there is substantial debate about what texts are genuinely his and which are spurious. See David Dunbar, "The Problem of Hippolytus of Rome: A Study in Historical-Critical Reconstruction," *Journal of the Evangelical Theological Society* 25 (1982): 63–74. Also see Ulrich Volp, "Hippolytus," *Expository Times* 120 (2009): 521–29.

[30]   Pseudo-Hippolytus, *Hippolytus on the Twelve*, as cited in *The Ante-Nicene Fathers: Translations of the Writings of the Fathers down to A.D. 325: Fathers of the Third Century*, ed. Alexander Roberts and James Donaldson, rev. A. Cleveland Coxe (Buffalo, NY: Christian Literature Co., 1885), 5:255.

[31]   There are different traditions that report Andrew died "on an olive tree," or "on a tree," or simply by crucifixion. There are even some later traditions that Andrew was crucified upside-down.

[32]   Wilhelm Schneemelcher, ed., *New Testament Apocrypha*, trans. R.M. Wilson (Louisville, KY: Westminster John Knox Press, 2003), 2:104.

[33]   The most reliable translation is by Dennis MacDonald. While MacDonald concedes that some parts of his reconstruction are conjectural, the martyrdom text is secure. Dennis R. MacDonald, *The Acts of Andrew and the Acts of Andrew and Matthias in the City of Cannibals* (Atlanta, GA: Scholars Press, 1990), ix.

for the martyrdom are more numerous and their testimony somewhat more homogeneous" when compared with the travels of Andrew.[34] And yet he notes that some of the early texts contain a few quick notes about his death, rather than a developed martyrdom account. Nevertheless, even though we have seen a variety of adaptations, the activity and death of Andrew in Patras was the goal of his voyage, and likely part of the original text.[35] All the recensions of the *Acts of Andrew* share his conflict with pagan authorities which leads to his death.[36]

Eusebius provides the earliest reference to the *Acts of Andrew*. He suggests the *Acts of Andrew*, as well as the *Acts of John* and other Apocryphal Acts, should be "cast aside as absurd and impious."[37] It should be noted that in rejecting the *Acts of Andrew*, Eusebius was not rejecting that it had *any* claim to historicity; he rejected it *theologically*. In the same section, Eusebius discusses the *Acts of Andrew*, he also rejects the Gospel of Peter as heretical. Yet he clearly believes the Gospel of Peter was correct to affirm the resurrection of Jesus as a historical fact, even though it also contained other material Eusebius rejected. The same may be true for the historical kernel in the *Acts of Andrew*. As a whole, the *Acts of Andrew* received a mixed reception in the early church—ranging from condemnation (Pope Innocent I) to adaptation and use for popular piety (Gregory of Tours).

Like the rest of the Apocryphal Acts, the *Acts of Andrew* contains clear legendary embellishment. Given that the sixth century Bishop Gregory of Tours combines the more legend-filled and fantastic *Acts of Andrew and Matthias* with the *Acts of Andrew*, some have concluded that it belonged to the original text.[38] But this seems unlikely.[39] The key question is whether or not the *Acts of Andrew* preserves a historical nucleus. Taken at its core, it reports the missionary travels of Andrew and his ministry and execution in Patras. While the *Acts of Peter, Paul, Thomas,* and *John* contain legendary accretion, they also preserve the most

---

[34] Fernando Lautaro Roig Lanzilotta, "The Apocryphal Acts of Andrew: A New Approach to the Character, Thought and Meaning of the Primitive Text" (PhD. diss., Rijksuniversiteit Groningen, 2004), 348.

[35] Hans Josef Klauck, *The Apocryphal Acts of the Apostles*, trans. Brian McNeil (Waco, TX: Baylor University Press, 2008), 114.

[36] Johannes Quasten, *The Beginnings of Patristic Literature*, Patrology, vol. 1 (Westminster, MD: Newman, 1950), 1:138.

[37] Eusebius, *Ecclesiastical History*, 3.25.6, as cited in *Nicene and Post-Nicene Fathers: Eusebius: Church History, Life of Constantine the Great, and Oration in Praise of Constantine*, ed. Philip Schaff and Henry Wace (New York: Christian Literature Co., 1890), 1:157.

[38] MacDonald, *The Acts of Andrew*, 22–47.

[39] Hilhorst and Lalleman provide 11 substantial differences between the two documents. They argue the *Acts of Andrew and Matthias* was likely written two centuries later than the *Acts of Andrew* (A. Hilhorst and Pieter J. Lalleman, "The Acts of Andrew: Is it Part of the Original Acts of Andrew?", in *The Apocryphal Acts of Andrew*, ed. Jan N. Bremmer [Leuven, Belgium: Peeters, 2000], 13).

reliable destination and fate for their respective apostles, including a natural death for John. External corroboration confirms that the various Acts likely got the fate of these apostles correct. Although the writer of the various Apocryphal Acts had creative license, he or she was also bound by known tradition. Is it not reasonable to conclude that the same is likely true for the *Acts of Andrew*, even though it is not possible to verify the claims externally in the same way as the other Apocryphal Acts?

For all their diversity, the five Apocryphal Acts share at least five structural similarities.[40] To these points, it could also be added that each Act builds toward and reaches its climax with the fate of the apostle. These similarities do not imply any special relationship between individual Acts, but they do show the authors followed a similar script and approach in chronicling the activities of each apostle. The authors clearly invent unbelievable stories for their respective apostles, but they are connected by a known historical tradition nonetheless.

The Apocryphal Acts were frequently grouped together because of their theology and genre. For instance, Eusebius condemns the various Apocryphal Acts together as a group, and the Manichaeans lumped them together in a special corpus they used as scripture instead of the biblical book of Acts. Given the similarities in structure and genre, we have no good reason to doubt that the *Acts of Andrew*—like the other four Apocryphal Acts—is a historical novel that preserved the known fate of the apostle Andrew toward the end of the second century.

Dvornik rejects this tradition because he finds it strange that Eusebius does not report any missionary travels of Andrew beyond Scythia, including his fate in Patras.[41] Given that Origen had been to Achaia, Dvornik finds it more likely that Andrew never made it there, and simply died in Scythia. But even if Dvornik is right, Andrew still may have died as a martyr in Scythia. In *The Contendings of the Apostles*, Budge records that Andrew died by crucifixion in Scythia.[42]

Dvornik suggests the facts are not quite as straightforward. While Eusebius clearly cites Origen as the source for his information in this section about the journeys of the apostles Thomas, Andrew, John, Peter, and Paul, he does not quote Origen specifically. Since Origen's *Commentary on Genesis* is not extant, it is not possible to determine in what manner Eusebius was utilizing his source. Eusebius could have been summarizing Origen, pulling out the information he felt necessary. He may have included all the information Origen wrote about, or merely part of it. It is at least possible Origen included it in his *Commentary*,

---

[40]   Pieter J. Lalleman, "The Acts of Andrew and the Acts of John," in *The Apocryphal Acts of Andrew*, ed. Jan N. Bremmer (Leuven, Belgium: Peeters, 2000), 141.

[41]   Ibid., 211.

[42]   E.A. Wallis Budge, *The Contendings of the Apostles: Being the Histories and the Lives and Martyrdoms and Deaths of the Twelve Apostles and Evangelists* (London: Oxford University Press, 1935), 181–85.

but Eusebius left it out for some unknown reason. This may seem strange, but Eusebius does discuss other known martyrs without including their deaths, so it is entirely plausible he would do the same with Andrew.[43]

Even if Origen did not include further information about Andrew in his original *Commentary*, it does not follow, as Dvornik suggests, that he knew nothing of the tradition. Maybe he wrote about it elsewhere. It is certainly fair to ask why Origen may not have included it, but it is unreasonable to assume silence here implies a false account and that Origen was completely unaware of such a tradition. The objection thus provides minimal reason to doubt the tradition of Andrew's death in Patras. Given the agnosticism concerning how Eusebius used his source, Dvornik is unwarranted in concluding definitively that the tradition regarding the martyrdom of Andrew did not exist in Achaia during the time of Origen.

Following Dvornik's lead, Lamont finds it strange that Luke, who likely wrote his Gospel in Achaia, never mentions the tradition that Andrew died in Patras, so Lamont and Dvornik conclude that Andrew likely never visited there.[44] However, this is also an argument from silence. As we have already seen, Luke leaves out seemingly important details such as the fate of Peter, Paul and James the brother of Jesus, because he had a different purpose for his writings from merely tracing the lives of the individual apostles. As interesting and important as the question of the fate of Andrew is to this investigation, it was not the primary or even a secondary matter for Luke. It is not surprising that Luke would ignore the fate of Andrew in Achaia.

Finally, we ought to consider the persecution of Christians in Greece during the time Andrew was traditionally put to death (*c.* AD 65–69). No record exists of formal state-directed persecution against Christians in Greece during this period. Yet the date falls directly during the time of the Neronian persecution in Rome. As noted previously, Christians were specifically targeted as scapegoats, starting with the fire in Rome in AD 64. Given the precedent set by Caesar at the capital of Rome, it is entirely plausible that a local governor used Christians as a scapegoat for some political reason as well. Or, if there was some local religious disturbance, such as the kind that lead to the persecution of Paul or the death of Jesus, a provincial governor may have put Andrew to death.

Determining the likelihood of the fate of Andrew is a difficult task. The evidence is clearly not as demonstrative as for Peter, Paul, and James. Although she considers the traditional fate for Andrew in Patras "not impossible," Ursula

---

[43]   As an example, Eusebius mentions Hippolytus of Rome (*Ecclesiastical History* 6.20, 22, 39) without mentioning the traditions of his martyrdom. Hippolytus was probably a disciple of Irenaeus, and thus may have been linked back to the apostles through Polycarp and John.

[44]   Lamont, *The Life of Saint Andrew*, 42.

Hall believes there is "no positive evidence to support it."[45] Her conclusion is understandable, and is certainly a reasonable inference from the evidence. Yet, while the evidence is admittedly weaker than for other apostles, there is at least *some* evidence that cannot be simply dismissed. I cannot believe that the earliest traditions of the works and fate of the apostle Andrew, an important and well-known figure in the first and second centuries, were *entirely fabricated*, unconnected to a reliable tradition.

We cannot dismiss the consistent and relatively early account of his fate by crucifixion. Some accounts differ as to where he was crucified, but there is broad agreement that he died in this manner.[46] There is no early contrary tradition claiming a natural death, which for an apostle as prominent as Andrew is not insignificant. Minimally, it must be deemed at least plausible that Andrew died as a martyr. While some scholars may be inclined to take a more critical view, the evidence seems to point ever so slightly towards the following conclusions:

1. Andrew engaged in missions—*very probably true* (*Acts of Andrew*; Origen, *Commentary on Genesis* vol. 3, in Eusebius, *Ecclesiastical History* 3.1; *Teachings of the Apostles*; Andrew had a missionary mindset [John 1:41, 6:8–9, 12:22]; geographical and chronological fit of various traditions; archaeological support; evidence the apostles generally engaged in missions).

2. Andrew went to Greece—*more probable than not* (*Acts of Andrew*; Philastrius, *de Haeresibus liber* 88; Gregory of Nazianzen, *Oration* 33.11; Jerome *Ad Marcellum*; Evodius, *de Fide contra Manichaeos*; Theodoretus, *Commentary on Psalm 116*).

3. Andrew experienced martyrdom—*more plausible than not* (*Acts of Andrew*; *Hippolytus on the Twelve Apostles* 2; Peter Chrysologus of Ravenna, Sermon 133: "Saint Andrew the Apostle"; lack of competing narrative; acceptance of tradition in the East and West).

---

[45]   Hall, *The Cross of Saint Andrew*, 14.

[46]   It is difficult to assess the merits of Andrew's death specifically by crucifixion. In one sense, it could have been invented to make his fate similar to both Jesus and his brother Andrew. There was certainly a tendency in the third and fourth centuries to give the apostles "fitting" deaths. On the other hand, there are multiple accounts of his crucifixion, even if they differ as to the location and whether or not he was executed on a cross or a tree. Death by crucifixion shows up in the earliest account, the *Acts of Andrew*. Crucifixion was a common penalty for criminals and other enemies of the state and so it is entirely believable Andrew was crucified for either creating disturbances or upsetting the proconsul, as the *Acts of Andrew* reports. Yet the tradition Andrew was crucified on an X-shaped cross is almost certainly false. It plays no role in the *Acts of Andrew*. There is no evidence the Romans crucified with such a cross, and the earliest record of the X-shaped cross being used for his death comes from the twelfth century. See Hall, *The Cross of St. Andrew*, 31, 73, 101.

Chapter 11
Martyrdom of James, Son of Zebedee

James, the son of Zebedee, one of the first disciples called by Jesus, is among the first three in each list of the apostles. In Mark, James is mentioned second after Peter (Mark 3:17), and in Matthew, Luke, and Acts he comes third (Matt 10:2; Luke 6:14; Acts 1:13). Since James is most often listed before John, and John is almost consistently referred to as "the brother of James," many scholars believe James was the elder brother.[1] James and John both left their fishing business and followed Jesus when he personally called them (Matt 4:21–22; Luke 5:10), although their quick response suggests possible earlier contact. He is often called James the Great, to differentiate him from James the Little (Mark 15:40), James, the son of Alphaeus (Mark 3:18), and James the brother of Jesus (Gal 1:19).

Along with John his brother and Peter, James was among the privileged circle of the apostles. He was present at the Mount of Olives (Mark 13:3), witnessed the raising of the daughter of Jairus (Mark 5:37–42) and the transfiguration (Mark 9:2–13; Matt 17:1–13; Luke 9:28–36), and joined Jesus in the Garden of Gethsemane (14:32–42). As noted in Chapter 8 on the apostle John, it is interesting that these three instances each relate to death—*preparing* for death (Jesus in Gethsemane), *rising* from the dead (Jairus's daughter), and *appearing* after death (Jesus, Moses, and Elijah). Considering that James saw the risen Jesus (John 21:1–2) as well, it is clear that he would have had tremendous confidence and firsthand convictions to face death as a follower of Jesus.

Given how prominent James was among the apostles, it is remarkable we do not have more information about him. Still, the New Testament provides some material, and stories and legends about him develop in the ensuing centuries. For instance, in Book 7 of his *Outlines*, Clement tells the story of a man brought into court with James who was so moved by his testimony that he also confessed Christ.[2] This story is likely legendary embellishment. Nevertheless, it is interesting that Clement does confirm the death of James by beheading as reported by Luke, even if he adds this additional tale. The tradition of his death, then, was firm by this time and taken for granted.

---

[1]   David Noel Freedman, ed., *The Anchor Bible Dictionary* (New York: Doubleday, 1992), s.v. "James," by Donald A. Hagner.

[2]   Eusebius, *Ecclesiastical History* 2.9.3, as cited in *Nicene and Post-Nicene Fathers: Eusebius: Church History, Life of Constantine the Great, and Oration in Praise of Constantine*, ed. Philip Schaff and Henry Wace (New York: Christian Literature Co., 1890), 1:111.

Other legendary accounts of the apostle James begin to crop up in the ensuing centuries. *The Apostolic History of Abdias* (sixth/seventh century) tells a story of James and his interaction with two pagan magicians who eventually confess Christ. *The Acts of Saint James in India* reports a tradition that he went to India along with Peter.[3] Given the late date of composition and the lack of any local accounts of their visit, Eastern and Western scholars are united in dismissing this latter account as legendary. James has also become the patron saint of Spain. According to the tradition, James preached in Spain, and returned to Judea shortly before his death. Given the short timespan between Pentecost and James's martyrdom, the trip to Spain seems unlikely. And since the earliest written record of James's visit to Spain is in the seventh century (*c.* AD 600), most scholars dismiss it as legendary.[4] The most likely reason apocryphal accounts are rare for James is because his martyrdom in Judea (AD 44) was so firmly entrenched in the early church and limited the trajectory of such stories.

While these missionary accounts are likely fictional, we have good reason to believe the death of James occurred while the apostles were on the brink of world missions. When Judas died, the apostles immediately appointed Matthias as successor (Acts 1:15–26), yet they did not reconstitute the Twelve after the execution of James (Acts 12:2). In fact, the death of James serves more as a backdrop for the protection of Peter and his departure to another place (12:6–17),[5] which began the expansion of the Gospel to the "ends of the earth" (1:8). Riesner observes:

> When Peter, as the leader among the twelve, now left the holy city and the holy land itself, now completely under the rule of Agrippa I, this marked a clear cut in the activity on behalf of Israel itself. This absence of any reestablishment of the circle of twelve to its entirety betrays a consciousness of living in a new age, one in which missionary efforts on behalf of the older people of God in Jerusalem and in the holy land no longer constituted the only task.[6]

Even though Jesus had earlier commanded the apostles to spread out and reach the world (1:8), the tipping point seemed to come at the death of James. With his death, persecution was no longer propagated by the religious leaders of the

---

[3]   E.A. Wallis Budge, *The Contendings of the Apostles: Being the Histories and the Lives and Martyrdoms and Deaths of the Twelve Apostles and Evangelists* (London: Oxford University Press, 1935), 246–52.

[4]   John Williams and Alison Stones, eds., *The Codex Calixtinus and the Shrine of St. James* (Tübingen, Germany: Gunter Narr Verlag, 1992), 41–42.

[5]   Hans Conzelmann, *Acts of the Apostles*, Hermeneia, trans. James Limburg, A. Thomas Krabel, and Donald H. Juel (Philadelphia, PA: Fortress Press, 1972), 93.

[6]   Rainer Riesner, *Paul's Early Period: Chronology, Mission, Strategy, Theology*, trans. Doug Stott (Grand Rapids, MI: Eerdmans, 1998), 121.

Jews, but by Herod Agrippa I, an official of the state. The apostles were forced to leave Jerusalem and begin reaching out to the "ends of the earth."

Jesus had predicted that James would suffer and die for his faith. In Mark 10:35–45, James and John approach Jesus, requesting that he give them what they ask for. After they request to reign with him, he tells them they must drink his "cup" (10:39). Scholars are split over whether this refers to suffering or death, but the passage's most natural reading indicates that Jesus is prophesying that they would both die for their faith. Questions remain about the fate of John, but the earliest evidence indicates Herod Agrippa had James put to death (Acts 12:2).

Evidence for the Martyrdom of James, Son of Zebedee

One of the most unexpected elements in the book of Acts is the brief mention of the death of James by King Agrippa: "About that time Herod the king laid violent hands on some who belonged to the church. He killed James the brother of John with the sword" (Acts 12:1–2). The brevity of this account is what makes it so unexpected. This is only the second reference to James in the entire book of Acts, apart from his mention in the list of the Twelve (1:13). Why did Luke mention him so briefly, especially since he was in the inner circle of Jesus? Given the amount of space dedicated to the martyrdom of Stephen (6:8–7:58), one would expect Luke to provide more information on the fate of James.

One possibility is that Luke simply did not know any more than he reports. But this seems unlikely, and raises a further question: How could he—and the church—have forgotten the tradition of such a prominent apostle? Controversial questions in the book of Acts typically raise issues that one would expect Luke to have less information about, such as private conversations or events that were distant geographically or chronologically.[7] But the death of James is an area in which Luke would be expected to have reliable information—since it would have been public knowledge.

We must remember that Acts is not strictly a book about the apostles *per se*, but about the spread of the Gospel to the "ends of the earth" (1:8). The title "Acts of the Apostles" is technically a misnomer. The apostles are only included in the narrative insofar as they advance the Gospel worldwide, in fulfillment of the theme of Acts. It may also be surprising that Acts does not report the deaths of Peter and Paul, but as demonstrated earlier, such reports were not integral to Luke's wider purpose. It may be puzzling why Luke does not include more about the fate of James. But the brief report indicates why Peter was arrested, which

---

[7]   Craig S. Keener, *Acts: An Exegetical Commentary* (Grand Rapids, MI: Baker, 2012), 1:102.

in turn shows his departure to another place and the shift in the narrative to the focus on the missions of Saul (13). The brief account of the death of James fits the pattern of Luke focusing on details necessary to advance his larger goal.

The brevity of the account may be unexpected, but it does serve to strengthen its reliability. It has the ring of authenticity, and lacks details of legendary development. This is clear when the narrative is compared with the execution of Stephen. Shelly Matthews suggests that the parallels in the Stephen episode are the result of the motif of *imitatio Christi*, rather than genuine historical concern.[8] While the historicity of Stephen is a separate matter from this inquiry, it is important to recognize that this critique would not apply to the death of James. No parallels are drawn between his death and Jesus. No legendary details creep into the narrative. In fact, quite the opposite is true. The account reads like an official execution.[9]

Why Was James Killed?

King Herod Agrippa, who ruled Judea in AD 41–44 and was the grandson of King Herod the Great, ordered the execution of James. After thirty-five years of direct Roman control through procurators, many Jews welcomed a Herodian ruler. Some of his admirers may have even considered him a potential Messiah.[10] Josephus records the fondness with which many remembered Agrippa I (*Antiquities of the Jews* 19.328–331). His popularity among the Jews may help explain why he specifically targeted Christians for persecution. Although he had seemingly tolerated Christians at the beginning of his reign, at some point "he laid violent hands on some who belonged to the church" with the specific intent of doing evil to them.[11]

King Herod Agrippa had James put to death by the sword, with the likely intent of snuffing out the movement from the top down. It may seem unlikely Agrippa would utilize death by sword rather than a more brutal method such as burning, impaling, or crucifixion. But as Keener notes, death by sword is not implausible since Josephus reports on other occasions that Agrippa showed mercy even to his enemies.[12]

---

[8]   Shelly Matthew, *Perfect Martyr: The Stoning of Stephen and the Construction of Christian Identity* (Oxford: Oxford University Press, 2010), 15–20.

[9]   James D.G. Dunn, *Beginning from Jerusalem: Christianity in the Making* (Grand Rapids, MI: Eerdmans, 2009), 2:209.

[10]   Wolf Wirgin, *Herod Agrippa 1: King of the Jews*, Monograph Series, vol. 10(A) (Leeds, England: Leeds University Oriental Society, 1968), 79.

[11]   Darrell L. Bock, *Acts*, Baker Exegetical Commentary on the New Testament (Grand Rapids, MI: Baker, 2007), 424.

[12]   Keener, *Acts*, 2:1872.

According to Jewish law, execution by sword was the punishment for murder or apostasy (*m. Sanhedrin* 9:1; Deut 13:6–18).[13] Herod lived as a faithful Jew, so he would naturally have been concerned to stop the growth of any heretical sect. According to Deuteronomy 13:6–18, if an individual entices the Jews to "go and serve other gods," then that person is to be stoned to death. But if that person entices the entire city to follow other gods, then that person is to be killed by the sword. Simon Kistemaker concludes: "In the eyes of Herod Agrippa, James had led the city of Jerusalem astray."[14] Agrippa seemingly had both political and religious reasons for having James killed by sword.

Brownrigg may be overstating the case when he concludes that the martyrdom account of James is "absolutely reliable,"[15] but he is right to emphasize that the tradition is early and consistent and has a very high historical probability of being true. Not only is the tradition of the martyrdom of James emphasized in the biblical record (Acts 12:2; Mark 10:39), it is also consistently affirmed by later church fathers from the second century onwards.[16]

Does Acts Record History?

Richard Pervo has challenged the idea that the genre of Acts is apologetic history. He believes the writing of Acts has more in common with ancient fiction than historiography. Pervo concludes: "Luke's achievement as a historian lies more in his success at creating history than in recording it."[17] In other words, he sees Acts as one kind of historical novel that contains much more fiction than history. On his view, there would be little reason to take the report of the death of James as historical, since Luke was more interested in advancing the early movement evangelistically than in reporting sober truth.

Pervo notes a number of the techniques that Acts shares with ancient fiction.[18] While these parallels are literarily insightful, his approach ignores the many features of ancient romances that are absent from Acts as well. Ben Witherington concludes: "The essential problem for Pervo is that he must

---

[13]   William J. Larkin, *Acts*, The IVP New Testament Commentary (Downers Grove, IL: InterVarsity Press, 1995), 182.

[14]   Simon J. Kistemaker, *Exposition of the Acts of the Apostles*, New Testament Commentary (Grand Rapids, MI: Baker, 1993), 433.

[15]   Ronald Brownrigg, *The Twelve Apostles* (New York: Macmillan, 1974), 94.

[16]   Clement of Alexandria, *Outlines* Book 7; Eusebius, *Ecclesiastical History* 2.9.1; Chrysostom, *Homilies on the Acts of the Apostles* 26; Gregory of Nyssa, *Homily 2: On Stephen*; Philip of Side, *Christian History*; *The Apostolic Acts of Abdias* (Latin text).

[17]   Richard I. Pervo, *Acts: A Commentary on the Book of Acts*, Hermeneia (Minneapolis, MN: Fortress Press, 2009), 18.

[18]   Ibid., 17.

define the ancient novel much too widely in order to include Acts within its compass, and he must strain to show that Acts has features that are *distinctive* of, not merely characteristic of, ancient novels."[19]

Witherington concedes that viewing Acts as a novel reveals some fruitful literary insights. Yet he says: "It must also be said that there are clearly some indisputable historical traditions being used in this section involving the death of James and Agrippa."[20] Even if Pervo were right about the genre of Acts, it would still likely follow that Acts 12:1–2 contains genuine historical tradition regarding the fate of James.

We have good reason, then, to believe that Acts is apologetic historiography.[21] And we have ample evidence that Acts is a generally reliable historical document and can be confirmed in most cases.[22] Bart Ehrman argues that the narrative structure of Acts, which focuses on chronicling the historical development of the Christian church, is closely related to other histories produced in antiquity.[23] While this does not definitively prove the account in Acts 12:1–2 is historical, it does mean it should get the benefit of doubt. If Luke can be confirmed as accurate on the accounts that can be investigated, it gives reason to trust his accounts when they cannot. The burden of proof is thus on those who doubt the early, consistent, and reliable tradition that James, the son of Zebedee was the first apostolic martyr.

1. James experienced martyrdom in Jerusalem under Herod Agrippa I—*highest possible probability* (Acts 12:1–2; Mark 10:39; Clement of Alexandria, *Outlines*, Book 7 [Eusebius, *Ecclesiastical History* 2.9]; Chrysostom, *Homilies on the Acts of the Apostles* 26; Gregory of Nyssa; *Homily 2 On Stephen*; Philip of Side, Papias fragment; lack of any competing tradition).

---

[19] Ben Witherington III, *The Acts of the Apostles: A Socio-Rhetorical Commentary* (Grand Rapids, MI: Eerdmans, 1998), 378; emphasis in original.

[20] Ibid., 381.

[21] Keener, *Acts*, 1:51–165.

[22] For instance, see C.K. Barrett, "The Historicity of Acts," *Journal of Theological Studies* 50:2 (1999): 515–34; Colin Hemer, *The Book of Acts in the Setting of Hellenistic History*, ed. Conrad H. Gempf (Winona Lake, IN: Eisenbrauns, 1990); Keener, *Acts*, 1:166–220.

[23] Bart D. Ehrman, *A Brief Introduction to the New Testament*, 3rd ed. (Oxford: Oxford University Press, 2013), 166.

Chapter 12
Martyrdom of Philip

The apostle Philip appears in the Synoptic tradition only in the lists of the apostles (Matt 10:3; Mark 3:18; Luke 6:14). He always appears fifth, behind Peter, Andrew, James, and John. Along with Peter and James, the son of Alphaeus, Philip is one of three apostles who always appear in the same position in the apostolic lists—first, fifth, and ninth respectively—which may indicate their leadership roles over their respective subgroups.[1] In Acts 1:13, Philip again appears fifth, but this time he is paired next to Thomas rather than Bartholomew. Philip is clearly among the middle-level apostles, and given his consistent primary listing among this group, he may have had some degree of prominence and responsibility within the Twelve.

The Scriptural Philip

John 1:43–48: The Call of Philip

Philip appears most frequently in the Gospel of John, which describes him as coming from Bethsaida, the "town of the apostles"[2] (John 1:44). He may have been a disciple of John the Baptist, since Jesus called him to discipleship near Bethany, where John was baptizing. The day after calling Peter and Andrew, Jesus went to Galilee and found Philip, and said to him: "Follow me" (John 1:43). The text does not specifically say that he chose to follow Jesus, but the implication is clear, since Philip immediately goes to Nathanael and proclaims that he has found the Messiah (1:45). Yet Nathanael responds with incredulity: "Can anything good come out of Nazareth?" Rather than giving an answer, Philip merely invites Nathanael to come and see Jesus in person and consider the evidence himself (1:46).

This brief episode of the call of Philip reveals three important things about his character. First, he was expecting the Messiah. He spoke of Jesus as the one

---

[1]   Beltran Villegas, "Peter, Philip, and James of Alphaeus," *New Testament Studies* 33 (1987): 292–94.

[2]   The Gospels specifically link Peter, Andrew, and Philip to Bethsaida. The association of the apostle Philip to this city is appropriate since Philip, son of Herod, governed the surrounding region. See Fred Strickert, *Philip's City: From Bethsaida to Julias* (Collegeville, MN: Liturgical Press, 2011), 47–48.

to whom the Old Testament Scriptures bore witness (cf. Luke 24:27). Second, Philip had a missionary mindset. As Andrew had brought Peter, and possibly Philip, to Jesus, Philip in turn witnesses to Nathanael. Third, Philip was a personal witness of Jesus and could act as a legal witness on his behalf.[3] Like the other apostles, he was an eyewitness of the *risen* Jesus (Acts 1:3), and was willing to suffer for that conviction (Acts 5:17).

John 6:1–15: Feeding the Five Thousand

Philip appears a second time in John's Gospel for the feeding of the five thousand (6:1–15), the only miracle story recorded in all four Gospels. In the Johannine account, there was not enough food for them to eat, so Jesus asked Philip: "Where are we to buy bread, so that these people may eat?" (6:5). Jesus decided to test Philip, even though he already knew how he would feed them. Philip replied: "Two hundred denarii worth of bread would not be enough for each of them to get a little." Even though John reports "the signs that he [Jesus] was doing on the sick" (6:2), Philip perceives the problem entirely on a human level, hopelessly wondering how they could produce the means to feed all the people. While it is not entirely clear why Jesus chose Philip, the point of Jesus's question was to determine whether Philip understood who he was. Although he does answer Jesus, clearly Philip, like the rest of the disciples, does not yet fully understand his mission or identity. Even though Jesus had turned water to wine at Cana (2:1–12), Philip failed to see that he could do the same with the fish and bread.

John 12:20–36: Some Greeks Seek Jesus

In this brief account, some Greeks come to see Jesus in Jerusalem during Passover. Josephus speaks of a large number of Greeks coming to worship at Passover, but of their not being allowed to offer sacrifices.[4] There is scholarly disagreement about the identity of the Greeks. But it is clear they were outsiders captivated by Jesus. The Greeks had become fascinated by the powerful stories of Jesus and wanted to meet him personally. They first come to Philip, who takes them to Andrew, who in turn brings them to Jesus. It seems likely the story singles out Philip and Andrew because they are the only two disciples with Greek names. Since Philip takes their request to Andrew rather than directly to Jesus, he seems to clearly understand his moderating role among the apostles.

---

[3]   George R. Beasley-Murray, *John*, Word Biblical Commentary, vol. 36 (Nashville, TN: Thomas Nelson, 1999), 29.

[4]   Josephus, *Wars* 6.426–427.

John 14:8–21: Jesus Answers Philip

The final passage involving Philip occurs during the Last Supper. Jesus was telling his disciples to believe in him since he is going to prepare a place for them in heaven. Thomas asks how they can know the way, and Jesus famously replies: "I am the way, and the truth, and the life. No one comes to the Father except through me. If you had known me, you would have known my Father also. From now on you do know him and have seen him" (John 14:6–7). Then Philip speaks up and says: "Lord, show us the Father, and it is enough for us" (14:8). Jesus gently rebukes Philip for not yet knowing him, and by extension, the Father (14:9–11).

As in the earlier case when Philip spoke up at the feeding of the five thousand, his response characterizes the ill-informed and dull-witted nature of the apostles who do not yet understand the full extent of who Jesus is. Philip wanted to see the Father with his physical eyes through some sort of theophany, as Moses experienced. But he failed to realize the far greater privilege he had personally been granted by being with Jesus.[5] Based on the criterion of embarrassment, this story has the ring of authenticity and is likely reliable. Tenney explains what this reveals about the character of Philip:

> If Thomas was a skeptic, Philip was a realist. Having determined in his thinking that the Father of whom Jesus spoke must be the Ultimate Absolute, Philip demanded that he and his associates might see him. Philip was materialistic; apparently abstractions meant little to him. Nevertheless he had a deep desire to experience God for himself. If he and the other disciples could only apprehend God with at least one of their senses, they would be satisfied.[6]

Traditions about Philip

Traditions about Philip emerge in the second century onward. One of the difficulties in knowing what traditions apply to the apostle Philip is that he seems to be frequently conflated with Philip the evangelist (Acts 6:5; 8:4–8; 21:8–9). One tradition identifies Philip as the disciple who requested to bury his father before following Jesus (Matt 8:21; Luke 9:56; Clement, *Stromata* 3.4.25; 4.9.73).[7] A Coptic *Gospel of Philip* is used by Gnostics and Manicheans

---

5   William Hendriksen, *Exposition of the Gospel According to John*, New Testament Commentary (Grand Rapids, MI: Baker, 1953), 2:269–70.

6   Merrill C. Tenney, *John*, in vol. 9 of *The Expositor's Bible Commentary*, ed. J.D. Douglas and Frank E. Gaebelein (Grand Rapids, MI: Zondervan, 1981), 145.

7   David Noel Freedman, ed., *Anchor Bible Dictionary* (New York: Doubleday, 1992), s.v. "Philip," by Wesley W. Isenberg.

which dates to the mid-fourth century, but is likely dependent upon an earlier Greek text. It is technically anonymous, and may bear the title "Philip" since he is the only apostle mentioned by name (73:9–14).[8] Philip also appears in other Gnostic writings, such as *Pistis Sophia* and the *Book of Jews*, as a mediator between their teachings and Christ. *The Letter of Philip to Peter* is a late second- or third-century document from the Nag Hammadi library that emphasizes the leadership role of Peter and the importance of suffering. Given that Philip is named fifth in the apostolic lists and his prominence in John, it should come as no surprise that he is a common figure in apocryphal texts of the second century onward. In fact, considering his influence in the Gospels, Acts, and non-canonical works of the second century onward, Christopher Matthews argues that Philip's name should be included among the select group of apostles who guaranteed the accurate transmission of the faith in the early Christian era.[9]

Missionary Travels of Philip

Later traditions place Philip in Parthia, Athens, Scythia—among the Anthropophagi[10]—and various cities in Asia for his missionary journeys. There is also a tradition by Isidore of Seville (AD 560–636) that the apostle Philip preached in France (*De ortu et obitu partum*, c. 72), but this tradition is difficult to substantiate.[11] The earliest and most consistent tradition places Philip in Hierapolis. In the early second century, Papias is the first to mention that Philip went to Hierapolis.[12] This finds further support in the writings of Polycrates and Gaius,[13] as well as later apocryphal works such as the *Acts of Philip* and *The Apostolic Acts of Abdias* (Book X). Thomas Schmidt says there is good reason to believe Philip preached in Hierapolis, but qualifies his position with the

---

    8   Ibid.
    9   Christopher R. Matthews, *Philip: Apostle and Evangelist* (Boston, MA: Brill, 2002), 1. It must be recognized that the arguments of Matthews rest upon his assumption that there was only one Philip in the early church, and thus traditions from the New Testament, early church fathers, and apocryphal texts all provide information for Philip. Therefore, if he is mistaken about there being one Philip, then his claim may be an overstatement about the significance of the apostle Philip in guarding early church traditions.
    10   The tradition that places Philip among the Anthropophagi is found in the third-/fourth-century *Manichaean Psalms* and the *Irish Biblical Apocrypha*.
    11   Els Rose, *Ritual Memory: The Apocryphal Acts and Liturgical Commemoration in the Early Medieval West (c. 500–1251)* (Leiden, The Netherlands: Brill, 2009), 128, 136–37.
    12   Papias, *Expositions of the Oracles of the Lord*, in Eusebius, *Ecclesiastical History* 3.39.9.
    13   The writings of both Polycrates and Gaius are recorded in Eusebius, *Ecclesiastical History* 3.31.2–5.

possibility that early church fathers conflated Philip the apostle with Philip the evangelist or that there was later confusion by Eusebius.[14]

There is no good reason to doubt that Philip engaged in missionary activity, even though there is debate about the particular locale. In his first appearance in the Gospel of John, Philip shows his missionary intent by inviting Nathanael to come and see the Messiah (1:45–46). Philip had seen the risen Jesus and personally received the commission to take the Gospel to the world (Matt 28:19–20; Acts 1:8). Given the general evidence the apostles engaged in missionary activity, as well as the variety of traditions from the second century onward, there is little reason to doubt Philip left Jerusalem to proclaim the Gospel.

Which Philip?

One of the difficulties in tracing the missionary endeavors and fate of the apostle Philip is the existence of Philip the evangelist in Acts, apparently a different figure than the apostle (6:1–6; 8:4–14, 26–40; 21:8–9). Given the number of stories in Acts about Philip the evangelist, Barclay concludes that more is known about him than about the apostle Philip.[15] Philip the evangelist has been suggested as the author of a number of anonymous New Testament documents of which authorship is unknown.[16] McBirnie concludes that there is no good reason to doubt that the apostle Philip ministered and met his fate in Hierapolis. Yet surprisingly, McBirnie makes no attempt to distinguish the apostle Philip from Philip the evangelist, and he may have conflated traditions concerning the two.

Acts 6:1–7

In the book of Acts, the apostle Philip only appears by name in the apostolic list (1:13). In Acts 6, the Twelve choose seven to help serve widows in the daily distribution of food. Among the seven are Philip and Stephen (6:5). The Twelve lay their hands on them in prayer, and commission them for service. In this passage, Luke is clearly distinguishing the two Philips, since he uses the term "twelve" to refer to the original apostles in contrast with the newly appointed "seven."

---

[14]   Thomas E. Schmidt, *The Apostles After Acts: A Sequel* (Eugene, OR: Cascade, 2013), 143.

[15]   William Barclay, *The Master's Men* (London: SCM Press, 1960), 84.

[16]   Philip the evangelist has been proposed as the author of the first 13 chapters of the Gospel of Mark, special material in Luke's Gospel (infancy stories, Sermon on the Plain, travel narrative in the middle section), the prime source for the Samaritan tradition in John, and the book of Hebrews. See F. Scott Spencer, *The Portrait of Philip in Acts*, Journal for the Study of the New Testament Supplement Series, vol. 67, ed. Stanley E. Porter (Sheffield, England: JSOT, 1992), 15–16.

Acts 8:14–25

The evangelist Philip appears again in Acts 8. After the martyrdom of Stephen, Christians were scattered throughout Judea and Samaria. While Saul is ravaging the church and the apostles remain in Jerusalem, Luke shifts the story to the missionary work of the evangelist Philip in Samaria, revealing that the preaching of the Gospel is not limited to the Twelve, but also includes Stephen and Philip. It is not merely the Twelve who take the Gospel from Jerusalem to Judea to Samaria and to "the ends of the earth" (Acts 1:8). Philip proclaimed Christ, performed many signs and wonders, and as a result, there was much joy in the city (8:6–8). Even Simon the magician believed when he saw the signs Philip performed (8:9–13).

When the Twelve heard about the work of God in Samaria, they sent Peter and John so they might receive the Holy Spirit (8:14–16). Two key observations are important. First, Peter and John realize that messianic salvation is universally offered to all, including the Samaritans.[17] While Philip was the author and initiator of salvation, the apostles completed the work of salvation in Samaria. Second, the mission of Philip is only complete when the apostolic witnesses, Peter and John, come to pray for the Holy Spirit. The need for apostolic prayers for the reception of the Holy Spirit is not set up as a normative pattern for new believers. Normally, the spirit comes by faith (Acts 2:38; 1 Cor 12:3, 13). Yet these are unique circumstances to indicate that God is breaking through old barriers in a new way.[18] If the Philip of this story were an apostle, he would have been able to lay hands on the Samaritans *himself* so they would receive the Holy Spirit. The fact that he needs an apostolic witness underscores that Luke does not view this Philip as a member of the Twelve, but as a separate evangelist.

Acts 8:26–40

The evangelist Philip appears as the main character in one more narrative, involving an Ethiopian eunuch (8:26–40). After Samaria, an angel guided Philip to head south to the road from Jerusalem to Gaza. He met an Ethiopian eunuch, a court official of the queen of Ethiopia (Nubia), reading the book of Isaiah. Philip shared with him the meaning of the passage, and then baptized him by the side of the road. Both Irenaeus and Eusebius report that the Ethiopian eunuch became a missionary to his own people.[19] Philip was taken away by the Lord and preached in multiple towns until he came to Caesarea.

---

[17] David G. Peterson, *The Acts of the Apostles*, Pillar New Testament Commentary (Grand Rapids, MI: Eerdmans, 2009), 285.

[18] Darrell L. Bock, *Acts*, Baker Exegetical Commentary on the New Testament (Grand Rapids, MI: Baker, 2007), 256–57.331.

[19] Irenaeus, *Against Heresies* 3.12.10; Eusebius, *Ecclesiastical History* 2.1.

Acts 21:8–9

The final time Philip the evangelist appears is roughly twenty years later, still living in Caesarea (Acts 21:8–9). In this passage, Luke is clearly referring to the evangelist Philip, since he refers to him as "one of the seven." This reference is the first indication the evangelist Philip has four daughters. The earlier passages involving Philip are written from the third-person perspective, but this latter passage appears in the "we" section, and thus provides incidental confirmation for its integrity. When these three passages are considered, Luke unmistakably considers the apostle and the evangelist to be separate individuals who share the name Philip.

It may seem strange that Luke would commit so much space in his narrative to the work of a figure who was not even an apostle. Still, if Luke were inventing the story, it seems far more likely he would have given credit for such an important missiological breakthrough to one of the apostles. The fact that he highlights the work of an otherwise obscure evangelist provides support for the credibility of the narrative.

Evidence from the Early Church

Luke clearly portrays the two Philips as separate individuals with distinct roles; however, confusion regarding their identities seems to arise in the second century, when traditions about Philip emerge in the writings of the early church fathers. Scholars take three general positions in identifying various traditions of Philip.

The Two Philips Were Blended in the Early Church

Papias, bishop of Hierapolis, wrote the earliest known non-canonical statement about Philip. Eusebius claims that Papias learned key truths about the faith from those who directly knew Jesus. He provides a direct quote from Papias:

> If, then, any one came, who had been a follower of the elders, I questioned him in regard to the words of the elders—what Andrew or what Peter said, or what was said by Philip, or by Thomas, or by James, or by John, or by Matthew, or by any other of the disciples of the Lord.[20]

---

[20] Papias, *Exposition of Oracles of the Lord,* as quoted in Eusebius, *Ecclesiastical History* 3.39.4a, as cited in *Nicene and Post-Nicene Fathers: Eusebius: Church History, Life of Constantine the Great, and Oration in Praise of Constantine,* ed. Philip Schaff and Henry Wace (New York: Christian Literature Co., 1890), 1:171.

Eusebius also reports that Papias personally heard miraculous stories from the daughters of the apostle Philip, who lived at Hierapolis.[21] Papias clearly refers to the apostle Philip, since he pairs him with Thomas, James, John, and Matthew.

Earlier in the *Ecclesiastical History*, Eusebius reports the missionary travels of Philip the "diaconate." Eusebius reports his preaching in Samaria, his success and fame, and his interaction with the Ethiopian eunuch.[22] Clearly, Eusebius understands this Philip to be the evangelist, not the apostle, since all these stories adhere with the accounts in Acts. But later, he seems to conflate the two. He cites a letter from the Ephesian bishop Polycrates that refers to John and Philip the apostle:

> For in Asia also great lights have fallen asleep, which shall rise again on the last day, at the coming of the Lord, when he shall come with glory from heaven and shall seek out all the saints. Among these are Philip, one of the twelve apostles, who sleeps in Hierapolis and his two aged virgin daughters, and another daughter who lived in the Holy Spirit and now rests at Ephesus."[23]

Then Eusebius quotes Proclus in the Dialogue of Gaius: "After him there were four prophetesses, the daughters of Philip, at Hierapolis in Asia. Their tomb is there and the tomb of their father."[24] Finally, Eusebius cites the biblical writer Luke to indicate that Philip and his daughters were at Caesarea.[25]

It is difficult to avoid the conclusion that Eusebius has confused traditions regarding the two different Philips, since clearly Eusebius believes that all three of the quotes he included in *Ecclesiastical History* refer to Philip the apostle. The first quotation by Polycrates is introduced specifically as referring to the apostle Philip. And before the second quote by Proclus, Eusebius says that he "speaks similarly about the deaths of Philip and his daughters." He gives no indication he is referring to a different Philip. In the final quotation, Eusebius clearly believes that the Philip who moved to Caesarea and was one of the seven was the apostle Philip, even though the passage in Acts is clear they are distinct. Tertullian seems

---

[21]   Eusebius, *Ecclesiastical History* 3.39.8–9. Eusebius apparently contradicts his own report about whether or not he met the apostles in person. In ibid. 3.39.1–4, Eusebius states that Papias was not a direct hearer of the apostles, but garnered their teachings from those who knew them firsthand. Yet in ibid. 3.39–8-9, he states that Papias directly knew the apostle Philip and his daughters.

[22]   Ibid. 2.1.10–14.

[23]   Polycrates (an epistle), in Eusebius, *Ecclesiastical History* 3.31.3, as quoted in Eusebius, *Ecclesiastical History* 3.39.4a, as cited in *Nicene and Post-Nicene Fathers: Eusebius: Church History, Life of Constantine the Great, and Oration in Praise of Constantine*, ed. Philip Schaff and Henry Wace (New York: Christian Literature Co., 1890), 1:162.

[24]   Eusebius, *Ecclesiastical History* 3.31.4.

[25]   Ibid. 3.31.5.

also to have confused the two Philips, attributing the baptism of the Ethiopian eunuch to an "apostle."[26] The Calendar of the Coptic and Armenian Churches commemorates Philip as "deacon and apostle."[27] A similar conflation may have also occurred in the *Letter of Peter to Philip* (second/third century), a Gnostic text that came to light in the Nag Hammadi collection.[28] And the *Acts of Philip* likely conflated traditions of the apostle Philip with the deacon and evangelist.[29] This is why most scholars conclude that both Philips were fused as one in later church tradition, although later medieval authors do distinguish them.[30] If this view is correct, it would be exceedingly difficult to know which traditions of his travels and fate accurately apply to the apostle Philip as opposed to the evangelist.

There Were Two Philips, Both with Daughters

In contrast, J.B. Lightfoot has provided four reasons why he believes the Philip at Hierapolis is the apostle, not the evangelist.[31] First, Polycrates (*c.* AD 130–196), the earliest witness, distinctly says that the apostle Philip resided in Hierapolis with his daughters and is buried there. Second, the subsequent historical account by Proclus is questionable in its authenticity, at least a quarter of a century later, and is suspicious in form—it reports four daughters instead of three. Third, the relationship between John and Philip would likely draw him to Asia after John. Incidents involving Philip had special interest for the writer of John as well as his audience. Fourth, Papias mentions Philip the apostle in his list of those he gathered stories from, but he never mentions Philip the evangelist. It seems natural, claims Lightfoot, that when Eusebius later mentions his interactions with the daughters of Philip, he is referring to the same person. Thus, Lightfoot concludes: "There is no improbability in supposing that both the Philips were married and had daughters."[32] Although often dismissed by contemporary scholars, this view deserves greater consideration than it typically receives. It may seem unlikely, but it is certainly not impossible. The second and third arguments above are somewhat speculative, but the first and last have some merit. That there were two Philips with daughters, and that the apostle Philip

---

26   Tertullian, *Concerning Baptism* 18.

27   Barclay, *The Master's Men*, 84.

28   Fred Lapham, *An Introduction to the New Testament Apocrypha* (New York: T. & T. Clark, 2003), 78–79.

29   Wilhelm Schneemelcher, ed., *New Testament Apocrypha*, trans. R.M. Wilson (Louisville, KY: Westminster John Knox Press, 2003), 2:469.

30   Rose, *Ritual Memory*, 126.

31   J.B. Lightfoot, *St. Paul's Epistles to the Colossians and to Philemon*, rev. ed. (Grand Rapids, MI: Zondervan, 1879), 46, accessed May 1, 2014, https://archive.org/details/saintpaulsepistl1880ligh.

32   Ibid., 46.

travelled to Hierapolis is certainly a live possibility. If this view were correct, it would provide some confidence that the apostle Philip met his fate in Hierapolis.

There Was Only One Philip

A final option for the identity of Philip is that there was only one Philip, who was *both* apostle and evangelist. In an extensive study on Philip, based upon his 1993 Harvard dissertation, Christopher Matthews suggests there was only one historical figure Philip, who was used by the early church in a variety of ways. Thus, the Gospels, Acts, early church fathers, as well as other non-canonical texts all refer to the same apostle Philip, who was also an evangelist.

To support his thesis, Matthews provides three primary arguments. First, he argues that the reason scholars largely agree that early church fathers confused the two Philips is because they accept Lukan priority.[33] According to Matthews, if scholars recognized that Papias was a contemporary of Luke, who was at least as reliable historically, then they would see that the evangelist and apostle are one and the same. Second, the available onomastic evidence for Palestine suggests it is quite unlikely two early Christian figures would both have the name Philip.[34] Third, the term "evangelist" for Philip does not exclude him also being an apostle.[35] Even Martin Hengel and F.F. Bruce concede the plausibility of this approach.[36]

Although this is certainly not an *impossible* reconciliation of the data, the question is whether it is the most *probable*. Significant questions can be raised against each of the points mentioned. First, while it is true that the case for two separate Philips rests largely upon Lukan priority, dismissing Luke is not so easily done. Against the consensus of most scholars, Matthews dates Papias before AD 110.[37] Even if this dating were correct, it is still at least a generation after standard dating for Acts. Although a strong case can be made for dating Acts in the 60s, many scholars date it to AD 80–90. Thus, it is minimally one generation *before* the writings of Papias. If the early dating of Acts is correct, as well as the later dating for Papias, they may even be two generations removed. While Papias undoubtedly falls within the living memory of the apostles, Matthews needs to provide solid reasons for dating Acts late and Papias early before scholars reject Lukan priority.

---

[33]   Matthews, *Philip*, 2, 15.

[34]   Ibid., 16–19.

[35]   Ibid., 93.

[36]   Martin Hengel, *Saint Peter: The Underestimated Apostle*, trans. Thomas H. Trapp (Grand Rapids, MI: Eerdmans, 2010), 118; F.F. Bruce, "Philip and the Ethiopian," *Journal of Semitic Studies* 34 (1989): 378.

[37]   Matthews, *Philip*, 31.

Second, the onomastic evidence indicates that Philip was not among the most common names for Jewish men of Palestine. It ranks sixty-first—seven instances from 330 BC to AD 200.[38] Nevertheless, the fact that it was borne by several Macedonian kings, including the father of Alexander the Great, as well as a son of Herod the Great suggests it was not entirely uncommon either.[39] The unlikelihood that Philip would be the name of two prominent early Christian figures, as Matthews suggests, must be considered in light of the entirety of onomastic evidence for the Twelve. Richard Bauckham has observed that the frequency of names for the Twelve fits nicely with the onomastic evidence of ancient Jewish Palestine.[40] When considered against the prominence of certain individuals named Philip and the overall accurate frequency of apostolic names in the wider Jewish culture, the claim that there was likely only one Philip loses its force. If numerous Philips appeared in the New Testament, the onomastic evidence would present concern, but the mere existence of *two* individuals named Philip, a name that is not entirely uncommon, provides minimal reason to overturn the Lukan tradition.

Third, these points must also be coupled with the unlikelihood that Luke would invent a fictional character named Philip. Why would Luke intentionally name a significant character Philip if the name is so unlikely, as Matthews suggests, when it could so easily lead to confusion? And more pressing, if Luke felt free to "to redescribe literarily or 'reinvent' known personalities or events in order to conform them to the needs of his narrative presentation,"[41] then why invent a non-apostolic character to preach so successfully, perform such powerful signs, and be the first to take the Gospel outside Judea? It seems far more likely Luke would have imparted this role to a member of the Twelve, or at least to a more prominent individual such as Paul, Timothy, or Barnabas. Craig Keener observes:

> Likewise, he [Luke] would hardly invent from whole cloth Philip's ministry to a Gentile (8:26–40), since he already has the standard, institutional version of the earliest Gentile mission in the Cornelius narrative (Acts 10–11). Assuming Philip was a fairly reliable informant (and he seems to have been trusted by Paul and Caesarean church, 21:8–10), Luke's account of Philip's ministry in 8:5–40 likely is Luke's rendition of genuine historical truth.[42]

---

[38] Richard Bauckham, *Jesus and the Eyewitnesses: The Gospels as Eyewitness Testimony* (Grand Rapids, MI: Eerdmans, 2006), 102.

[39] C.K. Barrett, *A Critical and Exegetical Commentary on the Acts of the Apostles* (New York: T. & T. Clark, 1994), 1:315.

[40] Bauckham, *Jesus and the Eyewitnesses*, 102.

[41] Matthews, *Philip*, 65.

[42] Craig S. Keener, *Acts: An Exegetical Commentary* (Grand Rapids, MI: Baker, 2013), 2:1,488.

Even though Jesus had personally commissioned the apostles to reach Samaria (Acts 1:8), Philip the evangelist, not one of the Twelve, fulfilled this command. It seems unlikely Luke would invent this narrative, and potentially cast the apostles in a negative light. The fact that Peter and John, who represented the apostles (cf. Acts 3:1–7; 4:20), came to approve of the ministry in Samaria shows that Luke viewed the apostle and evangelist as separate individuals.

The most likely reason Luke includes two separate Philips, and ascribes the traditions in Acts 6, 8, and 21 to the evangelist, is that this was the earliest account he received during his investigation (Luke 1:1–4; Acts 1:1–3). Comparing the various accounts of Philip in Acts, F. Scott Spencer concludes:

> Finally, the nexus between 8.1 and 8.4–5 sets apart the itinerant evangelist, Philip, from the company of apostles who remain in Jerusalem. This distinction goes back to 6.1–7 and becomes a critical factor in 8.14–25. Moreover, it eliminates any prospect of identifying Philip the evangelist with his apostolic namesake (Lk. 6.1; Acts 1.13).[43]

Nevertheless, if the traditions do in fact refer to one Philip, both apostle and evangelist, then there would be little reason to question his journey and death in Hierapolis. Still, while adopting this view would make the martyrdom of Philip in Hierapolis more likely, the evidence simply does not warrant it.

There is no easy answer to the question of the identity of the apostle Philip after the New Testament era. The existence of two Philips in Hierapolis is a live possibility that should not so easily be dismissed. Yet the majority position that early church fathers conflated the two Philips seems most probable, as this also happened with other apostles, such as Matthew and Matthias, and the various biblical figures named James.

Evidence for the Martyrdom of Philip

While the earliest church fathers, such as Papias, Polycrates, Proclus, and Eusebius, mention Philip the apostle in Hierapolis, none mentions his martyrdom.[44] They state that he lived, ministered, and died in Hierapolis, but not *how* he met his

---

[43]   Spencer, *The Portrait of Philip in Acts*, 34.

[44]   The one possible exception is a reference in the *Chronicle* by St. Jerome. Writing around AD 380, Jerome translated the *Chronicle* by Eusebius (*c.* AD 311) into Latin, adding some of his own content. It is difficult to know whether the reference to Philip is truly from Jerome since there were a number of medieval additions to the text. In his translation, Roger Pearse places it as a footnote, which indicates it was not in the reliable text. Nevertheless, under the 207th Olympiad, the *Patrologia Latina* version reads: "Philip, the apostle of Christ to the people in Hierapolis, a city of Asia, while preaching the Gospel, is nailed to a cross and

fate. Only so much can be drawn from the absence of a martyrdom account for Philip in the earliest church fathers, but it is undoubtedly noteworthy that the first account arises in the fourth-century apocryphal text the *Acts of Philip*.

Thanks to the work of François Bovon and Christopher Matthew, there is an almost complete version of the *Acts of Philip*, which was previously unavailable.[45] While the *Acts of Philip* was put into its final form in the late fourth century, some of the content derives from the second and third centuries, and it was likely written in Phrygia, perhaps in Hierapolis itself.[46] Like the other Apocryphal Acts, the *Acts of Philip* contains many bizarre legendary tales, but it likely retains a historical core. The *Acts of Philip* has many similarities to some of the earlier Acts. For instance, reminiscent of the *Acts of Peter*, Philip gives a speech on the cross and then is crucified upside-down. Nevertheless, Matthews properly cautions critics not to simply assume literary dependence and uncreative borrowing from these earlier works.[47]

The *Acts of Philip* begins with the apostle Philip departing Galilee for ministry. He travels through multiple cities performing miracles, casting out demons, preaching the Gospel, debating Jewish religious leaders, and eventually dying by crucifixion. Perhaps the most memorable story in the *Acts of Philip* occurs when Philip, Bartholomew, and Mariamne travel through the wilderness of the she-dragons.[48] A leopard comes out of the wilderness, prostrates himself at their feet, and shares that he had a change of heart and decided to spare a kid (young goat) rather than eat him. Philip prays for the leopard to receive a human heart, and invites him and the kid to join them on their journey.

The martyrdom account begins in Chapter 15, when Philip enters Hierapolis. Nicanora, the wife of the Proconsul Tyrannos, became a believer in Jesus after hearing Philip's preaching. Nicanora told her husband to repent from worshipping idols, but he became angry and demanded Philip and Bartholomew be tortured for their deception: "And he ordered Philip to be hung up and his ankles pierced through, and that iron instruments of torture be brought and passed through his heels, and that he be hung head downward before the temple on a tree."[49] Suddenly, the apostle John appears in the story. The people attempt to kill John as well, and Philip lashes out in anger, threatening to destroy them

---

stoned to death" (Jerome, *Chronicle*, trans. Roger Pearse and friends, accessed May 1, 2014, http://www.tertullian.org/fathers/jerome_chronicle_03_part2.htm).

[45]   François Bovon and Christopher R. Matthews, *The Acts of Philip: A New Translation* (Waco, TX: Baylor University Press, 2012).

[46]   Hans-Josef Klauck, *The Apocryphal Acts of the Apostles*, trans. Brian McNeil (Waco, TX: Baylor University Press, 2008), 233.

[47]   Matthews, *Philip*, 161.

[48]   *The Acts of Philip* 8.16–21.

[49]   Ibid. 15.19.

all.[50] Philip then curses the people, which results in the earth opening up and swallowing the entire temple, the Viper the people were worshipping, and about seven thousand men, plus women and children. The only place left standing was where the apostles stood. The Lord appears and castigates Philip for returning evil for evil, barring him outside paradise for forty days.[51] After giving a speech on the cross, Philip gives up his spirit. After forty days, Jesus appears in the form of Philip to give instruction to Bartholomew and Mariamne about where they are to minister next.

Later writers affirm the tradition of the martyrdom of Philip. For instance, Isidore of Seville says: "Afterwards, he [Philip] was stoned and crucified, and died in Hierapolis, a city of Phrygia, and having been buried with his corpse upright along with his daughters rests there." According to (Pseudo-)*Hippolytus on the Twelve*: "Philip preached in Phrygia, and was crucified in Hierapolis with his head downward in the time of Domitian, and was buried there."[52] The *Breviarum Apostolorum* (*c.* AD 600) and other apostolic lists of the Middle Ages depict Philip as a martyr as well: "Thereupon he [Philip] was crucified in Hierapolis in the province of Phrygia and he died lapidated. And there he rests with his daughters. And his feast day is celebrated on the first of May."[53] The *Irish Biblical Apocrypha* also contains an account of the crucifixion of Philip in Hierapolis. In this story, Philip preaches to the people and Jewish priests about Christ, and in an attempt to silence him, they cut out his tongue, beat him, and stone him. But they cannot cause him harm:

> Thereupon the people and priests ordered that the apostle should be crucified, since they failed to inflict any other death on him. A certain wicked cruel man among them came forward, and placed a deadly noose around the apostle's neck, and they hanged him then, after he had endured much pain, insult, and scourging, like his master, Jesus. Hierapolis, then, is the name of the city in which Philip the apostle was crucified. Great splendor and ministering angels were seen around the gallows when Philip expired, and the angels placed the soul of the apostle in the mansions of the kingdom of heaven in the glory of the angels, after his attainment of the crown of martyrdom.[54]

The tradition of Philip's martyrdom in Hierapolis finds some confirmation in the Martyrium of Philip, an ancient site that many believe was built on the place

---

50   Ibid. 8.25.

51   Ibid. 8.31.

52   If Hippolytus actually wrote this account, it would pre-date the *Acts of Philip*. But this has not been established, and many consider it spurious.

53   See translation in Rose, *Ritual Memory*, 136.

54   Marie Herbert and Martin McNamara, eds., *Irish Biblical Apocrypha* (Edinburgh: T. & T. Clark, 1989), 106–08.

where Philip was martyred.[55] Around AD 400, the Philip Martyrium was built outside the city of Hierapolis to mark the spot where the apostle was crucified according to the *Acts of Philip*. Yet at the same time Francesco D'Andria released his article on the Philip Martyrium, he announced that he had in fact found the tomb of the martyred apostle Philip, though not where expected.[56] Rather than on top of the Martyrium, it was located in a newly excavated church about forty yards away. While the body is gone, D'Andria believes the tomb originally held the remains of the apostle Philip.[57]

The tradition of the martyrdom of Philip, however, is not unanimous. In the Latin text of *The Apostolic Acts of Abdias* (Book X), Philip goes to Hierapolis to battle the Ebionites. He marries, and has two daughters who become evangelists in their own right. But rather than face martyrdom by crucifixion, he dies naturally aged 87. Like the apostle John, Philip experiences a peaceful death at an advanced age. John, Philip, and Thaddeus are the only three apostles whose apocryphal traditions end with their peaceful deaths. Although there are some points of contact between the *Acts of Philip* and Pseudo-Abdias (for example, the dragon), there is unlikely to be any textual relationship between these two works.[58] This may represent an independent line of tradition regarding the fate of Philip, and thus provides a significant counterexample to the crucifixion account in the *Acts of Philip*. In addition, there is a hymn from the medieval ages, *Fulget coruscans*, which describes a similar natural death for Philip as the collection of Pseudo-Abdias. Most hymns of this sort treat the apostles as martyrs, and most hymns of Philip give him a martyr's death, but in this hymn Philip dies peacefully after ministering in Scythia.

Since the *Acts of Philip* is likely the earliest source for the martyrdom of Philip, we must ask whether it retains a historical core. Certain details give it the aura of historical underpinning. First, the *Acts of Philip* includes a number of historical figures, such as the emperor Trajan, the high priest Ananias, and the 12 disciples. Second, it accurately depicts the missionary journeys of Peter to Rome, Thomas to India, Andrew to Achaea, John to Asia, and more.[59] Third,

[55] Francesco D'Andria, "Conversion, Crucifixion, and Celebration," *Biblical Archaeological Review* 37 (July/August 2011): 34–46.

[56] Biblical Archaeology Society, "Philip's Tomb Discovered—but Not Where Expected," *Biblical Archaeological Review* 38 (January/February 2012): 18.

[57] The Martyrium of Philip is interesting, and certainly demonstrates that there was a cult following surrounding the fate of the apostle Philip by the fourth century, perhaps even earlier. But given the lack of veneration or recognition of the site any earlier than the fourth century, it is difficult to consider the Martyrium positive evidence for his actual martyrdom by crucifixion in Hierapolis.

[58] Schneemelcher, *New Testament Apocrypha*, 2:473.

[59] *Acts of Philip* 8.1.

Philip meets his fate in Hierapolis, a destination multiple church fathers—from the second century onward—attest he visited.

Yet there are reasons to question whether or not the martyrdom account in *Acts of Philip* is historical. First, it was likely written in the fourth century, when many writings stop conserving historical material and resort to "pure legend and hagiography."[60] This does not mean the *Acts of Philip* necessarily contains an invented martyrdom account, but confidence that it is historical is greatly diminished. Second, the *Acts of Philip* likely did not circulate widely and was not well known.[61] Unlike the five primary Acts—Peter, Paul, Thomas, John, and Andrew—there are few external references to the *Acts of Philip*, and these are late.[62] Finally, Bovon notes:

> The companionship of Mariamne and Bartholomew with Philip is a distinguishing difference between this text and most ancient apocryphal Acts of the apostles, such as *Acts of John* and the *Acts of Andrew*. It brings the *Acts of Philip* closer to the "second wave" of noncanonical Acts (like the *Acts of Peter and Paul* or the *Acts of Andrew and Matthias*).[63]

Conclusion

While difficult to unravel, the traditions surrounding the apostle Philip present a consistent voice from the early second century attesting that he went to Hierapolis, though even this is compromised by the possibility that early church fathers conflated traditions about Philip the evangelist with the apostle Philip. While the first church fathers list Hierapolis as Philip's final destination, they do not mention his manner of death. The earliest source that mentions his fate is likely the *Acts of Philip*. While it may in fact report the actual martyrdom of Philip, it was written in the fourth or fifth century, when legend and fabrication often grew untethered by an historical anchor. In the case of Philip, counterbalancing evidence leads me to the following conclusion:

1. Philip engaged in missionary work outside Jerusalem—*very probably true* (general evidence for apostolic missions as found in Matt 28:18–20, Acts

---

[60]   Klauck, *The Apocryphal Acts of the Apostles*, 231.

[61]   Bovon and Matthews, *The Acts of Philip*, 12–14.

[62]   For example, the Manichaeans valued the five Apocryphal Acts more than the biblical Acts. While the Manichaean psalm book contains episodes from each of the five Apocryphal Acts, there are no references to the *Acts of Philip*. See Lapham, *An Introduction to the New Testament Apocrypha*, 132.

[63]   Bovon and Matthews, *The Acts of Philip*, 29.

1:8, and early non-canonical sources; Philip had a heart for evangelism, as seen in John 1:45; *Letter of Philip to Peter*; *Acts of Philip*).

2. Philip experienced martyrdom—*as plausible as not* (*Acts of Philip*; Isidore of Seville; *Hippolytus on the Twelve* 5; *Breviarum Apostolorum*; Philip Martyrium).

Chapter 13
Martyrdom of Bartholomew

Bartholomew appears as a member of the Twelve in every apostolic list (Matt 10:3; Mark 3:18; Luke 6:14; Acts 1:13). He appears sixth in the Synoptics, always after Philip, which may suggest they were close ministry partners or perhaps played a similar role among the apostles. In the canonical Acts, Bartholomew appears seventh after Thomas. While Bartholomew was not among the inner circle of disciples, his moderate place in the lists may indicate he was more prominent among the Twelve than others. As shown in Chapter 3, it seems reasonable to conclude that Bartholomew and Nathanael are different names for the same person.

Bartholomew is the subject of many later apocryphal and Gnostic writings such as the *Gospel of Bartholomew*, the *Acts of Andrew and Bartholomew* (Coptic), the *Acts of Bartholomew and Barnabas*, *The Questions of Bartholomew* (*c.* AD second–sixth century) and *The Book of the Resurrection of Jesus Christ by Bartholomew the Apostle* (AD fifth/sixth century). It may be surprising that these last two texts consider Bartholomew a central apostle who could bear such significant revelations about God. Yet Hans-Josef Klauck suggests these apocryphal traditions mark the fulfillment of the promise Jesus made to Nathanael (Bartholomew), whom he called an Israelite without deceit (John 1:47) who would "see greater things that these" (1:50).[1]

The Missionary Travels of Bartholomew

While the New Testament record of Bartholomew is bare, a variety of later tales, at least four primary traditions, report the missionary travels and fate of Bartholomew, which are not necessarily contradictory.[2] First, according to the *Acts of Philip*, Bartholomew traveled to Hierapolis and Lyconia to minister along with the apostle Philip. Even though he was nailed to the wall of the temple,

---

[1]   Hans-Josef Klauck, *Apocryphal Gospels: An Introduction*, trans. Brian McNeil (New York: T. & T. Clark, 2003), 99.

[2]   Brownrigg suggests Bartholomew may have first gone to Phrygia, then India, and finally to Armenia, where he was martyred. Ronald Brownrigg, *The Twelve Apostles* (New York: Macmillan, 1974), 136. The latter two points find confirmation in *Hippolytus on the Twelve* 6.

Bartholomew survived, unlike Philip, who has his ankles and feet pierced before being hung upside-down from a tree.

Second, Bartholomew traveled to Egypt. According to this tradition, when the apostles divided up countries for ministry, Bartholomew received a lot directing him to the Oases of Egypt. Unfamiliar with the country, Bartholomew appealed to Peter for help. Yet when they were denied entrance into Egypt, Peter sold Bartholomew as a slave to a camel owner. Bartholomew performed many miracles, preached the message of Jesus nightly, and eventually departed after three months. From there he left for Parthia, where he suffered martyrdom.[3]

Third, the Armenian Church has claimed Bartholomew as its patron saint for at least 1,400 years. In terms of the broader question of Christianity reaching Armenia, Nina Girosïan observes:

> The early appearance of Christianity coming to Armenia from Palestine by way of Syria and Mesopotamia is equally beyond doubt. The second century African church father Tertullian already listed the Armenians among the people who had received Christianity, and the mid-third century letter of Bishop Dionysios of Alexandria to an Armenian bishop named Meruzanes indicates a sizable community .... Consequently, it is now evidence that two currents of Christianity reached Armenia successively. The first came to the southern portion of the country closest to the original center of Palestine by way of Mesopotamia at a very early date. The second was brought to the northern Aršakuni Kingdom of Greater Armenia in the second decade of the fourth century.[4]

According to Orthodox Armenian historian Malachia Ormanian, the near instantaneous conversion of the whole of Armenia to Christianity at the beginning of the fourth century can only be explained by the pre-existence of a Christian community that had taken root in the country centuries earlier.[5] History records early persecutions in Armenia (*c.* AD 110, 230, 287) that could only have occurred if there were significant numbers of Armenian Christians

---

[3]   Given the similarities between this story and the *Acts of Thomas* (for example, apostle sold as a slave; talking serpent which is commanded by an apostle to suck the poison out of its victim), Schneemelcher believes the author used the *Acts of Thomas* and adapted it to an Egyptian situation. See Wilhelm Schneemelcher, *New Testament Apocrypha*, trans. R.M. Wilson (Louisville, KY: Westminster John Knox Press, 2003), 2:451–52.

[4]   Nina Girosïan, "The Aršakuni Dynasty (A.D. 12-[180?]-428)," in *The Armenian People from Ancient to Modern Times*, ed. Richard G. Hovannisian (New York: St. Martin's Press, 1997), 1:83.

[5]   Malachia Ormanian, *The Church of Armenia: Her History, Doctrine, Rule, Discipline, Liturgy, Literature, and Existing Condition*, ed. Terenig Poladian, trans. G. Marcar Gregory (London: A.R. Wombray, 1955), 7.

at that time.[6] Of course, while this does not prove that Bartholomew actually visited Armenia or that he was martyred there, it does provide a historical context that helps make the narrative plausible. According to the Armenian tradition, Bartholomew appeared after St. Thaddeus, who had preached the Gospel in Armenia beginning in AD 43 before suffering martyrdom at Artaz (*c.* AD 66). Bartholomew appeared around AD 60, and was martyred in AD 68 at Albanus.[7] According to the Roman Breviary,[8] Bartholomew was flayed alive and beheaded.[9] His tomb is venerated at Alpac (Bashkale), in southeast Armenia. Along with St. Thaddeus, Bartholomew is considered the "First Illuminator of Armenia." Even though this tradition is not as central to the Armenian Church as the Thomas tradition is for India, it is widely accepted as part of its history.[10]

Fourth, Bartholomew went to India. *The Martyrdom of Bartholomew* (*The Passion of Bartholomew*) reports the travels of Bartholomew to India, where he casts out a demon, heals the lunatic daughter of King Polymius, then converts the royal family to the faith. The heathen priests become enraged at Bartholomew and have him beaten, beheaded, and his body thrown into the sea. Although reminiscent of the features of Paul in the *Acts of Paul*, *The Martyrdom of Bartholomew* offers the earliest known description of the apostle Bartholomew:

> He has black curly hair, white skin, large eyes, straight nose, his hair covers his ears, his beard long and grizzled, middle height: he wears a white *colobium* with a purple stripe, and a white cloak with four purple "gems" at the corners: for twenty-six years he has worn these and they never grow old: his shoes have lasted

---

6   Ian Gillman and Hans-Joachim Klimkeit, *Christians in Asia before 1500* (Ann Arbor, MI: University of Michigan Press, 1999), 92.

7   Aziz S. Atiya, *History of Eastern Christianity* (South Bend, IN: University of Notre Dame Press, 1968), 315–16.

8   The Roman Breviary is a seventh- or early eighth-century composite work from earlier sources and authors. See Pierre Batiffol, *History of the Roman Breviary*, trans. Atwell M.Y. Baylay (New York: Longmans, Green, 1896), 1.

9   A. Le Houllier, "Bartholomew, Apostle St." *New Catholic Encyclopedia*, vol. 2 (New York: Catholic University of America Press, 1967), 132.

10   As a whole, the Armenian Church assumes the tradition to be true rather than feeling the need to defend it, as do many Indian scholars concerning the Thomas tradition. Many Armenian history books mention the tradition without providing historical evidence for how it is known to be true. For instance, in *Armenia: A Journey Through History*, Arra S. Avakian mentions the tradition of Bartholomew and Thaddeus visiting Armenia in a historical timeline of key events in Armenia, but begins the history of Christianity in Armenia at the turn of the third/fourth century, when Armenia became the first nation to officially embrace Christianity. It is somewhat surprising not to see any details about the journey of Bartholomew (and Thaddeus) to Armenia. See Arra S. Avakian, *Armenia: A Journey Through History* (Fresno, CA: Electric Press, 1998).

twenty-six years: he prays 100 times a day and 100 times a night: his voice is like a trumpet: angels wait on him: he is always cheerful and knows all languages.[11]

Eusebius offers support for the tradition that Bartholomew ministered in India. In the middle of the second century, Stoic philosopher Pantaenus became a Christian. Because of his zeal, he was sent east to India to preach the Gospel. To his apparent surprise, "he found the Gospel according to Matthew, which had anticipated his own arrival. For Bartholomew, one of the apostles, had preached to them, and left with them the writing of Matthew in the Hebrew language, which they had preserved till that time."[12] Jerome confirms this tradition.[13]

There is nothing surprising about Pantaenus finding Christians in India, since tradition reports the apostle Thomas went there a century earlier. The question is whether or not Bartholomew *personally* visited India. We have no reason to see Bartholomew and Thomas as rivals. Considering the size of India, it is not unlikely or impossible that two apostles would minister in different parts, or they could have ministered together. If Bartholomew ministered with Philip in Hierapolis, there is no reason why he could not have gone to India with Thomas as well. On the other hand, Kurikilamkatt suggests that Pantaenus may have misunderstood the local Christians, confusing "Mar Tholmai" with "Bartholomai."[14] If so, then the entire tradition was the result of a misunderstanding and there is no good reason to believe Bartholomew ever set foot ashore India. This is an interesting hypothesis, but it cannot be proven.

Given the tentative nature of the evidence, scholars disagree about whether Bartholomew journeyed to India. While the majority of scholarly opinion remains against it, a significant minority accepts it.[15] As noted in Chapter 9 on Thomas, there is nothing implausible about an apostle traveling to India in the late first century. The pressing question, of course, is whether or not it is *probable*.

While we have some positive evidence for Bartholomew's visit to India, the lack of a consistent Indian tradition as for Thomas challenges the tradition. Nevertheless, A.C. Perumalil suggests that the Bartholomew Christians

---

[11]   J.K. Elliott, *The Apocryphal New Testament* (Oxford: Oxford University Press, 2005), 518.

[12]   Eusebius, *Ecclesiastical History* 5.10.3, as cited in *Nicene and Post-Nicene Fathers*: *Eusebius: Church History, Life of Constantine the Great, and Oration in Praise of Constantine*, ed. Philip Schaff and Henry Wace (New York: Christian Literature Co., 1890), 1:225.

[13]   Jerome, *On Illustrious Men* 36.

[14]   James Kurikilamkatt, *First Voyage of the Apostle Thomas to India* (Bangalore, India: Asian Trading Corporation, 2005), 100.

[15]   A. Mathias Mundadan, *From the Beginning up to the Middle of the Sixteenth Century up to 1542*, History of Christianity in India, vol. 1 (Bangalore, India: Theological Publications in India, 1984), 65; C. Bernard Ruffin, *The Twelve: The Lives of the Apostles After Calvary* (Huntington, IN: Our Sunday Visitor, 1997), 117.

continued as a separate community until the coming of the Portuguese, when they became one with the Christians of Bombay.[16] Given the slight *positive* evidence for such an endeavor, Leslie Brown suggests the story of Pantaenus's visit and his discovery of a Gospel brought by Bartholomew may have credibility, but has been overwhelmed by the Thomas tradition.[17] The Indian tradition of Bartholomew may be lacking the requisite evidence to make it more probable than not, but we have at least some positive evidence that demands further research and analysis by both Western and Eastern scholars alike.

Nevertheless, the consistent testimony is that Bartholomew engaged in missionary work beyond Judea. There is no record that Bartholomew stayed in Jerusalem and died there. Every account has him traveling well beyond Judea, spreading the newfound faith. While there is disagreement over where he went and how he died, we have no good reason to doubt that he left Jerusalem to spread the Gospel of Christ. While the particular location(s) of the missions of Bartholomew may be difficult to discern, Bartholomew undoubtedly took the missionary charge of Jesus seriously.

Evidence for the Martyrdom of Bartholomew

Of the variety of traditions regarding the fate of Bartholomew, no known traditions hold that he rejected his faith or died peacefully, but there is significant variety about *how, where,* and *when* he experienced martyrdom. In the *Acts of Philip* (*c.* fourth/fifth century), Bartholomew travels with Philip to Hierapolis. While both apostles are tortured, Bartholomew is set free, yet the crucifixion of Bartholomew in Lyconia is predicted just before the execution of Philip.[18]

Martyrdom in Parthia

In the *Contendings of the Apostles*, Budge reports the tradition that Bartholomew met his fate in Naidas, Parthia.[19] According to this tradition, Bartholomew traveled to Naidas, a great city upon the sea, to minister to people who had no knowledge of God. Many turned to God in repentance. Bartholomew traveled around the country, preaching, healing, and casting out demons. However, as

---

[16] A.C. Perumalil, *The Apostles in India,* 2nd ed. (Dasarahalli, India: St. Paul Press Training School, 1971), 139–40.

[17] L.W. Brown, *The Indian Christians of St. Thomas* (Cambridge: Cambridge University Press, 1956), 63.

[18] *The Acts of Philip* 15.36.

[19] E.A. Wallis Budge, *The Contendings of the Apostles: Being the Histories and the Lives and Martyrdoms and Deaths of the Twelve Apostles and Evangelists* (London: Oxford University Press, 1935).

a result of Bartholomew's preaching, the wife of King Acarpus decided to stop sleeping with him. Furious, the king accused Bartholomew of sorcery and had him tossed into the sea in a sack full of sand.

Martyrdom in Armenia

As noted previously, according to the tradition of the Armenian Church, Bartholomew was martyred in AD 68 at Albanus. According to *Hippolytus on the Twelve* 6: "Bartholomew, again, preached to the Indians, to whom he also gave the Gospel according to Matthew, and was crucified with his head downward, and was buried in Allanum, a town of the great Armenia."[20] One difficulty in establishing the reliability of the Bartholomew tradition is how late it appears in Armenian historiography. The first reference is in the *History of Armenia* by Movsēs Xorenac'I (Moses of Khorene), who was born AD 410–415 and who probably wrote his *History* around AD 480. As a criticism of the tradition, Van Esbroeck notes that the oldest Armenian historians do not mention Bartholomew at all.[21] Yet it should be kept in mind that Movsēs Xorenac'I was the first Armenian historian to write a comprehensive history of Armenia, beginning with the most ancient events. Historians before Movsēs discussed particular events, whereas Movsēs wrote an entire history of Christianity in Armenia (for example, Agathangelos wrote his *History* on the life and times of Gregory the Illuminator).[22] Xorenac'I is the first historian who would be expected to mention Bartholomew, and in fact he did.

It is also important to remember that Armenia had no native literature until the conversion of the nation to Christianity in the early fourth century.[23] If Bartholomew in fact traveled to Armenia and experienced martyrdom, the tradition would have been transmitted orally, so early written records would not exist. Like that of all ancient people groups, Armenian literature was originally preserved orally through epic tales, legend, ritual songs, and lyric poetry. Although the exact date for the origin of oral history for Armenia is unknown, recorded events trace back to the ninth century BC, and possibly as early as the fifteenth

---

[20]   Pseudo-Hippolytus, *Hippolytus on the Twelve* 6, as cited in *The Ante-Nicene Fathers: Fathers of the Third Century*, ed. Alexander Roberts and James Donaldson, rev. A. Cleveland Coxe (Buffalo, NY: Christian Literature Co., 1885), 5:255.

[21]   Michael van Esbroeck, "The Rise of Saint Bartholomew's Cult in Armenia from the Seventh to the Thirteenth Centuries," in *Medieval Armenian Culture*, University of Pennsylvania Armenian Texts and Studies, vol. 6 (Chico, CA: Scholars Press, 1983), 162. Esbroeck suggests there were both political and religious reasons for why the Armenians claimed Bartholomew as their apostolic saint.

[22]   M. Chahin, *The Kingdom of Armenia* (New York: Dorset, 1987), 201.

[23]   Everett Ferguson, ed., *Encyclopedia of Early Christianity*, vol. 1 (New York: Garland, 1997), s.v. "Armenian Christian Literature," by Robin Darling Young.

century BC. According to the authors of *The Heritage of Armenian Literature*, epic tales that have been transmitted orally often contain a historical core.[24] They suggest that the origin of Christianity in Armenia is a "mixture of fact and fiction,"[25] and that there may be a historical core to the tradition that Thaddeus and Bartholomew both came as missionaries to Armenia, and that they both died as martyrs. The lack of early written records cannot count against this tradition since, regardless of their actual fates, this is exactly what should be found.

More significant for the Armenian tradition are doubts concerning the reliability of the *History* by Xorenac'I.[26] He is considered the "Father of Armenian History," and has been described as the Herodotus of Armenia. He undoubtedly preserved some sound and valuable material, but scholars are divided over how much his scholarship can be trusted. Various extreme positions have been taken, from hypercritical rejection to naive acceptance. Armenian scholar Aram Topchyan suggests a balanced approach:

> Consequently, what one should do nowadays is, firstly, to get rid of extreme mistrust and prevailing negative stereotypes, and, secondly, to continue extracting from the work of the longsuffering "father of Armenian historiography" as much useful information as possible. Such an approach seems even more mandatory against the background of today's balanced tendencies in the research of classical authors (tendencies applicable to ancient historiography as a whole), and given the absolute lack of any substitute for Xorenac'I's book in Armenian literature, especially for the pre-fourth century history.[27]

Nevertheless, it is worth noting that the relevant passage concerning Bartholomew is straightforward and contains no flowery details.[28] He makes no mention of the tradition Bartholomew was flayed to death, which first appeared around AD 600.[29] It simply reads: "There came then into Armenia the Apostle Bartholomew, who suffered martyrdom among us in the town of Arepan." Immediately afterward, Xorenac'I mentions the tradition that the apostle

---

[24]   Agop J. Hacikyan, *The Heritage of Armenian Literature*, ed. Gabriel Basmajian, Edward S. Franchuk, Nourhan Ouzounian (Detroit, MI: Wayne State University Press, 1999), 1:23.

[25]   Ibid., 1:75.

[26]   According to M. Chahin, most scholars criticize the work of Xorenac'I as inaccurate. Yet Chahin notes that many scholars use the narratives of Xorenac'I for further research and study. See Chahin, *The Kingdom of Armenia*, 201.

[27]   Aram Topchyan, *The Problem of Greek Sources of Movsēs Xorenac'I's History of Armenia* (Leuven, Belgium: Peeters, 2006), 15.

[28]   Movsēs Xorenac'I, *History of Armenia* Book IX: Martyrdom of Our Apostles.

[29]   Els Rose, *Ritual Memory: The Apocryphal Acts and Liturgical Commemoration in the Early Medieval West (c. 500–1251)* (Leiden, The Netherlands: Brill, 2009), 86–89.

Simon came to Persia and was martyred in Veriospore. Xorenac'I refrains from commenting on the reliability of the Simon tradition because he is not sure of the facts. He ensures his readers that he tells them only what is necessary and what he is certain about. Given the character of his presentation, then, we might reasonably believe Xorenac'I must have been quite confident that Bartholomew was martyred in Armenia.

Armenian scholar Malachia Ormanian believes the apostolic origins of the Armenian Church can be considered "an incontrovertible fact in ecclesiastical history."[30] While recognizing the facts are somewhat veiled historically, he provides three reasons why the tradition can be trusted. First, there are no historical improbabilities in Bartholomew and Thaddeus ministering and dying in Armenia. Second, all Christian churches in Armenia agree on his apostolic journey, preaching, and martyrdom in Armenia. Third, the name Albanus, which is the traditional site of his martyrdom, can be identified as Albacus. Ormanian writes:

> The apostolic origin, which is essential to every Christian Church, in order to place her in union with her Divine Founder, is claimed to be direct when that origin is traced back to the individual work of one of the apostles; it is indirect when it is derived from a Church which herself has a primitively apostolic basis. The Armenian Church can rightly lay claim to such a direct apostolic origin .... And if tradition and historic sources, which sanction this view, should give occasion for criticism, these have no greater weight than the difficulties created with regard to the origin of oter apostolic Churches, which are universally admitted as such.[31]

Martyrdom in India

The Martyrdom of Bartholomew, which likely originated in the fifth or sixth century and is today preserved in Greek, Latin, and Armenian,[32] reports yet another tradition of the fate of Bartholomew—that he traveled to India, was beaten with clubs, beheaded by heathen priests who complained to the king about him, and then his body was thrown into the sea—later manuscripts from the ninth and twelfth centuries incorporate the Armenian tradition that he was flayed to death.[33] From the fifth century onward, a variety of traditions report that Bartholomew met his fate in India.[34] The *Hieronymian Martyrology* (c. fifth century) also reports

---

[30]   Ormanian, *The Church of Armenia*, 4.

[31]   Ibid.

[32]   Elliott, *The Apocryphal New Testament*, 518

[33]   Rose, *Ritual Memory*, 84.

[34]   The reports that Bartholomew met his fate in India include Gregory of Tours (sixth century), St. Bede the Venerable (eighth century), Usuard of Sagermanum (ninth century), Odo, bishop of Vienne (ninth century), the Greek Menology of Constantinople (tenth

that Bartholomew was beheaded in Citerior, India, by order of King Astriagis. Perumalil believes that this is most likely Bombay (modern-day Mumbai), a port town in western central India. The claim that the body of Bartholomew was thrown into the sea matches this identification. According to Perumalil: "If the writer was inventing a mere fable, a coincidence of this kind would not have been found."[35] The same location is mentioned by Pseudo-Sophronius, a seventh-century writer.[36] A flourishing Christian community was found there in the sixth century. Thus, Perumalil concludes: "Hence in all probability the Apostle Bartholomew preached on the Kalyana [western] Coast of India, made converts and established a church that was still extant in the sixth century."[37]

The Historical Question

As with the case of other apocryphal accounts, the question is whether *The Martyrdom of Bartholomew* preserves historical material. That it appears much later than the primary Acts counts against the tradition. Other scholars are quite sanguine about the possibility that it contains a historical nucleus. Thomas Schmidt notes:

> The work is a fifth-century composition that, like other apocryphal works already described, may combine fabrication with a core of historical material. Certainly the pattern—healing, successful preaching (often involving an influential individual), then local reprisals—is familiar from the early chapters of Acts, and it formed a model for the spread of Christianity for almost a thousand years.[38]

The Martyrdom of Bartholomew contains names of two kings and three gods. Is there any reason to believe these names are historical? Given that names often undergo change over time, especially when foreigners pronounce Indian names, Perumalil suggests that Astaruth may be the Indian god Astarudra, Baldad may be Baladat (an incarnation of Vishnu) or Baladeva (older brother of Krishna), and Becher may be the Hellenized form of the Kanarese Bachiran.[39] As for the two kings, Perumalil notes that historical sources for this time are very meager. Yet the numismatic and inscriptional data suggest that when the *Martyrdom of*

---

century), and a Syrian tradition written by Amr (fourteenth century). See Perumalil, *The Apostles in India*, 133–35.

35   Rose, *Ritual Memory*, 114.

36   Ibid., 111.

37   Ibid.

38   Thomas E. Schmidt, *The Apostles After Acts: A Sequel* (Eugene, OR: Cascade, 2013), 150.

39   Perumalil, *The Apostles of India*, 118.

Bartholomew speaks of King Polymius, it refers to the Indian name Pulumayi, and that King Astreges may be identified as either Attrakan (of Pakrit) or Aristakarman (of the Puranas).[40]

A few important points stand out from analyzing traditions of the fate of Bartholomew. First, we have no record that he either recanted his faith or died peacefully, and we should consider the significance of his appearance in a decent number of apocryphal and Gnostic accounts. Second, the various accounts unilaterally agree that he died as a martyr. R.A. Lipsius notes the breadth of variation in the accounts of the death of Bartholomew:

> The gnostic legend of Bartholomew has him *crucified*, the Coptic narrative has him *put in a sack* full of sand then sunk in the sea, the local Armenian saga has him *beaten with clubs*, a fourth tradition, probably originating in Persia, has him *flayed*, and finally a fifth tradition has him *beheaded*.[41]

While there is substantial disagreement about how and where he met his fate, there is no disagreement he was executed for reasons tied to his faith.

Third, it is not necessarily the case that these accounts are true or false in their entirety. It may be that some traditions are completely false. It may also be the case that some traditions retain a historical kernel of his travels, but incorporate fictional details of his martyrdom. And some may contain an accurate rendering of both his travels *and* martyrdom. At this point, the data remain inconclusive, but simply because some of the accounts contain irreconcilable details, we should not dismiss them all as fictional.

Fourth, there is nothing implausible about the various means mentioned for his manner of death. Victims were regularly drowned, beaten, crucified, and even flayed to death.[42] Bartholomew could have been killed in any of these ways. In particular, death by flaying was one of the most painful and horrific methods of execution ever invented. Executioners would aim to remove the entire skin, peel by peel, while the victim was still alive. Victims who did not die from the flaying were often burned, impaled, or crucified. Flaying can be traced back long before the time of Christ, and was practiced in Turkey, China, and in many other Eastern countries.[43] While the record of Bartholomew's death by flaying is late, there is precedent for this kind of death during that time, and no reason to doubt its plausibility.[44]

---

[40]   Ibid., 126–29.

[41]   As translated and quoted in Hans-Josef Klauck, *The Apocryphal Acts of the Apostles*, trans. Brian McNeil (Waco, TX: Baylor University Press, 2008), 244.

[42]   Geoffrey Abbot, *Execution* (New York: St. Martin's Press, 2005).

[43]   Ibid., 113.

[44]   Although flaying was typically a form of punishment, there are other known reasons why it was administered to some. See Sarah Kay, "Original Skin: Flaying, Reading, and

Conclusion

Similar to other less prominent apostles, the evidence for the martyrdom of Bartholomew is mixed. There is disagreement about when, where, and how he died, but there is unanimity that Bartholomew met his fate by martyrdom. Yet it must be conceded that the first accounts are late. With these considerations in mind, the following probabilities seem most reasonable in regard to the missionary work and fate of Bartholomew:

1. Bartholomew engaged in missionary work outside Jerusalem—*very probably true* (Matt 28:18–20; Acts 1:8; *Hippolytus on the Twelve* 6; various traditions from Hierapolis, Lyconia, Egypt, Armenia, and India).
2. Bartholomew experienced martyrdom—*as plausible as not* (*History of Armenia* by Movsēs Xorenac'I; *Hippolytus on the Twelve* 6; *Martyrdom of Bartholomew*; *Hieronymian Martyrology*; *Contendings of the Apostles*).

Thinking in the Legend of Saint Bartholomew and Other Works," *Journal of Medieval and Early Modern Studies* 36 (2006).

Chapter 14
Martyrdom of Matthew

Matthew is probably best known as the author of the first Gospel. Given how central this Gospel has been historically and theologically, it may come as a surprise to many that Matthew is among the apostles of Jesus whom scholars know the least about. One author even refers to him as the "phantom apostle."[1] However, Edgar J. Goodspeed claims that more is known more about Matthew than any of the other apostles, except possibly Peter.[2] While this is likely an overstatement, there is *some* information about the life and travels of Matthew that enables the critical scholar to make a reasonable inference about the manner of his fate.

Matthew is one of the only apostles for whom there is an account of his call from Jesus (Matt 9:9). While Matthew's response to the call may seem sudden, he was likely familiar with Jesus, and had possibly even heard him teach on various occasions. His willingness to follow Jesus also demonstrated a great deal of faith. While fishermen could quite easily go back to their fishing business, Matthew gave up a high-paying job. After all, who would hire a former tax collector?

When Matthew received the call to follow Jesus, he was living and working in Capernaum, the home town of Peter, James, and John. Mark refers to him as "Levi the son of Alphaeus," which is probably another name for Matthew (Mark 2:14).[3] If this identification is correct, Matthew was likely a Levite, and would have been familiar with Jewish law and customs. He would also have been the brother of James, son of Alphaeus, another member of the Twelve. Regardless, Matthew was certainly a Jew. He was undoubtedly familiar with Jewish traditions and Scripture, and this is reflected in his Gospel.[4]

---

[1] C. Bernard Ruffin, *The Twelve: The Lives of the Apostles After Calvary* (Huntington, IN: Our Sunday Visitor, 1997), 135.

[2] Edgar J. Goodspeed, *Matthew: Apostle and Evangelist* (Philadelphia, PA: John C. Winston, 1959), 10.

[3] It was common for Jews to have multiple names in the first century. See Craig L. Blomberg, *Matthew*, The New American Commentary, vol. 22 (Nashville, TN: Broadman & Holman, 1992), 155. Nevertheless, Bauckham has noted the "virtually unparalleled phenomenon" of a Palestinian Jew bearing two common Semitic names. Thus, he judges it "implausible" that Matthew and Levi refer to the same person. See Richard J. Bauckham, *Jesus and the Eyewitnesses: The Gospels as Eyewitness Testimony* (Grand Rapids, MI: Eerdmans, 2006), 108–12.

[4] William Hendriksen, *Exposition of the Gospel According to Matthew*, Baker New Testament Commentary (Grand Rapids, MI: Baker, 1973), 96.

His name, from the Aramaic *mattai*, is a shortened form of the Hebrew *mattanyâ*, meaning "gift of Yahweh."[5] Twice Matthew appears seventh in the list of apostles (Mark 3:18; Luke 6:15), and twice he appears eighth (Matt 10:3; Acts 1:13). The Bible and early church history offer no physical description for Matthew. But Clement of Alexandria suggests he was a vegetarian who ate seeds, nuts, and vegetables.[6]

As a tax collector, Matthew was in the service of Herod Antipas, and so knew at least Greek and Aramaic—he would have spoken Aramaic and kept records in Greek. He would be required to keep written records of the money he collected, and possibly even knew shorthand.[7] Thus, Matthew must have had some formal education and training. Since he was employed through an unpopular government, which was sanctioned by Rome, he would have been profoundly resented and hated by patriotic Jews and the general populace.

R.T. France provides key insights as to the significance of Jesus choosing Matthew:

> For Jesus to call such a man to follow him was a daring breach of etiquette, a calculated snub to conventional ideas of respectability, which ordinary people no less than Pharisees might be expected to baulk at. Fishermen may not have been high in the social scale, but at least they were not automatically morally and religiously suspect; Matthew was. Almost as remarkable as Jesus' decision to call him is Matthew's confident response; he does not seem to have felt uncomfortable at being included in a preacher's entourage, though we are not told what the other disciples thought.[8]

Immediately after his call to discipleship, Matthew had Jesus over for dinner along with many other tax collectors and sinners (Mark 2:15). But when the Pharisees saw that he was reclining with such unsavory company, they protested to his disciples. When Jesus heard this, he replied: "Those who are well have no need of a physician, but those who are sick. I came not to call the righteous, but sinners" (Mark 2:17). A feast of this sort would likely minimally require a decent-sized home, so Matthew may have been a man of considerable financial means.[9]

---

[5] Catholic University of America Staff, ed., *New Catholic Encyclopedia*, vol. 9 (Washington, DC: Catholic University Press, 2003), s.v. "Matthew, Apostle, St.," by J.A. Lefrançois.

[6] Clement of Alexandria, *Paedagogus* 2.1.

[7] Hendriksen, *Exposition of the Gospel According to Matthew*, 95.

[8] R.T. France, *The Gospel of Matthew* (Grand Rapids, MI: Eerdmans, 2007), 351–52.

[9] Herbert Lockyer, *All the Apostles of the Bible* (Grand Rapids, MI: Zondervan, 1972), 121–22.

While a significant minority of scholars accept Matthean authorship for the first Gospel, the majority reject it—a principal reason being that the author of Matthew seems so closely to follow Markan material.[10] Yet Michael Wilkins observes: "But if Matthew did have access to Mark's Gospel, he would have known that Peter's apostolic reminiscences lay behind Mark's text, ensuring that Mark's Gospel was reliable and a ready source for reinforcing his own reminiscences about the life and works of Jesus Christ."[11] Wilkins also provides positive evidence for Matthean authorship of the first Gospel.[12] And Goodspeed offers internal evidence as well.[13] Nevertheless, even some conservative scholars remain tentative regarding the conclusions.[14]

Missions of Matthew

Eusebius reports that Matthew first preached to the Hebrews, then planned to go to other places as well.[15] It is not clear whether this was to Jews in Judea, those in the diaspora, or to both. Jerome confirms that Matthew was in Judea.[16] The church historian Socrates (born *c.* AD 379) reports that Matthew received the lot to go to Ethiopia.[17] *Hippolytus on the Twelve* places his fate in Hierees, Parthia. The *Acts of Andrew* has Matthew in Mermidona. Other traditions place him in Persia and Macedonia.[18] With such a variety of traditions regarding Matthew's itinerary, none falling within the window of living memory, we move cautiously, with exceeding difficulty, between legend and history. We have little reason to doubt that Matthew spent at least some time ministering in Palestine, as the earliest traditions report, but where else did he go? Thomas Schmidt suggests the traditions describing him in Ethiopia and Egypt may be the most reliable:

---

[10] For instance, see Luz Ulrich, *Matthew 1–7: A Commentary on Matthew 1–7*, ed. H. Koester, trans. James E. Crouch (Minneapolis, MN: Fortress Press, 2007), 59.

[11] Michael Wilkins, "Apologetics Commentary on the Gospel of Matthew," in *The Holman Apologetics Commentary on the Bible*, ed. Jeremy R. Howard (Nashville, TN: Broadman & Holman, 2013), 10.

[12] Ibid., 7–11. For the patristic evidence of Matthean authorship, see Papias, *Ecclesiastical History* 3.39.16; Irenaeus, *Against Heresies* 3.1.1; Origen, *Ecclesiastical History* 6.25.4; Eusebius, *Ecclesiastical History* 3.24.6; Jerome, *On Illustrious Men* 3.1.

[13] Goodspeed, *Matthew.*

[14] Blomberg, *Matthew,* 44.

[15] Eusebius, *Ecclesiastical History* 3.24.6.

[16] Jerome, *On Illustrious Men* 3.1.

[17] Socrates, *The Ecclesiastical History* 1.19.

[18] W.D. Davies and D.C. Allison, *Matthew 1–7*, International Critical Commentary (New York: T. & T. Clark, 1988), 146 n. 125.

The Nile was a convenient highway, there were land and sea routes into Arabia, and there were Jewish settlements throughout the region. Apostles could have traveled south beyond the borders of the empire just as they (more certainly) traveled to other compass points. The story of the Ethiopian eunuch (Acts 8:27–39) supports at least an awareness of the region and, perhaps, a connection to it through this early convert. Together, these factors support at least the possibility of an apostolic journey far up the Nile. Since Matthew is the only one of the Twelve with any traditional connection to the area; and since he is not strongly connected anywhere else, this account designates him the southernmost apostolic missionary.[19]

This rendition is certainly plausible, although it is difficult to determine its level of probability. The existence of seemingly distinct traditions of his sojourn to Ethiopia does count in its favor. Ruffin agrees, noting the lack of any reference of Matthew by Paul, which may suggest Matthew's sphere of activity was not in the Mediterranean.[20]

It is undoubtedly difficult to ascertain which missionary traditions are history and which are legend. Nevertheless, the consistent testimony of the patristic evidence is that Matthew ministered in Judea for a while, then went forth proclaiming the Gospel of Jesus Christ. We have no good reason to doubt that Matthew took seriously the last words of Jesus as recorded in the Gospel by his name: "And Jesus came and said to them, 'All authority in heaven and on earth has been given to me. Go therefore and make disciples of all nations, baptizing them in the name of the Father and of the Son and of the Holy Spirit'" (Matt 28:18–19). And as with the other apostles, Matthew was an eyewitness of the risen Jesus (Matt 28:16–17; Luke 24:36–49; John 20:19–23, 26–29; Acts 1:3) and was willing to suffer for his faith (Acts 5:17–32).

Evidence for the Martyrdom of Matthew

As with many of the other apostles, scholars differ in their assessment of the reliability of the martyrdom accounts of Matthew. When we look for ourselves and examine the evidence, we find that different traditions surround the fate of Matthew. According to *Hippolytus on the Twelve*, Matthew published his Hebrew Gospel in Jerusalem, then traveled to Parthia, where he "fell asleep." Given that *Hippolytus* cites the crucifixion of Peter, beheading of Paul, stoning of James, and the specific methods of execution for many of the other apostles, it seems likely

---

[19]   Thomas E. Schmidt, *The Apostles After Acts: A Sequel* (Eugene, OR: Cascade, 2013), 174.

[20]   Ruffin, *The Twelve*, 143.

he believed that Matthew died naturally, which is the most straightforward way to understand the passage. The entry in Isidore of Seville's *De ortu et obitu patrum* concurs that Matthew faced a natural death: "He preached the gospel first in Judea, and after that in Macedonia. He has his resting place in the mountains of the land of the Parthians."[21]

Yet numerous traditions report that Matthew died as a martyr. According to the fifth-century *Hieronymian Martyrology*, Matthew was martyred in the town of Tarrium, Persia.[22] Other medieval apostolic lists name Matthew as a martyr as well. For instance, the entry for Matthew in the *Breviarium Apostolorum* (c. AD 600) says: "He first preached the gospel in Judea, and after that in Macedonia, and he suffered martyrdom in Persia."[23]

Another account is found in the *Martyrdom of Matthew*, which was probably based on the Apocryphal Acts of Andrew and Matthias.[24] The story begins with Jesus appearing to the apostles in the form of a child. Matthew cannot recognize him, and simply assumes he is one of the children King Herod murdered in Bethlehem. Interestingly, Matthew is the only Gospel that records this story (Matt 2:16–18). After their commission, Matthew goes to Myrna, the city of man-eaters, to preach. While no record exists of a city called Myrna, there was a city called Myra not far from Ephesus.[25] Many people were converted, including many in the royal family, but King Phulbanus became upset when Matthew would not stop, so he ordered him burned to death. He sent soldiers, who captured Matthew and aimed to torture him to death with oil, brimstone, asphalt, and pitch. Matthew was temporarily spared from the flames, which destroyed 12 idols, killed many soldiers, and turned into a dragon that chased the king until he returned to Matthew pleading for help. Matthew eventually "gave up the ghost" by his own volition and then returned to life before ascending to heaven with two angels.

Another tradition reports the martyrdom of Matthew in Parthia.[26] According to this tradition, Matthew travels to the city of Apayanno, where he preaches and heals many. He meets a man who was thrown in jail when the ship he was guiding crashed and he lost all the possessions of the owner. Feeling compassion,

---

[21] Els Rose, *Ritual Memory: The Apocryphal Acts and Liturgical Commemoration in the Early Medieval West (c. 500–1251)* (Leiden, The Netherlands: Brill, 2009), 175.

[22] David Noel Freedman, ed., *The Anchor Bible Dictionary* (New York: Bantam Dell, 1992), s.v. "Matthew, Martyrdom of," by Kenneth G.C. Newport.

[23] Rose, *Ritual Memory*, 174.

[24] J.K. Elliott, *The Apocryphal New Testament* (Oxford: Oxford University Press, 2005), 520.

[25] W. Milton Timmons, *Everything About the Bible that You Never Had Time to Look Up* (Bloomington, IN: Xlibris, 2002), 487.

[26] E.A. Wallis Budge, *The Contendings of the Apostles: Being the Histories and the Lives and Martyrdoms and Deaths of the Twelve Apostles and Evangelists* (London: Oxford University Press, 1935), 109–14.

Matthew let him out of prison for two days and guided him to find a bag of gold that he could use to repay his debt. But after he brought the money to the ship owner, he was accused of stealing the money, and Matthew was summoned to give an account before the king. The king was profoundly angry with Matthew, and had his guards behead him and leave his body upon the ground so the birds could eat it.

Another tradition, from Book VII of the Latin Pseudo-Abdias, places Matthew in Naddaver, a city in Ethiopia, during the reign of King Aeglippus.[27] Matthew counteracted two magicians, performed many miracles, preached the Gospel, and built a massive church for the converts. The new king, Hirtacus, desired Matthew's help to persuade Ephigenia to marry him, but Matthew objected and proclaimed such an act sacrilege. Enraged, Hirtacus sent a soldier to pierce Matthew in the back while he prayed. Yet Matthew came back from the grave, Hirtacus committed suicide, and churches sprung up all throughout Ethiopia. The medieval martyrology of Hrabanus (9th century) offers a similar script: "When he had preached there [in Ethiopia] the word of God and converted many to the faith in Christ, at last a spy was sent by King Hirtacus, who killed him with a sword, thus making him a martyr of Christ."[28]

The accounts of the journey and fate of Matthew vary so significantly that it may be tempting to dismiss them all as legendary. In one tradition Matthew dies peacefully, but in other traditions he is burned, beheaded, or stabbed to death. Yet there may in fact be a gem of truth in one or some of the traditions. Currently, while it may not be possible to determine with any confidence which of those traditions contain a historical core, it would be pretentious to dismiss them all as fabrications. Kraeling suggests the martyrdom accounts of Matthew were invented since so many Christians had died for their faith, and it became incredible than any apostle other than John died naturally.[29] This may be true, but he should provide positive evidence to establish this as the most *reasonable* conclusion.

Analysis of the traditions surrounding the fate of Matthew reveals a few important insights. First, the earliest patristic sources mention nothing of his martyrdom. Neither Eusebius nor Jerome make any mention of the fate of Matthew, although they both mention his ministry in Palestine. This is admittedly an argument from silence, but it does raise the question of whether or not the tradition of his martyrdom existed or was known at this time. Thus, whether or not they contain a historical core, it must be acknowledged that the various martyrdom traditions for Matthew are late. No known traditions exist of the death of Matthew until roughly two centuries after the close of the period of living memory.

---

[27] Elliott, *The Apocryphal New Testament*, 530–31.
[28] Rose, *Ritual Memory*, 176.
[29] Emil G. Kraeling, *The Disciples* (Skokie, IL: Rand McNally, 1966), 165.

Second, there is widespread difference over *how* he died. According to various traditions, he died by burning, beheading with a sword, and stabbing with a spear. If there were agreement that Matthew died by execution, but disagreement about the method, then the issue of agreement might trump the particulars of how he died and reveal a historical core, but given the disagreement over whether or not he died peacefully or as a martyr, the disagreements over his method of execution are much more glaring.

Third, we have traditions that he died as a martyr as well as traditions that he died naturally. Unlike traditions of the fate of Peter or Paul, which unanimously indicate martyrdom in Rome, considerable disagreement exists as to whether or not Matthew died as a martyr. For instance, *Hippolytus on the Twelve* claims that Matthew "fell asleep" in Parthia, and the entry on Matthew in *De ortu et obitu patrum* seems to agree.

In the writings of Clement of Alexandria, we find one of the most frequently cited passages in favor of Matthew's natural death. In *The Stromata* 4.9, Heracleon says:

> That there is a confession by faith and conduct, and one with the voice. The confession that is made with the voice, and before the authorities, is what the most reckon the only confession. Not soundly: and hypocrites also can confess with this confession. But neither will this utterance be found to be spoken universally; for all the saved have confessed with the confession made by the voice, and departed. Of whom are Matthew, Philip, Thomas, Levi, and many others.[30]

Even though it is a minority position, many scholars take this passage as an indication these apostles did *not* die as martyrs, but experienced natural deaths.[31]

This interpretation, however, is less certain than many take it to be. First, it is not clear that the term "departed,"—undoubtedly a euphemism for death in this passage—requires a natural death, especially since the point is that all believers ("the saved") have confessed and then died. However, among the departed could also be those who testified before rulers and then were killed for their faith subsequently, but not before a magistrate. Second, Clement separates Levi and Matthew, whom the Gospels seem to take as the same person, which raises the question of whether Clement is passing on a reliable tradition. Third, it may be that Clement cites Heracleon, but does not necessarily endorse his conclusion. Clement often jots down statements from various sources indiscriminately.[32]

---

[30] Clement of Alexandria, *The Stromata* 4:9, as cited in *Ante-Nicene Fathers: Fathers of the Second Century: Hermas, Tatian, Athenagoras, Theophilus and Clement of Alexandria,* ed. Alexander Roberts and James Donaldson, rev. A. Cleveland Coxe (Buffalo, NY: Christian Literature Co., 1885), 2:422.

[31] Newport, *The Anchor Bible Dictionary,* s.v. "Matthew, Martyrdom of."

[32] A.E. Medlycott, *India and the Apostle Thomas* (London: Ballantyne, 1905), 121.

Fourth, if this passage were in fact indicating martyrdom, it might be an outlier that does not necessarily undermine the rest of the tradition. In the case of Thomas, we have an equally early and widespread tradition that he went to India and died as a martyr. It would be difficult to conclude that one vague passage by Clement (Heracleon) overturns this entire tradition. If Clement is wrong about Thomas, it raises questions regarding his conclusions about Matthew and Philip as well. Fifth, why is John not mentioned? If Clement's goal was to mention apostles who testify and stay faithful to the Gospel throughout their lives without dying as martyrs, then John would have been the perfect candidate. Furthermore, there is no straightforward way to take this passage that does not raise further unanswered questions. Elaine Pagels asks: "Is he [Clement] saying that martyrdom is fine for ordinary Christians, but not necessary for gnostics? Is he offering a rationale for gnostics to avoid martyrdom? If that is what he means, he avoids stating it directly: his comments remain ambiguous."[33]

Sixth, in the same document where Pseudo-Hippolytus claims that Clement died naturally, he mentions that Philip died as a martyr.[34] Therefore, either Pseudo-Hippolytus reports an entirely different tradition than Clement of Alexandria, or the passage in Clement does not indicate they died naturally. While some see this passage in Clement of Alexandria as evidence *against* martyrdom for Matthew, Philip, and Thomas, others see it as evidence *for* their martyrdom. The ambiguity of the passage leads me to consider it inconclusive.

Still, even if this interpretation is mistaken and Clement was reporting that Matthew died a natural death, Heracleon does indicate that the three apostles confessed Christ before the authorities and lived faithfully throughout their entire lives.[35] Heracleon confirms they stayed faithful to the end and never recanted or wavered in their faith. The sincerity of their belief in the risen Jesus is substantiated either way. With this analysis in mind, the following probabilities seem most reasonable in regard to the missionary work and fate of Matthew:

1. Matthew engaged in missionary work outside Jerusalem—*very probably true* (Matt 28:18–20; Acts 1:8; Eusebius *Ecclesiastical History* 3.24; Jerome, *On Illustrious Men* 3.1; Socrates, *The Ecclesiastical History* 1.19; *Hippolytus on the Twelve* 7; *The Acts of Andrew*; other later traditions).

2. Matthew experienced martyrdom—*as plausible as not* (*Hieronymian Martyrology*; *Breviarium Apostolorum*; *Martyrdom of Matthew*; [Latin] *Pseudo-Abdias*; *Contendings of the Apostles*; earliest accounts in the fifth century; disagreement over martyrdom and natural death).

---

33   Elaine Pagels, *The Gnostic Gospels* (New York: Random House, 1979), 97.
34   Pseudo-Hippolytus, *Hippolytus on the Twelve* 5.
35   Pagels, *The Gnostic Gospels*, 97.

Chapter 15
The Martyrdom of James, Son of Alphaeus

James, the son of Alphaeus, is one of the Twelve for whom the least is known. H.S. Vigeveno calls him "the unknown apostle."[1] He appears ninth in all four apostolic lists (Matt 10:3; Mark 3:18; Luke 6:15; Acts 1:13), which may indicate that he was a leader of the third group of apostles.[2] Even so, he was undoubtedly one of the minor apostles. We find no record of his calling to follow Jesus. Apart from the apostolic lists, James, son of Alphaeus, appears nowhere else in the New Testament.

There are six individuals named James in the New Testament, which contributes to some of the confusion surrounding the identity of James, the son of Alphaeus. Among the Twelve, two have the name James—the first, James, the son of Zebedee, was known as "James the Great"; the second, James, the son of Alphaeus, is often referred to as "James the Little." While some have suggested that this means he was less significant among the Twelve, Jewish parallels show it refers to his physical stature. However, the identification of James, son of Alphaeus, with James the Little rests upon the assumption that James, the son of Alphaeus, is the same individual as the son of Mary (Matt 27:56; Mark 15:40), which cannot be proven.

The father of Matthew (Levi) was also called Alphaeus (Mark 2:14). This has led some scholars to consider them brothers.[3] Yet according to the *Anchor Bible Dictionary*: "But since the evangelists seem eager to point out pairs of brothers among the Twelve (as in Peter and Andrew, James and John) but never refer to Matthew and James as brothers, this conclusion seems very improbable."[4]

Even though we have no individual biblical stories of James, son of Alphaeus, we know that, as one of Jesus's closest disciples, he personally traveled with Jesus for an extended period, granting him rare insights into and experiences of the life, character, and ministry of Jesus. He heard Jesus teach many times, witnessed

---

[1]   H.S. Vigeveno, *Thirteen Men Who Changed the World* (Glendale, CA: G/L Publications, 1967), 59.

[2]   Beltran Villegas, "Peter, Philip, and James of Alphaeus," *New Testament Studies* 33 (1987): 292–94.

[3]   For instance, McBirnie draws much of his information about James from his knowledge about Matthew, whom he presumes to be his brother. Yet if they are not brothers, then this information is misleading. William Steuart McBirnie, *The Search for the Twelve Apostles*, rev. ed. (Carol Stream, IL: Tyndale, 1973).

[4]   David Noel Freedman, ed., *The Anchor Bible Dictionary* (New York: 1992), s.v. "James," by Donald A. Hagner.

his miracles, and saw his ascension. He witnessed Jesus alive after he had been killed (1 Cor 15:5; Matt 28:16; Luke 24:36; John 20:19–23; Acts 1:3), and like the rest of the apostles, James, the son of Alphaeus, was willing to suffer for his belief in the resurrection (Acts 5:17–29).

The extra-biblical information on James, the son of Alphaeus, is also minimal. From the second century onward, James is simply mentioned in various lists of the Twelve, including the *Diatessaron* (8.11), the *Acts of Thomas* (1.1), and the *Constitutions of the Holy Apostles* (Homily XXXII). The Book of Common Prayer (sixteenth century) lists James, the son of Alphaeus, as the author of the canonical book of James, but most scholars reject this designation. There is no known Acts of James, and the only known Passion remains unpublished.[5]

The Mission and Martyrdom of James

Beyond the general missionary call for the Twelve, no specific early accounts record the travels of James. There is a tradition that James, the son of Alphaeus, established Christianity in Spain.[6] In the ninth century, the bishop of Iria claimed a star guided him to the burial spot of James. Ever since, James has been recognized as a patron saint of Spain. Given how late these traditions are, Schmidt suggests that James may have stayed in Jerusalem and been stoned to death by Jewish religious leaders who accused him of blasphemy.[7]

Death by Stoning

Schmidt suggests there is some historical precedent for the stoning to death of James in Jerusalem. *Hippolytus on the Twelve* 9 says: "And James the son of Alphæus, when preaching in Jerusalem, was stoned to death by the Jews, and was buried there beside the temple."[8] E.A. Wallis Budge reports a similar fate for James, although he does not mention the burial by the temple.[9] Both stories agree

---

[5]   François Bovon, "Byzantine Witness for the Apocryphal Acts of the Apostles," in *The Apocryphal Acts of the Apostles*, ed. François Bovon, Ann Graham Brock, and Christopher R. Matthews (Cambridge, MA: Harvard University Press, 1999), 91.

[6]   Myrtle Strode-Jackson, *Lives and Legends of Apostles and Evangelists* (London: Morrison & Gibb, 1928), 149.

[7]   Thomas E. Schmidt, *The Apostles After Acts: A Sequel* (Eugene, OR: Cascade, 2013), 115.

[8]   Pseudo-Hippolytus, *Hippolytus on the Twelve* 9, as cited in *Ante-Nicene Fathers: Translations of the Writings of the Fathers down to A.D. 325*, ed. Alexander Roberts and James Donaldson, rev. A. Cleveland Coxe (New York: Christian Literature Co., 1886), 5:255.

[9]   E.A. Wallis Budge, *The Contendings of the Apostles: Being the Histories and the Lives and Martyrdoms and Deaths of the Twelve Apostles and Evangelists* (London: Oxford University Press, 1935), 222.

that religious leaders had James stoned to death in Jerusalem. Although this was a common means of death for blasphemy (cf. Deut 13:1–18), it is difficult to avoid the conclusion that traditions surrounding James, the son of Alphaeus, were conflated with traditions regarding James the brother of Jesus. It is not impossible both were stoned to death in Jerusalem, but the fact that Pseudo-Hippolytus reports the crucifixion in Jerusalem and burial by the temple (which was reported much earlier for James the Just) makes it likely the traditions were conflated. The second fact that makes this tradition suspect is the line in Budge's account "may God curse them!" in reference to the Jews. While this could be a personal line Budge added to the tradition he received, it seems equally possible the tradition of the death of James by the Jews may have been invented to set up James as a saint and further depict the Jews as "God-killers."

Death by Crucifixion

Two traditions hold that James was crucified. The *Hieronymian Martyrology* (*c.* fifth century) places his journeys and crucifixion in Persia. The second tradition comes from Nicetas David, the Paphlagonian (b. ninth century), who wrote a number of homilies on different saints.[10] His *Oration octava*, on the life of James, the son of Alphaeus, provides little historical information about the life of James, son of Alphaeus.[11] The primary focus of the homilies was not to impart historical information, but to connect readers or hearers to the apostle through faith.[12] Yet Nicetas does make it clear that Christian spirituality is tied to history. Bovon explains:

> James is historically relevant on several accounts: as an eyewitness to Christ's miracles, as an adherent to Christ's words, as a participant in Christ's passion, and, after Christ's ascension, as an active apostle and martyr. Nicetas mentions all sorts of travels, agonies, humiliations, including persecution by the Jews and heathen uprisings against him. Finally, James is crucified.[13]

Nicetas tracks the travels of James through Eleutheropolis, Gaza, Tyre, and multiple smaller towns. The martyrdom account occurs in Ostrakine, Egypt. Like Andrew from the *Acts of Andrew* and Peter from the *Acts of Peter*, James gives a speech from the cross. Roughly four centuries later, Nikephoros Kallistos Xanthopoulos wrote his *Historia Ecclesiastica* and provided a similar story for

---

[10] Alexander Kazhdan, ed., *The Oxford Dictionary of Byzantium* (Oxford: Oxford University Press, 1991), s.v. "Niketas David Paphlagon," by Alexander Kazhdan.
[11] Bovon, "Byzantine Witness," 92.
[12] Ibid., 93.
[13] Ibid.

James, the son of Alphaeus. While there are some slight differences in the travel narratives, it is likely they both borrowed from an earlier source regarding James.[14]

Traditions surrounding the travels and fate of James are undoubtedly tentative. Nevertheless, the following points weigh in favor of the martyrdom of James. First, Jesus warned his disciples that they would suffer and be killed, just as Israel had done to the prophets (Matt 21:33–40, 22:6; 23:30–31, 34, 37; Mark 12:1–11; Luke 6:22–23; 11:47–50; 13:34; 20:9–18).

Second, some evidence suggests that some lesser-known apostles died as martyrs—this may include James, son of Alphaeus. In his *Letter to the Smyrneans* 3:1–2, Ignatius reports an appearance of Jesus to his disciples (reminiscent of Luke 24:39), who reach out and touch him. As a result, Ignatius claims: "they also despised death, for they were found to be beyond death." Ignatius seems to assume common knowledge that some of the apostles died as martyrs. He reports their willingness to suffer and die as a result of seeing the risen *physical* Jesus.

Further, in his *Letter to the Philippians* 9, Polycarp lists Ignatius, Paul, and "other apostles" as examples of those who have stayed faithful during persecution and who are now with the Lord:

> I exhort you all, therefore, to yield obedience to the word of righteousness, and to exercise all patience, such as ye have seen [set] before your eyes, not only in the case of the blessed Ignatius, and Zosimus, and Rufus, but also in others among yourselves, and in Paul himself, and the rest of the apostles. [This do] in the assurance that all these have not run in vain, but in faith and righteousness, and that they are [now] in their due place in the presence of the Lord, with whom also they suffered. For they loved not this present world, but Him who died for us, and for our sakes was raised again by God from the dead.[15]

The key part of this passage is when Polycarp refers to Paul "and the other apostles." To encourage the Philippians to remain faithful to death, Polycarp cites the examples of Ignatius, Zosimus, Rufus, Paul, and "other apostles" who remained faithful and are now "in the place they deserved, with the Lord, with whom they also suffered." I addition, the fourth-century Syrian Church father Aphrahat said:

> Great and excellent is the martyrdom of Jesus. He surpassed in affliction and in confession all who were before or after. And after Him was the faithful martyr

---

14   Ibid., 96.

15   Polycarp, *Letter to the Philippians* 9, as cited in *The Ante-Nicene Fathers: The Apostolic Fathers—Justin Martyr—Irenaeus*, ed. Alexander Roberts and James Donaldson, rev. by A. Cleveland Coxe (Buffalo, NY: Christian Literature Co., 1885), 1:35.

Stephen whom the Jews stoned. Simon (Peter) also and Paul were perfect martyrs. And James and John walked in the footsteps of their Master Christ. Also (others) of the apostles hereafter in diverse places confessed and proved true martyrs.[16]

Third, two independent traditions claim James, the son of Alphaeus, was martyred for his faith by stoning or by crucifixion. They disagree on *where* and *how*, but they agree he was martyred. Fourth, there is no record that James recanted his faith or died peacefully. Traditions are unanimous that he was a martyr.

Conclusion

These points are not insignificant, yet it must be conceded that the accounts of James are late and historically tentative. Beyond his membership in the Twelve, we know little else about James with any considerable degree of confidence. When all the facts are considered, the following seems to be the most reasonable conclusion with regard to the travels and fate of James, son of Alphaeus:

1. James, son of Alphaeus, engaged in missionary work outside Jerusalem— *very probably true* (Matt 28:18–20; Acts 1:8; general evidence for the Twelve engaging in missionary work; *Hieronymian Martyrology*; Nicetas David the Paphlagonian, *Oration octava*).
2. James, son of Alphaeus, experienced martyrdom—*as plausible as not* (*Hippolytus on the Twelve* 9; *Hieronymian Martyrology*; Nicetas David the Paphlagonian, *Oration octava*; Nikephoros Kallistos Xanthopoulos, *Historia Ecclesiastica*).

---

[16] Aphrahat, *Demonstration XXI: Of Persecution* (§ 23), as cited in *Nicene and Post-Nicene Fathers of the Christian Church*, ed. Philip Schaff and Henry Wace (New York: Christian Literature Co., 1898), 2:401.

Chapter 16
The Martyrdom of Thaddeus

We know little about the apostle Thaddeus. Along with Andrew and Philip, he was one of three apostles with a non-Hebrew name. Matthew and Mark place him tenth in their apostolic lists, right after James, the son of Alphaeus (Matt 10:3; Mark 3:18). Assuming Thaddeus and Judas, the son of James, are the same person, Luke places him eleventh, right before Judas Iscariot (Luke 6:16; Acts 1:13). It seems most likely that the names Thaddeus and Judas, son of James, do in fact refer to the same person.[1]

Thaddeus does appear under the name Judas in one story in the Gospel of John. During the upper-room discourse with the apostles, Judas, who is specifically identified as *not* Iscariot, asks Jesus a question: "'Lord, how is it that you will manifest yourself to us, and not to the world?'" (John 14:22b). Jesus answers by talking about love and obedience. He insists that anyone who loves him must obey his commands (14:23–24; cf. 8:51; 17:6; 21:15–17). Then Jesus promises the Holy Spirit will help them and teach them all things (14:25). As in the case of Philip and Thomas, who had just previously asked questions, the writer of John makes it clear that Judas also does not yet grasp the true identity of Jesus or the full purpose of his mission. Judas was likely expecting Jesus to make a public proclamation of his identity to convince the world that he was the awaited Messiah. He expected Jesus to show his glory in power, whereas Jesus would show his glory through his death and suffering (John 17:1–5).

Beyond this one question, we know almost nothing about Thaddeus's life both before and after the ascension. Nevertheless, there are a few areas of speculation surrounding his life. Some have argued that Thaddeus was a zealot, like Simon the Canaanite.[2] Whether or not Thaddeus was zealot, he was always placed next to Simon in the apostolic lists, which has led some to conclude they were close friends or ministry partners.[3] Others have argued that he was probably the son of James the Great,[4] and some have suggested that Levi is the

---

[1]   See Chapter 3.

[2]   Ronald Brownrigg, *The Twelve Apostles* (New York: Macmillan, 1974), 163–70.

[3]   Simon the Canaanite and Judas Thaddeus do appear together regularly in later traditions regarding their ministry travels and martyrdoms.

[4]   William Steuart McBirnie, *The Search for the Twelve Apostles*, rev. ed. (Carol Stream, IL: Tyndale, 1973), 150–52.

apostle Thaddeus.[5] These are certainly possibilities, but cannot be upheld with any high degree of confidence.

We do know that for an extended period Thaddeus traveled with Jesus during his public ministry. He heard Jesus teach, and witnessed his many miracles. Jesus considered him one of his trusted friends. For some unknown reason, Jesus believed Thaddeus would be a good follower who could help take the Gospel to the "ends of the earth" after his death. Thaddeus witnessed the risen Christ (1 Cor 15:5; Matt 28:16; Luke 24:36; John 20:19–23; Acts 1:3) and saw him ascend to the Father (Acts 1:9). And like the rest of the apostles, Thaddeus was willing to suffer for his belief in the resurrection (Acts 5:17–29).

Extra-Biblical Accounts of Thaddeus

An early story of Thaddeus, popular in Eastern churches and possibly dating from the end of the second century, has perplexed scholars for some time. According to Eusebius, people far and wide heard of the healing power of Jesus and hoped he would heal them of their sufferings.[6] As a result, King Abgar V (AD 13–50), ruler from the other side of the Euphrates, sent a letter to Jesus, pleading to be healed. Jesus sent him a personal response, promising his request would be fulfilled. Then the apostle Thomas sent Thaddeus, also an apostle and member of the Seventy, to Edessa to preach, evangelize, and heal Abgar. Eusebius claims there are written records that provide evidence of this in the archives of Edessa, the royal capital at that time. The story ends with Thaddeus preaching to all the citizens at Edessa, then refusing to accept money from Abgar.[7] Armenian historian Movsēs Xorenac'I also reports a similar story in his *History of Armenia* (XI–XIII), obviously borrowing from Eusebius. He also reports the fate of the apostle Thaddeus in Armenia (IX).

While the story bears all the marks of legend, Fred Lapham cautions critics "not to exclude the possibility that a simpler form of the tradition could be very much earlier, and on which, like many legends, is not entirely without historical foundation."[8] Rather than Thaddeus, the disciple Thomas sent may

---

5   Barnabas Lindars, "Matthew, Levi, Lebbaeus and the Value of the Western Text," *New Testament Studies* 4 (1958): 220–22.

6   Eusebius, *Ecclesiastical History* 1.13.1, as cited in *Nicene and Post-Nicene Fathers: Eusebius: Church History, Life of Constantine the Great, and Oration in Praise of Constantine*, ed. Philip Schaff and Henry Wace (New York: Christian Literature Co., 1890), 1:100. A similar version of the story is found in Jerome, *Homily on Matthew* 10.4. Jerome admittedly uses Eusebius as a source.

7   Eusebius, *Ecclesiastical History* 1.13.20.

8   Fred Lapham, *An Introduction to the New Testament Apocrypha* (New York: T. & T. Clark, 2003), 37.

have been Addai, who was not one of the Twelve. Addai also appears in the *First Apocalypse of James* (36.15–25), and later Greek writers may have confused him with Thaddeus. Nonetheless, even if this story involving King Abgar were true, it would reveal little about Thaddeus. The emphasis in the story is on the role he plays as an apostle, rather than his unique character as an individual. From what is known of the apostles, many of the others, if not *all* the others, could have performed the same function in Edessa as Thaddeus. But whether or not it is true, Thaddeus's mission to Edessa has been forever sealed into his legacy.

Travels and Fate of Thaddeus

A significant variety of traditions surround the travels and fate of Thaddeus. Schmidt notes: "Their [Simon's and Thaddeus's] traditional areas of missionary activity are literally all over the map, which may indicate either that they traveled extensively or that ignorance of their movements made them convenient subjects for invention."[9] It could be that some of these are true and others false. Traditions needs not be accepted or rejected in their entirety.

A Coptic tradition independent of either the Greek or Latin *Acts of Thaddeus*[10] reports that Thaddeus (Judas) preached and died in Syria.[11] According to the account, Peter joins Thaddeus as they preach, cast out evil spirits, and heal the wounded and sick. In their preaching, the apostles incorporate well-known teachings of Jesus (for example, The Rich Young Man, Mark 10:17–27). After their ministry was finished, Thaddeus died peacefully and Peter continued on his way.[12] However, a separate tradition exists of his ministry and fate in Syria, where Thaddeus is shot with arrows and stoned to death.[13]

Another tradition aims to account for the origin of Christianity in Edessa. Following the account in Eusebius, the (Greek) *Acts of Thaddeus* (fifth century) reports that Thaddeus went to Edessa to help heal the kingdom of Abgar (Abgarus).[14] In this account, Thaddeus finds Abgar already healed. After preaching the Gospel, he baptizes many Greeks, Syrians, and Armenians. He

---

[9]   Thomas E. Schmidt, *The Apostles after Acts: A Sequel* (Eugene, OR: Cascade, 2013), 162.

[10]   Wilhelm Schneemelcher, ed., *New Testament Apocrypha*, trans. R.M. Wilson (Louisville, KY: Westminster John Knox Press, 2003), 2:480.

[11]   E.A. Wallis Budge, *The Contendings of the Apostles: Being the Histories and the Lives and Martyrdoms and Deaths of the Twelve Apostles and Evangelists* (London: Oxford University Press, 1935), 296–306.

[12]   Ibid., 305.

[13]   William Smith and Henry Wace, eds., *Dictionary of Christian Biography* (London: William Clowes & Sons, 1887), s.v. "Thaddaeus," by Richard Adelbert Lipsius.

[14]   Schneemelcher, *New Testament Apocrypha*, 2:481.

destroys idols and builds churches throughout multiple cities in Syria. After traveling, preaching, and converting many to the faith, Thaddeus dies peacefully. This seems to be the same tradition as reported in *Hippolytus on the Twelve* 10: "Jude, who is also called Lebbaeus, preached to the people of Edessa, and to all Mesopotamia, and fell asleep at Berytus, and was buried there."[15]

In contrast to these stories, the Western tradition pairs Simon and Judas (Thaddeus) together as missionaries and martyrs. The (Latin) Pseudo-Abdias (*c.* AD sixth/seventh century)[16] places their activities in Persia, where they encounter the two sorcerers Zaroes and Afraxat (Aphraxat), whom Matthew had expelled from Ethiopia. As they travel throughout Egypt and Babylon, Simon and Judas win multiple spiritual disputes with the two magicians. Even though Simon and Judas spare their lives, the magicians continue to follow the apostles and heckle them in every city they enter. Nevertheless, the two apostles win many converts, ordain deacons, and found multiple churches. They even ordain Abdias, the supposed writer of these stories, who became bishop of Babylon. Kraeling reports an interesting part of the tradition, which may suggest a late second-century date for its composition (*passio Simonis et Judae*). As Simon and Judas traveled through Persia:

> one of their disciples, a man named Craton, is said to have written a long narrative
> in ten books about what they did and suffered during thirteen years of work in
> this field. Sextus Julius Africanus, a soldier who campaigned in Mesopotamia in
> AD 195 and became a friend of the rulers of Edessa, is said to have translated
> the narrative into Latin. It is from this quarter that the Latin *Martyrdom* must
> ultimately have derived its material concerning these apostles.[17]

The story further reports that the religious leaders in the city of Suinar, Persia, eventually arrest Simon and Judas, allowing them either to worship statues of the sun and moon, or die; they choose martyrdom, and are killed with swords.[18] After their deaths, a lightning bolt strikes the temple and splits it into three

---

[15]   Pseudo-Hippolytus, *Hippolytus on the Twelve* 10, as cited in *Ante-Nicene Fathers: Translations of the Writings of the Fathers down to A.D. 325*, ed. Alexander Roberts and James Donaldson, rev. A. Cleveland Coxe (New York: Christian Literature Co., 1886), 5:255.

[16]   The Pseudo-Abdias writings were collected some time in the sixth or seventh centuries. The *Passio Simonis et Judae* shows signs of familiarity with details of the fourth-century Persian kingdom, including ruler, religion, and the role of the magi. Thus, the *terminus post quem* for the origin of the *Passio* is the fourth century. More precise dating is unattainable. See Schneemelcher, *New Testament Apocrypha*, 2:482.

[17]   Emil G. Kraeling, *The Disciples* (Skokie, IL: Rand McNally, 1966), 212.

[18]   One version reports that they were killed, beaten with sticks, and stoned to death. This is why Simon and Judas are often depicted with stick in hand. See Brownrigg, *The Twelve Apostles*, 174.

parts. Zaroes and Afraxat are also struck, and their bodies are incinerated. The Latin *Hieronymian Martyrology* (*c.* fifth century) also reports the Persian city of Suinar as the place of their passion and death.

There is yet another Western tradition placing the ministry of Judas in Mesopotamia, and his death in Armenia. According to the *Breviarium Apostolorum* (*c.* AD 600), "Jude [Thaddeus], which means confessor, was a brother of James, and he preached in Mesopotamia and the inlands of Pontus. He is buried in the city Neritus in Armenia, and his feast is celebrated on 28 October."[19] In his *De ortu et obitu partum*, Isidore of Seville (AD 560–636) largely agrees with the rendition in the *Breviarium*:

> Jude, the brother of James, spread the gospel in Mesopotamia and in the inlands of Pontus, and with his teaching he domesticated the untamed and uncivilized people, as if they were wild beasts, and he submitted them to the faith in the Lord. He is buried in Berito, in Armenia.[20]

These traditions do not state that he died peacefully, but this seems to be the strong implication. Later Greek writers, however, state that infidels in the town of Arat pierced Thaddeus with arrows.[21]

Along with Bartholomew, Thaddeus is also considered one of the "First Illuminators of Armenia." Popular tradition considers him the first evangelist of Armenia, ministering from AD 43 to AD 66.[22] After including the story of Thaddeus and King Abgar, Movsēs Xorenac'I states that Thaddeus was martyred and his body buried in Artaz (Book IX).

While there is debate regarding the historicity of the Thaddeus tradition, Armenian scholar Malachia Ormanian considers the Thaddeus tradition and the apostolic origin of the Armenian Church an "incontrovertible fact in ecclesiastical history."[23] The Armenian tradition is ancient and unvarying that the apostle Thaddeus was one of its apostolic founders. He notes that the presumption of history is not opposed to this tradition, and that this is all that could be asked of the Armenian Church to prove its origin.[24] While traditions

---

[19] Els Rose, *Ritual Memory: The Apocryphal Acts and Liturgical Commemoration in the Early Medieval West (c. 500–1251)* (Leiden, The Netherlands: Brill, 2009), 222.

[20] Ibid., 223.

[21] Lipsius, s.v., "Thaddaeus."

[22] Aziz S. Atiya, *History of Eastern Christianity* (Notre Dame, IN: University of Notre Dame Press, 1968), 315.

[23] Malachia Ormanian, *The Church of Armenia: Her History, Doctrine, Rule, Discipline, Liturgy, Literature, and Existing Condition*, ed. Terenig Poladian, trans. G. Marcar Gregory (London: A.R. Wombray, 1955), 4.

[24] Ibid., 3.

regarding the ministry and fate of Bartholomew are unanimous in Armenia, traditions vary about Thaddeus. Louis Boettiger describes the various traditions:

> Some suppose him to have been the brother of St. Thomas, and according to these, he traveled to Ardaze by way of Edessa. There is an anachronism, however, in this tradition which would transfer the mission of Thaddeus to the second century. According to a second tradition he is not the brother of Thomas, but one St. Judas Thaddeus, surnamed Lebbeus, who also is said to have established a sanctuary of worship at Ardaze, a circumstance admitted by the Greek and Latin churches. The Armenian church places the time of this mission as a period of eight years from 35–43. That this has been done to lay a strong foundation for the claim of apostolic origin may be suspected, especially in view of the belief that apostolic origin is essential to every Christian church, in order, as stated by Ormanian, "to place her in union with her Divine Founder." The church, however, has us at its mercy, for conclusive evidence one way or another is lacking. Nevertheless, the fact of Thaddeus' mission to Armenia wherever and whenever it might have occurred, is undisputed.[25]

The Armenian Church is convinced Thaddaeus was the first evangelist in the country and that he died there as a martyr. The evidence may not be as strong as the Armenian Church insists, but it is not impossible.

Conclusion

As with the other minor apostles, the evidence for the missionary work and fate of Thaddeus is mixed. One difficulty in ascertaining traditions of Thaddeus is the uncertainty surrounding his identity. Possible confusion with Addai (*Doctrine of Addai*), as well as traditions involving Jude, the brother of Jesus, temper the confidence of these conclusions. As far as his fate is concerned, some traditions hold that Thaddeus died as a martyr, including death by the sword, stoning, beaten with sticks, shot with arrows, as well as some martyrdom accounts that do not describe his means of death. But there are also some accounts that he died peacefully. Accounts of his peaceful death and his martyrdom occur in *both* Eastern and Western traditions. There seem to be independent lines of his martyrdom, but also independent lines of his natural death. Traditions vary considerably as to when, how, why, where, and *whether* he died as a martyr, which could mean there was no known fate for Thaddeus and stories could be invented out of thin air to meet the theological needs of various communities.

---

[25]   Louis Angelo Boettiger, *Arminian Legends and Festivals*, Studies in the Social Sciences, vol. 14 (Minneapolis, MN: University of Minnesota Press, 1920), 29.

There could also be some truth in one or more of these traditions that remains amid the legendary exaggeration. The truth is elusive.

Here are some facts that are known. First, Jesus warned his disciples that they would suffer and be killed, just as Israel had done to the prophets (Matt 21:33–40; 22:6; 23:30–31, 34, 37; Mark 12:1–11; Luke 6:22–23; 11:47–50; 13:34; 20:9–18). Thaddeus expected to suffer and possibly die for his faith. He preached the Gospel with this knowledge in mind, willing to face persecution (Acts 5:17–29). Second, early traditions exist that many of the apostles were martyred.[26] Third, there are no stories that Thaddeus recanted his faith. Even if he did die peacefully, we have no good reason to doubt he lived his life faithfully as an eyewitness to the resurrection of Jesus Christ, even amid suffering and the prospect of death. With these facts taken into consideration, the following conclusions seem most reasonable:

1. Thaddeus engaged in missionary work outside Jerusalem—*very probably true* (Matt 28:18–20; Acts 1:8; general evidence for the Twelve engaging in missionary work; Eusebius, *Ecclesiastical History* 1.13; *Acts of Thaddeus*, Movsēs Xorenac'I, *History of Armenia*; *Pseudo-Abdias* [*passio Simonis et Judae*], *Hippolytus on the Twelve* 10; *Contendings of the Apostles*; various martyrologies).

2. Thaddeus experienced martyrdom—*as plausible as not* (martyrdom traditions include Movsēs Xorenac'I, *History of Armenia*; [Latin] *Pseudo-Abdias* [*passio Simonis et Judae*]; various martyrologies; non-martyr traditions include the *Acts of Thaddeus* [Greek]; *Hippolytus on the Twelve* 10; *Breviarium Apostolorum*; Isidore of Seville, *De ortu et obitu partum*).

---

[26] Ignatius, *Letter to the Smyrneans* 3.1–2; Polycarp, *Letter to the Philippians* 9; Aphrahat, *Demonstration XXI: Of Persecution*, §23. Since some traditions place the death of Thaddeus in Syria, Aphrahat would likely have been familiar with traditions of his fate.

Chapter 17
Martyrdom of Simon the Zealot

In the New Testament, Simon the Zealot appears only in the apostolic lists (Matt 10:4; Mark 3:18; Luke 6:15; Acts 1:13), eleventh in Matthew and Mark, and tenth in both Lukan lists. He is sometimes referred to as the "Simon the Cananaean" or "Simon the Canaanite," not to indicate he was from Canaan, but likely as the Aramaic equivalent of the Greek "zealot" (*zēlōtēs*). Simon, called the Zealot to distinguish him from Peter, is arguably the mirror-opposite of Peter in terms of what we know about his life, ministry, and fate.

Many scholars assume that Simon was called "Zealot" to indicate his affiliation with the party known as Zealots. As a fanatical Jewish sect, the Zealots vehemently resented Palestinian control by Rome. They were prepared to use violence to fight for Jewish independence. Their radicalism was one of the reasons Rome destroyed Jerusalem in AD 70. If Simon were indeed a Zealot, there would be much that could rightly be inferred about his character and temperament.

Some writers have built their entire persona of Simon on his supposed affiliation as a Zealot.[1] But Keener urges caution in this identification, since no evidence exists for a group of revolutionaries called zealots before AD 66.[2] The term *zēlōtēs* could simply refer to someone who was committed to the fulfillment of the law.[3] In fact, *zēlōtēs* is used many times in the New Testament without reference to the Zealots (for example, Acts 22:3; Gal 1:14; Acts 21:20; 1 Cor 14:12; Titus 2:14; 1 Peter 3:13). Simon may have been a member of the Zealots, but more likely he was zealous for the traditions of his predecessors and eagerly awaiting fulfillment of the law.

The extra-biblical information on Simon the Zealot is minimal. Records from the first few centuries of the church, including the *Diatessaron* (8.11), the *Acts of Thomas* (1.1), and the *Constitutions of the Holy Apostles* (Homily XXXII), simply mention him in various lists of the Twelve. But a variety of later legends arise about Simon—some possibly with a grain of truth, while others are pure

---

[1] H.S. Vigeveno, *Thirteen Men Who Changed the World* (Glendale, CA: G/L Publications, 1967), 53; Herbert Lockyer, *All the Apostles of the Bible* (Grand Rapids, MI: Zondervan, 1972), 164.

[2] Evidence seems to count against a unified revolutionary movement of Zealots in first-century Palestine. The term "Zealots" referred to a more limited group. See Craig S. Keener, *Acts: An Exegetical Commentary* (Grand Rapids, MI: Baker, 2012), 1:744.

[3] Eckhard J. Schnabel, *Early Christian Mission* (Downers Grove, IL: InterVarsity Press, 2004), 1:269.

invention. One legend claims Simon was one of the shepherds the angels visited to reveal the birth of Christ.[4] In the Byzantine Church, Simon is identified with Nathanael, who was from Cana (John 21:2). Later ecclesiastical tradition identified Judas of James and Simon the Zealot as the brothers of Jesus named "Judas and Simon" (Mark 6:3; Matt 13:55).

Even though Simon the Zealot only appears in the apostolic lists in the New Testament, he clearly personally traveled with Jesus for a lengthy period as one of his closest associates. Simon knew Jesus personally, and saw his life, character, and ministry firsthand. He heard Jesus teach, saw him perform miracles, and watched his ascension. He witnessed Jesus alive after he had been killed (1 Cor 15:5; Matt 28:16; Luke 24:36; John 20:19–23; Acts 1:3), and like the rest of the apostles, Simon the Zealot was willing to suffer for his belief in the resurrection (Acts 5:17–29).

Travels and Martyrdom

Eastern Traditions

Tracking Simon outside the New Testament is not an easy task. One difficulty is that Simon the Zealot is often confused with Simon, son of Clopas (cf. John 19:25), successor to the Jerusalem bishopric after James.[5] *Hippolytus on the Twelve* 11 seems to make this conflation: "Simon the Zealot, the son of Clopas, who is called Jude, became bishop of Jerusalem after James the Just, and fell asleep and was buried there at the age of 120."[6] The (Coptic) *Acts of Simon of Cananaean* also suffer from this confusion, which is common in the Eastern Church. According to this Apocryphal Act, Simon ministered in Jerusalem and Samaria. After being accused of magic, Trajan demands his crucifixion.[7] This is very similar to the version in the *Breviarium Apostolorum*, except it adds Egypt as part of his travels and places his fate during the reign of Emperor Hadrian:

> Simon Zelotes, which means "the zealous," was first called "the Cananean," burning with zeal for God. He was Peter's namesake and equal to him in honor. He received the guidance over Egypt and he is said to have held the chair of

---

[4]   C. Bernard Ruffin, *The Twelve: The Lives of the Apostles After Calvary* (Huntington, IN: Our Sunday Visitor, 1997), 145.

[5]   Eusebius, *Ecclesiastical History* 3.32.

[6]   *Hippolytus on the Twelve* 11, as cited in *The Ante-Nicene Fathers: Translations of the Writings of the Fathers down to A.D. 325*, ed. Alexander Roberts and James Donaldson, rev. A. Cleveland Coxe (New York: Christian Literature Co., 1886), 5:255.

[7]   Wilhelm Schneemelcher, ed., *New Testament Apocrypha*, trans. R.M. Wilson (Louisville, KY: Westminster John Knox Press, 2003), 2:479–80.

Jerusalem after James the Just. After a hundred and twenty years, he was worthy to suffer the martyrdom of passion through the cross during Hadrian's reign.[8]

Isidore of Seville has a similar story for the fate of Simon, but he places it under Trajan rather than Hadrian.[9]

Another Eastern tradition claims Simon the Zealot and Matthias came along with Andrew on his third missionary trip to Georgia. According to this late tradition, Matthias died in the town-fortress of Asparos. Simon the Zealot died later in Abkhazia, and was buried in Nikopsia. Reportedly, in the fourteenth and fifteenth centuries the remains of Simon were transferred to Anakopia.[10]

Western Traditions

The Western tradition, distinct from traditions found in the East, pairs Simon with Judas Thaddeus. The (Latin) *Passio Simonis et Judae* (Book VI of Pseudo-Abdias) considers Simon and Thaddeus apostles and martyrs in Persia. According to the tradition, they travel around preaching, performing miracles, and countering the magic of Zaroes and Arfaxat. Priests and others attack and kill them for refusing to offer sacrifices to the gods of the sun and moon. The author shows familiarity with the fourth-century Persian kingdom, which provides a *terminus post quem* for its origin.[11]

In the *History of Armenia*, Movsēs Xorenac'I confirms that Simon experienced martyrdom in Persia, although he mentions the city of Veriospore. Movsēs mentions that he is unsure of surrounding details, although he is confident of the martyrdom of Simon.[12] The *Hieronymian Martyrology* also mentions the martyrdom of Simon in Persia, although it mentions the city of Suinar. The ninth-century medieval martyrologies of Hrabanus, Florus, Ado, and Usuard also attribute a shared martyrdom for the two apostles.

Britain

One popular tradition reports that Simon—after Joseph of Arimathea was there in AD 36–39—evangelized Britain and was crucified there.[13] The earliest

---

[8]   Els Rose, *Ritual Memory: The Apocryphal Acts and Liturgical Commemoration in the Early Medieval West (c. 500–1251)* (Leiden, The Netherlands: Brill, 2009), 222.

[9]   Ibid., 223.

[10]   Giuli Alasania, "Twenty Centuries of Christianity in Georgia," *IBSU International Refereed Multi-Disciplinary Scientific Journal* 1 (2006): 117–18.

[11]   Schneemelcher, *New Testament Apocrypha*, 2:482.

[12]   Movsēs Xorenac'I, *History of Armenia* Book IX.

[13]   For an in-depth analysis of the tradition that Simon went to Britain, see George F. Jowett, *The Drama of the Lost Disciples* (Bishop Auckland, England: Covenant 2004), 149–60.

evidence comes from Dorotheus, bishop of Tyre (AD 300): "Simon Zelotes traversed all Mauritania, and the regions of the Africans, preaching Christ. He was at last crucified, slain, and buried in Britain"[14]

While this early fourth-century citation comes relatively late, it is not impossible Simon visited Britain. He would have traveled during the *Pax Romana* along fortified roads[15] in relative peace. If Thomas made it east to India, there is no reason in principle why Simon could not have ventured west to Britain.

Morgan claims there can be little doubt Simon visited Britain.[16] Schmidt, however, provides a more reasonable approach:

> What of Britain and Gaul? To a modern reader, they may seem so far from Judea that the notion of travel there, especially by apostles in the first century, can only be the stuff of legend. And granted, there are some outlandish traditions .... But is an apostolic missionary venture to the northern fringes of the empire out of the question? First century Roman roads were excellent, and it was a time of relative peace. By land, it is about 2,600 miles from Jerusalem to London. At [this pace], the journey could be made on foot in four months—or six months with fewer miles per day or longer stops. By sea, the journey is quicker, but perhaps more hazardous. Now, take a dozen young men determined to propagate the gospel throughout the empire and give them about fifty years to accomplish it (say AD 35–85), for a total of six hundred man years. Is it unreasonable to think of just one of those years devoted to Britain, and one more to Gaul?[17]

Admittedly, as far as the prospects of Simon visiting Britain are concerned, Schmidt provides the most optimistic scenario. No record exists of a church founded by Simon in Britain. And Bede the Venerable (eighth century) makes no reference to a visit by Simon in his *Ecclesiastical History of England*, although he does mention early Christians in Britain explaining how they got there. Modern history books of England often similarly describe Christians there in the early centuries without claiming to know when they first arrived.[18]

---

[14]   This quote is from Doretheus, *Synopsis de Apostol*, as found in Richard Williams Morgan, *St. Paul in Britain; Or, The Origin of British As Opposed to Papal Christianity* (Oxford: J.H. and Jas. Parker, 1861), 151.

[15]   Immediately after the invasion by Claudius, the Romans were active in building roads in Britain and other frontiers of the military districts. See Winston S. Churchill, *The Birth of Britain* (New York: Dodd, Mead & Co., 1956), 42.

[16]   Morgan, *St. Paul in Britain*, 150.

[17]   Thomas E. Schmidt, *The Apostles after Acts: A Sequel* (Eugene, OR: Cascade, 2013), 163–64.

[18]   For instance, see A.R. Birley, "Britons and Romans *c.* 100 BC–AD 409," in *The Cambridge Historical Encyclopedia of Great Britain and Ireland*, ed. Christopher Haigh

Tertullian mentions Christians in Britain at the end of the second century.[19] We have good reason to believe, then, that Christianity had arrived in Britain by the late second century, but evidence for its existence there in the first century is much more difficult to ascertain. While Simon might possibly have traveled to Britain, evidence is scant. The fact that British scholars largely ignore his visit is a sign it may be apocryphal.

Some scholars believe Simon may have gone to Britain, but doubt, as Dorotheus reports, his crucifixion there, because crucifixion was a Roman, not British, practice. Therefore, they conclude, his death by crucifixion was most likely invented as a copycat of the fate of Jesus. This may be true, but it is not entirely unreasonable that Simon could have been crucified in Britain. While Rome and Britain first came into contact during the two brief expeditions of Julius Caesar in 55 and 54 BC, lowland Britain was officially brought under Roman hegemony during the reign of Claudius in AD 43. Because of trade, however, Roman influence was felt throughout Britain long before the invasion by Claudius.[20] Many times the Romans dealt harshly with the British to establish their control.[21] The evidence is late and questionable, but it is not entirely impossible that the Romans crucified Simon in Britain.

Conclusion

Simon the Zealot is an apostle for whom there is simply little reliable information. He traveled with Jesus, and witnessed his life, ministry, and resurrection, and he proclaimed that truth and was willing to suffer for it, but beyond that, the information is minimal. We do know, however, that history has often confused Simon the Zealot with Simon, son of Clopas (cf. John 19:25). As with the other apostles (for example, Philip), this confusion makes it difficult to judge what traditions genuinely apply to the apostle. Second, a variety of traditions exist which tell of his journeys as well as his fate. He is said to have traveled to Jerusalem, Samaria, Egypt, Persia, Armenia, Britain, Gaul, and more. It could be that Simon was particularly *zealous* for the Lord, and traveled to many or even all of these places, or various churches could simply have invented stories about Simon since there were no reliable traditions at the time. Third, a variety of means for his fate claim he was crucified, slain with a sword, hacked to death

---

(Cambridge: Cambridge University Press, 1985), 13; W. E. Lunt, *History of England*, 4th ed. (New York: Harper & Brothers, 1957), 28.

[19] Tertullian, *An Answer to the Jews* 7.4.

[20] George Clark, *English History: A Survey* (Oxford: Oxford University Press, 1971), 19.

[21] Walter Phelps Hall, *A History of England and the British Empire*, 3rd ed. (New York: Ginn & Co., 1953), 7.

with an axe, and even died peacefully. Both Eastern and Western accounts of his supposed crucifixion exist, but given that crucifixion was a common means of execution and that hagiographers wanted to paint the apostles similarly to the crucified Christ, this only has so much evidential value. Finally, we have no strong local traditions for Simon, as seen for Thomas in India or Bartholomew and Thaddeus in Armenia.

Wherever scholars land on the fate of Simon, it must be conceded that there is a significant gap in knowledge within the first few centuries of the church. Clearly, he might have died as a martyr. Jesus warned his apostles of coming persecution, and they publicly followed a crucified savior—a criminal in the Roman Empire. There is also evidence that some of the lesser apostles died as martyrs,[22] but it is also possible he died peacefully. Given the breadth of the data, the following conclusions seem most reasonable regarding the travels and fate of Simon the Zealot:

1. Simon the Zealot engaged in missionary work outside Jerusalem— *very probably true* (Matt 28:18–20; Acts 1:8; general evidence for the Twelve engaging in missionary work; [Coptic] *Acts of Simon Cananaean*; Dorotheus, *Synopsis de Apostol*; *Breviarium Apostolorum*; Movsēs Xorenac'I, *History of Armenia*; *Hieronymian Martyrology*; *Pseudo-Abdias* [*passio Simonis et Judae*]).

2. Simon the Zealot experienced martyrdom—*as plausible as not* (martyrdom traditions include Dorotheus, *Synopsis de Apostol*; Movsēs Xorenac'I, *History of Armenia*; [Latin] *Pseudo-Abdias*; *Breviarium Apostolorum*; later martyrologies).

---

[22] Ignatius, *Letter to the Smyrneans* 3.1–2; Polycarp, *Letter to the Philippians* 9; Aphrahat, *Demonstration XXI: Of Persecution*, §23.

Chapter 18
Martyrdom of Matthias

While knowledge of the final four apostles is undoubtedly limited, information about Matthias may be the most scarce. He appears only once in the New Testament, when he is chosen to replace Judas among the 12 apostles (Acts 1:12–25). The name Matthias is a shortened version of Mattathias, which means "Gift of God." He has been suggested as a possible candidate for the Beloved Disciple.[1] According to Eusebius, Matthias was a member of the Seventy before being chosen as an apostle.[2] Many of the earliest extra-biblical citations simply refer to his replacing Judas without providing further information about his life and ministry.[3] Some early accounts where the apostles are assigned places of ministry do not even include Matthias.[4]

According to Clement of Alexandria, Matthias taught the importance of fighting against the flesh, not yielding to pleasure, and building up the soul through faith and knowledge.[5] Another interesting account comes from Hippolytus of Rome, who claims that Matthias gave secret teachings from the Lord to Basilides and Isidore. Hippolytus does not mention the content of the discourses, but twice mentions that Matthias was the source of the secret teachings of Jesus.[6]

Origen and Eusebius both mention a *Gospel of Matthias*, likely composed some time before the third century.[7] Scholars debate whether this is the same document referred to by Clement of Alexandria as *Traditions of Matthias*. No traces of its contents remain, but Eusebius considered it to be heretical,[8] and in the early fifth century it was repudiated and condemned by Pope Innocent I.[9]

---

[1]   Eric L. Titus, "The Identity of the Beloved Disciple," *Journal of Biblical Literature* 69 (1950): 323–28.

[2]   Eusebius, *Ecclesiastical History* 1.12.3. Pseudo-Hippolytus also affirms that Matthias was one of the Seventy. See *Hippolytus on the Twelve* 12.

[3]   Irenaeus, *Against Heresies* 2.20.2; Clement of Alexandria, *Stromata* 6.13; Origen, *Contra Celsum* 2.65.

[4]   *Diatessaron* 8.11; *Acts of Thomas* 1.1.

[5]   Clement of Alexandria, *Stromata* 3.24.25–26.

[6]   Hippolytus, *Refutation of All Heresies* Book VII, chap. 8.

[7]   Wilhelm Schneemelcher, ed., *New Testament Apocrypha*, trans. R.M. Wilson (Louisville, KY: Westminster John Knox Press, 2003), 2:19.

[8]   Eusebius, *Ecclesiastical History* 3.25.

[9]   Els Rose, *Ritual Memory: The Apocryphal Acts and Liturgical Commemoration in the Early Medieval West (c. 500–1251)* (Leiden, The Netherlands: Brill, 2009), 47.

Even though the *Gospel of Matthias* was pseudepigraphal, its existence reveals, in the first two centuries of the church, a significant interest in the life of Matthias compared to some of the other lesser-known apostles. While it is not impossible early traditions existed regarding Matthias, it is equally probable that little was known about him, inviting hagiographers to invent stories about his escapades without fear of reprisal. Arie Zwiep concludes that these accounts are historical fictions and provide no reliable data about Matthias.[10]

One of the difficulties in tracing traditions of Matthias is that he was often confused with the apostle Matthew. For instance, in the *Book of the Resurrection of Jesus Christ*, a Coptic text attributed to Bartholomew, Matthias is referred to as the rich man who left everything to follow Jesus. This is likely a conflation with Levi-Matthew, the tax collector (cf. Matt 9:9). According to Clement of Alexandria, Zaccheus and Matthias refer to the same person, the chief tax collector,[11] yet this is incredible, since Zaccheus was not with Jesus from the baptism of John, and we have no record he was a witness of the resurrection (cf. Acts 1:21–22). According to the early third-century Nag Hammadi text *The Book of Thomas the Contender*, a man named "Mathaias," which could be Matthias or Matthew, wrote down the secret words of the resurrected Lord Jesus to his brother Jude Thomas.

Biblical Evidence: Acts 1:12–25

As noted previously, Matthias appears in the New Testament only when he replaces Judas as the twelfth apostle. There were three criteria for consideration as an apostle.[12] This standard serves to ensure the teachings and traditions of Jesus are passed on faithfully (cf. 1:1–3). First, an apostle must be one who continually followed Jesus. Second, he must have begun following Jesus at the baptism of John and stayed with him until the ascension. Third, he must be a witness of his resurrection (1:21–22).

The apostles narrow potential apostolic replacements down to two: Justus (Joseph) Barsabbas and Matthias. The disciples cast lots, and they fall to Matthias, but he is never mentioned again in the New Testament. Some have suggested there was a mistake in the election of Matthias, and that Paul should have been selected.[13] However, John Stott notes: "But Luke gives no hint at all

---

[10]   Arie W. Zwiep, *Judas and the Choice of Matthias* (Tübingen, Germany: Mohr Siebeck, 2004), 163.

[11]   Clement of Alexandria, *Stromata* 4.6.35.2.

[12]   James D.G. Dunn, *The Acts of the Apostles*, Narrative Commentaries, ed. Ivor H. Jones (Valley Forge, PA: Trinity Press International, 1996), 20.

[13]   Morgan G. Campbell, *The Acts of the Apostles* (Grand Rapids, MI: Revell, 1924), 19–20.

that a mistake was made, in spite of the fact that Paul was obviously his hero. Besides, Paul did not have the fuller qualification which Peter laid down."[14] Karl Heinrich Rengstorf argues that the names of both apostolic candidates belong to the old pre-Lukan stock of tradition. Given that Acts does not show personal interest in Matthias, and his quick rise to a particular dignity, Rengstorf concludes that the Lukan account of the selection of Matthias has the ring of authenticity.[15]

Even though he was not mentioned in the Gospels, Matthias saw the life and ministry of Jesus just as closely as the other apostles. He traveled with Jesus, saw him preach, watched him heal the sick and demon-possessed, and was a witness of his resurrection (Acts 1:22). Origen even surmised that the appearance to the Twelve in 1 Corinthians 15:5 included Matthias.[16] Regardless, as with the other apostles, he was arrested and thrown in prison for preaching about Jesus. As a member of the Twelve, Matthias was beaten for his faith, but continued to proclaim the risen Christ. He was clearly willing to suffer for his belief that Jesus was the expected Messiah, who had risen on the third day.

Travels and Martyrdom

One of the earliest accounts of the travels of Matthias is found in the *Acts of Andrew and Matthias* (AD fifth century).[17] Some believe this was likely part of the original *Acts of Andrew*, but this is unlikely.[18] Yet the *Acts of Andrew and Matthias* is not meant to replace the *Acts of Andrew*; it offers an additional story containing a missionary episode of Andrew and Matthias. There is uncertainty, however, whether the story is about Matthias or Matthew.

The story begins with Matthias (Matthew) being assigned to preach in the city of Myrmidonia, the city of cannibals. The word *Anthropophagi* comes from a combination of the Greek words *anthropos* (man) and *phagein* (eat). It can

---

[14]   John R.W. Stott, *The Message of Acts* (Downers Grove, IL: InterVarsity Press, 1990), 58.

[15]   Karl Heinrich Rengstorf, "The Election of Matthias: *Acts 1.15ff,*" in *Current Issues in New Testament Interpretation*, ed. William Klassen and Graydon F. Snyder (New York: Harper & Brothers, 1962), 182. Reginald Fuller makes the case why there is no good reason that the choice of Matthias cannot be used as evidence for the historicity of the Twelve. See Reginald Fuller, "The Choice of Matthias," in *Studia Evangelica*, ed. Elizabeth A. Livingston (Berlin, Germany: Akademie-Verlag, 1973), 6:140–46.

[16]   Origen, *Contra Celsus* 2.65.

[17]   Also known as *Andrew and Matthias among the Anthropophagi*.

[18]   A. Hilhorst and Pieter J. Lalleman, "The Acts of Andrew: Is it Part of the Original Acts of Andrew?" in *The Apocryphal Acts of Andrew*, ed. Jan N. Bremmer (Leuven, Belgium: Peeters, 2000), 13.

be broadly defined as human beings eating the flesh of fellow humans.[19] When Matthias came to the city, they drugged him and threw him in prison, intending to eat him in three days' time. But Jesus restored his sight and assured him that Andrew would come and rescue him. Andrew arrived and together they healed other blind men in prison. Although Andrew stayed to preach in Myrmidonia, a cloud took Matthias and his disciples to a city in the east where they met Peter.

This story clearly has fanciful elements that may have been invented for a theological purpose. Schneemelcher suggests the stigmatization of cannibalism may be interpreted as a renunciation of any consumption of meat.[20] Nevertheless, it is not entirely impossible that Andrew and Matthias journeyed together to a land known for cannibalism. Cannibalism was not uncommon in the ancient world. There are records of cannibalistic practices in distant lands hundreds of years before the time of Christ and for hundreds of years after. In the fifth century BC, Herodotus describes how the Issedonians serve the dead body of a man's father at a banquet along with the flesh from a sacrificed sheep.[21] In his *Natural History*, Pliny the Elder later wrote that the Scythians fed on human flesh.[22]

Another Eastern tradition claims that Simon the Zealot and Matthias joined Andrew on his third missionary trip to Georgia. According to this tradition, Matthias died in the town-fortress of Asparos.[23] Given the existence of two separate traditions pairing Andrew and Matthias, there may in fact be a historical core to their ministry partnership.

In the apocryphal traditions of the fate of Matthias, he is consistently confused with Matthew, yet one tradition is uniquely for Matthias, which involves a tomb of the apostle at a church in the Benedictine abbey in Trier, Germany. According to the tradition, the remains of Matthias were sent by Constantine to Treves, but were lost under debris during the Norman onslaught. They were later rediscovered, and now lie in Germany, except the skull, which is in Italy.[24]

Another tradition reports the preaching and death of Matthias in Judea. *Hippolytus on the Twelve* 12 says: "And Matthias, who was one of the seventy, was numbered along with the eleven apostles, and preached in Jerusalem, and fell asleep and was buried there."[25] Pseudo-Hippolytus does not mention that Matthias died peacefully, but this is the natural interpretation of the term "fell

---

[19]   Lewis Petrinovich, *The Cannibal Within* (New York: Aldine De Gruyter, 2000), 4.

[20]   Schneemelcher, *New Testament Apocrypha*, 2:445.

[21]   Herodotus, *The History of Herodotus* 4.26; cf. 1.217.

[22]   Pliny the Elder, *Natural History* 7.2.

[23]   Giuli Alasania, "Twenty Centuries of Christianity in Georgia," *IBSU International Refereed Multi-Disciplinary Scientific Journal* 1 (2006): 117–18.

[24]   Ernst Haenchen, *The Acts of the Apostles: A Commentary* (Oxford: Blackwell: 1971), 162 n. 5.

[25]   Pseudo-Hippolytus, *Hippolytus on the Twelve* 12, as cited in *The Ante-Nicene Fathers: Translations of the Writings of the Fathers down to A.D. 325: Fathers of the Third Century*, ed.

asleep." Budge reports the tradition that Matthias preached in Damascus, but died peacefully in Judea after the "men of the city" seized him and tried to burn him alive.[26] Schmidt believes Matthias and James, son of Alphaeus, likely died early, either in Jerusalem or nearby.[27] He concludes that Matthias may have died by stoning at the hands of the chief priests and Pharisees. In *Sacred and Legendary Art*, Anna Jameson records a similar tradition that Matthias preached the Gospel in Judea and was killed at the hands of the Jews. But rather than dying by stoning, she reports that he was killed either by an axe or a lance.[28]

One popular tradition reports that Matthias journeyed to Ethiopia, where he preached and then died as a martyr, which Byzantine Church historian Nicephorus Callistus Xanthopoulos (Nikephoros Kallistos Xanthopoulos) first recorded in his fourteenth-century *Ecclesiastical Historiae* (2.40).[29] Nicephorus depends largely upon early church historians such as Eusebius, Socrates, Sozomenos, Theodoret of Cyrrhus, and Evagrios Scholastikos.[30] Since none of these writers mentions the fate of Matthias in Ethiopia, Nicephorus probably did not transmit an unknown but reliable tradition of his fate. In his *Ecclesiastical History* (1.19), Socrates mentions that Matthew was assigned Ethiopia, but he makes no mention of Matthias. It seems more probable that Nicephorus conflated the traditions of Matthias and Matthew than that he somehow retained an independent, reliable tradition of the fate of the apostle Matthias in Ethiopia.

One final source must be evaluated concerning the fate of Matthias, from the Babylonian Talmud *Sanhedrin* 43a (*c.* AD fourth/fifth century):

> Our Rabbis taught: Yeshu had five disciples, Matthai, Nakai, Nezer, Buni and Todah. When Matthai was brought [before the court] he said to them [the judges], Shall Matthai be executed? Is it not written, *Matthai* [when] *shall I come and appear before God?* Thereupon they retorted: Yes, Matthai shall be executed, since it is written, *When Matthai* [when] *shall* [he] *die and his name perish.*[31]

Alexander Roberts and James Donaldson, rev. A. Cleveland Coxe (Buffalo, NY: Christian Literature Co., 1885), 5:255.

[26] E.A. Wallis Budge, *The Contendings of the Apostles: Being the Histories and the Lives and Martyrdoms and Deaths of the Twelve Apostles and Evangelists* (London: Oxford University Press, 1935), 241–45.

[27] Thomas E. Schmidt, *The Apostles After Acts: A Sequel* (Eugene, OR: Cascade, 2013), 115.

[28] Anna Brownell Jameson, *Sacred and Legendary Art* (New York: Longmans, Green, 1891), 1:254.

[29] Nicephorus Callistus Xanthopoulos, *Ecclesiastical Historiae* 2.40.

[30] Alexander Kazhdan, ed., *The Oxford Dictionary of Byzantium* (Oxford: Oxford University Press, 1991), s.v. "Xanthopoulos, Nikephoros Kallistos," by Alice-Mary Talbot.

[31] Rabbi I. Epstein, trans., *The Babylonian Talmud: Seder Nezikin in Four Volumes* (London: Soncino, 1935), 3:282.

This particular passage follows a section about Jesus. While there is some debate among scholars whether or not certain rabbinical passages refer to Jesus, there is almost universal agreement that *Sanhedrin* 43a refers to Jesus of Nazareth. The context reveals that "Yeshu" was charged with practicing sorcery and leading Israel astray, witnesses were called, and he was hanged on the eve of Passover. Still, the historical value of this passage is questionable. While it is not entirely *impossible* that it retains at least the fossils of an older tradition about Jesus and his disciples, even conservative scholars consider it a "dubious source" and "unlikely" to contain independent testimony related to the historical Jesus.[32] At best, it is a late Jewish account that affirms the existence of Jesus.[33]

While some scholars have suggested this passage may provide evidence for the fate of Matthias, we have serious reasons to question its applicability. First, it is a late source. No rabbinic writings from the first or second century AD exist during the period of living memory. Second, historical questions were not the primary concern in early rabbinic literature such as the Mishnah and Talmud.[34] Third, this particular passage is more concerned with polemic against Christianity than providing an objective account of history.[35]

Even if this passage were historically reliable, there would still be reason to question its relevance to the fate of Matthias. For one thing, it is not clear that "Matthai" refers to the apostle Matthias. It could be a reference to the apostle Matthew. Or since "Matthew" was a common name,[36] it could be a reference to an entirely unknown follower of Jesus. This is made more likely since four other unknown disciples of Jesus are mentioned along with Matthai: Nakai, Nezer, Buni, and Todah. This passage simply cannot provide any confident information as to the fate of the apostle Matthias.

Conclusion

Even though we know very little about Matthias, some important observations can be made about his life and fate. First, as the twelfth apostle, he was a witness of Jesus during his entire ministry as well as of his resurrection (Acts 1:21–22). Second, along with the other apostles, he proclaimed the Gospel publicly and

---

[32]   Craig Evans, "Jesus in Non-Christian Sources," in *Studying the Historical Jesus: Evaluations of the State of Current Research*, ed. Bruce Chilton and Craig Evans (Leiden, The Netherlands: Brill, 1998), 443–50.

[33]   John P. Meier, *A Marginal Jew* (New York: Doubleday, 1991), 1:96.

[34]   Robert E. Van Voorst, *Jesus Outside the New Testament* (Grand Rapids, MI: Eerdmans, 2000), 104.

[35]   Meier, *A Marginal Jew*, 1:95.

[36]   Margaret Williams, "Palestinian Jewish Personal Names in Acts," in *The Book of Acts in its Palestinian Setting*, ed. Richard Bauckham (Grand Rapids, MI: Eerdmans, 1995), 91.

was willing to suffer for his faith (Acts 5:17–42). Third, we have a variety of historically questionable stories about Matthias, appearing in late traditions of the church fathers and in Gnostic sources such as *The Gospel of Matthias*. Fourth, some traditions report Matthias died as a martyr, while others report he died peacefully. Methods of his execution include burning, stoning, and stabbing with either an axe or a lance. And yet *none* of them are even close to the period of living memory.

The tentative nature of the evidence does not mean Matthias died peacefully. After all, Jesus made it clear that his disciples would be persecuted for their faith (Matt 21:33–40; 22:6; 23:30–31, 34, 37; Mark 12:1–11; Luke 6:22–23; 11:47–50; 13:34; 20:9–18). He was fully aware that his public proclamation of the risen Christ might cost him his life, and he embraced it willingly. In addition, early traditions maintain that many of the apostles were martyred, which could have included Matthias.[37] With all the evidence in mind, the following conclusions seem most reasonable:

1. Matthias engaged in missionary work outside Jerusalem—*very probably true* (Matt 28:18–20; Acts 1:8; general evidence for the Twelve engaging in missionary work; variety of traditions that Matthias ministered in Judea, Damascus, Georgia, Scythia, and Ethiopia).

2. Matthias experienced martyrdom—*as plausible as not* (Babylonian Talmud *Sanhedrin* 43a; Nicephorus Callistus Xanthopoulos, *Ecclesiastical Historiae* II.40; later traditions that he was stoned or killed with an axe or a sword; non-martyr traditions *Hippolytus on the Twelve* 12; E.A. Wallis Budge, *The Martyrdom of Saint Matthias*; later traditions that he died naturally).

---

[37] Ignatius, *Letter to the Smyrneans* 3.1–2; Polycarp, *Letter to the Philippians* 9; Aphrahat, *Demonstration XXI: Of Persecution*, §23.

Chapter 19

Conclusion

So far, the evidence for the martyrdom of the apostles has been carefully examined. We have convincing evidence Peter, Paul, James, the son of Zebedee, and James, the brother of the Lord, died as martyrs. It is more probable than not that Thomas died as a martyr, and Andrew warrants a designation of more plausible than not for his fate. And the scant evidence for some of the lesser-known apostles, such as Simon the Zealot and Matthias, makes it difficult to determine their fates with any confidence. The critical point is not that we might establish the martyrdom of all the apostles; rather, their willingness to suffer and die for their firsthand witness of the risen Jesus—this is of foremost importance. The evidence shows that some really died as martyrs, and that none recanted.

The consistent testimony of the New Testament and the earliest sources shows that the apostles were witnesses of the risen Jesus and willingly suffered for the proclamation of the Gospel. No evidence exists that any wavered in their faith or commitment. Of course, this does not mean they were necessarily right, but it does mean they really thought Jesus had risen from the grave, and they bet their lives on it.

But before bringing our investigation to a close—and to distinguish the singular importance of their fates—it is important to consider two common objections.

Objection 1: Others Have Died for Their Beliefs

Clearly, many people throughout history have died for their beliefs. As a form of political protest, for example, Buddhist monks have participated in self-immolation.[1] And on September 11, 2001, 19 radical Muslims hijacked four planes and, killing themselves in the process, attacked and killed thousands of people. Clearly, the willingness to die on their parts shows the sincerity of their beliefs. Muslim radicals believed they were following the commands of the Qur'an and would be rewarded in the afterlife; Buddhist monks believed their

---

[1] Anthony Boyd, "Buddhist Monk Sets Himself on Fire to Protest against the Slaughter of Cattle in Sri Lanka," *The Daily Mail*, May 24, 2013, accessed May 7, 2014, http://www.dailymail.co.uk/news/article-2330398/Buddhist-monk-sets-protest-slaughter-cattle-Sri-Lanka.html.

sacrifice would save more lives in the future or lead to political freedom. Given these Muslim radicals and Buddhists were just as sincere as the apostles, should their claims be considered reliable as well?

But this objection misses a key difference between the deaths of the apostles and modern martyrs. Modern martyrs[2] die for what they sincerely believe to be true, but their knowledge comes secondhand from others. For instance, Muslim terrorists who attacked the Twin Towers on 9/11 were not eyewitnesses of any miracles by Mohammed. In fact, they were not eyewitnesses of *any* events of the life of Mohammed. Rather, they lived over thirteen centuries later. No doubt the Muslim radicals acted out of sincere belief, but their convictions were received secondhand, at best, from others. They did not know Mohammed personally, see him fulfill any prophecy, nor witness him doing any miracles such as walking on water, healing the blind, or rising from the dead. There is a massive difference between willingly dying for the sake of the religious ideas accepted from the testimony of others (Muslim radicals) and willingly dying for the proclamation of a faith based upon one's own eyewitness account (apostles). The deaths of the 19 terrorists provide no more evidence for the truth of Islam than my death would provide for the truth of Christianity. My martyrdom would show I really believed it, but nothing more.

In contrast to the beliefs of these Buddhist monks and Muslim radicals and any other modern martyrs, including Christians, the beliefs of the apostles was not received secondhand, but from personal experience with the risen Jesus (Acts 1:21–22; 1 Cor 15:5–8). They proclaimed what they had seen and heard with their own eyes and ears, not stories received from others (Acts 1:3; 2:22–24). Peter not only claims that he was an eyewitness, but that the events took place in public and that his audience had full knowledge of them. The events were not in secret in a corner. These Buddhist monks and Muslim terrorists were certainly willing to suffer and die for a faith they received secondhand, but the apostles were willing to suffer and die for what they had seen with their own eyes.

If Jesus had not risen from the grave and appeared to his apostles, they alone would have known the falsity of his claims. In other words, if the resurrection did not happen, the apostles would have willingly suffered and died for something they knew was false. While people are willing to die for what they believe is true, it is a stretch to think *all* the apostles were willing to suffer and die for a claim they *knew* was false. The suffering and deaths of the apostles testify to the sincerity of their beliefs that they had seen the risen Jesus.

In *Ancient Christian Martyrdom*, Candida Moss objects to the claim that the deaths of Christians uniquely provide evidence for Christianity: "For much of

---

[2]   The term "modern martyrs" refers to those who die in the present age for their beliefs. Technically, Muslim terrorists would not qualify as *martyrs*, since they are actively murdering people, rather than being put to death for the proclamation of their faith.

the Christian era, martyrdom was viewed as particular to Christianity and as an indication of Christianity's unique possession of religious truth. If Christians alone were prepared to die for their beliefs, it was thought, then there must be something special about Christianity."[3] Moss is certainly right that people of all religious persuasions have been willing to die for their beliefs; however, this is not the argument. The argument presented here rests uniquely upon the apostles as eyewitnesses to the risen Christ. They were willing to die because they had seen the risen Jesus and *knew* death was not the end. Yes, others have died for a *secondhand* faith, but only the apostles died for what they saw *firsthand*.

Objection 2: The Apostles Were Executed Against Their Wills

Could it be possible the apostles were killed unwillingly? Maybe they recanted their faith, rejected the risen Jesus, but were killed anyway. There are a few problems with this suggestion. First, not a shred of evidence exists that any apostle wavered in or recanted his faith—excluding Judas. The uniform testimony from Acts and the early church fathers upholds that they willingly suffered for proclaiming the risen Jesus. Second, the apostles were killed in diverse places, at diverse times, and in diverse ways. If the apostles were all rounded up and killed together, this objection might have some merit. But this is simply not the case. The deaths of the apostles likely took place over a span of about sixty years (AD 42–c. AD 103) and hundreds of miles apart—possibly even *thousands*. Some of the apostles were known to have died (for example, James, the son of Zebedee), yet the others continued to proclaim the Gospel. Given the diverse stories of their travels and fates, it is inconceivable they all unwillingly suffered and died for their faith. In reality, there is no good reason to believe this is true for *any* of them.

Third, if an apostle did recant his faith, it is hard to imagine there would not have been at least one mention of it in history. Historian Michael Licona notes:

> We may also expect that a recantation by any of the disciples would have provided ammunition for Christian opponents like Celsus and Lucian in the third quarter of the second century, the former of which wrote against the church while the latter wrote of the Christian movement in a pejorative manner. Thus to suggest that the disciples did not willingly suffer for their message would be to posit a scenario greatly lacking in plausibility.[4]

---

[3]   Candida R. Moss, *Ancient Christian Martyrdom* (New Haven, CT: Yale University Press, 2012), 23.

[4]   Michael R. Licona, *The Resurrection of Jesus: A New Historiographical Approach* (Downers Grove, IL: InterVarsity Press, 2010), 371.

Summary of Our Investigation

The willingness of the apostles to suffer and die for their faith provides a critical step in establishing their sincerity and reliability as the first witnesses to the resurrected Jesus. This final section contains summaries of the key findings, and draws some general conclusions from this investigation. These initial points portray the context, which provides a general expectation for the martyrdom of the apostles. The final section includes summary findings of the individual apostles and draws some final conclusions

Six points emerge as most relevant for this investigation. First, the Christian movement was a resurrection movement since its inception: that is, "to believe in Jesus" always meant "to believe that he had risen from the grave, conquering death and sin." No evidence exists that the earliest Christians considered the resurrection secondary; rather, the centrality of the resurrection in the earliest creeds, which pre-date the writing of the New Testament books (for example, Rom 1:3–4; 4:24b–25; 1 Thess 4:14; 1 Cor 15:3–7), shows just the opposite— that the resurrection, its historical reality, itself grounded faith in Jesus as Messiah. The resurrection also held a central place in the apostolic *kerygma* as represented in the sermon summaries in Acts (Acts 2:24). From the earliest records of the Christian faith to the writings of the Apostolic Fathers, it is evident the apostles had a *resurrection* faith.

Second, the 12 apostles were the first witnesses to the resurrection, and launched the initial missionary movement from Jerusalem. The missionary efforts of the apostles are supported by both internal and external evidence. They had been with Jesus at least from his baptism until the ascension, and they were eyewitnesses of Jesus after his death (Acts 1:21–22). Paul and James the brother of the Jesus were not members of the Twelve, but they were eyewitnesses of the resurrection (1 Cor 15:7–8) who were willing to suffer and die for their beliefs. After Pentecost, the apostles boldly proclaimed that Jesus is the risen Messiah, even though they were threatened, persecuted, thrown in jail, and martyred (Acts 4:1–22; 5:18–32; 7:54–60; 12:2).

Third, Christians were persecuted in the early church. Jesus had predicted his followers would be persecuted (Matt 10:16–23; Mark 13:9; John 15:18–27; 16:2–3, 33), and that they would suffer and die like Israel had done to the prophets (Matt 21:33–40; 22:6; 23:30–31, 34, 37; Mark 12:1–11; Luke 6:22–23; 11:47–50; 13:34; 20:9–18). Paul not only suffered deeply for proclaiming the Gospel (2 Cor 6:4–9), he also taught that Christians should expect to suffer as well (Rom 8:35–36; 1 Thess 3:3–4; Phil 1:29; 2 Tim 4:5). The expectation of persecution and suffering is a central theme throughout the entirety of the New Testament. Specifically, persecution began in Israel, in Jerusalem, among their own countrymen (as reported in the book of Acts), who turned Jesus over to face crucifixion and threatened, beat, and killed some of the first Christians

(Acts 4:13–22; 5:40; 7:54–60). Roman persecution began during the reign of Nero, the first emperor to use state power against Christians. Once Christians were officially condemned for *the name* by Nero, nothing prevented other provincial governors from punishing Christians in their districts for "deviant" behavior. Christians were largely persecuted for three reasons: following a crucified "criminal," practicing apparently bizarre rituals, and refusing to pay homage to the Roman gods.

Fourth, although there is no early evidence *each* of the apostles died as martyrs, some general claims make their individual martyrdoms more likely than not.[5]

Fifth, the apostles were willing to suffer and die for their faith. The apostles began healing the sick and proclaiming Christ at Pentecost. The consistent reason they gave is that Jesus appeared to them personally over a lengthy period of time (Acts 1:3). They were threatened, beaten, thrown in prison, and killed for their faith, and yet they refused to back down because they obeyed God rather than men (Acts 5:29). Whether or not all the apostles actually died as martyrs, they all willingly proclaimed the risen Jesus with full knowledge it could cost them their lives.

Sixth, there are no accounts that any of the apostles recanted their faith. If any of the apostles were known to have abandoned their faith under pressure, the enemies of the church would have seized this opportunity to discount the burgeoning movement. And yet not a single account exists that *any* of the Twelve, including Paul and James, recanted their belief that Jesus had appeared to them alive after his death. This is not insignificant evidence for the martyrdom of the apostles.

The Individual Apostles

As for the individual apostles, the historical evidence leads to the following assessments regarding the likelihood of their martyrdoms:

1. Peter—*the highest possible probability*
2. Paul—*the highest possible probability*
3. James, brother of Jesus—*very probably true*
4. John, the son of Zebedee—*improbable*
5. Thomas—*more probable than not*
6. Andrew—*more plausible than not*
7. James, son of Zebedee—*the highest possible probability*
8. Philip—*as plausible as not*

---

[5] Ignatius, *Letter to the Smyrneans* 3.1–2; Polycarp, *Letter to the Philippians* 9; Aphrahat, *Demonstration XXI: Of Persecution* §23.

9. Bartholomew—*as plausible as not*
10. Matthew—*as plausible as not*
11. James, son of Alphaeus—*as plausible as not*
12. Thaddeus—*as plausible as not*
13. Simon the Zealot— *as plausible as not*
14. Matthias—*as plausible as not.*

In sum, there are three apostles in the category of *the highest possible probability*, one that is *very probably true*, one that is *more probable than not*, one that is *more plausible than not*, seven that are *as plausible as not*, and one that is *improbable*. Thus, of the 14 apostles, six are at least *more plausible than not*, seven are *as plausible as not*, and only one, John, is lower than *plausible*. More evidence may arise some day that would alter these findings, but currently Table 19.1 shows the most reasonable conclusions.

Table 19.1   Martyrdom probabilities

Highest possible probability	Very probably true	More probable than not	More plausible than not	As plausible as not	*Improbable*
Peter Paul James, son of Zebedee	James, brother of Jesus	Thomas	Andrew	Philip Matthew Thaddeus Bartholomew James, son of Alphaeus Simon the Zealot Matthias	John, son of Zebedee

The willingness of the apostles to suffer and die for their faith contributes significantly to resurrection research. While alone it does not *prove* the resurrection is true, it does show the apostles sincerely believed it. They were not liars. As Blaise Pascal once said: "I only believe histories whose witnesses are ready to be put to death" (822).[6] The apostles proclaimed the risen Jesus to skeptical and antagonistic audiences with full knowledge they would likely suffer and die for their beliefs. All the apostles suffered and were "ready to be put to death," and we have good reason to believe some of them actually faced

---

6   Blaise Pascal, *Pensées*, trans. A.J. Krailsheimer (London: Penguin, 1995), 249.

execution. There is no evidence they ever wavered. Their convictions were not based on secondhand testimony, but personal experience with the risen Jesus, whom they truly believed was the risen Messiah, banking their lives on it. It is difficult to imagine what more a group of ancient witnesses could have done to show greater depth of sincerity and commitment to the truth.

Bibliography

Books

Aageson, James W. *Paul, the Pastoral Epistles, and the Early Church*, edited by Stanley E. Porter. Peabody, MA: Hendrickson, 2008.

Abbot, Geoffrey. *Execution*. New York: St. Martin's Press, 2005.

Achtemeier, Paul. *1 Peter*. Hermeneia. Minneapolis, MN: Fortress Press, 1996.

Akin, Daniel L. *1, 2, 3 John*. The New American Commentary, vol. 38. Nashville, TN: Broadman & Holman, 2001.

Allison, Dale C. *Resurrecting Jesus: The Earliest Christian Tradition and its Interpreters*. New York: T. & T. Clark, 2005.

Aphrahat. *Demonstration XXI: Of Persecution* (§ 23). In vol. 13 of *Nicene and Post-Nicene Fathers of the Christian Church*, edited by Philip Schaff and Henry Wace, 392–401. Buffalo, NY: Christian Literature Co., 1898.

Atiya, Aziz S. *History of Eastern Christianity*. Notre Dame, IN: University of Notre Dame Press, 1968.

Avakian, Arra S. *Armenia: A Journey Through History*. Fresno, CA: Electric Press, 1998.

Baldwin, Matthew C. *Whose Acts of Peter? Text and Historical Context of the Actus Vercellensis*. Tübingen, Germany: Mohr Siebeck, 2005.

Barclay, William. *The Master's Men*. London: SCM Press, 1960.

Barnett, Paul. *The Birth of Christianity: The First Twenty Years*. Grand Rapids, MI: Eerdmans, 2005.

——— . *Jesus and the Rise of Early Christianity*. Downers Grove, IL: InterVarsity Press, 1999.

Barrett, C.K. *Acts of the Apostles*. Hermeneia, vol. 1. New York: T. & T. Clark, 1994.

——— . *Acts of the Apostles*. Hermeneia, 2nd ed., vol. 2. New York: T. & T. Clark, 2004.

——— . *A Critical and Exegetical Commentary on the Acts of the Apostles*. Vol. 1. New York: T. & T. Clark, 1994.

——— . *The Gospel According to St. John: An Introduction with Commentary and Notes on the Greek Text*. 2nd ed. Philadelphia, PA: Westminster, 1978.

Batiffol, Pierre. *History of the Roman Breviary*. Translated by Atwell M.Y. Baylay. New York: Longmans, Green, 1896.

Bauckham, Richard J. *Jesus and the Eyewitnesses: The Gospels as Eyewitness Testimony*. Grand Rapids, MI: Eerdmans, 2006.

———. *Jude and the Relatives of Jesus in the Early Church*. Rev. ed. New York: T. & T. Clark, 2004.

———. *Jude, 2 Peter*. Word Biblical Commentary, vol. 50. Nashville, TN: Thomas Nelson, 1983.

Bauer, W. *Das Johannes-Evangelium*. Tübingen, Germany: Mohr-Siebeck, 1933.

Beasley-Murray, George, R. *John*. Word Biblical Commentary, vol. 36. Nashville, TN: Thomas Nelson, 1999.

Becker, Jürgen. *Paul: Apostle to the Gentiles*. Translated by O.C. Dean, Jr. Louisville, KY: John Knox Press, 1993.

Bernard, John Henry. *Studia Sacra*. London: Hodder & Stoughton, 1917.

Bernheim, Pierre-Antoine. *James, Brother of Jesus*. London: SCM Press, 1997.

Blomberg, Craig L. *Can We Still Believe the Bible?* Grand Rapids, MI: Baker, 2014.

———. *The Historical Reliability of John's Gospel*. Downers Grove, IL: InterVarsity Press, 2001.

———. *Matthew*. The New American Commentary, vol. 22. Nashville, TN: Broadman & Holman, 1992.

Bock, Darrell L. *Acts*. Baker Exegetical Commentary on the New Testament. Grand Rapids, MI: Baker, 2007.

———. *Blasphemy and Exaltation in Judaism: The Charge against Jesus in Mark 14:53–65*. Grand Rapids, MI: Baker, 2000.

Bockmuehl, Markus. *Simon Peter in Scripture and Memory*. Grand Rapids, MI: Baker, 2012.

Boettiger, Louis Angelo. *Arminian Legends and Festivals*. Studies in the Social Sciences. Vol. 14. Minneapolis, MN: University of Minnesota Press, 1920.

Boismard, Marie-Émile. *Le Martyre de Jean L'apôtre*. Pende, France: J. Gabalda, 1996.

Borchert, Gerald L. *John 1–11*. The New American Commentary, vol. 25A. Nashville, TN: Broadman & Holman, 1996.

———. *John 12–21*. The New American Commentary, vol. 25B. Nashville, TN: Broadman & Holman, 2002.

Bovon, François, and Christopher R. Matthews. *The Acts of Philip: A New Translation*. Waco, TX: Baylor University Press, 2012.

Bowersock, G.W. *Martyrdom and Rome*. New York: Cambridge University Press, 1995.

Brown, L.W. *The Indian Christians of St. Thomas*. Cambridge: Cambridge University Press, 1956.

Brown, Raymond E. *The Community of the Beloved Disciple: The Life, Loves, and Hates of an Individual Church in New Testament Times*. Mahwah, NJ: Paulist, 1979.

Brownrigg, Ronald. *The Twelve Apostles*. New York: Macmillan, 1974.

Bruce, F.F. *The Epistle to the Galatians*. The New International Greek Testament Commentary. Grand Rapids, MI: Eerdmans, 1982.

———. *Paul: Apostle of the Heart Set Free*. Grand Rapids, MI: Eerdmans, 2000.

———. *Peter, Stephen, James and John: Studies in Non-Pauline Christianity*. Grand Rapids, MI: Eerdmans, 1979.

———. *Philippians*. New International Biblical Commentary. Peabody, MA: Hendrickson, 1989.

Bryan, Christopher. *The Resurrection of the Messiah*. Oxford: Oxford University Press, 2011.

Buchholz, Dennis D. *Your Eyes Will Be Opened: A Study of the Greek Ethiopic Apocalypse of Peter*. Atlanta, GA: Scholars Press, 1988.

Budge, E.A. Wallis. *The Contendings of the Apostles: Being the Histories and the Lives and Martyrdoms and Deaths of the Twelve Apostles and Evangelists*. London: Oxford University Press, 1935.

Bultmann, Rudolf K. *The Gospel of John: A Commentary*. Translated by G.R. Beasley-Murray, R.W.N. Hoare, and J.K. Riches. Hoboken, NJ: Blackwell, 1971.

———. *Theology of the New Testament*. Vol. 1. Translated by Kendrick Grobel. New York: Charles Scribner's Sons, 1951.

Butz, Jeffrey. *The Brother of Jesus and the Lost Teachings of Christianity*. Rochester, VT: Inner Traditions, 2005.

Cairns, Earle E. *Christianity Through the Centuries: A History of the Christian Church*. 3rd ed. Grand Rapids, MI: Zondervan, 1996.

Cameron, Ron. *Sayings Traditions in the Apocryphon of James*. Harvard Theological Studies 34. Cambridge, MA: Harvard University Press, 2004.

Campbell, Morgan G. *The Acts of the Apostles*. Grand Rapids, MI: Fleming H. Revell, 1924.

Carson, D.A. *The Gospel According to John*. The Pillar New Testament Commentary. Grand Rapids, MI: Eerdmans, 1991.

Cassidy, Richard J. *Paul in Chains: Roman Imprisonment and the Letters of St. Paul*. New York: Crossroads, 2001.

Chahin, M. *The Kingdom of Armenia*. New York: Dorset, 1987.

Chapman, John. *John the Presbyter and the Fourth Gospel*. Oxford: Clarendon Press, 1911.

Charles, Robert Henry. *The Ascension of Isaiah*. London: A. & C. Black, 1900.

———. *A Critical and Exegetical Commentary on the Revelation of St. John*. International Critical Commentary. New York: Charles Scribner's Sons, 1920.

———, ed. and trans. *Pseudepigrapha of the Old Testament*. Vol. 2. Oxford: Clarendon Press, 1913.

Charlesworth, James H. *The Beloved Disciple.* Harrisburg, PA: Trinity Press International, 1995.

Chilton, Bruce. *Rabbi Paul: An Intellectual Biography.* New York: Doubleday, 2004.

———, and Jacob Neusner, eds. *The Brother of Jesus: James the Just and His Mission.* Louisville, KY: Westminster John Knox Press, 2001.

Churchill, Winston S. *The Birth of Britain.* New York: Dodd, Mead & Co., 1956.

Clark, Sir George. *English History: A Survey.* Oxford: Oxford University Press, 1971.

Claypool, John R. *The First to Follow: The Apostles of Jesus.* Harrisburg, NY: Morehouse, 2008.

Clement of Alexandria. *Stromata, Miscellanies.* In vol. 2 of *The Ante-Nicene Fathers: Translations of the Writings of the Fathers down to A.D. 325*, edited by Alexander Roberts and James Donaldson, revised by Cleveland Coxe, 299–569. Buffalo, NY: Christian Literature Co., 1885.

Click, E. Dale. *The Inner Circle.* Lima, OH: CSS, 2000.

Conzelmann, Hans. *Acts of the Apostles.* Hermeneia, edited by Eldon Jay Epp. Translated by James Limburg, A. Thomas Krabel, and Donald H. Juel. Philadelphia, PA: Fortress Press, 1972.

Coxe, A. Cleveland. *Ante-Nicene Fathers: Translations of the Writings of the Fathers down to A.D. 325*, edited by Alexander Roberts and James Donaldson. Grand Rapids, MI: Eerdmans, 1997.

Craig, William Lane. *Assessing the New Testament Evidence for the Historicity of the Resurrection of Jesus.* Lewiston, NY: Edwin Mellen Press, 1989.

Cullman, Oscar. *The Earliest Christian Confessions.* Translated by J.K.S. Reid. London: Lutterworth Press, 1949.

———. *The Johannine Circle.* Translated by John Bowden. Philadelphia, PA: Westminster, 1976.

———. *Peter: Disciple, Apostle, Martyr.* Waco, TX: Baylor University Press, 2011.

Culpepper, R. Alan. *The Johannine School: An Evaluation of the Johannine-School Hypothesis Based on an Investigation of the Nature of Ancient Schools.* Society of Biblical Literature Dissertation Series 26. Missoula, MT: Scholars Press, 1975.

———. *John, the Son of Zebedee: The Life of a Legend.* Minneapolis, MN: Fortress Press, 2000.

Cureton, William. *Ancient Syriac Documents.* London: Williams & Norgate, 1864.

Cyprian. *The Treatises of Cyprian.* In vol. 5 of *The Ante-Nicene Fathers: Translations of the Writings of the Fathers down to A.D. 325*, edited by Alexander Roberts and James Donaldson, revised by Cleveland Coxe, 421–596. Buffalo, NY: Christian Literature Co., 1885.

D'Cruz, F.A. *St. Thomas, the Apostle in India: An Investigation on the Latest Researches in Connection with the Time-Honored Tradition Regarding the Martyrdom of St. Thomas in Southern India*. Madras, India: Hoe & Co., 1922.

Davies, W.D., and D.C. Allison. *Matthew 1–7*. International Critical Commentary. New York: T. & T. Clark, 1988.

de Ste. Croix, G.E.M. *Christian Persecution, Martyrdom, and Orthodoxy*. Edited by Michael Whitby and Joseph Streeter. Oxford: Oxford University Press, 2006.

Drews, Arthur, and Frank R. Zindler. *The Legend of Saint Peter: A Contribution to the Mythology of Christianity*. Austin, TX: American Atheist Press, 1997.

Dunn, James D.G. *The Acts of the Apostles*. Narrative Commentaries, edited by Ivor H. Jones. Valley Forge, PA: Trinity Press International, 1996.

———. *Beginning from Jerusalem: Christianity in the Making*. Vol. 2. Grand Rapids, MI: Eerdmans, 2009.

Dvornik, Francis. *The Idea of Apostolicity in Byzantium and the Legend of the Apostle Andrew*. Cambridge, MA: Harvard University Press, 1958.

Eastman, David L. *Paul the Martyr: The Cult of the Apostle in the Latin West*. Atlanta, GA: Society of Biblical Literature, 2011.

Edwards, James R. *The Gospel According to Mark*. The Pillar New Testament Commentary. Grand Rapids, MI: Eerdmans, 2002.

Ehrman, Bart D., ed. and trans. *The Apostolic Fathers*. 2 vols. Cambridge, MA: Harvard University Press, 2004–2005.

———. *A Brief Introduction to the New Testament*. 3rd ed. Oxford: Oxford University Press, 2013.

———. *Peter, Paul, and Mary Magdalene: The Followers of Jesus in History and Legend*. Oxford: Oxford University Press, 2006.

Eisler, Robert. *The Enigma of the Fourth Gospel*. London: Methuen, 1938.

The Epistle of the Apostles. In *The Apocryphal New Testament*, edited by J.K. Elliott, 557–88. Oxford: Oxford University Press, 2009.

Epstein, Rabbi I., trans. *The Babylonian Talmud: Seder Nezikin in Four Volumes*. London: Soncino, 1935.

Eusebius. *The Church History*. Translated by Paul L. Maier. Grand Rapids, MI: Kregel, 2007.

———. *Ecclesiastical History*. In vol. 2 of *Nicene and Post-Nicene Fathers*, edited by Philip Schaff and Henry Wace, 81–388. New York: Christian Literature Co., 1890.

Evans, Craig A. *Ancient Texts for New Testament Studies*. Grand Rapids, MI: Baker, 2005.

Fee, Gordon D. *1 and 2 Timothy, Titus*. New International Biblical Commentary. Peabody, MA: Hendrickson, 1988.

Firth, C.B. *An Introduction to Indian Church History*. Delhi, India: ISPCK, 1961.

Fitzmyer, Joseph A. *The Gospel According to Luke I–IX: Introduction, Translation, and Notes*. The Anchor Bible, vol. 28. Garden City, NY: Doubleday, 1981.

France, R.T. *The Gospel of Matthew*. Grand Rapids, MI: Eerdmans, 2007.

Frend, W.H.C. *Martyrdom and Persecution in the Early Church*. Oxford: Blackwell, 1965. Corrected ed. Cambridge: James Clark, 2008.

Frykenberg, Eric. *Christianity in India: From Beginnings to the Present*. Oxford: Oxford University Press, 2008.

Gillman, Ian, and Hans-Joachim Klimkeit. *Christians in Asia Before 1500*. Ann Arbor, MI: University of Michigan Press, 1999.

Gonzalez, Justo. *The Early Church to the Dawn of the Reformation*. The Story of Christianity. Revised and updated ed. Vol. 1. New York: HarperCollins, 2010.

Goodspeed, Edgar J. *Matthew: Apostle and Evangelist*. Philadelphia, PA: John C. Winston, 1959.

———. *The Twelve: The Story of Christ's Apostles*. Philadelphia, PA: John C. Winston, 1957.

Grant, Michael. *Saint Peter: A Biography*. New York: Scribner, 1994.

Green, Bernard. *Christianity in Ancient Rome: The First Three Centuries*. New York: T. & T. Clark, 2010.

Green, Gene. *The Letter to the Thessalonians*. The Pillar New Testament Commentary. Grand Rapids, MI: Eerdmans, 2002.

Green, Michael. *The Second Epistle General of Peter and the General Epistle of Jude*. Tyndale New Testament Commentaries. Rev. ed. Grand Rapids, MI: Eerdmans, 1987.

Greenhough, J.G. *The Apostles of Our Lord*. New York: A.C. Armstrong & Son, 1904.

Guthrie, Donald. *The Pastoral Epistles: An Introduction and Commentary*. Grand Rapids, MI: Eerdmans, 1996.

Habermas, Gary R. *The Historical Jesus: Ancient Evidence for the Life of Christ*. Joplin, MO: College Press, 1997.

Hacikyan, Agop J. *The Heritage of Armenian Literature*, vol. 1, edited by Gabriel Basmajian, Edward S. Franchuk, and Nourhan Ouzounian. Detroit, MI: Wayne State University Press, 1999.

Haenchen, Ernst. *The Acts of the Apostles: A Commentary*. Oxford, Blackwell: 1971.

Hall, Ursula. *The Cross of St. Andrew*. Edinburgh: Birlinn, 2006.

Hall, Walter Phelps. *A History of England and the British Empire*. 3rd ed. New York: Ginn & Co., 1953.

Hartin, Patrick J. *James of Jerusalem: Heir to Jesus of Nazareth*. Collegeville, MN: Liturgical Press, 2004.

Hawthorne, Gerald F. *Philippians*. Word Biblical Commentary, vol. 43. Nashville, TN: Thomas Nelson, 2004.

Haykin, Michael A.G. *Rediscovering the Church Fathers*. Wheaton, IL: Crossway, 2011.

Helyer, Larry R. *The Life and Witness of Peter*. Downers Grove, IL: InterVarsity Press, 2012.

Hemer, Colin. *The Book of Acts in the Setting of Hellenistic History*, edited by Conrad H. Gempf. Winona Lake, IN: Eisenbrauns, 1990.

Hendriksen, William. *Exposition of the Gospel According to John*. New Testament Commentary. Grand Rapids, MI: Baker, 1953.

———. *Exposition of the Gospel According to Mark*. New Testament Commentary. Grand Rapids, MI: Baker, 1975.

———. *Exposition of the Gospel According to Matthew*. Baker New Testament Commentary. Grand Rapids, MI: Baker, 1973.

Hengel, Martin. *Crucifixion*. Philadelphia, PA: Fortress Press, 1977.

———. *The Johannine Question*. Translated by John Bowden. Philadelphia, PA: Trinity, 1989.

———. *Saint Peter: The Underestimated Apostle*. Translated by Thomas H. Trapp. Grand Rapids, MI: Eerdmans, 2010.

Herbert, Marie, and Martin McNamara, eds. *Irish Biblical Apocrypha*. Edinburgh: T. & T. Clark, 1989.

Herron, Thomas J. *Clement and the Early Church of Rome: On the Dating of Clement's First Epistle to the Corinthians*. Steubenville, OH: Emmaus Road, 2008.

Hill, Charles E. *From the Lost Teaching of Polycarp*. Tübingen, Germany: Mohr Siebeck, 2006.

Hillyer, Norman. *1 and 2 Peter, Jude*. New International Biblical Commentary. Peabody, MA: Hendrickson, 1992.

Holmes, Michael, W., ed. and trans. *The Apostolic Fathers: Greek Texts and English Translation*. 3rd ed. Grand Rapids, MI: Baker, 2007.

Hooker, Morna D. *The Gospel According to St. Mark*. Black's New Testament Commentary. London: A. & C. Black, 1981.

Hosten, H. *Antiquities from San Thomé and Mylapore*. Mylapore, India: The Diocese of Mylapore, 1936.

Ignatius. *Epistle to the Romans*. In vol. 1 of *The Apostolic Fathers*, edited and translated by Bart D. Ehrman, 69–83. Cambridge, MA: Harvard University Press, 2003.

———. Ignatius. *To the Ephesians*. In vol. 1 of *The Apostolic Fathers*. Edited and translated by Bart D. Ehrman, 219–41. Cambridge, MA: Harvard University Press, 2003.

———. *To the Philadelphians.* In vol. 1 of *The Apostolic Fathers*, edited and translated by Bart D. Ehrman, 283–95. Cambridge, MA: Harvard University Press, 2003.

———. *To the Smyrneans.* In vol. 1 of *The Apostolic Fathers*, edited and translated by Bart D. Ehrman, 285–95. Cambridge, MA: Harvard University Press, 2003.

———. *To the Trallians.* In vol. 1 of *The Apostolic Fathers*, edited and translated by Bart D. Ehrman, 257–69. Cambridge, MA: Harvard University Press, 2003.

Inch, Morris. *12 Who Changed the World: The Lives and Legends of the Disciples.* Nashville, TN: Thomas Nelson, 2003.

Incigneri, Brian C. *The Gospel to the Romans: The Setting and Rhetoric of Mark's Gospel.* Biblical Interpretation Series, vol. 65. Leiden, The Netherlands: Brill, 2003.

Irenaeus. *Against Heresies* 3.2–3. In vol. 1 of *The Ante-Nicene Fathers: Translations of the Writings of the Fathers down to A.D. 325*, edited by Alexander Roberts and James Donaldson, revised by A. Cleveland Coxe, 315–568. Buffalo, NY: Christian Literature Co., 1885.

Jameson, Anna Brownell. *Sacred and Legendary Art.* Vol. 1. New York: Longmans, Green, 1891.

Jenkins, Philip. *Hidden Gospels.* Oxford: Oxford University Press, 2001.

Jewett, Robert. *A Chronology of Paul's Life.* Philadelphia, PA: Fortress Press, 1979.

Josephus. *Antiquities of the Jews.* In *The Works of Josephus.* New Updated Version. Translated by William Whiston. Peabody, MA: Hendrickson, 1987.

———. *The Wars of the Jews.* In *The Works of Josephus: Complete and Unabridged.* Translated by William Whiston. Peabody, MA: Hendrickson, 1987.

Jowett, George F. *The Drama of the Lost Disciples.* Bishop Auckland, England: Covenant, 2004.

Keating, Daniel. *First and Second Peter, Jude.* Grand Rapids, MI: Baker, 2011.

Keay, John. *India: A History.* New York: Atlantic Monthly, 2000.

Keener, Craig S. *Acts: An Exegetical Commentary.* Vol. 1. Grand Rapids, MI: Baker, 2012.

———. *Acts: An Exegetical Commentary.* Vol. 2. Grand Rapids, MI: Baker, 2013.

———. *A Commentary on the Gospel of Matthew.* Grand Rapids, MI: Eerdmans, 1999.

———. *The Gospel of John: A Commentary.* 2 vols. Peabody, MA: Hendrickson, 2003.

———. *The Historical Jesus of the Gospels.* Grand Rapids, MI: Eerdmans, 2009.

———. *The IVP Bible Background Commentary: New Testament.* Downers Grove, IL: InterVarsity Press, 1993.

Kistemaker, Simon J. *Exposition of the First Epistle to the Corinthians*. New Testament Commentary. Grand Rapids, MI: Baker, 1993.

———. *New Testament Commentary: Exposition of the Acts of the Apostles*. Grand Rapids, MI: Baker, 1990.

Klauck, Hans-Josef. *The Apocryphal Acts of the Apostles*. Translated by Brian McNeil. Waco, TX: Baylor University Press, 2008.

———. *Apocryphal Gospels: An Introduction*. Translated by Brian McNeil. New York: T. & T. Clark, 2003.

Klijn, A.F.J. *The Acts of Thomas: Introduction, Text, and Commentary*. Leiden, The Netherlands: Brill, 2003.

Knight, Jonathan. *Disciples of the Beloved: The Christology, Social Setting and Theological Context of the Ascension of Isaiah*. Sheffield, England: Sheffield Academic Press, 1996.

Köstenberger, Andreas J. *John*. Baker Exegetical Commentary on the New Testament. Grand Rapids, MI: Baker, 2004.

Kraeling, Emil G. *The Disciples*. Skokie, IL: Rand McNally, 1966.

Kruger, Michael J. *The Canon Revisited*. Wheaton, IL: Crossway, 2012.

Kruse, Colin G. *John: An Introduction and Commentary*. Edited by Leon Morris. Tyndale New Testament Commentaries. Downers Grove, IL: InterVarsity Press, 2003.

Kurikilamkatt, James. *First Voyage of the Apostle Thomas to India*. Bangalore, India: Asian Trading Corporation, 2005.

Lamont, Stewart. *The Life of Saint Andrew*. London: Hodder & Stoughton, 1997.

Lane, William L. *The Gospel According to Mark*. Grand Rapids, MI: Eerdmans, 1974.

Lapham, Fred. *An Introduction to the New Testament Apocrypha*. New York: T. & T. Clark, 2003.

———. *Peter: The Myth, the Man, and the Writings*. New York: T. & T. Clark, 2003.

Larkin, William J. *Acts*. The IVP New Testament Commentary. Downers Grove, IL: InterVarsity Press, 1995.

LaSor, William. *Great Personalities of the New Testament*. Westwood, NJ: Fleming H. Revell, 1952.

Lewis, Naphtali, and Meyer Reinhold, eds. *Roman Civilization: Selected Readings*. 3rd ed. Vol. 2. New York: Columbia University Press, 1990.

Licona, Michael R. *The Resurrection of Jesus: A New Historiographical Approach*. Downers Grove, IL: InterVarsity Press, 2010.

Lightfoot, J.B. *St. Paul's Epistles to the Colossians and to Philemon*. Rev. ed. Grand Rapids, MI: Zondervan, 1880. Accessed May 1, 2014. https://archive.org/details/saintpaulsepistl1880ligh.

Lincoln, Andrew T. *The Gospel According to Saint John*. Black's New Testament Commentary. New York: Hendrickson, 2005.

Lockyer, Herbert. *All the Apostles of the Bible*. Grand Rapids, MI: Zondervan, 1972.

Longenecker, Richard. *Acts*. In vol. 9 of *The Expositor's Bible Commentary*, edited by Frank E. Gaebelein, 205–573. Grand Rapids, MI: Zondervan, 1981.

Lord, F. Townley. *The Master and His Men: Studies in Christian Enterprise*. London: Carey, 1927.

Luedemann, Gerd. *Opposition to Paul in Jewish Christianity*. Translated by M. Eugene Boring. Minneapolis, MN: Fortress Press, 1983.

Lunt, W.E. *History of England*. 4th ed. New York: Harper & Brothers, 1957.

MacDonald, Dennis R. *The Acts of Andrew and the Acts of Andrew and Matthias in the City of Cannibals*. Atlanta, GA: Scholars Press, 1990.

Mack, Burton L. *Who Wrote the New Testament? The Making of the Christian Myth*. New York: HarperCollins, 1995.

Maclean, Arthur John. *The Ancient Church Orders*. Piscataway, NJ: Gorgias, 2004.

Marcus, Joel. *Mark 8–16: A New Translation with Introduction and Commentary*. The Anchor Yale Bible. New Haven, CT: Yale University Press, 2009.

Martin, Francis, ed. *Acts*. Ancient Christian Commentary on Scripture. Downers Grove, IL: InterVarsity Press, 2006.

The Martyrdom of Isaiah. In vol. 2 of *Pseudepigrapha of the Old Testament*, edited and translated by R.H. Charles, 154–62. Oxford: Clarendon Press, 1913.

Matthew, Shelly. *Perfect Martyr: The Stoning of Stephen and the Construction of Christian Identity*. Oxford: Oxford University Press, 2010.

Matthews, Christopher R. *Philip: Apostle and Evangelist*. Boston, MA: Brill, 2002.

Mayer, Marianna. *The Twelve Apostles*. New York: Phyllis Fogelman, 2000.

McBirnie, William Steuart. *The Search for the Twelve Apostles*. Rev. ed. Carol Stream, IL: Tyndale, 1973.

McRay, John. *Paul: His Life and Teaching*. Grand Rapids, MI: Baker, 2003.

Medlycott, A.E. *India and the Apostle Thomas*. London: Ballantyne, 1905.

Meier, John P. *A Marginal Jew*. 5 vols. New York: Doubleday, 1991–2015.

Meinardus, Otto F.A. *St. Paul's Last Journey*. New Rochelle, NY: Caratzas Brothers, 1979.

Menachery, George, ed. *The St. Thomas Christian Encyclopaedia of India*. Vol. 1. Madras, India: BNK Press, 1982.

Merrill, Eugene H. *Deuteronomy*. New American Commentary, vol. 4. Nashville, TN: Broadman & Holman, 1994.

———. *Signature in The Cell*. New York: HarperCollins, 2009.

Michaels, J. Ramsey. *The Gospel of John*. Grand Rapids, MI: Eerdmans, 2010.

Middleton, Paul. *Radical Martyrdom and Cosmic Conflict in Early Christianity.* New York: T. & T. Clark, 2006.

Mingana, Alphonse. *The Early Spread of Christianity in India.* Manchester: Manchester University Press, 1926.

Moffett, Samuel Hugh. *Beginnings to 1500.* A History of Christianity in Asia. Vol. 1. New York: HarperCollins, 1992.

Moo, Douglas J. *The Letter of James.* The Pillar New Testament Commentary. Grand Rapids, MI: Eerdmans, 2000.

———. *2 Peter and Jude.* The NIV Application Commentary. Grand Rapids, MI: Zondervan, 1996.

Morgan, Richard Williams. *St. Paul in Britain; Or, The Origin of British As Opposed to Papal Christianity.* Oxford: J.H. and Jas. Parker, 1861.

Morris, Leon. *The Gospel According to John.* Rev ed. Grand Rapids, MI: Eerdmans, 1995.

———. *The Gospel According to Matthew.* The Pillar New Testament Commentary. Grand Rapids, MI: Eerdmans, 1992.

Moss, Candida R. *Ancient Christian Martyrdom.* New Haven, CT: Yale University Press, 2012.

———. *The Myth of Persecution: How Early Christians Invented a Story of Martyrdom.* New York: HarperCollins, 2013.

Most, Glenn W. *Doubting Thomas.* Cambridge, MA: Harvard University Press, 2005.

Mounce, William D. *Pastoral Epistles.* Word Biblical Commentary, vol. 46. Nashville, TN: Thomas Nelson, 2000.

Mundadan, A. Mathias. *From the Beginning up to the Middle of the Sixteenth Century up to 1542.* History of Christianity in India. Vol 1. Bangalore, India: Theological Publications in India, 1984.

Murphy-O'Connor, Jerome. *Paul: A Critical Life.* Oxford: Oxford University Press, 1996.

———, *Paul: His Story.* Oxford: Oxford University Press, 2004.

Musurillo, Herbert. *The Acts of the Christian Martyrs.* London: Oxford University Press, 1972.

Neill, Stephen. *Christian Missions.* Baltimore, MD: Penguin, 1964.

———. *A History of Christianity in India: The Beginning to AD 1707.* Cambridge: Cambridge University Press, 1984.

Newman, Barclay M., and Philip Stine. *Matthew: A Handbook on the Gospel of Matthew.* New York: United Bible Societies, 1988.

Neyrey, Jerome H. *2 Peter, Jude: A New Translation with Introduction and Commentary.* The Anchor Yale Bible. New Haven, CT: Yale University Press, 1993.

Novak, Ralph Martin, Jr. *Christianity and the Roman Empire.* Harrisburg, PA: Trinity Press, 2001.

O'Connor, Daniel W. *Peter in Rome: The Literary, Liturgical, and Archaeological Evidence*. New York: Columbia University Press, 1969.

Ormanian, Malachia. *The Church of Armenia: Her History, Doctrine, Rule, Discipline, Liturgy, Literature, and Existing Condition*, edited by Terenig Poladian. Translated by G. Marcar Gregory. London: A.R. Wombray, 1955.

Pagels, Elaine. *The Gnostic Gospels*. New York: Random House, 1979.

Painter, John. *Just James: The Brother of Jesus in History and Tradition*. Columbia, SC: University of South Carolina Press, 1997.

Pargiter, F.E. *Ancient Indian Historical Tradition*. London: Oxford University Press, 1922.

Paley, William. *A View of the Evidences of Christianity*. London: John W. Parker & Son, 1859.

Pascal, Blaise. *Pensées*. Translated by A.J. Krailsheimer. London: Penguin, 1995.

Patrick, James. *Andrew of Bethsaida and the Johannine Circle*. New York: Peter Lang, 2013.

Penner, Myron B., ed. *Christianity and the Postmodern Turn: Six Views*. Grand Rapids, MI: Brazos, 2005.

Perkins, Pheme. *Peter: Apostle for the Whole Church*. Minneapolis, MN: Fortress Press, 2000.

Perumalil, A.C. *The Apostles in India*. 2nd ed. Dasarahalli, India: St. Paul Press Training School, 1971.

Pervo, Richard I. *Acts: A Commentary on the Book of Acts*. Hermeneia. Minneapolis, MN: Fortress Press, 2009.

———. *The Making of Paul: Constructions of the Apostle in Early Christianity*. Minneapolis, MN: Fortress Press, 2010.

Peterson, David G. *The Acts of the Apostles*. Pillar New Testament Commentary. Grand Rapids, MI: Eerdmans, 2009.

Peterson, Peter M. *Andrew, Brother of Simon Peter: His History and His Legends*. Leiden, The Netherlands: Brill, 1958.

Petrinovich, Lewis. *The Cannibal Within*. New York: Aldine De Gruyter, 2000.

Pobee, John S. *Persecution and Martyrdom in the Theology of Paul*. Journal for the Study of the New Testament Supplement Series, edited by Bruce D. Chilton. Sheffield, England: JSOT Press, 1985.

Podipara, Placid J. *Thomas Christians*. Bombay, India: Darton, Longman & Todd, 1970.

———. *The Thomas Christians and Their Syriac Treasures*. Alleppey, South India: Praksam, 1974.

Polhill, John B. *Acts*. The New American Commentary, vol. 26. Nashville, TN: Broadman & Holman, 1992.

Pope Benedict XVI. *The Apostles*. Huntington, IN: Our Sunday Visitor, 2007.

Quasten, Johannes. *The Beginnings of Patristic Literature*. Patrology, vol 1. Westminster, MD: Newman, 1950.

Rapske, Brian. *The Book of Acts and Paul in Roman Custody*, edited by Bruce W. Winter. Grand Rapids, MI: Eerdmans, 1994.

Rapson, Edward James. *The Cambridge History of India*. Vol. 1. London: Cambridge University Press, 1922.

Reese, Ruth Anne. *2 Peter and Jude*. Grand Rapids, MI: Eerdmans, 2007.

Rengstorf, Karl Heinrich. *Apostolate and Ministry: The New Testament Doctrine of the Office of the Ministry*. Concordia Heritage Series. Translated by Paul D. Pahl. St. Louis, MO: Concordia, 1969.

Rice, Tamara. *The Scythians*. New York: Frederick A. Praeger, 1957.

Ridderbos, Herman N. *The Gospel According to John: A Theological Commentary*. Translated by John Vriend. Grand Rapids, MI: Eerdmans, 1997.

Riesner, Rainer. *Paul's Early Period: Chronology, Mission, Strategy, Theology*. Translated by Doug Stott. Grand Rapids, MI: Eerdmans, 1998.

Roberts, Alexander, and James Donaldson, eds. *Hippolytus on the Twelve*. In vol. 5 of *The Ante-Nicene Fathers: Translations of the Writings of the Fathers down to A.D. 325: Fathers of the Third Century*, revised by A. Cleveland Coxe, 255–56. Buffalo, NY: Christian Literature Co., 1885.

Roberts, Alexander, James Donaldson, Phillip Schaff, and Henry Wace, eds. *Nicene and Post-Nicene Fathers of the Christian Church*. Vol. 6. New York: Christian Literature Co., 1896.

Robinson, John A.T. *The Priority of John*, edited by J.F. Coakley. London: SCM Press, 1985.

Roetzel, Calvin. *Paul: The Man and the Myth*. Minneapolis, MN: Fortress Press, 1999.

Rooney, John. *Shadows in the Dark: A History of Christianity in Pakistan Up to the 10th Century*. Rawalpindi, Pakistan: Christian Study Centre, 1984.

Rose, Els. *Ritual Memory: The Apocryphal Acts and Liturgical Commemoration in the Early Medieval West (c. 500–1251)*. Leiden, The Netherlands: Brill, 2009.

Rosenblatt, Marie-Eloise. *Paul the Accused: His Portrait in the Acts of the Apostles*. Collegeville, MN: Liturgical Press, 1995.

Ross, Peter. *Saint Andrew: The Disciple, the Missionary, the Patron Saint*. New York: The Scottish American, 1886.

Ruffin, C. Bernard. *The Twelve: The Lives of the Apostles After Calvary*. Huntington, IN: Our Sunday Visitor, 1997.

Saint Jerome. *On Illustrious Men*. Translated by Thomas P. Halton. Washington, DC: Catholic University of America Press, 1999.

Sanders, E.P. *The Historical Figure of Jesus*. New York: Penguin, 1993.

––––––. *Jesus and Judaism*. London: SCM Press, 1985.

Sanders, J.N. *A Commentary on the Gospel According to St. John*. Black's New Testament Commentary. London: A. & C. Black, 1968.

Schaff, Philip. *History of the Christian Church*. Vol. 1. Grand Rapids, MI: Eerdmans, 1955.

Schmidt, Thomas E. *The Apostles After Acts: A Sequel.* Eugene, OR: Cascade, 2013.

Schnabel, Eckhard J. *Early Christian Mission: Paul and the Early Church*. 2 vols. Downers Grove, IL: InterVarsity Press, 2004.

Schneemelcher, Wilhelm, ed. *The Acts of Peter and the Twelve Apostles.* In *New Testament Apocrypha*. Vol. 2. Writings Relating to the Apostles; Apocalypses and Related Topics. Translated by R.M. Wilson. Louisville, KY: Westminster John Knox Press, 2003.

———, ed. *The Acts of Thomas*. In *New Testament Apocrypha*. Vol. 2. Writings Relating to the Apostles; Apocalypses and Related Topics. Translated by R.M. Wilson. Louisville, KY: Westminster John Knox Press, 2003.

Schnelle, Udo. *Apostle Paul: His Life and Theology*. Translated by M. Eugene Boring. Grand Rapids, MI: Baker, 2003.

Schoedel, William R. *Ignatius of Antioch: A Commentary on the Letters of Ignatius of Antioch*. Philadelphia, PA: Fortress Press, 1985.

Shanks, Monte A. *Papias and the New Testament*. Eugene, OR: Pickwick, 2013.

Smith, Asbury. *The Twelve Christ Chose*. New York: Harper & Row, 1958.

Smith, Terence V. *Petrine Controversies in the Early Church*. Tübingen, Germany: J.C.B. Mohr, 1985.

Snyder, Glenn E. *Acts of Paul: Formation of a Pauline Corpus*, edited by Jörg Frey. Tübingen, Germany: Mohr Siebeck, 2013.

Spencer, F. Scott. *The Portrait of Philip in Acts*. Journal for the Study of the New Testament Supplement Series. Vol. 67, edited by Stanley E. Porter. Sheffield, England: JSOT, 1992.

Stein, Robert. *Luke*. The New American Commentary, vol. 24. Nashville, TN: Broadman & Holman, 1992.

Stott, John R.W. *The Message of Acts*. Downers Grove, IL: InterVarsity Press, 1990.

Strickert, Fred. *Philip's City: From Bethsaida to Julias*. Collegeville, MN: Liturgical Press, 2011.

Strode-Jackson, Myrtle. *Lives and Legends of Apostles and Evangelists.* London: Morrison & Gibb, 1928.

Tajra, Harry W. *The Martyrdom of St. Paul.* Eugene, OR: Wipf & Stock, 1994.

Tenney, Merrill C. *John*. In vol. 9 of *The Expositor's Bible Commentary*, edited by J.D. Douglas and Frank E. Gaebelein, 1–205. Grand Rapids, MI: Zondervan, 1981.

Tertullian. *The Apology*. In vol. 3 of *The Ante-Nicene Fathers: Translations of the Writings of the Fathers down to A.D. 325*, edited by Alexander Roberts and James Donaldson. Revised and translated by A Cleveland Coxe, 17–55. Buffalo, NY: Christian Literature Co., 1885.

————. *On Baptism*. In vol. 3 of *The Ante-Nicene Fathers: Translations of the Writings of the Fathers down to A.D. 325*, edited by Alexander Roberts and James Donaldson. Revised and translated by A Cleveland Coxe, 669–97. Buffalo, NY: Christian Literature Co., 1885.

————. *Scorpiace*. In vol. 3 of *The Ante-Nicene Fathers: Translations of the Writings of the Fathers down to A.D. 325*, edited by Alexander Roberts and James Donaldson. Revised and translated by A Cleveland Coxe, 633–48. Buffalo, NY: Christian Literature Co., 1885.

Thapar, Romila. *A History of India*. Vol. 1. New York: Penguin, 1966.

Thiede, Carsten. *Simon Peter: From Galilee to Rome*. Grand Rapids, MI: Zondervan, 1988.

Thiselton, Anthony C. *The First Epistle to the Corinthians: A Commentary on the Greek Text*. Grand Rapids, MI: Eerdmans, 2000.

Thomas, Christine M. *The Acts of Peter: Gospel Literature, and the Ancient Novel*. Oxford: Oxford University Press, 2003.

Timmons, W. Milton. *Everything About the Bible that You Never Had Time to Look Up*. Bloomington, IN: Xlibris, 2002.

Tisserant, Eugene. *Eastern Christianity in India*. Calcutta, India: Orient Longmans, 1957.

Topchyan, Aram. *The Problem of Greek Sources of Movsēs Xorenac'I's*. History of Armenia. Leuven, Belgium: Peeters, 2006.

Torrey, Charles Cutler, ed. and trans. *The Lives of the Prophets: Greek Text and Translation*. Philadelphia, PA: Society of Biblical Literature and Exegesis, 1946.

Ulrich, Luz. *Matthew 1–7: A Commentary on Matthew 1–7*. Edited by H. Koester. Translated by James E. Crouch. Minneapolis, MN: Fortress Press, 2007.

Vadakkekara, Benedict. *Origin of India's St. Thomas Christians: A Historiographical Critique*. Delhi, India: Media House, 1995.

Van Voorst, Robert E. *The Ascents of James: History and Theology of a Jewish-Christian Community*. Society of Biblical Literature Dissertation Series 112. Atlanta, GA: Scholars Press, 1989.

————. *Jesus Outside the New Testament*. Grand Rapids, MI: Eerdmans, 2000.

Vigeveno, H.S. *Thirteen Men Who Changed the World*. Glendale, CA: G/L Publications, 1967.

Vinson, Richard B., Richard F. Wilson, and Watson E. Mills. *1 and 2 Peter*. Smyth & Helwys Bible Commentary. Macon, GA: Smyth & Helwys.

Von Wahlde, Urban C. *The Gospels and Letters of John*. Eerdmans Critical Commentary. Vol. 2. Grand Rapids, MI: Eerdmans, 2010.

Wallace, Daniel B. *The Basics of New Testament Syntax*. Grand Rapids, MI: Zondervan, 2000.

Weidmann, Frederick W. *Polycarp and John: The Harris Fragments and Their Challenge to the Literary Traditions*. Notre Dame, IL: Notre Dame Press, 1999.

Weinrich, William C. *Spirit and Martyrdom: A Study of the Work of the Holy Spirit in Contexts of Persecution and Martyrdom in the New Testament and Early Christian Literature*. Washington, DC: University Press of America, 1981.

Weiss, Johannes. *A History of the Period A.D. 30–150*. Vol. 2. Translated by Frederick C. Grant. New York: Harper & Brothers, 1937.

Westcott, B.F. *The Gospel According to St. John: The Authorized Version with Introduction and Notes*. London: Cambridge University Press, 1882.

Williams, Francis E. *The Nag Hammadi Library in English*, edited by James M. Robinson. Rev. ed. San Francisco, CA: HarperCollins, 1990.

Williams, John, and Alison Stones, eds. *The Codex Calixtinus and the Shrine of St. James*. Tübingen, Germany: Gunter Narr Verlag, 1992.

Wilson, A.N. *Paul: The Mind of the Apostle*. New York: W.W. Norton, 1997.

Wirgin, Wolf. *Herod Agrippa 1: King of the Jews*. Monograph Series, vol. 10(A). Leeds, England: Leeds University Oriental Society: 1968.

Witherington, Ben, III. *The Acts of the Apostles: A Socio-Rhetorical Commentary*. Grand Rapids, MI: Eerdmans, 1998.

———. *The Gospel of Mark: A Socio-Rhetorical Commentary*. Grand Rapids, MI: Eerdmans, 2001.

———. *What Have They Done with Jesus?* New York: HarperCollins, 2006.

Workman, Herbert B. *Persecution in the Early Church*. Cincinnati, OH: Jennings & Graham, 1906.

Wrede, William. *Paul*. London: Philip Green, 1907.

Wright, N.T. *The Resurrection of the Son of God*. Minneapolis, MN: Fortress Press, 2003.

Zahn, Theodor. *Introduction to the New Testament*. Vols. 2, 3. Translated by Melancthon Jacobus. Edinburgh: T. & T. Clark, 1909.

Zwiep, Arie W. *Judas and the Choice of Matthias*. Tübingen, Germany: Mohr Siebeck, 2004.

Articles and Book Chapters

Alasania, Giuli. "Twenty Centuries of Christianity in Georgia." *IBSU International Refereed Multi-Disciplinary Scientific Journal* 1 (2006): 117–29.

Alexandrou, George, and Nun Nectaria McLees. "The Astonishing Missionary Journeys of the Apostle Andrew." *Road to Emmaus* 4 (2010): 3–55.

Ash, Marinell, and Dauvit Brown. "The Adoption of Saint Andrew as Patron Saint of Scotland." In *Medieval Art and Architecture in the Diocese of St Andrews*, edited by John Higgit, 1–6. London: British Archaeological Association, 1994.

Badham, F.P. "The Martyrdom of St. John." *American Journal of Theology* 4 (1899): 729–40.

Barrett, C.K. "The Historicity of Acts." *Journal of Theological Studies* 50:2 (1999): 515–34.

Barton, Stephen C. "Paul as Missionary and Pastor." In *The Cambridge Companion to St. Paul*, edited by James D.G. Dunn, 34–50. Cambridge: Cambridge University Press, 2003.

Bauckham, Richard J. "For What Offence Was James Put to Death?" In *James the Just and Christian Origins*, edited by Bruce Chilton and Craig A. Evans, 199–232. Leiden, The Netherlands: Brill, 1999.

———. "James and Jesus." In *The Brother of Jesus: James the Just and His Mission*, edited by Bruce Chilton and Jacob Neusner, 100–37. Louisville, KY: Westminster Knox, 2001.

———. "James and the Jerusalem Church." In *The Book of Acts in its Palestinian Setting*, edited by Richard Bauckham, 415–80. Grand Rapids, MI: Eerdmans, 1995.

———. "The Martyrdom of Peter in Early Christian Literature." In *Rise and Decline of the Roman World*, edited by Wolfgang Haase and Hildegard Temporini, Part II, vol. 26, 539–95. New York: Walter De Gruyter, 1992.

Benario, Herbert W. "The Annals." In *A Companion to Tacitus*, edited by Victoria Emma Pagán 114–15. Chichester, England: Wiley-Blackwell, 2012.

Biblical Archaeology Society. "Philip's Tomb Discovered—but Not Where Expected." *Biblical Archaeological Review* 38 (January/February 2012): 18.

Birley, A.R. "Britons and Romans *c*. 100 BC–AD 409." In *The Cambridge Historical Encyclopedia of Great Britain and Ireland*, edited by Christopher Haigh, 5–53. Cambridge: Cambridge University Press, 1985.

Bock, Darrell. "Apologetics Commentary on the Acts of the Apostles." In *The Holman Apologetics Commentary on the Bible*, edited by Jeremy Royal Howard, 635–48. Nashville, TN: Broadman & Holman, 2013.

Bockmuehl, Markus. "Peter's Death in Rome? Back to Front and Upside Down." *Scottish Journal of Theology* 60 (2007): 1–23.

———. "Syrian Memories of Peter: Ignatius, Justin, and Serapion." In *The Image of the Judaeo-Christians in Ancient Jewish and Christian Literature: Papers Delivered at the Colloquium of the Institutum Judaicum, Brussels 18–19 November, 2001*, edited by P.J. Tomson and D. Lambers-Petry, 124–46. Tübingen, Germany: Mohr Siebeck, 2001.

Bolyki, János. "Martyrium Pauli." In *The Apocryphal Acts of Paul and Thecla*, edited by Jan N. Bremmer, 92–106. Kampen, The Netherlands: Kok Pharos, 1996.

———. "Miracle Stories in the Acts of John." In *The Apocryphal Acts of John*, edited by Jan N. Bremmer, 15–35. Kampen, The Netherlands: Kok Pharos, 1995.

Bovon, François. "Byzantine Witness for the Apocryphal Acts of the Apostles." In *The Apocryphal Acts of the Apostles*, edited by François Bovon, Ann Graham Bock, and Christopher R. Matthews, 87–98. Cambridge, MA: Harvard University Press, 1999.

———. "Canonical and Apocryphal Acts of Apostles." *Journal of Early Christian Studies* 11 (Summer 2003): 166–94.

———, and Eric Junod, "Reading the Apocryphal Acts of the Apostles." *Semeia* 38 (1986): 161–71.

Boyd, Anthony. "Buddhist Monk Sets Himself on Fire to Protest against the Slaughter of Cattle in Sri Lanka." *The Daily Mail*, May 24, 2013. Accessed May 7, 2014. http://www.dailymail.co.uk/news/article-2330398/Buddhist-monk-sets-protest-slaughter-cattle-Sri-Lanka.html.

Brandon, S.G.F. "The Death of James the Just: A New Interpretation." In *Studies in Mysticism and Religion Presented to Gershom G. Scholem on His Seventieth Birthday by Pupils, Colleagues, and Friends*, 57–69. Jerusalem, Israel: Central Press, 1967.

Bremmer, Jan N. "The Acts of Thomas: Place, Date, and Women." In *The Apocryphal Acts of Thomas*, edited by Jan N. Bremmer, 74–90. Leuven, Belgium: Peeters, 2001.

———. "Magic, Martyrdom and Women's Liberation in the Acts of Paul and Thecla." In *The Apocryphal Acts of Paul and Thecla*, edited by Jan N. Bremmer, 36–59. Kampen, Netherlands: Kok Pharos, 1996.

———. "Women, Magic, Place, and Date." In *The Apocryphal Acts of Peter*, edited by Jan N. Bremmer, 1–20. Leuven, Belgium: Peeters, 1998.

Bruce, F.F. "Paul in Rome: 5 Concluding Observations." *Bulletin of the John Rylands Library* 50:2 (1968): 270.

———. "Philip and the Ethiopian." *Journal of Semitic Studies* 34 (1989): 377–86.

Callahan, Allan Dwight. "Dead Paul: The Apostle as Martyr in Philippi." In *Philippi at the Time of Paul and After His Death*, edited by Charalambos Bakirtzis, 67–84. Eugene: OR: Wipf & Stock, 2009.

Carey, Greg. "The *Ascension of Isaiah*: An Example of Early Christian Narrative Polemic." *Journal for the Study of Pseudepigrapha* 9 (1998): 65–78.

Craig, William Lane, and Bart D. Ehrman. "Is There Historical Evidence for the Resurrection of Jesus?" Debate at Holy Cross, Worcester, MA, March

28, 2006. Accessed November 5, 2013. http://www.reasonablefaith.org/is-there-historical-evidence-for-the-resurrection-of-jesus-the-craig-ehrman.

Czachesz, István. "The Gospel of Peter and the Apocryphal Acts of the Apostles." In *Das Petrusevangelium als Teil antiker Literatur*, edited by T. Nicklas and T.J. Kraus, 248–61. Berlin, Germany: W. De Gruyter: 2007.

D'Andria, Francesco. "Conversion, Crucifixion, and Celebration." *Biblical Archaeological Review* 37 (July/August 2011): 34–46.

Dassmann, Ernst. "Archaeological Traces of Early Christian Veneration of Paul." In *Paul and the Legacies of Paul*, edited by William S. Babcock, 281–306. Dallas, TX: Southern Methodist University Press, 1990.

Davis, Guy M., Jr. "Was Peter Buried in Rome?" *Journal of Bible and Religion* 20:3 (July 1952): 167–71.

Dehandschutter, Boudewijn. "Example and Discipleship: Some Comments on the Biblical Background of the Early Christian Theology of Martyrdom." In *Polycarpiana: Studies on Martyrdom and Persecution in Early Christianity*, edited by J. Leemans, 221–27. Leuven, Belgium: Leuven University Press, 2007.

———. "Example and Discipleship: Some Comments on the Biblical Background of the Early Christian Theology of Martyrdom." In *The Impact of Scripture in Early Christianity*, edited by J. den Boeft and M.L. van Poll-van de Lisdonk, 20–26. Boston, MA: Brill, 1999.

———. "Some Notes on 1 Clement 5, 4–7." In *Fructus Centesimus: Mélanges offerts à Gerard J.M. Bartelink à l'ccasion de son soixantecinquième anniversaire*, edited by A.A.R. Bastiaensen, A. Hilhorst, and C.H. Kneepkens, 189–94. Dordrecht, The Netherlands: Kluwer, 1989.

———. "Some Notes on 1 Clement 5, 4–7." *Instrumenta Patristica* 19 (1989): 83–89.

Dunbar, David. "The Problem of Hippolytus of Rome: A Study in Historical-Critical Reconstruction." *Journal of the Evangelical Theological Society* 25 (1982): 63–74.

Edwards, M.J. "Martyrdom and the First Epistle of John." *Novum Testamentum* 31 (1989): 164–71.

Edwards, William D., Wesley J. Gabel, Floyd E. Hosmer. "On the Physical Death of Jesus Christ." *Journal of the American Medical Association* 255 (March 1986): 1,455–63.

Eliav, Yaron Z. "The Tomb of James, Brother of Jesus, as *Locus Memoriae*." *Harvard Theological Review* 97 (2004): 35–59.

Erho, Ted. "New Ethiopic Witnesses to some Old Testament Pseudepigrapha." *Bulletin of the School of Oriental and African Studies* 76 (February 2013): 75–97.

Evans, Craig A. "Jesus and James Martyrs of the Temple." In *James the Just and Christian Origins*, edited by Bruce Chilton and Craig A. Evans, 233–49. Leiden, The Netherlands: Brill, 1999.

———. "Jesus in Non-Christian Sources." In *Studying the Historical Jesus: Evaluations of the State of Current Research*, edited by Bruce Chilton and Craig Evans, 443–50. Leiden, The Netherlands: Brill, 1998.

Farquhar, John N. "The Apostle Thomas in North India." In *Bulletin of the John Rylands Library*. Vol. 11. Manchester: Manchester University Press, 1926.

———. "The Apostle Thomas in South India." In *Bulletin of the John Rylands Library*. Vol. 11. Manchester: Manchester University Press, 1927.

Frend, W.H.C. "Persecution: Genesis and Legacy." In *The Cambridge History of Christianity: Origins to Constantine*, edited by Margaret M. Mitchell and Frances M. Young, 503–23. New York: Cambridge University Press, 2006.

Fuller, Reginald. "The Choice of Matthias." In *Studia Evangelica*, vol 6, edited by Elizabeth A. Livingston, 140–46. Berlin, Germany: Akademie-Verlag, 1973.

Girosïan, Nina. "The Aršakuni Dynasty: A.D. 12-[180?]-428." In *The Armenian People from Ancient to Modern Times*, vol. 1, edited by Richard G. Hovannisian, 63–94. New York: St. Martin's Press, 1997.

Goulder, Michael D. "Did Peter Ever Go to Rome?" *Scottish Journal of Theology* 57 (2004): 377–96.

Haacker, Klaus. "Paul's Life." In *The Cambridge Companion to St. Paul*, edited by James D.G. Dunn, 19–33. Cambridge: Cambridge University Press, 2003.

Hagner, Donald A. "James." In *The Anchor Bible Dictionary*, vol. 3, edited by David Noel Freedman, 616–18. New York: Bantam Dell, 1992.

Hedrick, Charles W., trans. "The Second Apocalypse of James." In *The Nag Hammadi Library in English*, edited by James M. Robinson, 249–55. Leiden, The Netherlands: E.J. Brill, 1977.

Hilhorst, A. "Tertullian on the Acts of Paul." In *The Apocryphal Acts of Paul and Thecla*, edited by Jan N. Bremmer, 150–63. Kampen, Netherlands: Kok Pharos, 1996.

———, and Pieter J. Lalleman. "The Acts of Andrew: Is it Part of the Original Acts of Andrew?" In *The Apocryphal Acts of Andrew*, edited by Jan N. Bremmer, 1–14. Leuven, Belgium: Peeters, 2000.

Hill, Charles E. "The Man Who Needed No Introduction: A Response to Sebastian Moll." In *Irenaeus: Life, Scripture, Legacy*, edited by S. Parvis and P. Foster, 95–104. Minneapolis, MN: Fortress Press, 2012.

———. "Papias of Hierapolis." *The Expository Times* 117 (2006): 309–15.

Huxley, George. "Geography in the *Acts of Thomas*." *Greek, Roman, and Byzantine Studies* 24 (1983): 71–80.

Isenberg, Wesley W. "Philip." In *The Anchor Bible Dictionary*, vol. 5, edited by David Noel Freedman, 311–13. New York: Doubleday, 1992.

Jackson, F.J. Foakes. "Evidence for the Martyrdom of Peter and Paul in Rome." *Journal of Biblical Literature* 46 (1927): 74–78.

Jerome. *Chronicle*. Translated by Roger Pearse and friends. *The Tertullian Project*, 2005. Accessed May 1, 2014. http://www.tertullian.org/fathers/jerome_chronicle_03_part2.htm.

Jones, F. Stanley. "The Martyrdom of James in Hegesippus, Clement of Alexandria, and Christian Apocrypha, Including Nag Hammadi: A Study of Textual Relations." *Society of Biblical Literature Seminar Papers* 29 (1990): 323–27.

Karttunen, Klaus. "On the Contacts of South India with the Western World in Ancient Times, and the Mission of the Apostle Thomas." In *South Asian Religion and Society*, edited by Asko Parpola and Bent Smidt Hansen, 189–204. Richmond, England: Riverdale, 1986.

Kay, Sarah. "Original Skin: Flaying, Reading, and Thinking in the Legend of Saint Bartholomew and Other Works." *Journal of Medieval and Early Modern Studies* 36 (2006): 35–73.

Kazhdan, Alexander, ed. *The Oxford Dictionary of Byzantium*. Oxford: Oxford University Press, 1991.

Koester, Helmut. "Ephesos in Early Christian Literature." In *Ephesos: Metropolis of Asia: An Interdisciplinary Approach to its Archaeology, Religion, and Culture*, edited by Helmut Koester, 119–40. Valley Forge, PA: Trinity Press International, 1995.

Köstenberger, Andreas J. "Apologetics Commentary on the Gospel of John." *The Holman Apologetics Commentary on the Bible*, edited by Jeremy Royal Howard, 504–634. Nashville, TN: Broadman & Holman, 2013.

———, and Stephen O. Stout. "'The Disciple Jesus Loved': Witness, Author, Apostle—a Response to Richard Bauckham's *Jesus and the Eyewitnesses*." *Bulletin for Biblical Research* 18:2 (2008): 209–32.

Lalleman, Pieter J. "The Acts of Andrew and the Acts of John." In *The Apocryphal Acts of Andrew*, edited by Jan N. Bremmer, 140–48. Leuven, Belgium: Peeters, 2000.

Lampe, G.W.H. "Martyrdom and Inspiration." In *Suffering and Martyrdom in the New Testament*, edited by William Horbury and Brian McNeil, 118–35. New York: Cambridge University Press, 1981.

Le Houllier, A. "Bartholomew, Apostle St." In *New Catholic Encyclopedia*. Vol. 2, 131–32. New York: Catholic University of America Press, 1967.

Lefrançois, J.A. "Matthew, Apostle, St." In *New Catholic Encyclopedia*, vol. 9, 2nd ed., edited by Thomas Carson and Joann Cerrito, 353. Washington, DC: Catholic University Press, 2003.

Licheli, Vakhtang. "St. Andrew in Samtskhe—Archaeological Proof?" In *Ancient Christianity in the Caucasus*, edited by Tamila Mgaloblishvili, 25–37. New York: Curzon Press, 1998.

Lindars, Barnabas. "Matthew, Levi, Lebbaeus and the Value of the Western Text." *New Testament Studies* 4 (1958): 220–22.

Lindemann, Andreas. "Paul in the Writings of the Apostolic Fathers." In *Paul and the Legacies of Paul*, edited by William S. Babcock, 25–45. Dallas, TX: Southern Methodist University Press, 1990.

Lipsius, Richard Adelbert. "Thaddaeus." In *Dictionary of Christian Biography*, vol. 4, edited by William Smith and Henry Wace, 875–76. London: William Clowes & Sons, 1887.

MacDonald, Dennis R. "Apocryphal and Canonical Narratives about Paul." In *Paul and the Legacies of Paul*, edited by William S. Babcock, 55–70. Dallas, TX: Southern Methodist University Press, 1990.

MacRae, George W. "Whom Heaven Must Receive Until the Time: Reflections on the Christology of Acts." *Interpretations* 27 (April 1973): 151–65.

Maier, Paul. "The Myth of Persecution: A Provocative Title, an Overdone Thesis." *Christian Research Journal* 36 (2013): 52–56.

McGrath, James F. "History and Fiction in the Acts of Thomas: The State of the Question." *Journal for the Study of Pseudepigrapha* 17 (2008): 297–311.

McLaren, James S. "Ananus, James, and Earliest Christianity. Josephus' Account of the Death of James." *Journal of Theological Studies* 52 (2001): 1–25.

McLees, Nectarias. "Witness for an Apostle: The Evidence for St. Thomas in India." *Road to Emmaus* 6 (2005): 47–61.

Meeks, Wayne A. "Social and Ecclesial Life of the Earliest Christians." In *The Cambridge History of Christianity: Origins to Constantine*, edited by Margaret M. Mitchell and Frances M. Young, 145–77. Cambridge: Cambridge University Press, 2006.

Meinardus, Otto F.A. "Paul's Missionary Journey to Spain: Tradition and Folklore." *The Biblical Archaeologist* 41 (1978): 61–63.

Misset-Van De Weg, Magda. "'For the Lord Always Takes Care of His Own': The Purpose of the Wondrous Works and Deeds in the *Acts of Peter.*" In *The Apocryphal Acts of Peter*, edited by Jan N. Bremmer, 97–101. Leuven, Belgium: Peeters, 1998.

Myers, Edward P. "Martyr." In *Eerdmans Dictionary of the Bible*, edited by David Noel Freedman, 862–63. Grand Rapids, MI: Eerdmans, 2000.

Myllykoski, Matti. "James the Just in History and Tradition: Perspectives of Past and Present Scholarship, Part I." *Currents in Biblical Research* 5:1 (2006): 73–122.

———. "James the Just in History and Tradition: Perspectives of Past and Present Scholarship, Part II." *Currents in Biblical Research* 6:1 (2007): 11–98.

Newport, Kenneth G.C. "Matthew, Martyrdom of." In *The Anchor Bible Dictionary*, vol. 3, edited by David Noel Freedman, 643–44. New York: Bantam Dell, 1992.

Norris, Frederick W. "Acts of Andrew." In *Encyclopedia of Early Christianity*, vol. 1, edited by Everett Ferguson, 10–11. New York: Garland, 1997.

Norris, Richard A., Jr. "Apocryphal Writings and Acts of the Martyrs." In *The Cambridge History of Early Christian Literature*, edited by Frances Young, Lewis Ayres, and Andrew Louth, 28–37. Cambridge: Cambridge University Press, 2004.

Painter, James. "Who Was James? Footprints as a Means of Identification." In *The Brother of Jesus*, edited by Bruce Chilton and Jacob Neusner, 10–65. Louisville, KY: Westminster John Knox Press, 2001.

Pesthy, Monika. "Cross and Death in the Apocryphal Acts of the Apostles." In *The Apocryphal Acts of Peter*, edited by Jan N. Bremmer, 123–33. Leuven, Belgium: Peeters, 1998.

Powell, Mark Allan. "Martyr." In *HarperCollins Bible Dictionary*, edited by Mark Allan Powell, 606–07. Rev. ed. New York: HarperCollins, 2011.

Price, Robert M. "Would the Apostles Die for a Lie?" *Free Inquiry* 21 (Fall 2001): 20.

Quispel, Gilles. "The Fourth Gospel and the Judaic Gospel Tradition." In *Gnostica, Judaica, Catholica. Collected Essays by Gilles Quispel*, edited by Johannes Van Oort, 475–48. Leiden, The Netherlands: Brill, 2008.

Rengstorf, Karl Heinrich. "The Election of Matthias: *Acts 1.15ff.*" In *Current Issues in New Testament Interpretation*, edited by William Klassen and Graydon F. Snyder, 178–92. New York: Harper & Brothers, 1962.

Robinson, Donald Fay. "Where and When Did Peter Die?" *Journal of Biblical Literature* 64, no. 2 (June 1945): 255–67.

Rose, Els. "Apocryphal Tradition in Medieval Latin Liturgy: A New Research Project Illustrated with the Case of the Apostle Andrew." *Apocrypha* 15 (2004): 115–38.

Russell, Donald A. "Plutarch." In *The Oxford Classical Dictionary*, 4th ed., edited by Simon Hornblower, Antony Spawforth, and Esther Eidinow, 1165. Oxford: Oxford University Press, 2012.

Schnabel, Eckhard J., trans. "Canon Muratori." Paper presented at the annual meeting of the Evangelical Theological Society, Baltimore, MD, November 20, 2013.

Schwartz, Daniel R. "The End of the Line: Paul in the Canonical Book of Acts." In *Paul and the Legacies of Paul*, edited by William S. Babcock, 3–24. Dallas, TX: Southern Methodist University Press, 1990.

Sellew, Philip. "Thomas Christianity: Scholars in Quest of a Community." *The Apocryphal Acts of Thomas*, edited by Jan N. Bremmer, 11–35. Leuven, Belgium: Peeters, 2001.

Sider, Robert D. "Literary Artifice and the Figure of Paul in the Writings of Tertullian." In *Paul and the Legacies of Paul*, edited by William S. Babcock, 99–120. Dallas, TX: Southern Methodist University Press, 1990.

Smallwood, E. Mary. "High Priests and Politics." *Journal of Theological Studies* 13 (1962): 14–34.

Smaltz, Warren M. "Did Peter Die in Jerusalem?" *Journal of Biblical Literature* 71:4 (December 1952): 211–16.

Smith, Carl B. "Ministry, Martyrdom and Other Mysteries: Pauline Influence on Ignatius of Antioch." In *Paul and the Second Century*, edited by Michael F. Bird and Joseph R. Dodson, 37–56. New York: T. & T. Clark, 2011.

Smith, Jonathan Z. "Birth Upside Down or Right Side Up?" *History of Religions* 9 (1970): 286–93.

Smith, Morton. "The Report About Peter in I Clement V. 4." *New Testament Studies* 7 (1960–61): 86–88.

Talbot, Alice-Mary. "Xanthopoulos, Nikephoros Kallistos." In *The Oxford Dictionary of Byzantium*, edited by Alexander Kazhdan, 2207. Oxford: Oxford University Press, 1991.

Thapar, Romila. "Historical Traditions in Early India: c. 1000 B.C. to c. AD 600." *The Oxford History of Historical Writing*, edited by Andrew Feldherr and Grant Hardy, 553–58. Oxford: Oxford University Press, 2011.

Thomas, Christine M. "The 'Prehistory' of the Acts of Peter." In *The Apocryphal Acts of the Apostles*, edited by François Bovon, Ann Graham Bock, and Christopher R. Matthews, 39–62. Cambridge, MA: Harvard University Press, 1999.

Titus, Eric L. "The Identity of the Beloved Disciple." *Journal of Biblical Literature* 69 (1950): 323–28.

Trompf, G.W. "On Why Luke Declined to Recount the Death of Paul: Acts 27–28 and Beyond." In *Luke–Acts: New Perspectives from the Society of Biblical Literature Seminar*, edited by Charles H. Talbert, 225–39. New York: Crossroad, 1984.

Valantasis, Richard. "Narrative Strategies and Synoptic Quandaries: A Response to Dennis MacDonald's Reading of *Acts of Paul* and *Acts of Peter*." *Society of Biblical Literature Seminar Papers* (1992): 234–39.

Van Belle, Gilbert. "Peter as Martyr in the Fourth Gospel." In *Martyrdom and Persecution in Late Antique Christianity: Festschrift Boudewijn Dehandschutter*, edited by J. Leemans, 281–309. Leuven, Belgium: Peeters, 2010.

Van den Bosch, Lourens P. "India and the Apostolate of St. Thomas." In *The Apocryphal Acts of Thomas*, edited by Jan N. Bremmer, 125–48. Leuven, Belgium: Peeters, 2001.

Van Esbroeck, Michael. "The Rise of Saint Bartholomew's Cult in Armenia from the Seventh to the Thirteenth Centuries." In *Medieval Armenian Culture*, University of Pennsylvania Armenian Texts and Studies, vol. 6, edited by Thomas J. Samuelian and Michael E. Stone, 161–78. Chico, CA: Scholars Press, 1983.

Villegas, Beltran. "Peter, Philip, and James of Alphaeus." *New Testament Studies* 33 (1987): 292–94.

Volp, Ulrich. "Hippolytus." *Expository Times* 120 (2009): 521–29.

Ward, Roy Bowen. "James of Jerusalem in the First Two Centuries." In *Aufstieg Und Niedergang Der Römischen Welt*, 779–812. Berlin, Germany: Walter de Gruyter, 1992.

Wenham, John. "Did Peter Go to Rome in AD 42?" *Tyndale Bulletin* 23 (1972): 94–102.

Wilkins, Michael. "Apologetics Commentary on the Gospel of Matthew." In *The Holman Apologetics Commentary on the Bible*, edited by Jeremy R. Howard, 15–198. Nashville, TN: Broadman & Holman, 2013.

Williams, Francis E. "The Apocryphon of James (I, 2)." In *The Nag Hammadi Library in English*, edited by James M. Robinson, 29–37. Leiden, The Netherlands: Brill, 1977.

Williams, Margaret. "Palestinian Jewish Personal Names in Acts." In *The Book of Acts in its Palestinian Setting*, edited by Richard Bauckham, 79–114. Grand Rapids, MI: Eerdmans, 1995.

Winter, Paul. "Josephus on Jesus." *Journal of Historical Studies* 1 (1968): 289–302

Witherington, Ben, III. "The Martyrdom of the Zebedee Brothers." *Biblical Archaeology Review* 33 (May/June 2007): 26.

Young, Robin Darling. "Armenian Christian Literature." In *Encyclopedia of Early Christianity*, vol. 1, edited by Everett Ferguson, 118. New York: Garland, 1997.

Dissertations

Dunn, Peter Wallace. "The *Acts of Paul* and the Pauline Legacy in the Second Century." Ph.D. diss., Queens College, Cambridge, 1996.

Haxby, Mikael Caley Grams. "The *First Apocalypse of James*: Martyrdom and Sexual Difference." Ph.D. diss., Harvard University, 2013.

Lanzilotta, Fernando Lautaro Roig. "The Apocryphal Acts of Andrew: A New Approach to the Character, Thought and Meaning of the Primitive Text." Ph.D. diss., Rijksuniversiteit Groningen, 2004.

Little, Henry D. "The Death of James, the Brother of Jesus." Ph.D. diss., Rice University, 1971.

Wespetal, Thomas J. "Martyrdom and the Furtherance of God's Plan: The Value of Dying for the Christian Faith." Ph.D. diss., Trinity Evangelical Divinity School, 2005.

Index